Conference Proceedings of the Society for Experimental Mechanics Series

Series Editor

Kristin B. Zimmerman
Society for Experimental Mechanics, Inc.,
Bethel, USA

The Conference Proceedings of the Society for Experimental Mechanics Series presents early findings and case studies from a wide range of fundamental and applied work across the broad range of fields that comprise Experimental Mechanics. Series volumes follow the principle tracks or focus topics featured in each of the Society's two annual conferences: IMAC, A Conference and Exposition on Structural Dynamics, and the Society's Annual Conference & Exposition and will address critical areas of interest to researchers and design engineers working in all areas of Structural Dynamics, Solid Mechanics and Materials Research.

Brandon Dilworth · Timothy Marinone · Jon Furlic
Editors

Topics in Modal Analysis & Parameter Identification I, Vol. 9

Proceedings of the 43rd IMAC, A Conference and Exposition on Structural Dynamics 2025

River Publishers

Published, sold and distributed by:

River Publishers
Broagervej 10
9260 Gistrup
Denmark

www.riverpublishers.com

ISBN 97887-438-0154-2 (Hardback)

ISBN 97887-438-0166-5 (eBook)

https://doi.org/10.13052/9788743801542

Conference Proceedings of the Society for Experimental Mechanics

An imprint of River Publishers

Preface

Topics in Modal Analysis & Parameter Identification I represents one of twelve volumes of technical papers presented at the 43rd IMAC, A Conference and Exposition on Structural Dynamics, organized by the Society for Experimental Mechanics, and held February 10-13, 2025. The full proceedings also include volumes on Nonlinear Structures & Systems; Dynamics of Civil Structures; Model Validation and Uncertainty Quantification; Dynamic Substructuring & Transfer Path Analysis; Special Topics in Structural Dynamics & Experimental Techniques; Computer Vision & Laser Vibrometry; Dynamic Environments Testing; Sensors & Instrumentation and Aircraft/Aerospace Testing Techniques; Data Science in Engineering; and Structural Health Monitoring 7 Machine Learning.

Each collection presents early findings from experimental and computational investigations on an important area within Structural Dynamics. Topics in Modal Analysis and Parameter Identification represents papers on enabling technologies for dynamic systems and applications of Modal Analysis in specific application areas.

The organizers would like to thank the authors, presenters, session organizers, and session chairs for their participation in this track.

Editor:
Brandon Dilworth–*MIT Lincoln Laboratory, MA, USA;* Timothy Marinone–*ATA Engineering, Inc., CA, USA;* Jon Furlich–*ATA Engineering, Inc., CA, USA.*

Contents

Chapter 1
The Energy Spectrum for the Detection of Harmonic Components in Ambient Vibration Tests

Mona Amer and Carlos E. Ventura

Abstract Operational modal analysis is a widely used technique to determine modal parameters from ambient vibration tests of civil and mechanical engineering structures. Speed-synchronous structural responses from rotating machines superimpose the ambient vibration responses and harm the successful identification of modal parameters. These so-called harmonics can be falsely identified as structural characteristics if not treated appropriately. A new technique for the identification of harmonics in ambient vibration data has been recently introduced and is discussed in more detail considering different applications such as an axial compressor, a wind turbine, and a ship. The mass-drawn energy spectrum is a measure used in earthquake engineering for the quantification of the energy introduced by ground motion. It can serve as a measure for potential structural damage. As harmonics have a much higher signal energy than structural modes, they can be distinguished in the frequency domain as sharp peaks. The proposed technique can thus be used to remove these components from the frequency spectrum before the consecutive modal analysis. The advantage is that frequencies, which do not result from the main rotation of the system but might be subjected to auxiliary equipment or the power circuit can be successfully identified as well. By means of the proposed approach, modal properties can be determined with greater confidence.

Keywords Operational modal analysis · Speed synchronous vibration · Earthquake engineering · Modal identification · Energy spectrum

Introduction

The modal identification of rotating machines in operation is still considered a challenge because speed-synchronous vibrations superimpose the measured output of a system in operation. These speed-synchronous vibrations, so-called harmonics, can be falsely identified as structural characteristics by established modal identification techniques if no appropriate action is taken. In the literature, various approaches to deal with these harmonics can be found. They can be categorized into four different types [1]. Statistical criteria, pre-processing techniques, extended identification methods, and input-independent identification techniques can be distinguished. Examples for these different types are the excess value [1], time-synchronous averaging [2], modified stochastic subspace identification [3], or transmissibility based operational modal analysis [4], just to name a few. These approaches were applied to systems under laboratory conditions or specific use cases with a unique set of operating conditions. Often limitations of the different procedures were experienced. For this reason, it is necessary to adapt an application-specific procedure, which takes into account the different boundary conditions of the system under investigation. A combination, which includes the identification and removal of harmonics, has proven successful when applied to a high-speed axial compressor [5]. A core quantity in this proposed technique represents the energy spectrum, which is a measure originally derived from earthquake engineering. It can provide insights into the presence of harmonics. Its effectiveness will be discussed more in detail using three different examples of application. The main advantage is that harmonics from other sources than the operated rotor can be identified as well, as will be shown in the results section.

Mona Amer · Carlos E. Ventura
Department of Civil Engineering, The University of British Columbia, Vancouver, BC V6T 1Z4
e-mail: mona.amer@ubc.ca; ventura@civil.ubc.ca

Brandon Dilworth et al. (eds.), *Topics in Modal Analysis & Parameter Identification I, Vol. 9*, Conference Proceedings of the Society for Experimental Mechanics Series, https://doi.org/10.13052/9788743801542-1

Methodology

The mass-drawn energy spectrum is a measure that is typically used in earthquake engineering. It classifies the energy introduced by ground motion into the structure and can be used as a measure for potential structural damage [6]. A single degree of freedom (DOF) system with the well-known equation of motion $\ddot{q} + 2D\omega\dot{q} + \omega^2 q = -\ddot{y}$, where D describes the damping, ω the natural circular frequency of the system, q the displacement of the excited single DOF system, respectively $\dot{q}$ the velocity, $\ddot{q}$ the acceleration, and $\ddot{y}$ the ground acceleration, is assumed. The mass-drawn input energy is defined as

$$E_I = \frac{E}{m} = \int_{-\infty}^{\infty} \ddot{y}\dot{q}dt, \tag{1}$$

with the energy E and the mass m. The velocity $\dot{q}$ can be calculated using different techniques. In this work, the numerical method proposed by Nigam and Jennings using a state-space representation is applied for the calculation. The single steps can be found in [7]. The calculation is based on time-discretized dimensions. To identify the harmonics, a low damping value, e.g. 1%, is assumed. The measured response acceleration of the structure serves as input for the ground acceleration $\ddot{y}$ in the previous equation. The procedure of calculating the energy spectrum for a single DOF system is depicted in Fig. 1.

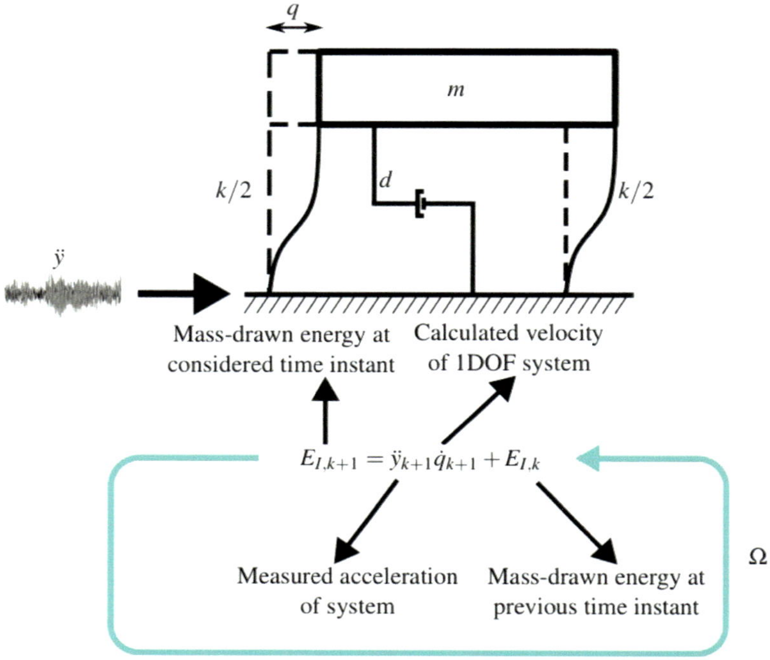

Fig. 1 Calculation of energy spectrum.

The different entities to calculate E_I are explained in Fig. 1. The blue arrow refers to the frequency range, for which the input energy is calculated so that the user obtains the energy spectrum in dependence of the pre-defined frequency vector. This can then be depicted as a function of the frequency in the frequency domain. The arrow can thus be interpreted as a loop, since the calculation is performed for each entry of the frequency vector. The single calculation steps are summarized as follows:

1. Calculation of the velocity $\dot{q}$, e.g. using the method by Nigam and Jennings [7],
2. Calculation of the discretized input energy $E_{I,k}$ at discrete time instants t_k over a designated frequency vector of interest: $E_{I,k+1} = \ddot{y}_{k+1}\dot{q}_{k+1} + E_{I,k}$,
3. Illustration of E_I dependent on the selected frequency range. The dominant peaks can be interpreted as disturbing signal components mainly from sources that cause harmonic vibrations.

The peaks in the energy spectrum represent the harmonics present in the operated system. The harmonics are characterized by a much higher signal energy than the structural modes and can thus be distinguished in the energy spectrum. This will be shown below by means of multiple use cases.

Results

The proposed method for the identification of harmonics is shown and discussed by means of three use cases that all consist of rotating components, more specifically an axial compressor, a wind turbine and a vessel in operation. In the following section, it is shown that harmonics can be identified unambiguously and efficiently using the proposed criterion.

Axial compressor

The axial compressor test rig, see Fig. 2, used for the following investigations consists of single stage rotor configuration with adjustable vanes and can be operated up to a nominal rotor speed of 17,100 rpm. The compressor has been operated and data has been acquired at different constant speeds as well as during run-up and run-down. The test rig has been equipped with 49 uniaxial acceleration sensors equally distributed over all the structure's components. The high sampling frequency of 25.6 kHz, which is needed for unbalance analysis in operation, is later downsampled, since the frequency range up to 150 Hz is of main interest. The critical speed of the rotor, representing a bending mode, is around 115 Hz. Details on the test setup can be found in [5]. Measurements for the constant speeds are usually three minutes long and for ramp-up and ramp-down around seven minutes long. The focus in the following analysis is on the constant rotational speeds, since the data from the ramp-downs and ramp-ups can be only analyzed in sections due to the large data size. Calculating the energy spectrum for a section of the run-down, will only show the mean rotational frequency during this duration as the dominant peak in the energy spectrum. Since the rotational speed is constantly varying, the peak is wide-banded showing a frequency content of multiple rotational frequencies around the mean rotational frequency. Analyzing a longer duration of the run-down shows the maximum rotor speed of 17,100 rpm or 285 Hz to be the most dominant peak, since the rotor speed changes slowly in the beginning of the run-down.

Fig. 2 Axial compressor test rig at the Institute of Turbomachinery and Fluid-Dynamics, Leibniz University Hannover.

In Fig. 3, the calculated energy spectrum is compared for three different constant rotational speeds. At first, the energy spectrum is calculated for each channel individually and can then be averaged over multiple sensors to capture a more representative behavior of the harmonic influence in operation. In the following case, it is averaged over nine sensors representing all instrumented components of the compressor test rig.

The first harmonic can be clearly identified for all three depicted rotational speeds and has been labeled accordingly. For the rotational speed of 3,900 rpm, other influences are visible in the energy spectrum. Since the structure couldn't be completely electromagnetically isolated, the power circuit acts as a source that causes harmonic response vibrations. For this reason, the user can observe dominant peaks at 50 Hz and 100 Hz (respectively the first and second harmonic of the power frequency in Europe). An additional dominant peak is visible in the lower frequency range. It also plays a role in the modal identification, since it is detected as a stable mode by the algorithms, but it does not represent a physical mode. Further investigations reveal that this frequency belongs to a local mode of the foundation, which should not be mistaken as a system mode and can thus be ignored in the data evaluation. This frequency, therfore, represents a noise mode.

The power frequency plays a less significant role for higher rotational speeds, since the signal energy of the first rotor harmonic is much more dominant, as can be seen in Fig. 3b looking at the high amplitudes of nearly 600 J/kg. Therefore, other influences than the first rotor harmonic don't play a role in this data set.

In Fig. 3c, next to the first rotor harmonic, a second effect becomes recognizable. This belongs to the third harmonic of the motor, which causes harmonic response vibrations of the system. Through the gearbox ratio of 1:13, this is transformed

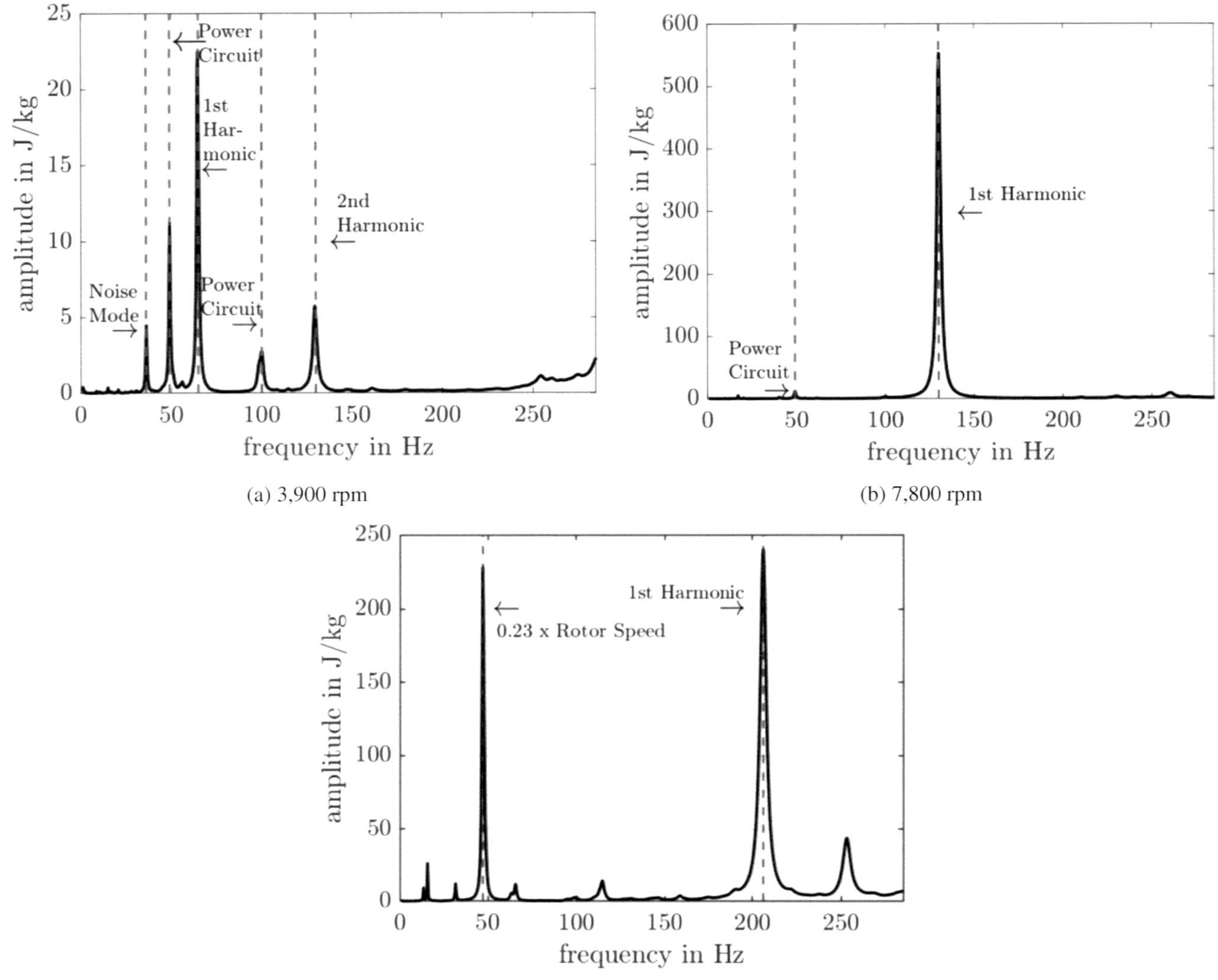

(a) 3,900 rpm (b) 7,800 rpm

(c) 12,360 rpm

Fig. 3 Energy spectrum of three different rotational speeds of the axial compressor investigated.

to 0.23 × first harmonic of the rotor, which the user can observe in the energy spectrum. This frequency has been already observed in the tip timing system used for the vibration analysis of the turbomachinery blades in operation. Due to the energy spectrum, this frequency can be excluded from the modal identification. This is especially important for even higher rotational speeds, since this frequency gets closer to the first natural frequency of the system and can thus be easily mistaken as a structural mode.

It is remarkable that each rotor speed investigated leads to a different amplitude level of the highest peak in the energy spectrum. This fact underlines that each relevant operating point should be studied individually and that there is no general cutoff value, which differentiates between structural mode and harmonics. However, it can be stated that all significant peaks in the studied energy spectra of the axial compressor belong to disturbing effects and do not represent a structural characteristic of the system. The advantage of this method is that it can also identify harmonics, which are associated with other sources than the rotor of the main system like auxiliary units with rotating components or the power circuit.

Wind turbine

The second data set is derived from a wind turbine, which is operated in the South of Chile. It was equipped with four triaxial velocity sensors from Tromino, which can be used for seismic measurements. A schematic setup of the sensors is depicted in

Fig. 4. The data was acquired during a 20 hours test with a sampling frequency of 128 Hz. The rotational speed information is sparse, since there is only one time stamp each ten minutes. Therefore, the sections chosen for the analysis can contain rotor speed variations. For the analysis, data sections were selected that had the same average rotor speed for more than two consecutive time stamps to ensure a sufficient length of the data set. For the analysis, two data sets with an average rotor speed of 9 rpm over 30 minutes and 10.5 rpm over 80 minutes were used. The energy spectrum resulting from this data is depicted in Fig. 5.

Fig. 4 Sensor setup on wind turbine.

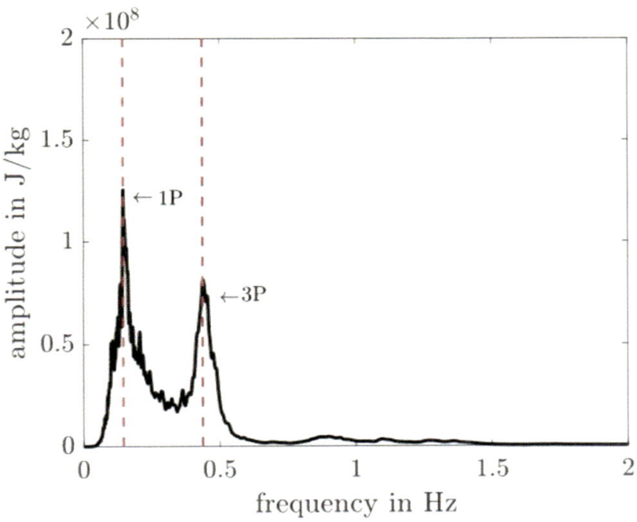

(a) 9 rpm

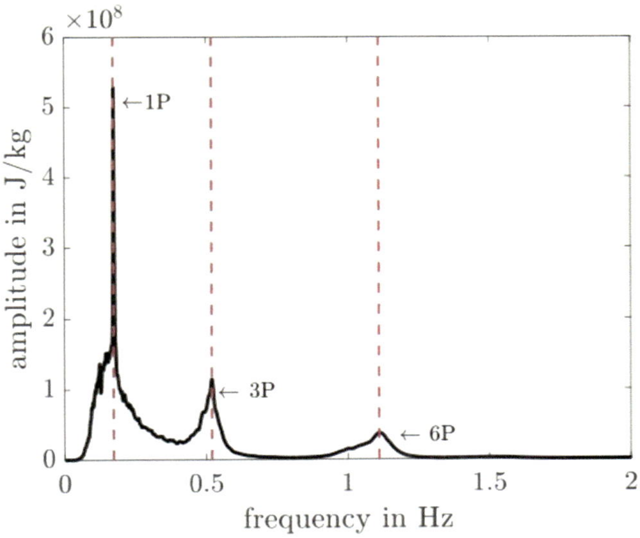

(b) 10.5 rpm

Fig. 5 Energy spectrum of three different rotational speeds of the wind turbine investigated.

The energy spectrum is averaged over all four sensors taking into account each of the channels measuring in North-South direction. In this data, the first, third, and sixth harmonic, also called 1p, 3p, and 6p in case of a wind turbine, are dominant. As expected, the influence of the first rotor harmonic and the third one according to the number of blades have the strongest superimposing character on the data. Other effects do not seem to play a dominant role for this use case. A rotor speed variability can be observed on the basis of the wide-spread peaks in the frequency domain in Fig. 5. The amplitude level of the input energy is more than 3×10^5 higher than the previous use case investigated. This fact demonstrates the strong influence of the rotation in the data and the necessity for appropriate tools to deal with these influences, since the harmonic frequency content is close to structural frequencies that have been identified in standstill condition without any rotation.

Ship

Next, data from a ship, shown in Fig. 6, excited by the running engine, is analyzed. The ship has a four bladed propeller with a controllable pitch and is equipped with 16 uniaxial sensors collecting data for a duration of 90 minutes with a sampling frequency of 128 Hz. It is, thus, expected to see a dominant influence of the first and fourth harmonic due the number of blades.

Fig. 6 Ship excited periodically from running propellers [8].

The influence of the different harmonics is represented by four different sensor channels in Fig. 7. On the one hand, strongly varying amplitude levels can be observed for the different channels. On the other hand, for each sensor other harmonics play the most dominant role in the energy spectrum. The distance of the sensor from the engine plays a significant role for the influence of the harmonics in the captured data. Channel 1 shows that the harmonics have a comparable influence as the structural modes. The signal energy of the harmonics is, in this case, not much higher than that of the structural modes and can thus not be distinguished from the structural components in the measured data. This looks very different for Channel 2, Channel 7, and Channel 8, also represented in Fig. 5. For these channels, only the influence of the harmonics resulting from the running propeller are dominant in the energy spectrum. Channel 2 in Fig. 7b shows the most significant influence resulting from the first rotor harmonic and a much more reduced influence from the fifth harmonic. In channel 7, the most significant influence comes from the fourth harmonic indicating that the sensor is located close to the propeller and the four blades lead to the strong influence that can be observed. The amplitude of the fourth harmonic is also more than four times higher than the amplitude of the first harmonic for channel 2. A mixture of the influence of multiple harmonics, can be observed for channel 8 in Fig. 7d. Next to the first harmonic, which is the most dominant, the fourth, fifth, and sixth harmonic can be clearly identified from the energy spectrum and will likely have an influence on the modal identification of this data.

In Fig. 8, the energy spectrum is represented as an average of six channels according to the previous application cases. Similarly to the results from channel 8, four dominant harmonic frequencies can be distinguished. As Fig. 8 represents an average, the amplitude level of each harmonic signal varies compared to the results from channel 8. The fourth harmonic, corresponding to the number of propeller blades, has the highest amplitude level. The comparison between the energy spectrum calculated for single channels depicted in Fig. 7 and an average over multiple, characteristic channels in Fig. 8 underlines the benefit of such an illustration, since single channels might not be representative for the influence of the

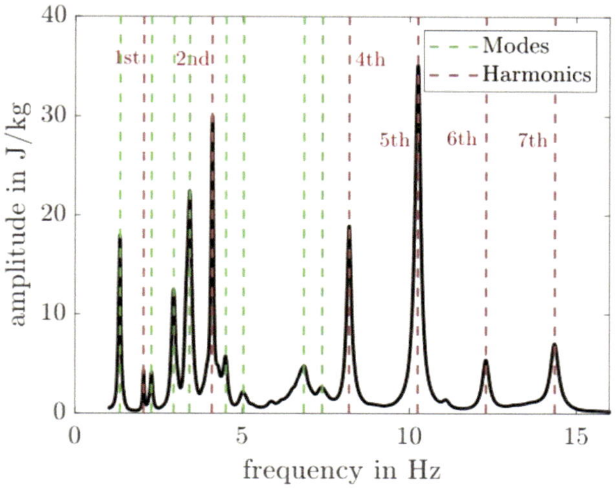

(a) Channel 1

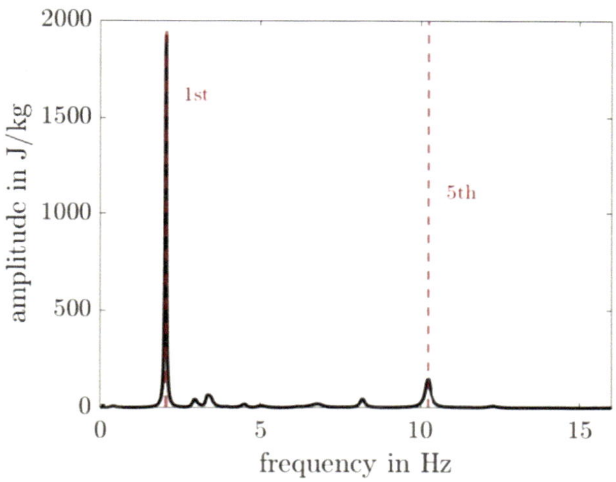

(b) Channel 2

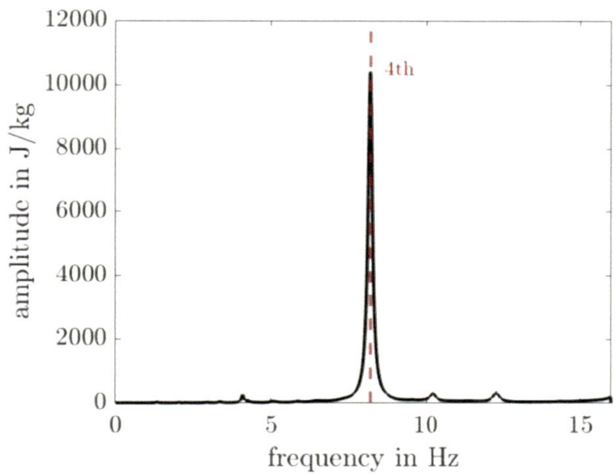

(c) Channel 7

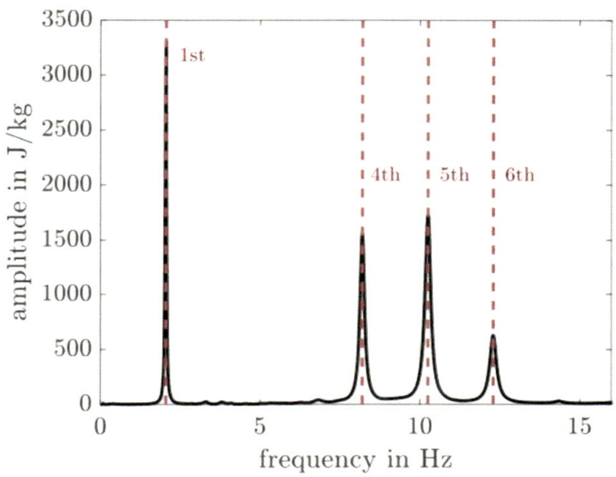

(d) Channel 8

Fig. 7 Energy spectrum of ship with running propellers calculated for four different sensor channels – green dotted lines represent structural modes; red dotted lines represent harmonics.

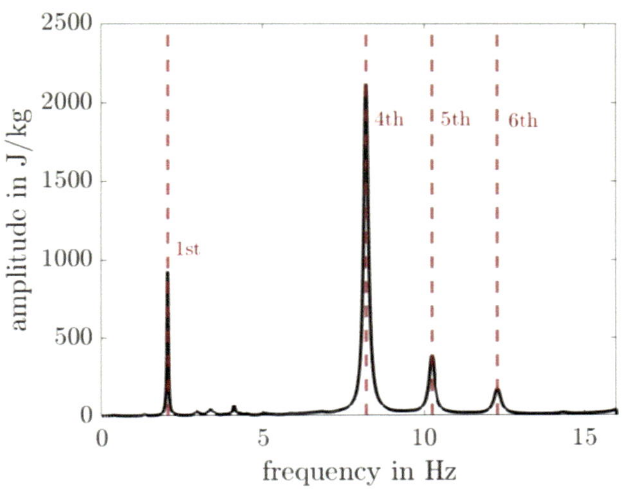

Fig. 8 Energy spectrum calculated from the ship data averaged over six channels.

harmonics on the overall structural behavior, see Fig. 7a. Considering a single channel can be misleading, since the influence of harmonics can be underestimated or overestimated. The influence of the harmonics is also evident when performing the data analysis since they can be clearly identified as thin sharp peaks in the power spectral density of the measured signal, cf. [8].

Comparison

From all of the three use cases, it can be observed that the influence of harmonic signal content in the measured structural responses can be clearly identified by means of the energy spectrum, described in the methodology section. It can be concluded that there is no generalized cutoff value for the amplitude, which decides whether a peak belongs to a harmonic or not. The amplitude of the peaks depend on the energy level of the harmonic vibrations for the individual use case. In comparison to other criteria like the probability density function, which can assess whether a selected mode is truly a structural mode or a harmonic, the energy spectrum is unambiguous at least when sufficient channels are considered. Taking the average over multiple test channels is therefore recommended to obtain a reliable representation. The energy spectrum therefore represents a supplement to the existing tools, which deal with harmonic system responses in ambient vibration tests.

Conclusions

A criterion for the distinction of harmonic signal content in measured structural responses usually used as input for operational modal analysis has been introduced and applied to different applications of machines. Three use cases of systems with rotating components in operation have been analyzed by means of the energy spectrum to obtain an insight into the harmonic effects present in the data. Depending on the application, the amplitude level of the calculated input energy for a single degree of freedom system will vary as it can be concluded from the comparison of the three use cases. Overall, the dominant harmonic frequencies superimposing the stochastic response could be clearly identified using the energy spectrum. In conclusion, there is no need for a cutoff value to differentiate between structural modes and harmonics, since the harmonic signal energy exceeds the level of structural modes by far. The reliable identification of harmonics will allow a robust extraction of modal parameters by means of well-established techniques for the modal identification of systems in operation.

Acknowledgments The authors would like to kindly thank the Institute of Turbomachinery and Fluid-Dynamics at Leibniz University Hannover, Germany and especially the head of institute Prof. Dr.-Ing. J. R. Seume for access to the axial compressor test rig, which enabled the test data acquisition in operation representing a large part of this study. In addition, the authors would like to thank Tómas Núñez and the company TNA Engineering as well as Sven-Erik Rosenow, Santiago Uhlenbrock, and Günther Schlottmann, for providing the wind turbine and ship data.

References

1. Motte, K., Weijtjens, W., Devriendt, C., and Guillaume, P. "Operational modal analysis in the presence of harmonic excitations: a review". In Dynamics of Civil Structures, Volume 2: Proceedings of the 33rd IMAC, A Conference and Exposition on Structural Dynamics, 2015, pages 379-395. Springer (2015)
2. Combet, F. and Gelman, L. "An automated methodology for performing time synchronous averaging of a gearbox signal without speed sensor". Mechanical systems and signal processing, 21(6):2590-2606 (2007)
3. Dong, X., Lian, J., Yang, M., and Wang, H. "Operational modal identification of offshore wind turbine structure based on modified stochastic subspace identification method considering harmonic interference". Journal of Renewable and Sustainable Energy, 6(3):033128 (2014)
4. Weijtjens, W. "Advanced methods for estimating and monitoring the modal parameters of operational systems subjected to non-white excitation". PhD thesis, Vrije Universiteit Brussel (2014)
5. Amer, M., Ventura, C.E., Maroldt, N., Seume, J.R., and Wallaschek, J. "Modal parameter estimation of turbomachinery in operation taking into account friction damping". Mechanical Systems and Signal Processing, 216:111414 (2024)
6. Ordaz, M., Huerta, B., and Reinoso, E. "Exact computation of input-energy spectra from Fourier amplitude spectra". Earthquake Engineering & Structural Dynamics, 32(4):597-605 (2003)
7. Nigam, N.C. and Jennings, P.C. "Calculation of response spectra from strong-motion earthquake records". Bulletin of the Seismological Society of America, 59(2):909-922 (1969)
8. Rosenow, S.E., Uhlenbrock, S., and Schlottmann, G. "Parameter extraction of ship structures in presence of stochastic and harmonic excitations". In Proceedings of the International Operational Modal Analysis Conference (IOMAC 2007), volume 4, page 01 (2007)

Chapter 2
Parametrising the Virtual Point Transformation and a Nonlinear Estimation Framework for Determining an Unknown Force

Julian Staiger and Frank Naets

Abstract This article examines the estimation of a force applied to a rigid interface using a model that does not explicitly consider such force. It discusses linear model-based estimation and proposes a novel approach based on a nonlinear augmented state-space model using the Virtual Point Transformation method. The proposed methodology is experimentally validated on an automotive-grade rubber mount component, showing superior performance compared to linear estimation approaches.

Keywords Virtual point transformation · Inverse load identification · Nonlinear estimation · Virtual sensing

Introduction

The problem of determining forces transmitted from sources to receivers, such as from an engine to a vehicle chassis, was historically treated by experimental Transfer Path Analysis (TPA) [1, 2] methods. In this context, the forces transmitting through connecting elements, e.g. rubber mounts, are of paramount importance due to the prominence of the structure-borne noise path in many applications. To determine inputs and outputs at inaccessible locations, Van der Seijs et al.proposed the Virtual Point Transformation (VPT) to transform a set of measured inputs and outputs [3]. However, TPA techniques are exploited in the frequency domain, compromising their usability for real-time calculations, direct use in control, and dealing with time-varying or nonlinear systems.

Recently, it has been proposed by the authors in [4, 5] to determine forces transmitting through connecting elements, such as rubber bushings, using an Augmented Kalman Filter (AKF) under the assumption of local rigid behaviour at the interfaces. This estimation is achieved by applying the VPT method to determine state-space models whose inputs are transformed into inaccessible virtual points. It makes estimating forces transmitting through connecting elements possible using measured data.

An unknown force's amplitude, position, and direction are essential in mechanical applications. Forces transmitted through connecting elements, such as rubber bushings, are crucial as they are the main pathway of structure-borne noise. It is essential to assess how effectively the bushing isolates vibrations by determining the forces transmitted through it. Furthermore, the position and direction of forces on each side of a bushing can affect its durability, leading to increased vibration, noise, or mechanical failure. Understanding these forces can also aid active control strategies employing advanced bushings. The existing literature primarily focuses on identifying unknown forces acting on mechanical systems at known locations, while forces transmitting through components or applied at unknown structure positions are less identified.

Obtaining State-Space Mdels from Experimental Data

The model-based estimation framework applied in this research utilises an experimental state-space model. The method that will be used to identify the state-space model from experimentally acquired data was originally proposed in [6]. This approach is composed of three different steps. 1) The Frequency Response Functions (FRF) of the structure of interest

Julian Staiger · Frank Naets
Department of Mechanical Engineering, KU Leuven, 3001 Heverlee, Belgium; Flanders Make@KU Leuven, 3001 Heverlee, Belgum
e-mail: Julian.Staiger@kuleuven.be; frank.naets@kuleuven.be

Brandon Dilworth et al. (eds.), *Topics in Modal Analysis & Parameter Identification I, Vol. 9*, Conference Proceedings of the Society for Experimental Mechanics Series, https://doi.org/10.13052/9788743801542-2

must be measured. 2) System identification algorithms, such as Polyreference least-squares complex frequency-domain (PolyMAX) [7] and Maximum Likelihood-Modal Model Method (ML-MM) [8], must be exploited to determine modal parameters from the measured set of FRFs. 3) As a final step, a complete state-space model representative of the dynamics of the structure of interest is constructed.

A complete state-space model can be defined by the in-band modal parameters (i.e. poles, mode shapes and modal participation factors) together with Residual Compensation Modes (RCM) determined from the lower and upper residual matrices to account for the out-of-band dynamic contributions as outlined by Dias et al.[9]. In this way, a complete state-space model, whose FRFs approximate the measured FRFs, can be defined as follows:

$$\dot{\tilde{\mathbf{x}}}(t) = \tilde{\mathbf{A}}\tilde{\mathbf{x}}(t) + \tilde{\mathbf{B}}\mathbf{u}(t) \tag{1}$$

$$\mathbf{y}(t) = \tilde{\mathbf{C}}\tilde{\mathbf{x}}(t) + \tilde{\mathbf{D}}\mathbf{u}(t), \tag{2}$$

where, $\mathbf{u}(t) \in \mathbb{R}^{n_i \times 1}$ is the vector of inputs while $\mathbf{y}(t) \in \mathbb{R}^{n_o \times 1}$ denotes the output vector constituted by displacements. Matrices $\tilde{\mathbf{A}} \in \mathbb{C}^{n \times n}$, $\tilde{\mathbf{B}} \in \mathbb{C}^{n \times n_i}$, $\tilde{\mathbf{C}} \in \mathbb{C}^{n_o \times n}$ and $\tilde{\mathbf{D}} \in \mathbb{C}^{n_o \times n_i}$ are the state, input, output and feedthrough matrices, respectively, with n representing the number of states and n_i,n_o the number of inputs and outputs respectively. These state-space matrices are given as follows:

$$\tilde{\mathbf{A}} = \begin{bmatrix} \mathbf{\Lambda}_{ib,RCM} & 0 \\ 0 & \mathbf{\Lambda}^H_{ib,RCM} \end{bmatrix} = \begin{bmatrix} \mathbf{\Lambda}_{ib} & 0 & 0 & & & \\ 0 & \mathbf{\Lambda}_{LR} & 0 & & \ddots & \\ 0 & 0 & \mathbf{\Lambda}_{UR} & & & \\ & & & \mathbf{\Lambda}^H_{ib} & 0 & 0 \\ & \ddots & & 0 & \mathbf{\Lambda}^H_{LR} & 0 \\ & & & 0 & 0 & \mathbf{\Lambda}^H_{UR} \end{bmatrix},$$

$$\tilde{\mathbf{B}} = \begin{bmatrix} \mathbf{L}_{ib,RCM} \\ \mathbf{L}^H_{ib,RCM} \end{bmatrix} = \begin{bmatrix} \mathbf{L}_{ib} \\ \mathbf{L}_{LR} \\ \mathbf{L}_{UR} \\ \mathbf{L}^H_{ib} \\ \mathbf{L}^H_{LR} \\ \mathbf{L}^H_{UR} \end{bmatrix}, \quad \tilde{\mathbf{C}} = \begin{bmatrix} \mathbf{\Psi}_{ib,RCM} & \mathbf{\Psi}^H_{ib,RCM} \end{bmatrix} = \begin{bmatrix} \mathbf{\Psi}_{ib} & \mathbf{\Psi}_{VP,LR} & \mathbf{\Psi}_{VP,UR} & \mathbf{\Psi}^H_{ib} & \mathbf{\Psi}^H_{VP,LR} & \mathbf{\Psi}^H_{VP,UR} \end{bmatrix} \tag{3}$$

with subscripts $\bullet_{LR}$ and $\bullet_{UR}$ denoting matrices composed of modal parameters associated with the RCMs exploited to, respectively, model the dynamic contribution of the lower and upper out-of-band modes. For a detailed discussion on the definition of these sets of RCMs, the reader is referred to [6, 9, 10]. It is also worth noticing that $\tilde{\mathbf{D}}$ is a null matrix for measured displacements [11, 4] but kept in Eq. (2) and subsequently for the sake of continuity of notation.

Joint Input-State-Position-Estimation Based on Parametrized IDMs

We consider a general geometrical reduction of a force acting on a rigid interface to a virtual point, as illustrated in Fig. 1. The contributions in the virtual point **m** can be expressed as a function of the acting force, its position and direction of action as:

$$\mathbf{m} = \bar{\mathbf{R}}^p_f(\mathbf{p}))^T f = \begin{bmatrix} 1 & 0 & 0 \\ 0 & 1 & 0 \\ 0 & 0 & 1 \\ 0 & -r_z & r_y \\ r_z & 0 & -r_x \\ -r_y & r_x & 0 \end{bmatrix} \begin{bmatrix} e_x \\ e_y \\ e_z \end{bmatrix} f = \begin{bmatrix} e_x \\ e_y \\ e_z \\ -r_z e_y + r_y e_z \\ r_z e_x - r_x e_z \\ -r_y e_x + r_x e_y \end{bmatrix} f. \tag{4}$$

with the parameter vector given as $\mathbf{p} = \begin{bmatrix} e_x & e_y & e_z & r_x & r_y & r_z \end{bmatrix}^T$ and $\bar{\mathbf{R}}^p_f(\mathbf{p}))$ can be understood as an Parametrized Interface Deformation Mode (PIDM). In this way, the parametrised expression given in Eq. (4) can be used to obtain the following nonlinear state-space representation:

$$\dot{\tilde{\mathbf{x}}}(t, \mathbf{p}) = \tilde{\mathbf{A}}_{VP}\tilde{\mathbf{x}}(t) + \tilde{\mathbf{B}}\mathbf{T}^T_f(\bar{\mathbf{R}}^p_f(\mathbf{p}))^T f(t), \tag{5}$$

$$\mathbf{y}(t, \mathbf{p}) = \tilde{\mathbf{C}}_{VP}\tilde{\mathbf{x}}(t) + \tilde{\mathbf{D}}\mathbf{T}^T_f(\bar{\mathbf{R}}^p_f(\mathbf{p}))^T f(t). \tag{6}$$

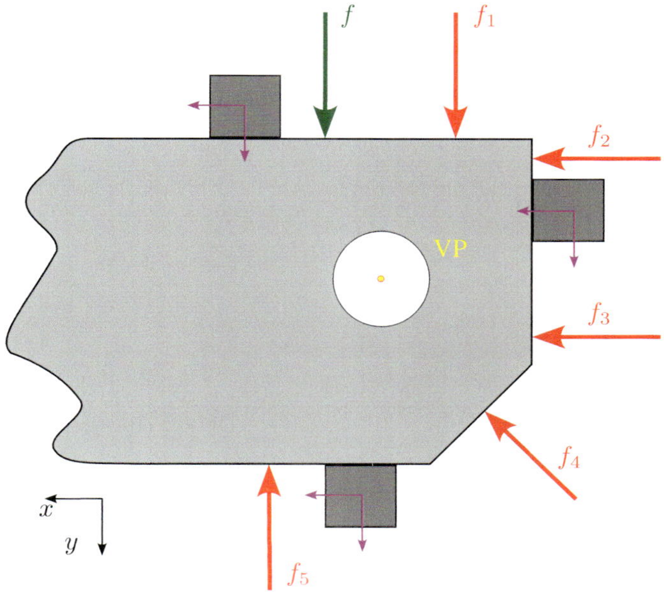

Fig. 1 Transforming the inputs of a given state-space model into a virtual point of interest and arbitrarily applied force f.

The system presented in Eqs. (5) and (6) is nonlinear due to its dependence on the parameter vector $\mathbf{p}$. At this point, to jointly estimate the parameter vector alongside the system states and the input, the state vector of the system as given in Eqs. (5) and (6) will be augmented to define the augmented model, including the dynamics states, the unknown parameters and force. To define this augmented system, the time evolution of the parameters and inputs must be modelled. A Zeroth Order Random Walk (ZORW) model will be used for both the parameters and inputs as given hereafter:

$$\dot{\mathbf{p}}(t) = \mathbf{0} + \mathbf{w}_p, \tag{7}$$

$$\dot{f}(t) = 0 + w_f, \tag{8}$$

where $\mathbf{w}_p$ and w_f are Gaussian variables with $\mathbf{w}_p \sim \mathcal{N}(0, \mathbf{Q}_p) \in \mathbb{R}^{n_p \times 1}$ and $w_f \sim \mathcal{N}(0, \mathbf{Q}_f) \in \mathbb{R}$ respectively. The deterministic-stochastic nonlinear augmented system can, thus, be denoted in short-hand notation as:

$$\dot{\tilde{\mathbf{x}}}_a(t) = \mathbf{g}(\tilde{\mathbf{x}}, \mathbf{p}, f) + \mathbf{w}_{a,NL}, \tag{9}$$

$$\mathbf{y}(t) = \mathbf{h}(\tilde{\mathbf{x}}, \mathbf{p}, f) + \mathbf{v}, \tag{10}$$

with

$$\tilde{\mathbf{x}}_a = \begin{bmatrix} \tilde{\mathbf{x}} \\ \mathbf{p} \\ f \end{bmatrix}, \quad \mathbf{g}(\tilde{\mathbf{x}}, \mathbf{p}, f) = \begin{bmatrix} \tilde{\mathbf{A}}_{VP}\tilde{\mathbf{x}} + \tilde{\mathbf{B}}_{VP}(\bar{\mathbf{R}}_f^p(\mathbf{p}))^T f \\ \mathbf{0} \\ 0 \end{bmatrix}, \quad \mathbf{w}_{a,NL} = \begin{bmatrix} \mathbf{w}_x \\ \mathbf{w}_p \\ w_f \end{bmatrix}, \quad \text{and} \quad \mathbf{h}(\tilde{\mathbf{x}}, \mathbf{p}, f) = \left[\tilde{\mathbf{C}}_{VP}\tilde{\mathbf{x}} + \tilde{\mathbf{D}}_{VP}(\bar{\mathbf{R}}_f^p(\mathbf{p}))^T f\right]. \tag{11}$$

The augmented system presented in Eqs. (9) and (10) is nonlinearly dependent on the set of unknown parameters included in $\mathbf{p}$. Linear estimation approaches like the linear Kalman filter can not be employed directly to estimate the states, inputs and parameters. Hence, a novel nonlinear Kalman filter, the Dual Augmented Extended Kalman Filter (DAEKF), introduced in [5], finds application in this article.

Results

The reconstruction results of a force applied by a shaker on a rigid interface attached to a rubber bushing as outlined in [5] are shown in Figure 2. Along with the estimation based on the nonlinear model introduced in Section also, two linear estimations are compared (details can be found in [5]). The three configurations which are compared are:

- Config.1: Linear AKF, defined with the unreduced model composed of 12 reference forces.

- Config.2: Linear AKF, defined with a virtual point reduced model estimating six virtual point contributions $\hat{\mathbf{m}}_{VP}$ belonging to the considered virtual point.
- Config.3: DAEKF estimation employing a nonlinear model as established in Eqs. (9) and (10) yielding an estimate of the force acting at the unknown position.

Analysing Fig. 2, it is evident that the applied force is best reconstructed by configuration 3. This trend is visible in the time- and frequency-domain and validates the performance of the nonlinear model and the use of the DAEKF.

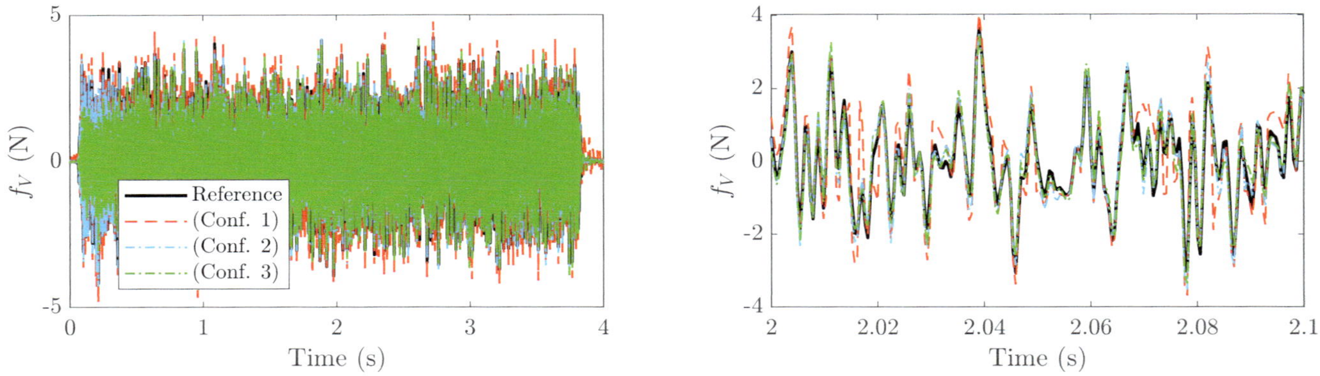

(a) Time-domain estimation of the force applied by the shaker.

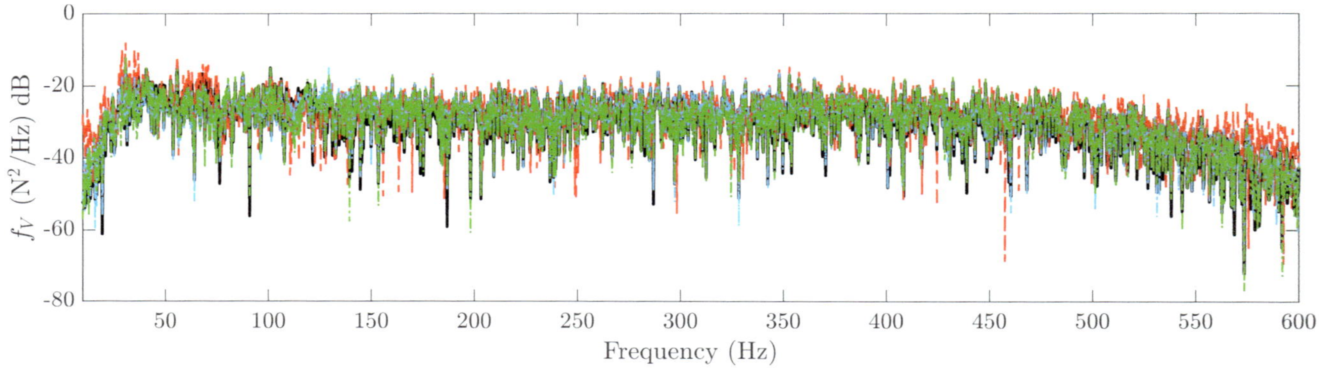

(b) Frequency-domain estimation of the force applied by the shaker.

Fig. 2 Time- and frequency-domain estimation results for the reference force f.

Conclusion

This paper compares three methodologies to determine an unknown force applied on a rigid interface while introducing the concept of PIDMs. Two of these approaches are based on linear AKF schemes, while the other employs a nonlinear augmented model defined via VPT by exploiting PIDMs. For estimation with the nonlinear model, the recently proposed DAEKF approach finds application in this article. The results obtained using a linear AKF based on the unreduced model showed the least accurate fit in both frequency and time domains when reconstructing the experimentally applied force. However, this was followed by the configuration using the same AKF with the virtual point reduced model. The reported results indicate that the strategy using the defined augmented nonlinear system combined with the DAEKF outperforms the previous two configurations, proving more suitable for determining an unknown force applied on a rigid interface.

Acknowledgments The authors gratefully acknowledge the European Commission for its support of the Marie Skłodowska Curie program through the ETN ECO DRIVE project (GA 858018).

References

1. Gajdatsy, P., Janssens, K., Desmet, W., and Van Der Auweraer, H. "Application of the transmissibility concept in transfer path analysis". *Mechanical Systems and Signal Processing*, 24(7):1963–1976 (2010)
2. Mas, P., Sas, P., and Wyckaert, K. "Indirect force determination based upon matrix inversion : A study on statistical and deterministic accuracy" (1994)
3. Van Der Seijs, M.V., Van Den Bosch, D.D., Rixen, D.J., and De Klerk, D. "An improved methodology for the virtual point transformation of measured frequency response functions in Dynamic Substructuring". In *ECCOMAS Thematic Conference - COMPDYN 2013: 4th International Conference on Computational Methods in Structural Dynamics and Earthquake Engineering, Proceedings - An IACM Special Interest Conference*, pages 4334–4347 (2013)
4. Staiger, J., Dias, R.S., Martarelli, M., Zucchini, A., and Naets, F. "Advancements and frequency domain error analysis for state-input estimation in virtual points via the augmented Kalman filter". *Submitted to Mechanical Systems and Signal Processing*, (in review) (2024)
5. Staiger, J., Dias, R.S., Vanpaemel, S., and Naets, F. "A parametrised virtual point reduction estimation framework for determining an unknown force, its direction and position of action". *Journal of Sound and Vibration*, 612 (2025)
6. Elkafafy, M. and Peeters, B. "Robust Identification of Stable MIMO Modal State Space Models". In Dilworth, B.J., Marinone, T., and Mains, M., editors, *Topics in Modal Analysis & Parameter Identification, Volume 8*, pages 81–95, Cham (2023) Springer International Publishing.
7. Peeters, B., Van Der Auweraer, H., Guillaume, P., and Leuridan, J. "The PolyMAX frequency-domain method: A new standard for modal parameter estimation?". *Shock and Vibration*, 11(3-4) (2004)
8. El-Kafafy, M., Peeters, B., Guillaume, P., and De Troyer, T. "Constrained maximum likelihood modal parameter identification applied to structural dynamics". *Mechanical Systems and Signal Processing*, 72-73 (2016)
9. Dias, R., Martarelli, M., and Chiariotti, P. "State-Space domain Virtual Point Transformation for State-Space identification in Dynamic Substructuring". In *Proceedings of the International Conference on Noise and Vibration Engineering*, pages 1627–1638 (2022)
10. Dias, R.S., Martarelli, M., and Chiariotti, P. "Including connecting elements into the Lagrange multiplier state-space substructuring formulation". *Journal of Sound and Vibration*, 546:117445 (2023)
11. Lembregts, F., Leuridan, J., and Van Brussel, H. "Frequency domain direct parameter identification for modal analysis: State space formulation". *Mechanical Systems and Signal Processing*, 4(1) (1990)

Chapter 3
Extracting 3D Mode Shapes from Cell Phone Videos

Shawn Richardson and Mark Richardson

Abstract Most power plants, oil refineries, and manufacturing plants worldwide have implemented machinery health monitoring programs for assessing the health of their rotating machinery and associated equipment. Digital vibration signals are the primary data used to detect and diagnose mechanical faults in machinery and equipment. A cell phone is a low-cost, non-contacting measurement device that can be used to accurately record the vibration of a machine during its operation. Everyone has a cell phone handy for making vibration measurements.

In this paper, it is shown how 3-dimensional (**3D**) Operational Modal Analysis (**OMA**) mode shapes of a rotating machine are calculated from a cell phone video using two curve fitting steps. First, the 2-dimensional (**2D**) **OMA** mode shapes of the machine are obtained by curve fitting a set of **ODS-FRFs** which were calculated from **TWFs** extracted from a cell phone video.

In the second step, **3D FEA** mode shapes of the machine are curve-fit to the **2D OMA** mode shapes to create **3D OMA** mode shapes. Starting with a cell phone video, this two-step curve fitting process yields accurate **3D OMA** mode shapes that can be used to characterize and diagnose the health of rotating machinery. This is demonstrated in a companion paper [1].

Keywords Time Waveform (**TWF**) · Digital Fourier Transform (**DFT**) · Operational Modal Analysis (**OMA**) mode shape · Finite Element Analysis (**FEA**) mode shape · Operating Deflection Shape (**ODS**) · Degree of Freedom (**DOF**) · Auto Power Spectrum (**APS**) · Cross Power Spectrum (**XPS**) · **ODS-FRF** (**APS** and **Phase** of an **XPS**) · Structural Dynamics Modification (**SDM**).

Rotating Machine

In a previous paper [2], **ODS's** were extracted from cell phone videos ***for nine different unbalance cases*** of the rotating machine shown in Figure 1. This machine has a variable speed motor connected to the rotor with a rubber belt. The motor speed was adjusted so that the rotor speed was ***approximately*** **1000 RPM** throughout all the cell phone video recordings. The video from one of those ***nine different unbalance cases*** was used for this paper.

Introduction

In previous papers [1] - [3] we illustrated the use of a new method for extracting vibration **TWFs** from frames of a cell phone video. In this paper we introduce a two-step curve fitting process for calculating **3D** mode shapes of a rotating machine from the **2D** mode shapes calculated from a cell phone video.

In the first curve fitting step, the **2D** mode shapes of the machine are obtained by using traditional digital signal processing methods together with **FRF-based** curve fitting. In the second curve fitting step, **3D** mode shapes of the machine are calculated by curve fitting its **2D** mode shapes with **3D FEA** mode shapes. To perform this second curve fitting step, a simple **FEA** model of the rotating machine was constructed in three steps using the Structural Dynamics Modification (**SDM**) method [4].

To calculate the **FEA** mode shapes, first an **FEA** model of one of the bearing blocks of the machine was created, and its **FEA** mode shapes were calculated. Then an **FEA** model of the baseplate was created, and its **FEA** mode shapes were calculated.

Shawn Richardson · Mark Richardson
Vibrant Technology, Inc., Centennial, CO
e-mail: shawn.richardson@vibetech.com; mark.richardson@vibetech.com

Brandon Dilworth et al. (eds.), *Topics in Modal Analysis & Parameter Identification I, Vol. 9*, Conference Proceedings of the Society for Experimental Mechanics Series, https://doi.org/10.13052/9788743801542-3

Fig. 1 Rotating Machine & Unbalance Screws Added to Its Rotors.

Next, ***very stiff*** **FEA springs** were attached between both bearing blocks and the baseplate, as shown in Figure 8. Then **SDM** was used to calculate the new mode shapes of the two bearing blocks firmly attached to the base plate. One of the new mode shapes is shown in Figure 8. Finally, **FEA** spring elements were attached between the corners of the baseplate and the fixed tabletop on which the rotating machine rested, and the new mode shapes of that model were calculated using **SDM** again.

Finally, a second curve fitting step was used to calculate the **3D OMA** mode shapes of the rotating machine from its **2D OMA** mode shapes. The **2D OMA** mode shapes were obtained by curve fitting the **ODS-FRFs** which were calculated from the cell phone video.

This two-step curve fitting process, curve fitting **ODS-FRFs** followed by curve fitting the **2D OMA** mode shapes with **3D FEA** mode shapes, can be used to calculate the **3D OMA** mode shapes of any rotating machine or test article when a cell video of it is recorded while it is vibrating.

TWFs & DFTs

A rectangular grid of points with rectangular surfaces attached between them is created when a video is processed in MEscope [8]. Frames of the video are attached to this surface during animated display of Video ODS's. Using a rectangular point grid, millions of pixels in each frame of a cell phone video are processed to extract TWFs for the horizontal & vertical deflections of thousands of points in the point grid. Grid points with little or no motion, (like background points), are hidden and their linked TWFs are removed from further analysis. A point grid with background points hidden is shown in Figure 2.

A DFT is calculated from each TWF that is extracted from the video. Time-based ODS's are displayed in animation from the TWFs using a sweeping Line cursor. Frequency-based ODS's are displayed in animation from the DFTs using sine dwell modulation of the ODS at the cursor position. The magnitude & phase of the ODS at selected grid points can also be displayed, as shown in Figure 2.

ODS-FRFs

A unique frequency domain function, called an **ODS-FRF,** can be calculated from each response **TWF** extracted from a video. A set of **ODS-FRFs** calculated from the **TWFs** is typically more accurate than **DFTs** because ***spectrum averaging*** can be used to reduce extraneous noise from the **ODS-FRFs**.

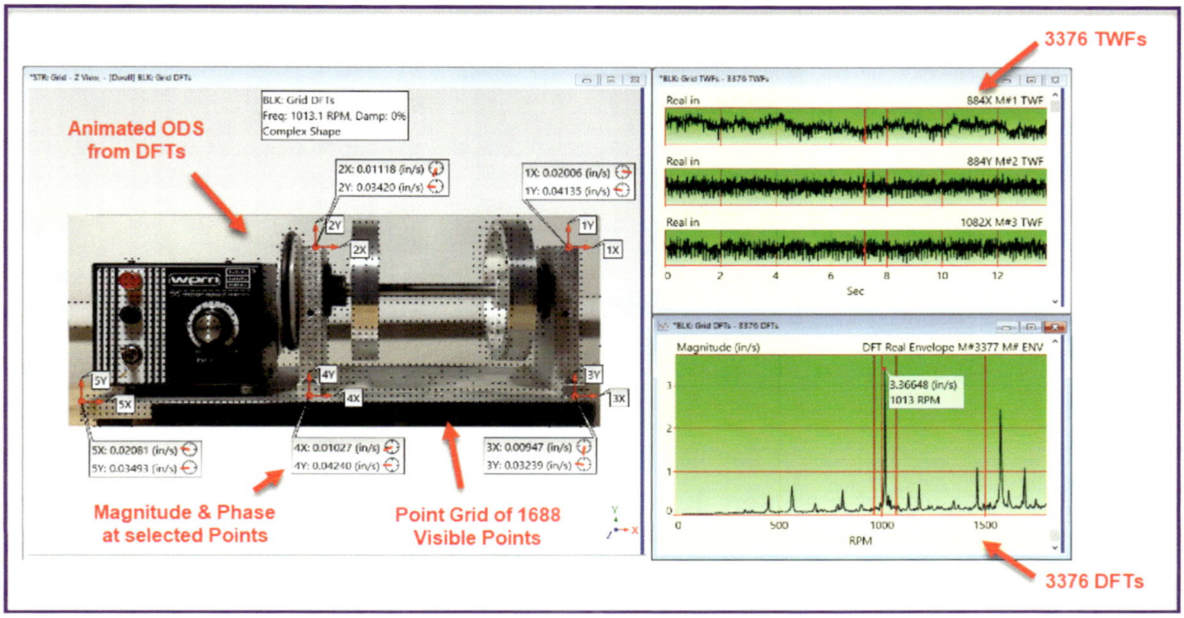

Fig. 2 First-Order ODS Animated from DFTs.

The ***magnitude*** of an **ODS-FRF** is the **APS** of the ***response*** **DOF** at a grid point. The ***phase*** of the **ODS-FRF** is the ***phase of the*** **XPS** between the ***response*** **DOF** and the **DOF** of any ***reference*** grid point.

ODS-FRFs carry the ***same displacement units*** as the response **TWFs** from which they are calculated. But because it is a frequency domain function, an **ODS-FRF** can be ***accurately differentiated to velocity units*** by multiplying it by the frequency variable.

Vibration in ***velocity units*** is commonly used by vibration analysts to quantify vibration levels in rotating equipment.

One of the laws of the **FFT** algorithm is that **Δf = 1/T**, where **Δf** is the ***frequency difference between samples*** of an **ODS-FRF**, and **T** is the ***time length*** of **TWF** data from which the **ODS-FRF** was calculated. For example, if an **ODS-FRF** is calculated from **TWF** data over a **15 second** period, the frequency resolution (**Δf**) of the **ODS-FRF** is **60/15 = 4 RPM**.

To increase the frequency resolution of an **ODS-FRF**, **TWF** data over a ***longer period*** **T** is required. Therefore, the video from which the **TWFs** are extracted must be recorded over a ***longer period*** **T**.

Aliased Order Peaks

A limitation of any video recording is that ***anti-alias filtering cannot be used*** to remove high-frequency signals from the video.

Without anti-alias filtering, machine order peaks ***greater than one-half the sampling frequency***, (called **Fmax**), are ***folded around*** **Fmax** and appear at lower frequencies in the **ODS-FRFs**, as shown in Figure 3.

All machine-order resonance peaks between **Fmax & 2x Fmax** are folded around (***wrapped around***) **Fmax** and appear at lower frequencies in the frequency band **(0 to Fmax)**. Aliasing of higher frequencies occurs in both **DFTs** and **ODS-FRFs**.

The **ODS-FRF** shown in Figure 3 was calculated from a **TWF** that was extracted from a video that was sampled at **60 fps**, or **3600 RPM**. Therefore, the **Fmax** of the **ODS-FRF** is **1800 RPM**. The first-order peak is at the machine running speed and is clearly visible at **1014 RPM**. The second order resonance peak should be at **2028 RPM** and third order resonance peak should be at **3042 RPM,** but they are both ***folded around*** **1800 RPM** and are clearly visible ***at lower frequencies*** in the **ODS-FRF**.

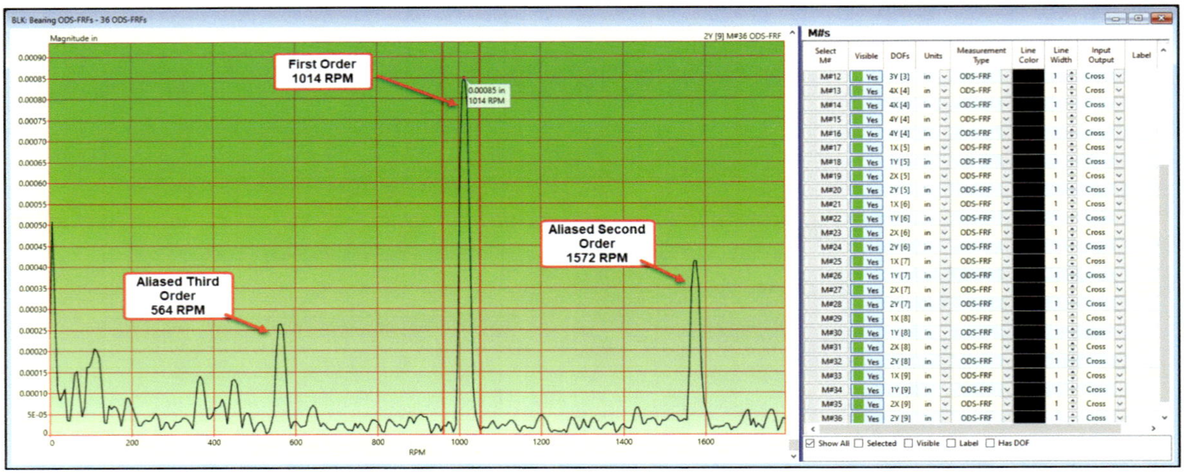

Fig. 3 ODS-FRF Showing First Three Order Peaks.

The aliased frequency of an order higher than **Fmax** can be calculated from **Fmax** and the expected order frequency.

- **Second order** aliased frequency 1800 - (2028 - 1800) **1572 RPM**
- **Third order** aliased frequency 1800 - (3042 - 1800) **558 RPM**

The **ODS-FRF** in Figure 3 was calculated from a **TWF** with ***a 10-second length***. Therefore **Δf = (1/10) Hz or 60/10 = 6 RPM** and the aliased frequency of the third order peak is ***within one*** **(Δf)** of its calculated value.

Curve Fitting The ODS-FRFs

ODS-FRFs can be curve-fit using an **FRF-based** curve fitter if they have been filtered with a special window. In MEscope [8] this filter is called a ***DeConvolution window***. This filter reshapes an **ODS-FRF** so that it more closely resembles an **FRF** and therefore can be curve fit using **FRF-based** curve fitting. An **FRF-based** curve fit of an **ODS-FRF** is shown in Figure 4. In the upper left-hand graph, the **red curve fitting function** is overlaid on a magnitude plot of the **ODS-FRF**.

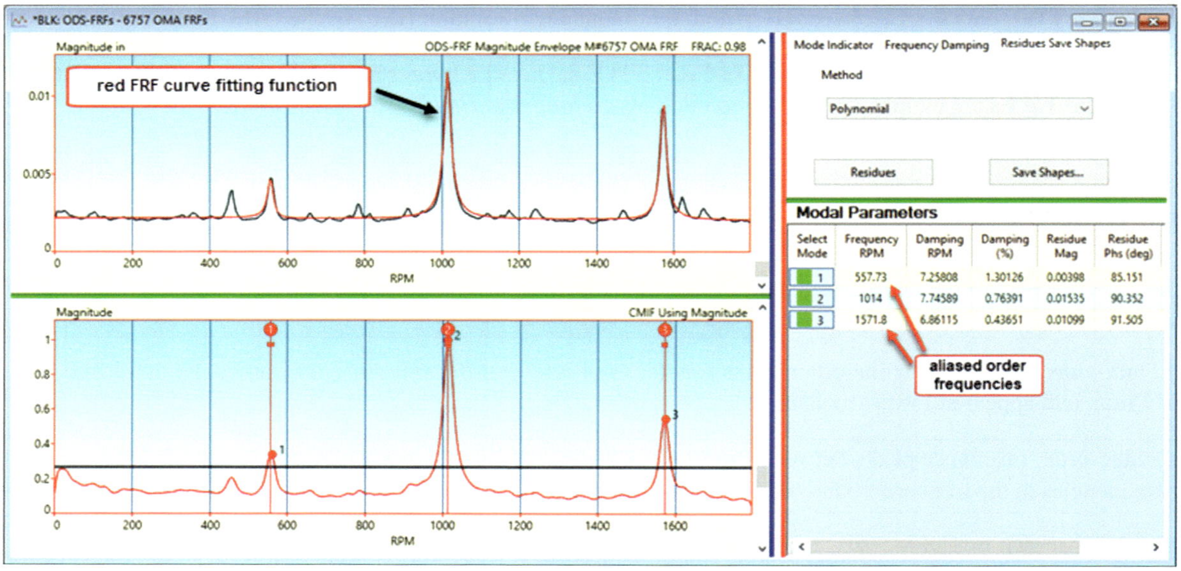

Fig. 4 Curve Fit of ODS-FRFs.

The aliased frequencies of the second and third orders are correctly estimated by curve fitting the **ODS-FRFs**.

Damping Removal

DeConvolution windowed is necessary before using an **FRF-based** curve fitter on a set of **ODS-FRFs**. But DeConvolution windowing ***adds a known amount of damping*** to each **OMA** mode shape. Therefore, following **FRF-based** curve fitting, when the **OMA** mode shapes are stored into a Shape Table in MEscope [8], the damping added by DeConvolution windowing is removed from them. This is shown in Figure 5.

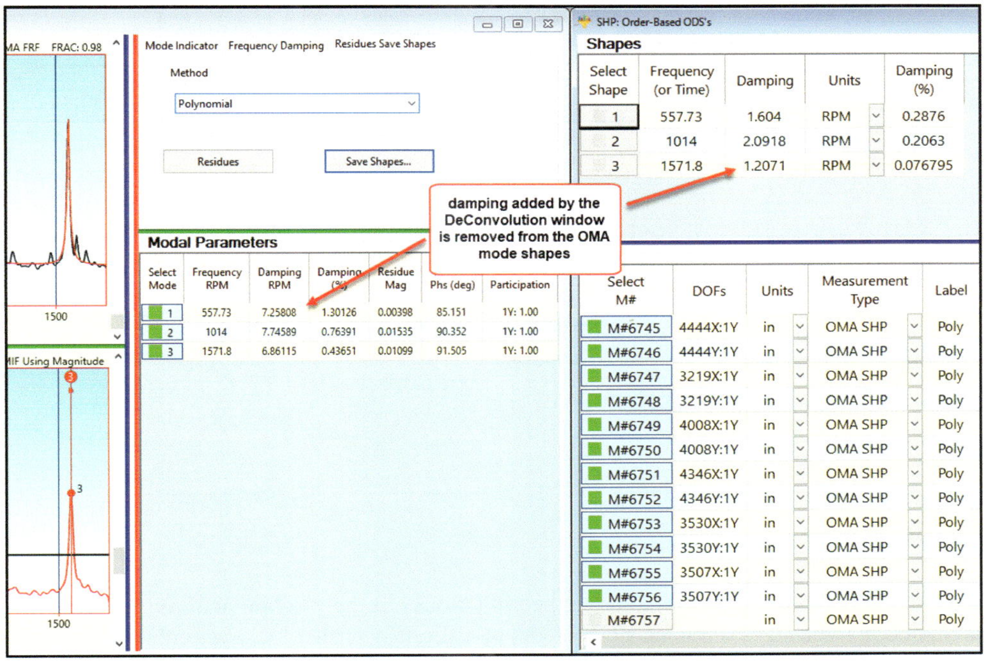

Fig. 5 DeConvolution Window Damping is Removed when OMA Mode Shapes are Saved.

Animating the OMA Mode Shapes on the Point Grid

After the **2D OMA** modes shapes are saved in a Shape Table, they can be differentiated from ***displacement to velocity*** units. The three **OMA** mode shapes are shown in figure 6.

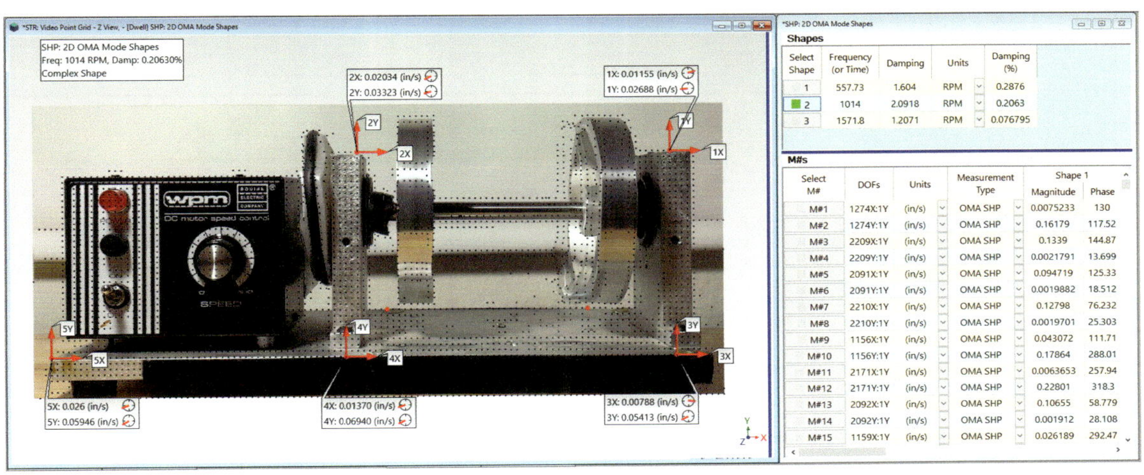

Fig. 6 Animated Display of 1014 RPM OMA Mode Shape on the Point Grid.

Structural Dynamics Modification (SDM)

SDM [4] is a modeling algorithm also referred to as ***"eigenvalue modification"***. Starting with the mode shapes of an unmodified mechanical structure, **SDM** calculates the ***new mode shapes*** resulting from making ***physical modifications*** to the structure by adding **FEA** elements between points on a model of the structure. Modifications are modeled with industry-standard finite elements. The inputs and outputs of **SDM** are depicted in Figure 7.

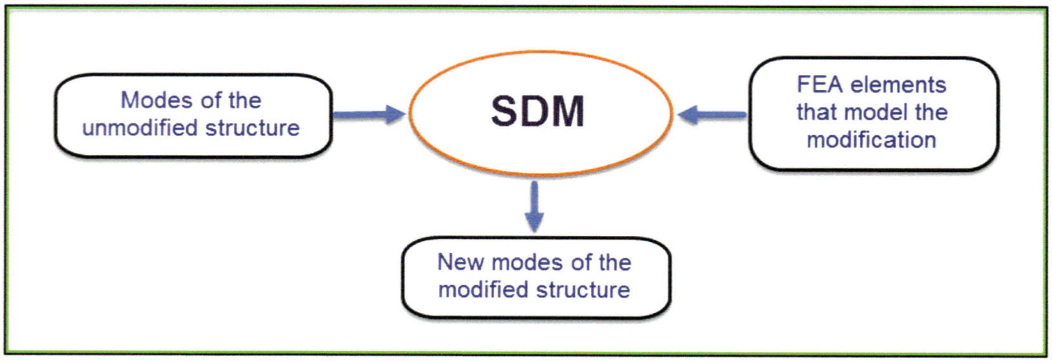

Fig. 7 Structural Dynamics Modification (SDM).

FEA Mode Shapes

The mode shapes of an **FEA** model of the baseplate & bearing blocks of the machine with rubber mounts resting on a fixed tabletop were calculated in three steps. First, an **FEA** model of a single bearing block was created, and its **FEA** mode shapes were calculated. Then, an **FEA** model of the baseplate was created, and its **FEA** mode shapes were calculated. Then **SDM** was used to model the attachment of both bearing blocks to the baseplate using ***very stiff*** **FEA spring elements**. This is depicted in Figure 8.

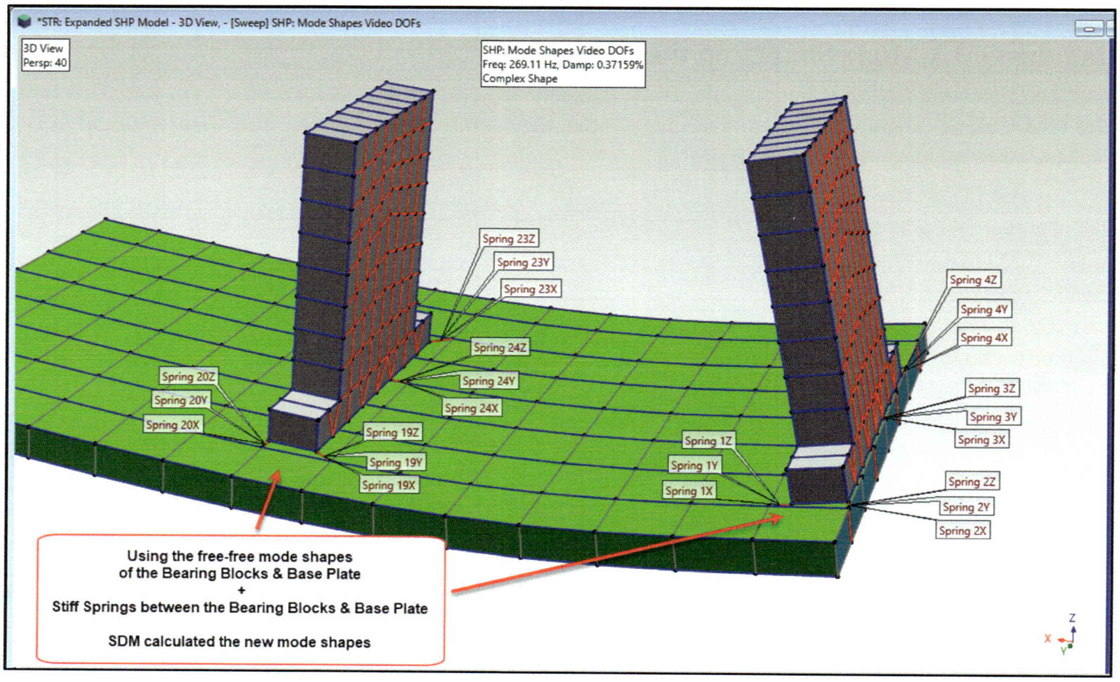

Fig. 8 Bearing Blocks Attached to the Baseplate With Very Stiff FEA Springs.

Next, to model the machine resting on a ***fixed*** tabletop, four **FEA spring elements** were added between each corner of the baseplate and a ***fixed ground point*** below the corner. Then **SDM** was used again to calculate the **FEA** mode shapes of the machine resting on the tabletop, as shown in Figure 9.

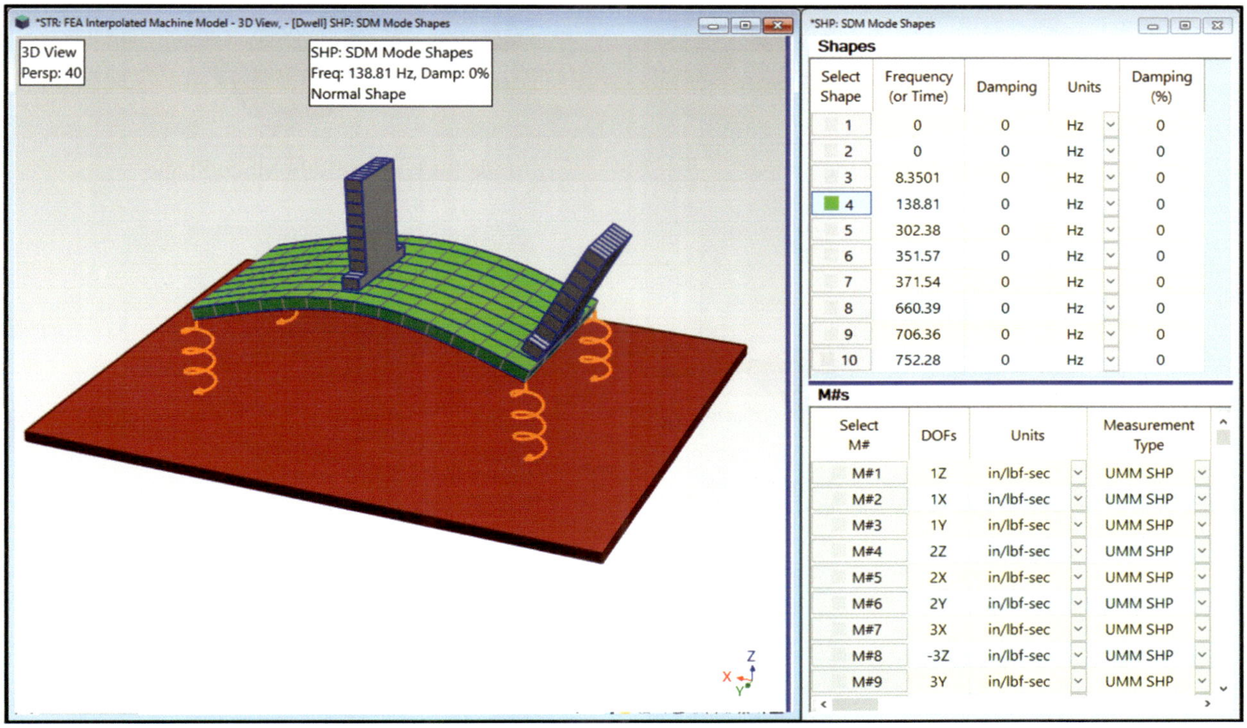

Fig. 9 Baseplate & Bearing Blocks Attached to the Fixed Tabletop With FEA Springs.

A stiffness of **10,000 lbs/inch** was used for each of the corner **FEA** spring elements. Using a different stiffness would change the frequencies of the **FEA** modes, but not their mode shapes. Only the **3D FEA** mode shapes are used to curve fit the **2D OMA** mode shapes, not their frequencies.
Admittedly, a much more accurate **FEA** model of the rotating machine could be created, but the **3D** mode shapes of this simplified model are sufficient for calculating **3D OMA** mode shapes by curve fitting the **2D OMA** mode shapes of the machine.

The ***ten lowest-frequency*** **FEA** mode shapes of the machine resting on a fixed tabletop with rubber mounts are shown in Figure 10.

Since damping was not modeled in the **FEA** models, all the mode shapes shown in Figure 10 have ***zero damping*** in them.

The ***first two*** mode shapes also have ***zero frequency***, and the ***third mode*** has a frequency ***nearly equal to zero.*** Since there is no bending of them in the baseplate or bearing blocks, these first three mode shapes in Figure 10 are called ***rigid-body*** mode shapes.

The first three mode shapes exhibit ***rigid-body*** deflection of the machine on its rubber mounts. The first two mode shapes are ***translational*** deflections in two directions and the third mode shape is ***rotational*** motion on the rubber mounts. All the other higher-frequency modes exhibit bending of the baseplate & bearing blocks; hence they are called ***flexible-body*** mode shapes.

Curve Fitting FEA Mode Shapes to 2D OMA Mode Shapes

In this second curve fitting step **3D OMA** mode shapes are calculated by curve fitting the **3D FEA** mode shapes of the machine to its **2D OMA** mode shapes. The **3D FEA** mode shapes of the baseplate & bearing blocks mounted with springs to a fixed base are curve fit to the **2D OMA** mode shapes obtained from curve fitting the **ODS-FRFs**.

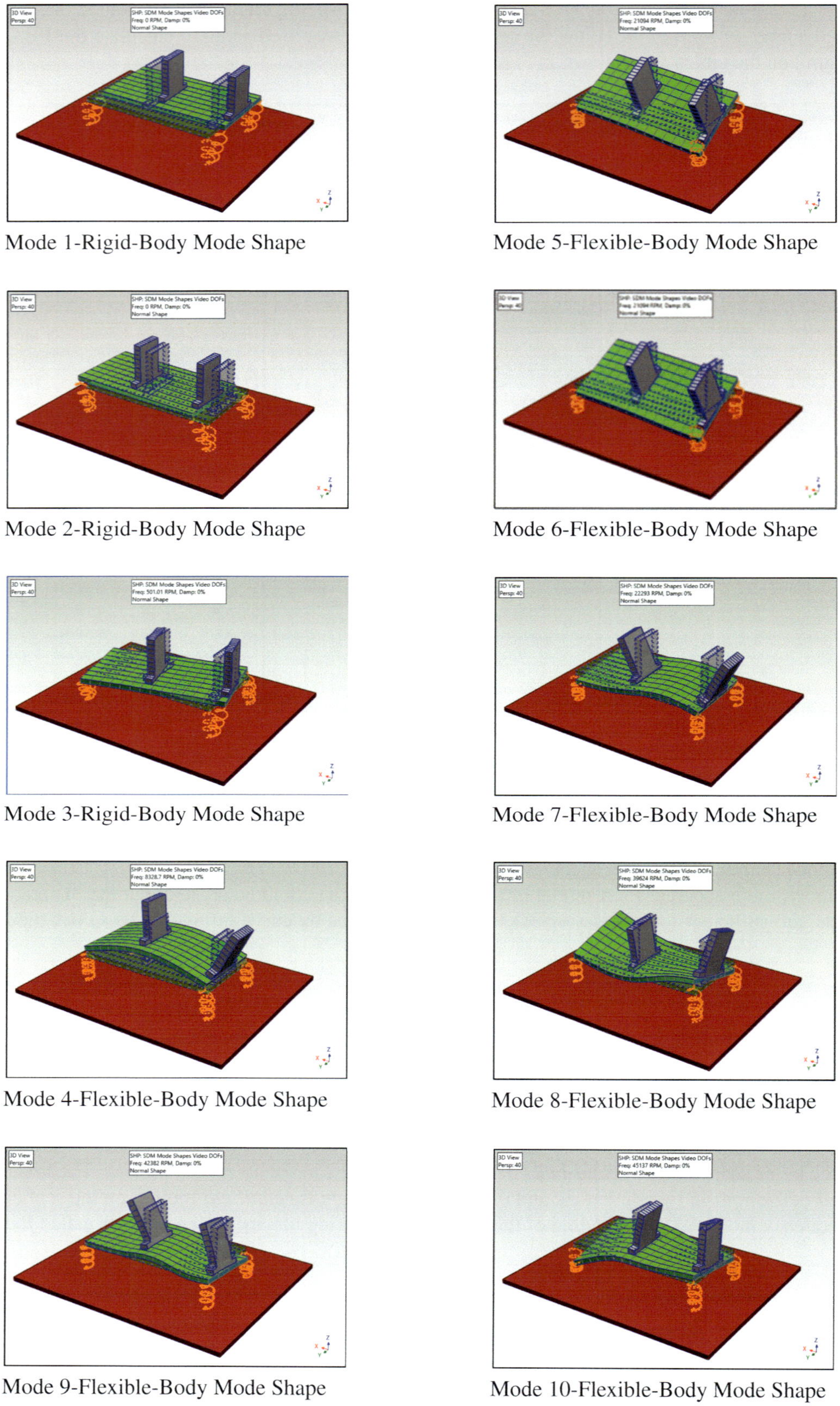

Mode 1-Rigid-Body Mode Shape

Mode 5-Flexible-Body Mode Shape

Mode 2-Rigid-Body Mode Shape

Mode 6-Flexible-Body Mode Shape

Mode 3-Rigid-Body Mode Shape

Mode 7-Flexible-Body Mode Shape

Mode 4-Flexible-Body Mode Shape

Mode 8-Flexible-Body Mode Shape

Mode 9-Flexible-Body Mode Shape

Mode 10-Flexible-Body Mode Shape

Fig. 10 FEA Mode Shapes of the Baseplate & Bearing Blocks on a Fixed Base

To curve fit the **3D** mode shapes to the **2D** mode shapes, five points on the video point grid were given the ***same point numbers*** as the ***five closest points*** on the **3D FEA** model, when viewed from the same direction as the video recording. The ***common numbered points*** are shown on the **FEA** model and on the point grid in Figure 11.

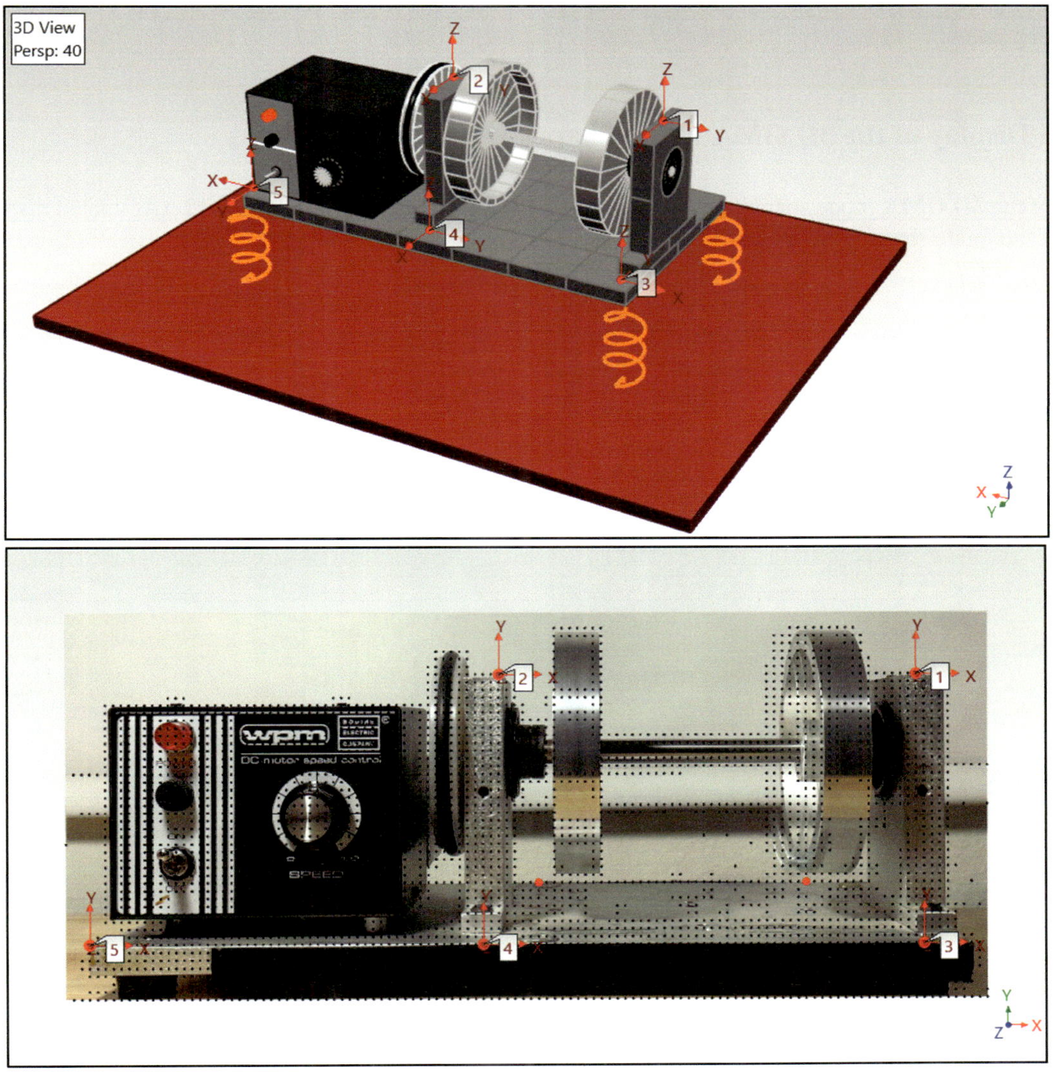

Fig. 11 FEA Model and Video Point Grid Showing Five Common Points.

The **FEA** mode shapes were curve-fit to the experimental **OMA** mode shapes using ***10 common*** shape **DOFs**, horizontal & vertical deflection at each of the five common points. This ***least-squared-error*** curve fitting yields a complex-valued ***participation*** of each **3D FEA** mode shape in each **2D OMA** mode shape. Then the **3D OMA** mode shapes are calculated using the ***participation*** of each **FEA** mode shape in each **OMA** mode shape.

- The **2D OMA** mode shapes have **6756 DOFs** in them, defining the **X & Y** motion at **3378 visible points** in the point grid
- The **3D FEA** mode shapes have **1938 DOFs** in them, defining the **X, Y & Z** motion at **646 points** in the **FEA** model

These are typical numbers of points for a video point grid and a simple **FEA** model of the baseplate & bearing blocks connected to a fixed base with rubber mounts.

- ***Least-sqaured-error*** curve fitting was performed using the ***10 common*** **DOFs** between the **2D OMA** shapes and the **3D FEA** mode shapes
- **3D OMA** mode shapes were calculated using the ***participation*** of each **FEA** mode shape in each **OMA** mode shape

Points must be chosen on the **FEA** model which are ***"close"*** to being in the ***same plane*** as the points chosen in the video point grid.

2D mode shape components from the **two red points** on the far side of the baseplate in the point grid cannot be used in this curve fitting step because ***their deflections would be less than the deflections*** of the **3D FEA** mode shapes at those corresponding points.

Animated Display of the 3D OMA Mode Shapes

Animation of the **3D OMA** mode shape of the first order at **1014 RPM** is shown in Figure 12. (Animated display shows the deflection of the mode shape more clearly.)

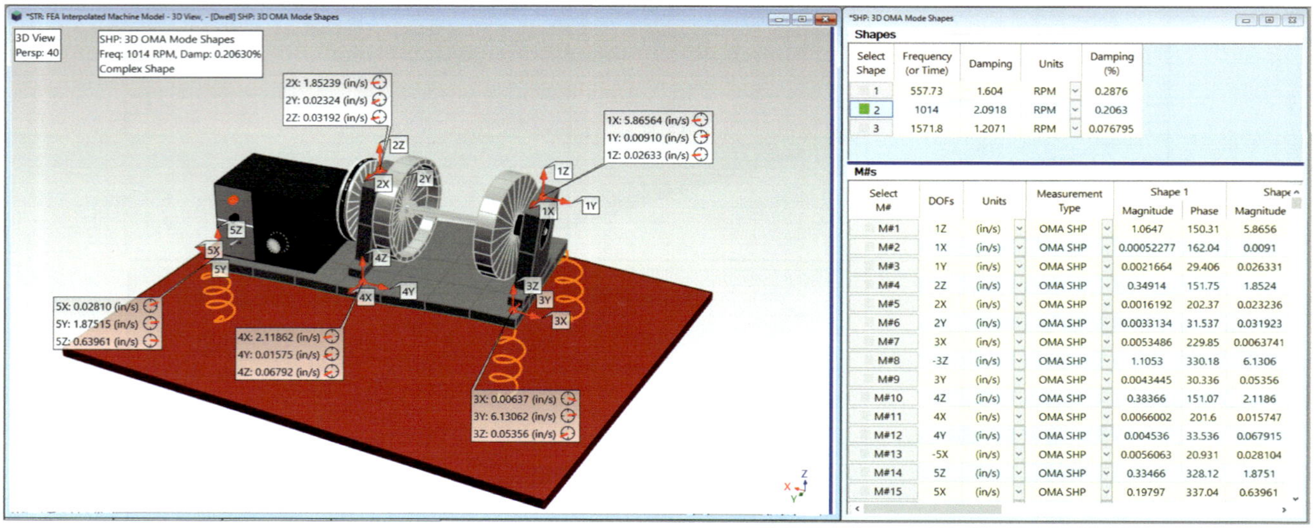

Fig. 12 Animated Deflection of the First-Order OMA Mode Shape.

Modal Participation

The participation of the **10 FEA** mode shapes in each **3D OMA** mode shape is shown in Figure 13. All the **3D OMA** mode shapes are ***very similar in shape*** because the **FEA** mode shapes ***participate nearly the same*** in each **3D OMA** mode shape, as shown in Figure 13. Only the ***magnitudes*** of the participation bars are different.

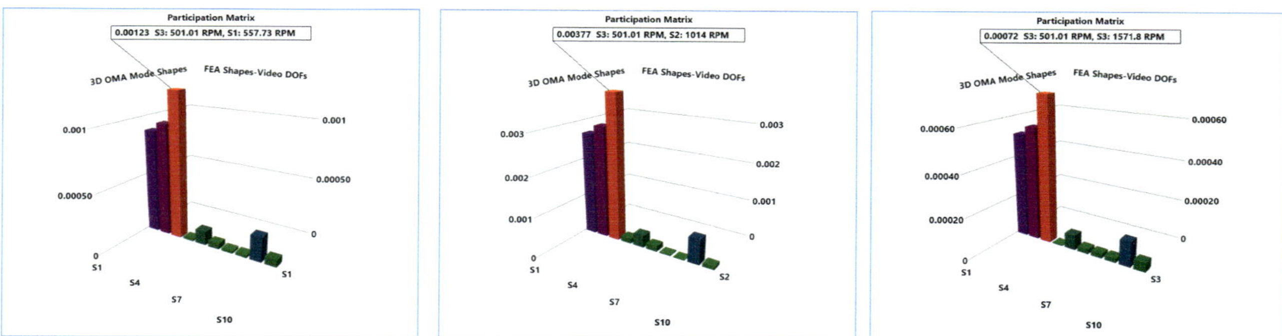

Fig. 13 Participation of FEA Mode Shapes in Each Order-Based OMA Mode Shape.

It can be concluded from Figure 13 that the mode shapes of the ***same three natural resonances dominate*** the first three orders of the machine's deflection at **1000 RPM**.

But re-examining the mode shapes in Figure 10, the first three **FEA** mode shapes define the ***rigid-body motion of the machine bouncing on its rubber mounts*** due to the unbalance forces from the rotors. All the remaining seven ***flexible-body*** mode shapes participate in the resonant vibration of the first three orders, with the ***ninth mode shape*** having the largest participation among the seven. From Figure 10 the deflection of the ninth resonance shows the bearing blocks rocking back and forth in phase with one another. These results agree with our intuition.

Conclusions

In this paper, we introduced a new method for curve fitting the **2D** mode shapes of a rotating machine to obtain its **3D** mode shapes. First, **ODF-FRFs** were calculated from the **TWFs** that were extracted from a **16-second-long** cell phone video of the rotating machine. Then, **2D OMA** mode shapes of a rotating machine were obtained by applying **FRF-based** curve fitting to the **ODS-FRFs**.

The **ODS-FRFs** contained the peaks of the ***first three orders*** of the rotating machine, two of them aliased about the **1800 RPM Fmax** of the **ODS-FRFs**. The **2D OMA** mode shapes obtained by curve fitting the **ODS-FRFs** were the mode shapes of the first three machine orders.

Then **3D FEA** mode shapes of the bearing blocks & baseplate of the machine resting on springs attached to a fixed tabletop were calculated in a series of steps. First an **FEA** model of a bearing block was constructed, and its mode shapes were calculated. Likewise, an **FEA** model of the baseplate was constructed, and its mode shapes were calculated. Then both bearing blocks were attached to the baseplate using very stiff springs. Finally, **SDM** was used to calculate the mode shapes of the baseplate & bearing blocks resting with rubber mounts on a fixed tabletop.

Finally, **3D OMA** mode shapes of the machine were calculated in a second curve fitting step by curve fitting **10 FEA** mode shapes of the machine to the **2D OMA** mode shapes of the machine. The participation of each **FEA** mode shape in each **3D OMA** mode shape gave results that satisfied our intuition.

These results verify **one of the laws of modal analysis**, namely that,

- All vibration can be represented as a ***summation of mode shapes***

References

1. S. Richardson, M. Richardson "Using Mode Shapes Derived from Cell Phone Videos to Monitor the Health of Rotating Machinery" IMAC XLII, January 29 - February 1, 2024, Orlando, FL.
2. B. Schwarz, S. Richardson, P. McHargue, M. Richardson "Using Modal Analysis and ODS Correlation to Identify Mechanical Faults in Rotating Machinery" IMAC XLII, January 29 - February 1, 2024, Orlando, TX.
3. D. Ambre, B. Schwarz, S. Richardson, M. Richardson, "Using Cell phone Videos to Diagnose Machinery Faults" IMAC XLI, , Austin, TX, February 13-16, 2023.
4. D. Formenti, M, Richardson, "Modal Modeling and Structural Dynamics Modification" Vibrant Technology, Inc., February 3, 2020.
5. B. Schwarz, S. Richardson, J. Tyler, R. Spears, M. Richardson, "Post-Processing ODS Data from a Vibration Video" IMAC XXXVIII Houston, TX, February 10-13, 2020.
6. B. Schwarz, M.H. Richardson, "Measurements Required for Displaying Operating Deflection Shapes" Proceedings of IMAC XXII, January 26, 2004
7. "B. Schwarz, P. McHargue, M. Richardson "Using SDM to Train Neural Networks for Solving Modal Sensitivity Problems" 14th IMAC Conference, Dearborn, MI, February 1996
8. MEscope^{TM} is a trademark of Vibrant Technology, Inc. www.vibetech.com

Chapter 4
Mode Shape Extraction Using Direct Field Acoustic Noise Test Data

Kevin Napolitano, Dr. Michael Yang, Eric Friedlander, and Dale Schick

Abstract Direct field acoustic noise (DFAN) testing involves the placement of loudspeakers around a structure for acoustic qualification tests. It is becoming more prevalent because it allows the testing to be performed in situ, which reduces or eliminates the test article transportation costs that arise from testing in an acoustic reverberation chamber. DFAN testing could provide an even greater value proposition if it could be used as a source of excitation for modal survey tests. This paper describes DFAN testing and how it can be used for modal survey tests and then uses DFAN test data from a demonstration test article to extract modes using operational modal analysis methods with measured, output-only cross spectra and cross spectra generated from frequency response functions to remove the time-delay-induced phase shift.

Keywords Modal testing · Parameter estimation · Direct field acoustic noise

Introduction

Direct field acoustic noise (DFAN) testing is increasingly used as the preferred method for performing acoustic tests because it is less expensive than traditional reverberant chamber tests. The value proposition associated with DFAN testing systems could be further enhanced if the DFAN speakers could also be used as sources for modal survey tests, especially for exciting acoustically active modes.

A DFAN system developed by Acoustic Research Systems (ARS) generates a diffuse acoustic field by ensuring that all acoustic devices in the test setup are driven by true random sources that are independent of each other. The amplitude of each speaker is set independently based on the test requirements placed on the microphone that controls it. The control microphones are placed such that each speaker has a microphone that is significantly closer than the other microphones, thereby ensuring that the response of each control microphone is dominated by a single speaker.

The fact that each source is truly independent is advantageous for modal testing because the sound pressure levels can be set such that they mostly satisfy the assumptions associated with operational modal testing (i.e., they are independent and constant over the frequency range of interest [1]). Furthermore, acoustic excitation techniques have been used to extract modes of a flat disk [3].

This paper demonstrates the feasibility of using a DFAN system to conduct a modal survey test on a demonstration test article using both output-only cross-spectra test data as well as cross spectra generated from frequency response functions (FRFs) with control microphones as references. It gives a background of DFAN testing and then describes how the equipment was used as sources for exciting the test article, how the resulting data was processed, and how the processed data was analyzed to extract modal parameters (shapes, frequency, and damping). Finally, the test results are presented and discussed.

Kevin Napolitano · Dr. Michael Yang
ATA Engineering, Inc., San Diego, California, 92128, USA
e-mail: kevin.napolitano@ata-e.com; myang@ata-e.com

Eric Friedlander · Dale Schick
Acoustic Research Systems, Shepherdstown, West Virginia, 25443
e-mail: eric@acousticrs.com; d.schick@acousticrs.com

Brandon Dilworth et al. (eds.), *Topics in Modal Analysis & Parameter Identification I, Vol. 9*, Conference Proceedings of the Society for Experimental Mechanics Series, https://doi.org/10.13052/9788743801542-4

Background of DFAN Testing

The history of DFAN testing began with the use of concert loudspeakers available in the late 1990s and early 2000s, which were designed to carry acoustic energy long distances with several band-pass filters. This type of testing required separate subwoofers, midrange, and high-frequency speakers. Using multiple loudspeaker drivers worked well for live sound but caused many challenges when trying to reproduce the intense energy propagated by the fairing of a large launch vehicle. DFAN technology has since evolved to mitigate these challenges and simplify the overall design into a more efficient test system. The system utilized for this study was the first to be designed specifically for the purpose of DFAN testing, its development and qualification having been discussed in previously published literature [1]. With the development of an acoustic device that can operate safely and efficiently at extremely high output levels, without the need for drive signal manipulation or integration of various discrete band-pass devices, uniform and highly repeatable acoustic field conditions can now be easily created. For the purpose of modal extraction, this acoustic generation system enables the creation of an acoustic field that is highly predictable and can be sustained at a high level for long periods of time with stability, and it has the advantage of adequately exciting the test article while extending the number of measurement averages to reveal modes in the infrasonic frequency range. The consistency of the DFAN system also allows for modal surveys to be run at different sound pressure levels, which can reveal nonlinearities in the structural response that can often occur with complex structures.

Another advantage to this type of system is scalability. The creation of a somewhat diffuse field requires only three devices, and incorporating additional devices fed with stochastic sources only increases the quality of diffusivity and spatial uniformity [1]. Currently, systems have been scaled from three to ninety units with adequate structural excitation in all configurations.

In traditional modal testing, the excitation is imparted to the structure using shakers and/or impact hammers, both of which require access to and contact with the structure. A third method of excitation, the focus of this paper, is a noncontact method of excitation. By exciting the entire structure with an acoustic field, components that could otherwise be damaged by contact-driven excitation or which are out of reach can be energized. An optical lens, for instance, may shatter with local excitation or lack response when traditional localized methods are used. Acoustic energy, on the other hand, will not only safely energize the spacecraft structure, but also the local fixturing of the optical lens as well as the lens itself. This benefit can also be extended to solar arrays, reflectors, antennas, and other spacecraft components.

For traditional structural components, which are less sensitive to impact and shaker excitation, there is still some benefit with the acoustic excitation method. First, impacts can be difficult to repeat in terms of amplitude consistency. Since many impacts are necessary to create clean FRFs for processing, the repeatability of the acoustic energy from one average to the next, along with the sheer number of them, has an advantage over the hammer method. Second, shakers require bonding of long, flexible rods (known as stingers) to the structure to adequately transfer the energy. Mounting the shaker and bonding the stinger provide added complexity and risk to the structure. The acoustic method, however, oftentimes only needs to be rolled up next to the test article, and the air already surrounding the test article is used to transmit vibration energy to the test article.

One key aspect of acoustic testing is that it typically focuses on the audible frequency range, about 20 Hz to 20 kHz. The ARS Neutron acoustic device (Fig. 1) utilized for this study, as designed for typical DFAN testing applications, has an operating frequency range that is optimized for testing from 20 Hz to 10 kHz. When utilizing a DFAN test system for modal extraction, it is important to consider how the system might excite modes that fall below the typical audible frequency range. From the standpoint of DFAN system design, the generation of infrasonic frequencies to an amplitude of significance requires not only special considerations to be made in the design and construction of the acoustic device but also a complete signal chain from sound generation source to microphone capture that supports the generation and acquisition of infrasonic frequencies.

While it is possible to address these challenges, one advantage of utilizing a purpose-built full-range acoustic device for in situ modal extraction is that the inherent efficiency of the acoustic device in the very-low-frequency (VLF) range allows it to generate significant and stable acoustic excitation, even as the frequency range of interest approaches the lower extension of the optimal operating bandwidth. This efficiency combined with a long acoustic exposure time allows the acoustic device utilized for this study to provide adequate excitation of modes in the infrasonic range, without the need to employ exotic methodologies.

Fig. 2 compares the low-frequency section of an ARS Neutron to the low-frequency section of a typical front-radiating concert subwoofer. The higher acoustic efficiency allows the device to more easily couple the excitation of the drivers to the air surrounding the test article, which, in turn, provides more energy for longer durations of time and with more incoherent sources to approximate a diffuse acoustic field. Note that regardless of approach, the efficiency of acoustic devices as they near infrasonic frequencies tends to decline.

Fig. 1 ARS Neutrons configured in six stacks of two (6 × 2).

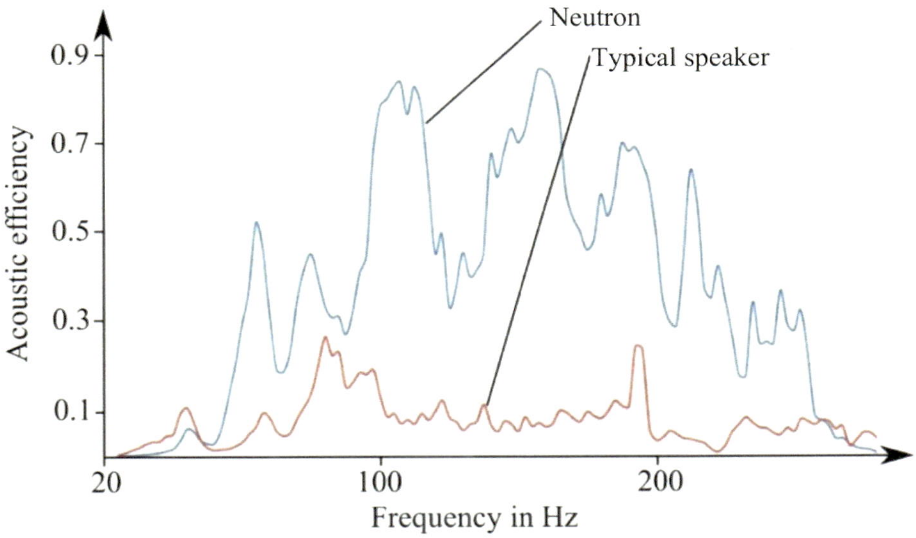

Fig. 2 Low-frequency acoustic efficiency of Neutron vs. typical front-radiating loudspeaker.

Test Article and Data Collection

A test article was designed, fabricated, and tested to demonstrate that both acoustic and modal testing can be performed while the test article is in one configuration, which is ideally on a head expander of an environmental shaker [4]. The test article, shown in Fig. 3, is a loose representation of a satellite bus with acoustically active panels mounted on a base plate that represents a head expander of an environmental shaker. The test article is mounted on four rubber mounts that rest on two portable sawhorses. The number of accelerometers mounted to the test article was minimized to make the test article as easily deployable as practicable but still observe primary bending, torsion, axial, and panel modes.

A total of 34 accelerometers were mounted on the test article. The accelerometers were placed in such a way as to measure the rigid body motion of the base, the rigid body motion of the upper box, and the relative motion between the

Fig. 3 Test article (left) and test display model with accelerometer measurement degrees of freedom (right).

bottom of the box and the base. Two accelerometers per surface were mounted in order to measure the out-of-plane motion of the four side panels and the top panel. Motion of unmeasured degrees of freedom (DOFs) in the test display model were estimated assuming that the base and the box move as independent rigid bodies.

One limitation of using data from environmental tests is that the total testing time is often short compared to the data collection time involved with a traditional modal survey [5].The short testing time forces the engineer to either not have enough frames of data to generate smooth frequency-domain data or not have a tight enough frequency resolution to adequately observe resonant peaks. Since the objective of this effort is to use acoustic speakers as sources for a modal survey test, data was collected for a total of 10 minutes at a low acoustic input level.

Data Processing

After the 10 minutes of random data was collected, the time-history data was processed into acceleration cross spectra and microphone sound pressure to acceleration FRFs using 20 s frames with an associated frequency spacing of 0.05 Hz, a Hanning window, and 95% overlap. Frequency-domain functions were calculated from 0 to 1.6 kHz. The full cross-spectra matrix was 34 accelerometers by 34 accelerometers, and the FRF matrix was 34 accelerometers by 12 microphones.

An overlay of the first two singular values of the accelerometer cross-spectra matrix vs. the singular values of a cross-spectra matrix generated from the FRF assuming unit microphone inputs is presented in Fig. 4. The peaks in the singular values are the observable modes. Generally, the singular values of the FRF-generated cross-spectra matrix are cleaner but

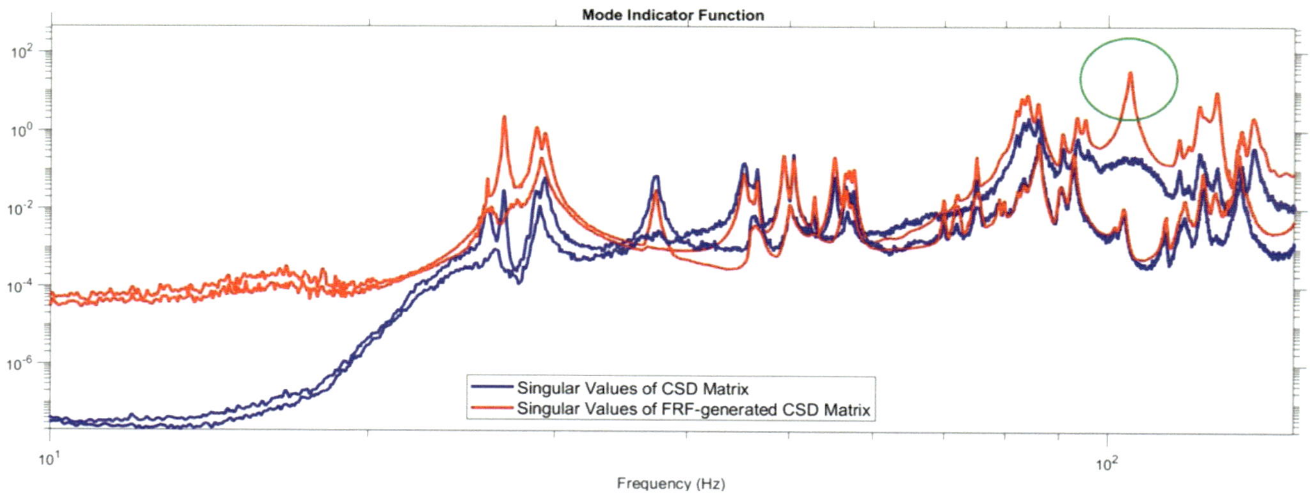

Fig. 4 Comparison of singular values of accelerometer cross-spectra matrix (CSD) vs. singular values of FRF-generated cross-spectra matrix.

most modes are observable from both sets. There is one mode near 104 Hz that is observable in the FRF-generated cross-spectra singular values but not as observable in the accelerometer cross-spectra singular values. The discrepancy could have been due to being a fictitious mode where there is cross talk between the speakers and the control microphones that causes a notch in the source-to-microphone FRF [6] or it could have been a mode where the impedance does not allow the microphone pressure to fully apply to the structure, leading to the mode not being fully observable in the cross spectra. This feedback effect is typical of many modal survey tests with shakers where the force spectra dips at a resonant frequency because the structure is too flexible to accept the full shaker load. Subsequent tap testing verified that the mode was real.

Modal Extraction from Acoustic Test: Operational Modal Analysis

The baseline assumption in operational modal analysis (OMA) is that the input cross-spectra matrix is constant over the frequency range of interest for which modes are extracted. With this assumption in place, several frequency- and time-domain methods have been proposed to extract modal parameters by manipulating the cross-spectra density matrix [2]. Since the DFAN system used in this effort controls the sound pressure of microphones mounted directly in front of the acoustic excitation sources, this assumption mostly holds true. Fig. 5 shows the power spectral density (PSD) functions for

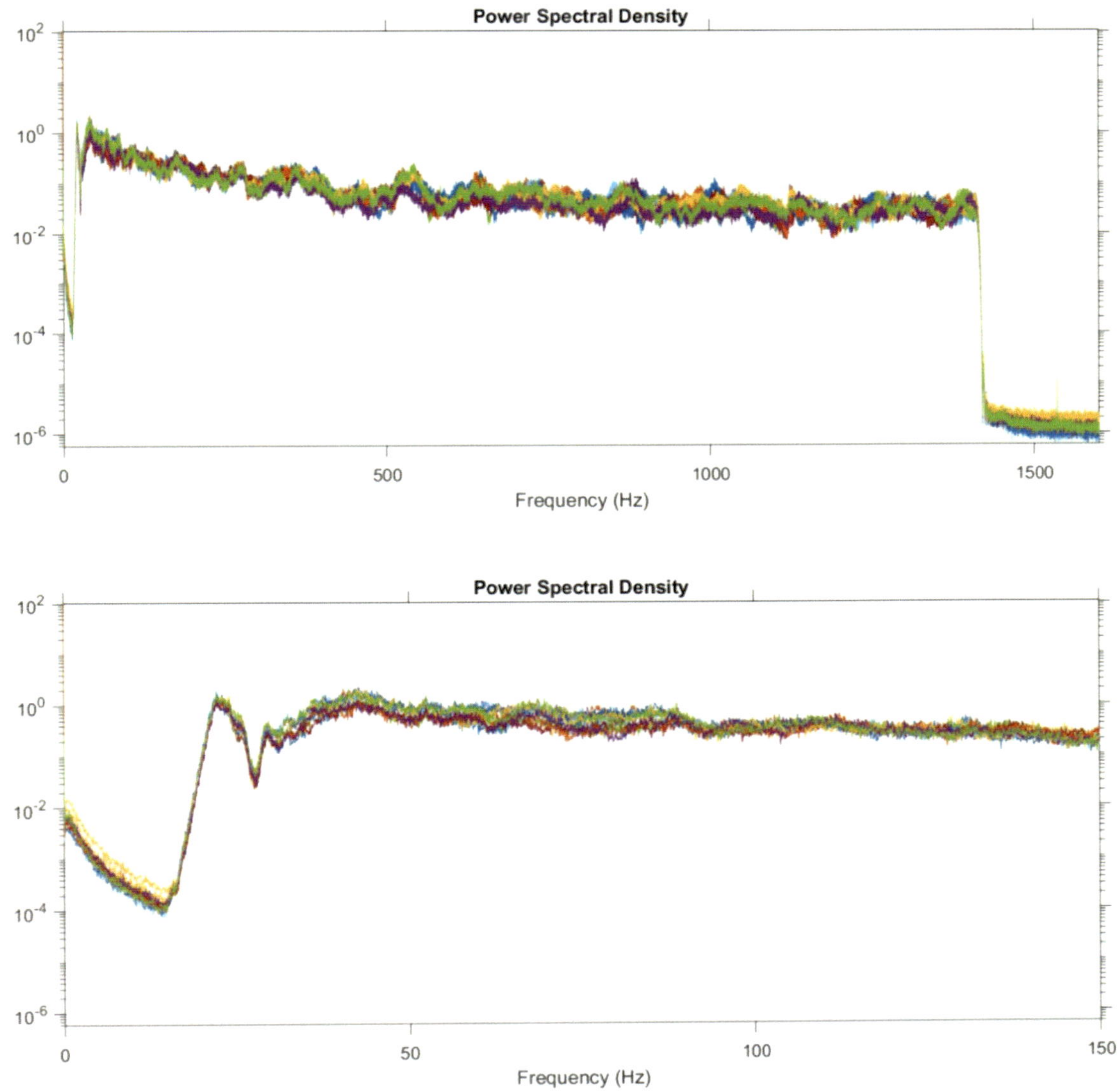

Fig. 5 PSDs of all control microphones. Full frequency range (top) and 0–150 Hz (bottom).

all six control microphones. For this test, the low-frequency power was boosted as high as practicable in order to excite the lower-frequency modes below 30 Hz as much as possible. The singular values of the control microphone cross-spectra density matrix (Fig. 6) shows that, while the control sound pressure is consistent over all frequencies, there is some feedback from the structure at around 104 Hz and 125 Hz such that the sound pressure is not fully independent at all frequencies.

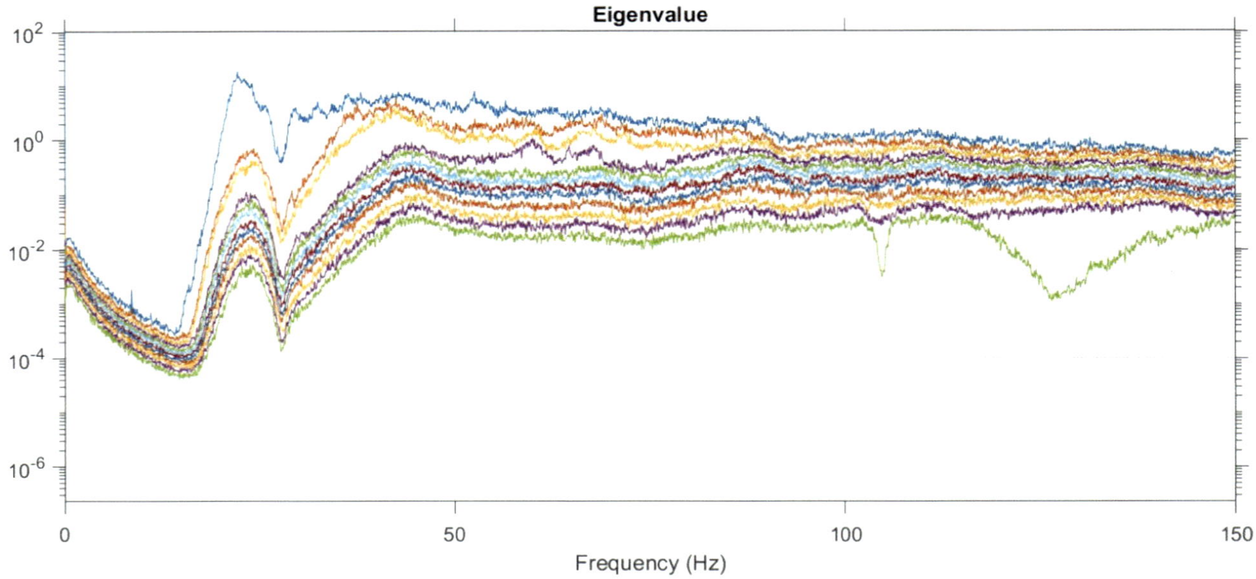

Fig. 6 Singular values of all control microphones.

Modes were extracted from the test data using a standard frequency-domain modal analysis tool by exploiting the fact that, as shown in Fig. 7, there are four complementary poles (two with positive damping and two with negative damping) when analyzing cross spectra instead of just two (both with positive damping) when analyzing FRF [7].

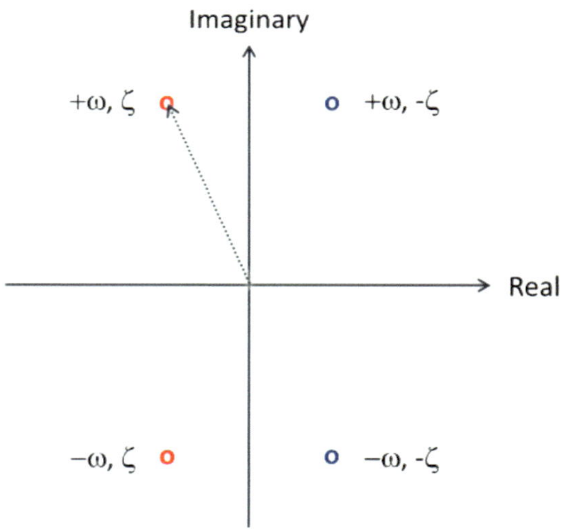

Fig. 7 Poles associated with cross spectra (blue and red) and FRFs (red).

The full 34 $\times$ 34 acceleration cross-spectra matrix was calculated, and then a coordinate transformation was applied to the DOFs associated with the columns using the first seven singular vectors from a concatenated array containing the cross-spectra matrices from 20 to 150 Hz. The resulting 34 $\times$ 7 cross-spectra matrix was then analyzed to extract mode shapes. A narrowband fit of each resonant frequency or set of closely spaced frequencies was then performed to extract modal parameters, including shape, frequency, and damping. The modal parameters were verified by overlaying the power spectrum mode indicator function of the cross-spectra matrix to the power spectrum mode indicator function of the cross-spectra matrix synthesized from the modal parameters. An overlay of the test vs. synthesized functions is presented in Fig. 8.

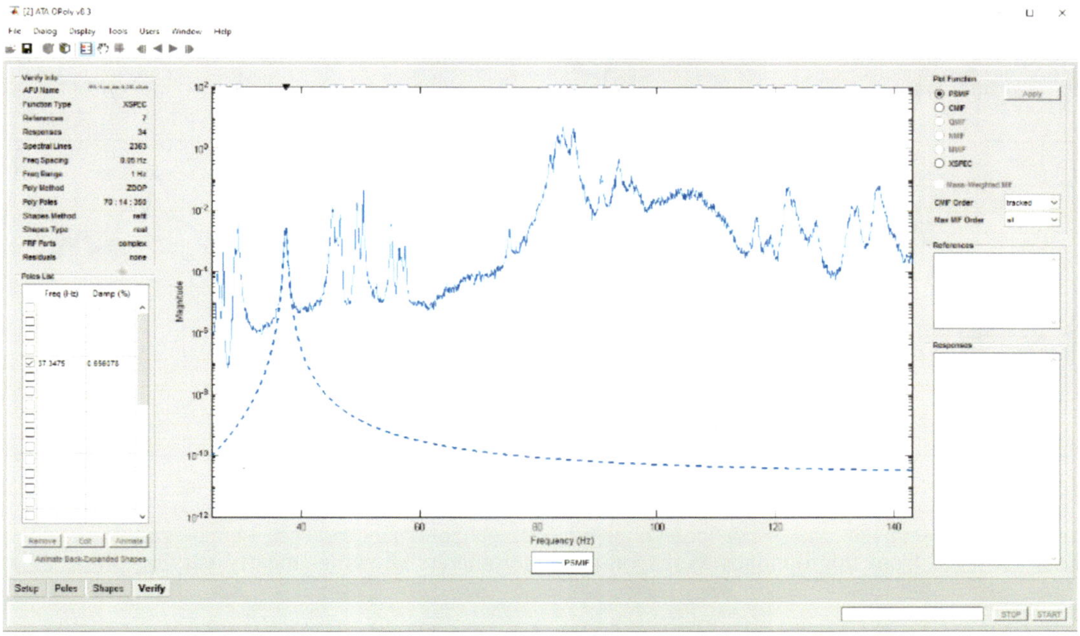

Fig. 8 Overlay of test vs. synthesized cross-spectra power spectrum mode indicator function verifies modal parameter extraction.

It was also noticed that low-order modes from 5.7 to 17.6 Hz of the test article resting on the rubber mounts and sawhorses were observable in some of the acceleration PSDs (Fig. 9). Note that the base and test article are moving in and out of phase for the rigid body vertical and first vertical modes, respectively. Each set of cross spectra was used to extract the observable mode using a single DOF.

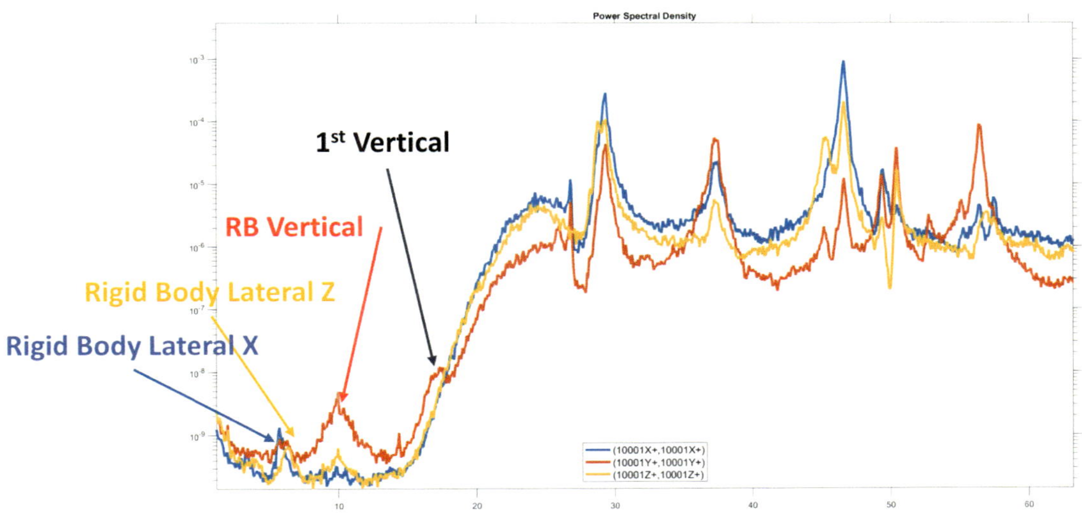

Fig. 9 Low-frequency lateral and vertical rigid body (RB) modes and first vertical modes observable in PSD data.

Modal Extraction from Acoustic Test: FRFs

The acoustically excited FRFs have a phase that varies linearly as a function of frequency associated with a time delay of the sound pressure traveling from the source to the test article (Fig. 10).

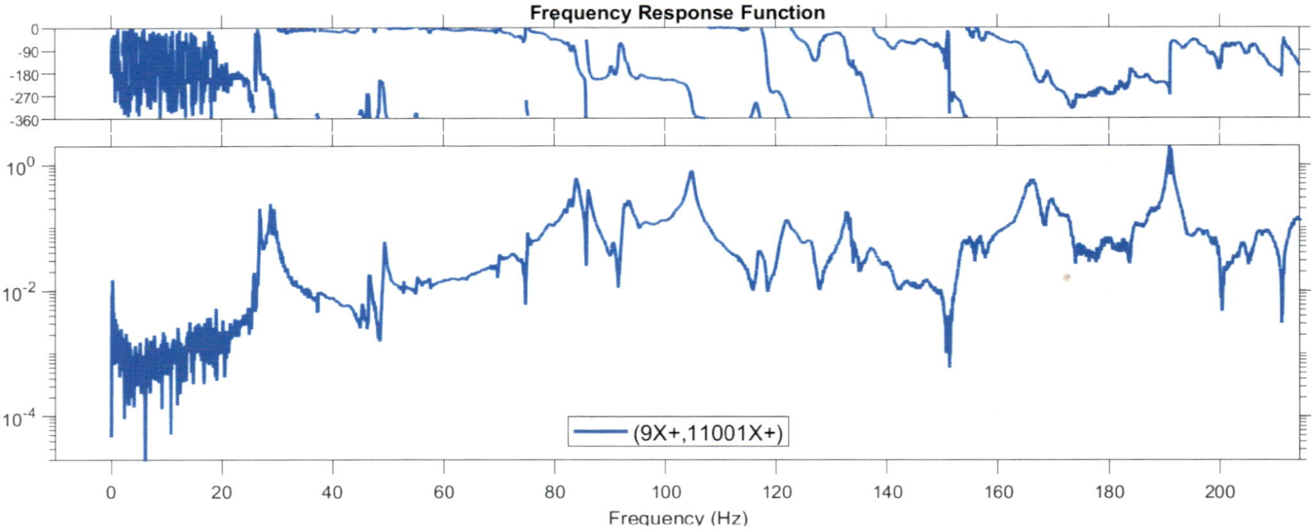

Fig. 10 Example FRF from microphones to response accelerometers showing linearly varying phase as a function of frequency.

While these FRF can still be used to extract complex modes to a reasonable degree, this paper uses the same OMA as above to calculate real modes directly. In this case, the FRFs were used to generate a full acceleration cross-spectra matrix by assuming that the reference autospectrum matrix for the microphones was equal to the identity matrix at all frequencies. Essentially,

$$[S_{YY}] = [H_{YX}]\,[S_{XX}]\,[H_{YX}]^H = [H_{YX}]\,[I]\,[H_{YX}]^H = [H_{YX}]\,[H_{YX}]^H, \tag{1}$$

where Y is associated with outputs, X is associated with microphone inputs, $[S_{YY}]$ is the FRF-generated output cross-spectra matrix, $[H_{YX}]$ is the FRF matrix from the inputs to the outputs, and $[S_{XX}]$ is the input cross-spectra matrix.

In doing so, the phase variation in the FRF is removed, since the phasing relationship of the accelerometers should be mostly real at resonance. An example of the FRF-generated cross spectra for several DOFs is presented in Fig. 11.

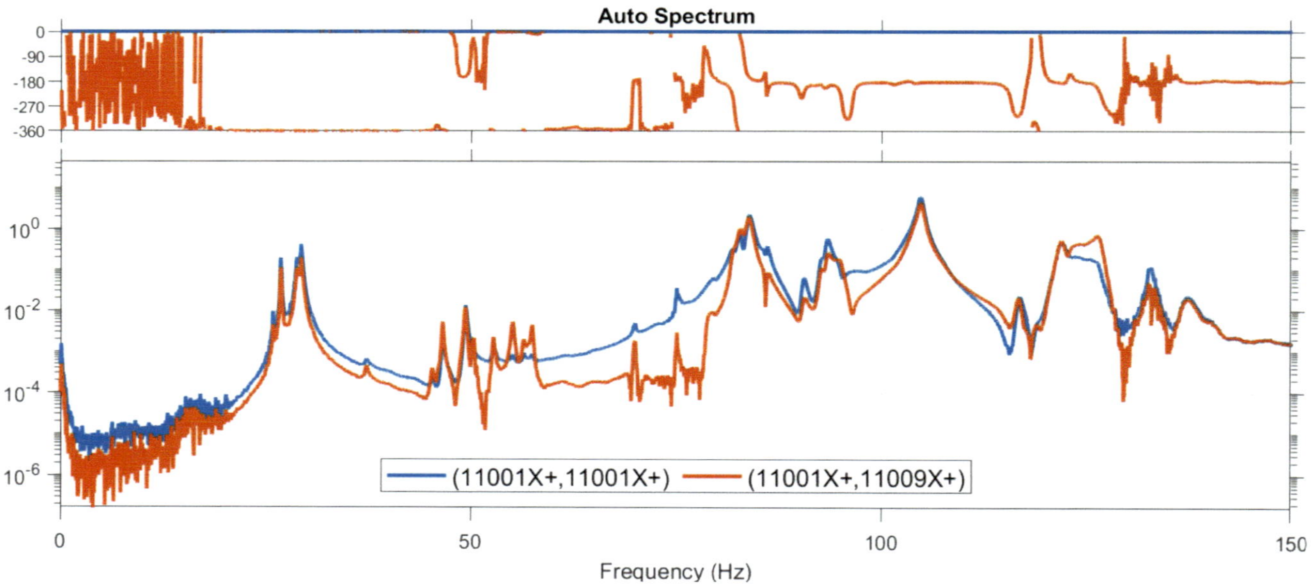

Fig. 11 Example FRF-generated cross-spectra matrix. Note that response is mostly real at resonant frequencies.

Once the data has been converted to the acceleration cross-spectra format, the same process as described in the OMA section was used.

Modal Extraction Results

Table 1 presents modal analysis results from using measured acceleration cross-spectra data and FRF-generated cross spectra for modes from 25 to 60 Hz as well as the 105 Hz mode. The 105 Hz mode is an actual mode that was verified through tap testing. Overall, both methods worked well for cases where the modes were well observed in the functions. There was one discrepancy in the cross-MAC at the low-observable 52 Hz mode, and for most cases the damping predictions were higher for the cross-spectra data than for the FRF-generated data.

Table 1 Modal extraction results: acceleration cross spectra vs. FRF-generated cross spectra.

	Acceleration Cross Spectra		FRF-Generated Cross Spectra		Ratio		
Mode Number	Frequency Hz	Damping %Crit	Frequency Hz	Damping %Crit	OMA/FRF Frequency	OMA/FRF Damping	Cross MAC
1	25.89	0.64	25.93	0.43	1.00	1.49	97
2	26.82	0.29	26.84	0.21	1.00	1.40	100
3	28.84	0.64	28.81	0.50	1.00	1.28	100
4	29.40	0.70	29.35	0.52	1.00	1.33	99
5	37.35	0.66	37.40	0.50	1.00	1.32	100
6	45.30	0.45	45.29	0.53	1.00	0.84	100
7	46.54	0.21	46.58	0.25	1.00	0.87	99
8	49.37	0.32	49.37	0.30	1.00	1.05	99
9	50.39	0.22	50.41	0.26	1.00	0.85	99
10	52.62	0.38	52.76	0.13	1.00	2.88	78
11	55.13	0.29	55.12	0.31	1.00	0.94	100
12	56.41	0.30	56.44	0.30	1.00	1.00	97
13	56.89	0.38	56.88	0.37	1.00	1.02	98
14	57.46	0.28	57.48	0.28	1.00	0.98	100
15	106.01	3.04	104.74	0.50	1.01	6.08	98

Plots of the first four modes are presented in Fig. 12. The first two modes are the primary modes of the side panels. The fifth mode is the primary mode of the top panel, and the fifteenth mode is the 104 Hz mode.

Additionally, low-frequency lateral and vertical modes of the test article on isolators extracted from the acceleration cross-spectra data are presented in Table 2. The relatively high damping values are likely due to the interaction between the primary modes and the heavily damped rubber mounts. The first lateral rocking mode is shown in Fig. 13.

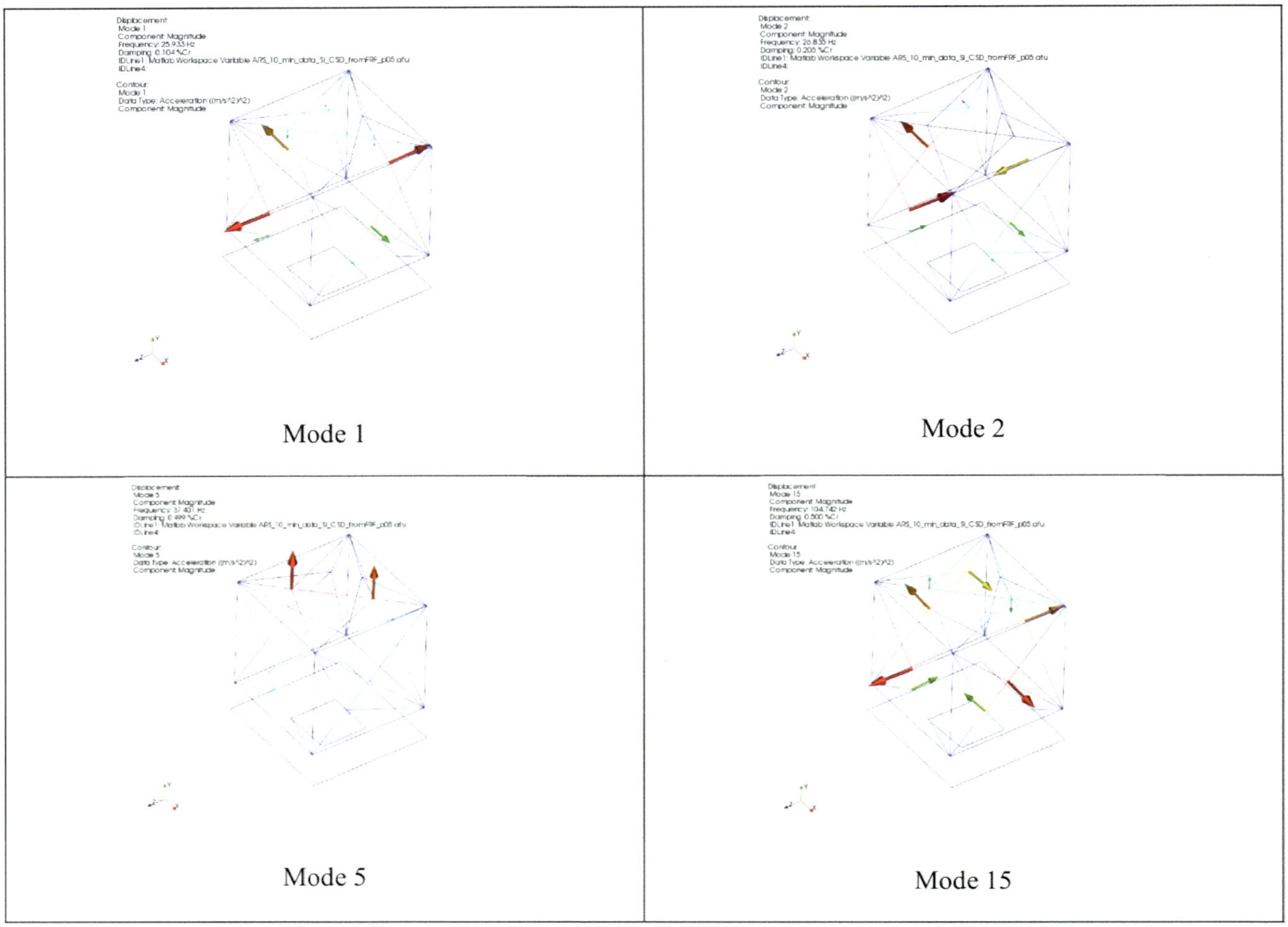

Fig. 12 Example back-expanded plots for modes 1, 2, 5, and 15.

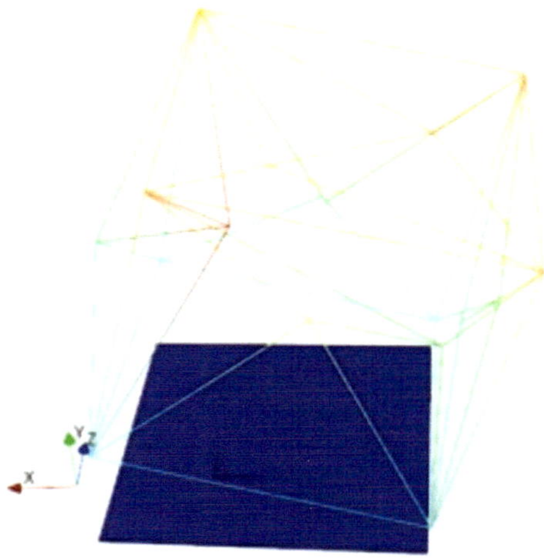

Fig. 13 First low-frequency mode – primary lateral X.

Table 2 Low-frequency OMA results.

Mode Number	Frequency Hz	Damping %Crit
1	5.76	3.06
2	6.24	5.58
3	9.92	1.67
4	17.1	1.62

Summary and Observations

This paper verifies the feasibility of extracting mode shapes from accelerometers excited by DFAN acoustic noise. In addition to using OMA on measured acceleration cross-spectra matrices, FRF-generated cross-spectra matrices were used to extract modal parameters. While both methods were able to extract many modes, the FRFs better characterize a poorly excited mode near 52 Hz and better estimate damping of a mode near 104 Hz. Likewise, OMA was able to extract estimates of mode shapes at low frequencies where the input sound pressure was not active.

References

1. Schick, D., Hoffman, T., Friedlander, E., and Kinsella, E., "Verifying a Novel Approach to Acoustic Testing: Acoustic Devices & Control Systems," *32nd Aerospace Testing Seminar*, Los Angeles, CA, 2020.
2. Crowley, J.R., Klosterman, A.L., Rocklin, G.T., and Vold, H., "Direct Structural Modification Using Frequency Response Functions," *Proceedings of the Second International Modal Analysis Conference*, Orlando, Florida, February 1984, pp. 58–65.
3. Peeters, B., Alvarez Blanco, M., Musella, U., Waimer, S., Di Lorenzo, E., and Carrella, A., "Identifying the Structural Behaviour of a Specimen During Spacecraft Acoustic Testing by Operational Modal Analysis," *7th International Operational Modal Analysis Conference*, 2017 May10–12, Ingolstadt – Germany.
4. Napolitano, K., "Fixed Base Modal Testing of the SWFO Sensor Platform on an Environmental Shaker," *Spacecraft and Launch Vehicle Dynamic Environments Workshop*, June 2023.
5. Napolitano, K.L., "Maximizing the Quality of Shape Extractions from Base Shake Modal Tests," In: Mains, M.L., Dilworth, B.J. (eds) Topics in Modal Analysis & Testing, Volume 8. Conference Proceedings of the Society for Experimental Mechanics Series. Springer, Cham. 2020. https://doi.org/10.1007/978-3-030-12684-1_12.
6. Yang, M., and Napolitano, K., "Simulation of Modal Survey Using Direct Field Acoustic Noise as Inputs," *43rd International Modal Analysis Conference*, Orlando, FL, 2025.
7. Fladung, W.F., "Why Don't We Just Use the Cross Spectra for Operational Modal Analysis?" *43rd International Modal Analysis Conference*, February 10–13, 2025.

Chapter 5
Simulation of Modal Survey Using Direct Field Acoustic Noise as Inputs

Kevin Napolitano and Dr. Michael Yang

Abstract Direct field acoustic noise (DFAN) testing involves mounting several sets of acoustic sources around a structure to provide inputs for acoustic qualification tests. It is becoming more prevalent because it is often less expensive than traditional reverberant chamber testing while also allowing acoustic tests to be performed at the test article facility, which reduces or eliminates test article transportation costs. This effort discusses the ability of acoustic analysis software packages to simulate acoustic modal survey tests so that the viability of using DFAN sources can be assessed well before a modal survey test is conducted.

Keywords Modal testing ·Parameter estimation ·Direct field acoustic noise ·Pretest analysis

Introduction

Direct field acoustic noise (DFAN) acoustic environmental testing involves placing a number of acoustic sources, usually a set of large speakers that together cover the acoustic frequency range of interest, around a structure and then controlling their excitation levels to meet required acoustic levels for the test.

DFAN testing has been gaining popularity as a way to perform acoustic environmental tests on structures when it saves a program schedule and budget compared to testing in a reverberant chamber. Further schedule and budget could be saved if DFAN sources could also be used as exciters in modal survey tests.

The objective of this paper is to perform pretest analysis on a finite element model (FEM) using acoustic sources as inputs. The FEM and acoustic source models were used to model the test setup of a demonstration article [1], shown in Fig. 1. Twelve Acoustic Research Systems (ARS) Neutron speaker systems are, in stacks of two, are evenly placed in a

Fig. 1 Demonstration article inside 6 × 2 configuration of ARS Neutron acoustic sources.

Kevin Napolitano · Dr. Michael Yang
ATA Engineering, Inc., San Diego, California, 92128, USA
e-mail: kevin_napolitano@yahoo.com; myang@ata-e.com

Brandon Dilworth et al. (eds.), *Topics in Modal Analysis & Parameter Identification I, Vol. 9*, Conference Proceedings of the Society for Experimental Mechanics Series, https://doi.org/10.13052/9788743801542-5

circle around the test article. Twelve control microphones are mounted, one in front of each speaker, to control speaker output to a predefined output level. This demonstration test was performed at Experior Laboratories in Oxnard, California, using a Neutron DFAN system provided by ARS.

This paper describes the NASTRAN FEM, modeling of the acoustic sources using Wave6 vibroacoustic analysis software, and processing of the analysis results to determine which modes are observable from the acoustic inputs and highlights some issues that may need to be accounted for during a modal survey test.

Baseline Nastran Model

The test article simulates a spacecraft on the head expander of a vertical base shaker. The FEM and test display model of the test article are shown in Fig. 2. The isolators between the base plate and the sawhorses represent the airbags used to keep the head expander at a specific height under load, and the sawhorses represent the complicated dynamics of the shaker table system.

Fig. 2 FEM (left) and test display model (right) showing accelerometer locations.

The FEM includes the demonstration article, its rubber isolators at the base, and the sawhorses used to support the test article at an optimal height for the acoustic sources. The FEM has approximately 230,000 elements and 236,000 nodes. The rubber isolators are represented with spring elements.

The objectives of the pretest analysis were to 1) select sensors to measure all test article modes up to 100 Hz (with the exception of local sawhorse modes, which were decoupled from the test article due to the isolators), 2) measure the base at the bottom of the test article, and 3) locate enough accelerometers to observe the six rigid body deformations as well as the first flexible mode of the base. To this end, 94 test degrees of freedom (DOFs) were selected using engineering judgement and conventional sensor up-selection and down-selection algorithms [1]. Static condensation (i.e., Guyan reduction) of the mass and stiffness matrices down to these test locations was then performed, and the 94-DOF mass matrix was used in the following orthogonality calculations.

Ideally, for aerospace modal tests the off-diagonal terms of the self-orthogonality matrix during pretest analysis are minimized as much as practicable. For this analysis, the majority of the off-diagonal terms were under 5%, with the maximum off-diagonal value being 9%. While these results may not be acceptable for some modal survey tests, they were good enough that the modes could be observed and differentiated from each other.

Acoustic Source Modeling

A simulation of a DFAN test with a 2 × 6 configuration of ARS Neutron speakers was performed using Wave6. A FEM of the test article was imported into Wave6 as finite element (FE) subsystem. The fluid (air) and speaker loading were simulated with the boundary element method (BEM). The calibrated Neutron speaker sources were not directly used because the

Table 1 FEM self-orthogonality matrix.

FEM Self Orthogonality Table

FEM Shapes

FEM Shapes		1	2	3	4	5	6	7	8	9	10	11	12	13	14	15	16	17	18	19	20	21	22	23	24	25	26	27	28	29	30	31	32	33	34	35
		3.84	3.91	6.06	6.20	6.90	8.78	17.82	19.97	20.26	23.02	25.06	27.39	27.58	42.64	44.02	47.51	48.85	50.43	53.23	54.29	58.79	61.14	62.94	65.28	75.35	76.58	80.91	84.34	87.57	87.67	90.96	93.74	95.16	99.43	100.43
1	3.84	100																																		
2	3.91		100																																	
3	6.06			100																																
4	6.20				100																															
5	6.90					100																														
6	8.78						100																													
7	17.82							100																												
8	19.97								100																											
9	20.26									100																										
10	23.02										100																									
11	25.06											100																								
12	27.39												100																							5
13	27.58													100																						
14	42.64														100																				5	7
15	44.02															100										5										
16	47.51																100									7										
17	48.85																	100									7									6
18	50.43																		100																	
19	53.23																			100																
20	54.29																				100															
21	58.79																					100							5							
22	61.14																						100			5										
23	62.94																							100												
24	65.28																								100											
25	75.35															5	7						5			100										
26	76.58																	7									100								8	
27	80.91																											100							5	
28	84.34																					5							100							
29	87.57																													100						
30	87.67																														100					
31	90.96																															100		5		
32	93.74																																100			
33	95.16																															5		100		
34	99.43														5												8	5							100	9
35	100.43											5		7			6																		9	100

version of Wave6 at the time of this writing only allowed for random analysis using those sources. Instead, rigid fluid surfaces were used to represent the fronts of the stacked speakers. These are idealized surfaces with effectively infinite impedance that will reflect incoming sound waves perfectly (i.e., without loss or distortion). A single monopole was placed at the center of each speaker face. Virtual microphones were placed in locations corresponding to those in the test configuration. Fig. 3

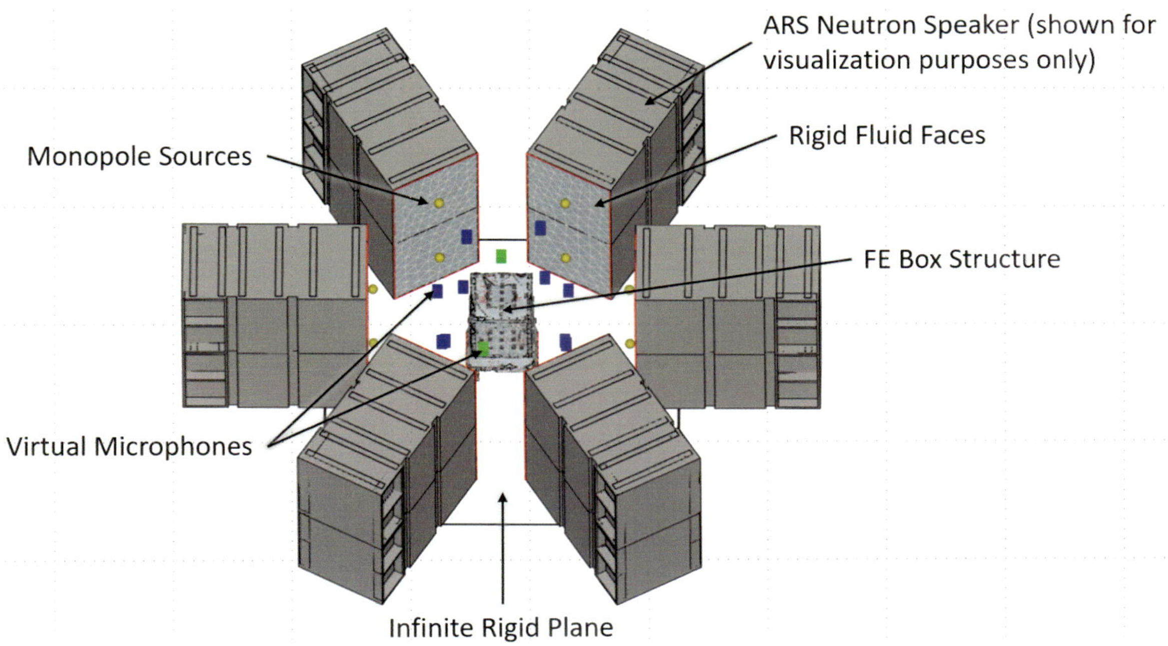

Fig. 3 Wave6 FE/BEM model (with ARS Neutron speakers shown for visualization purposes only). The blue and green squares represent control and monitor microphones, respectively.

illustrates the Wave6 model with the ARS Neutrons shown for visualization purposes. However, since these speaker sources were not explicitly used in the analysis, Fig. 4 is a more accurate representation of the fluid surfaces in the model.

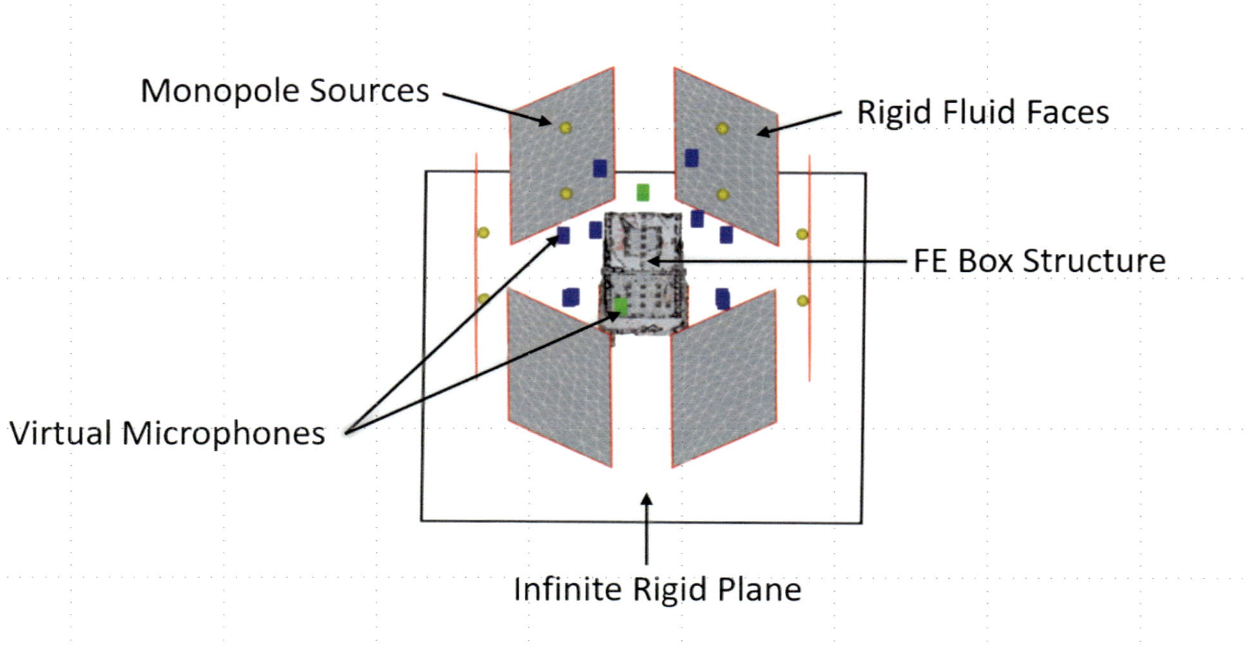

Fig. 4 Wave6 FE/BEM model with all structural and fluid components shown.

A separate load case was defined for each of the twelve monopole sources. Each monopole source was defined to have a sound power of 1+0i lbf-in/s at all frequencies. The model was solved deterministically from 1 to 367 Hz in 0.05 Hz increments. The frequency spacing was chosen for convenience and to match the spacing from the test. The structural FEM was given a structural damping loss factor of 1.0% at all frequencies, which corresponds to a 0.5% viscous damping value. The following responses were recovered:

- Acceleration (y) responses at 88 nodes on the FEM which correspond to the accelerometer locations on the physical test article. All translations were recovered in the global (CS 0) coordinate system.
- The modal amplitudes (q) for each of the structural modes.
- The field pressure (p) at the virtual microphone locations.

The results for each load case are placed in a column vector such that the response for all twelve load cases are $[y]$, $[q]$, and $[p]$, where the rows of each matrix correspond to their respective DOFs and the columns are associated with each load case.

Since each source consisted of a unit input, the output responses $[y]$, $[q]$, and $[p]$, are equal to their respective frequency response function (FRF) matrices $[H_{ys}]$, $[H_{qs}]$, and $[H_{ps}]$, where the subscript s refers to the acoustic sources. The microphone responses can be partitioned to the control microphones, $[c]$, which is also the FRF matrix associated with the control microphones $[H_{cs}]$.

All results were exported in HDF5 format and then imported into MATLAB for further processing in ATA's IMAT^{TM} software.

The modal amplitudes were used to calculate $[S_{qq}]$, the modal cross-spectral density matrix. This is a square matrix with the number of rows and columns equal to the number of *in vacuo* structural modes (i.e., structural modes that are not influenced by the surrounding fluid). It represents the random contribution of the structural modes at each frequency if each monopole source was used to excite the structure in an uncorrelated manner. $[S_{qq}]$ at each analysis frequency is calculated as

$$[S_{qq}] = [H_{qs}]\,[S_{ss}]\,[H_{qs}]^H,$$

where $[S_{ss}]$ is the identity matrix because each monopole has unit input and is assumed to be uncorrelated from the other monopoles. The superscript H denotes the Hermitian, or complex conjugate transpose. The diagonal of $[S_{qq}]$ can be plotted as a function of frequency to estimate how efficiently each structural mode is excited, as shown in Fig. 5.

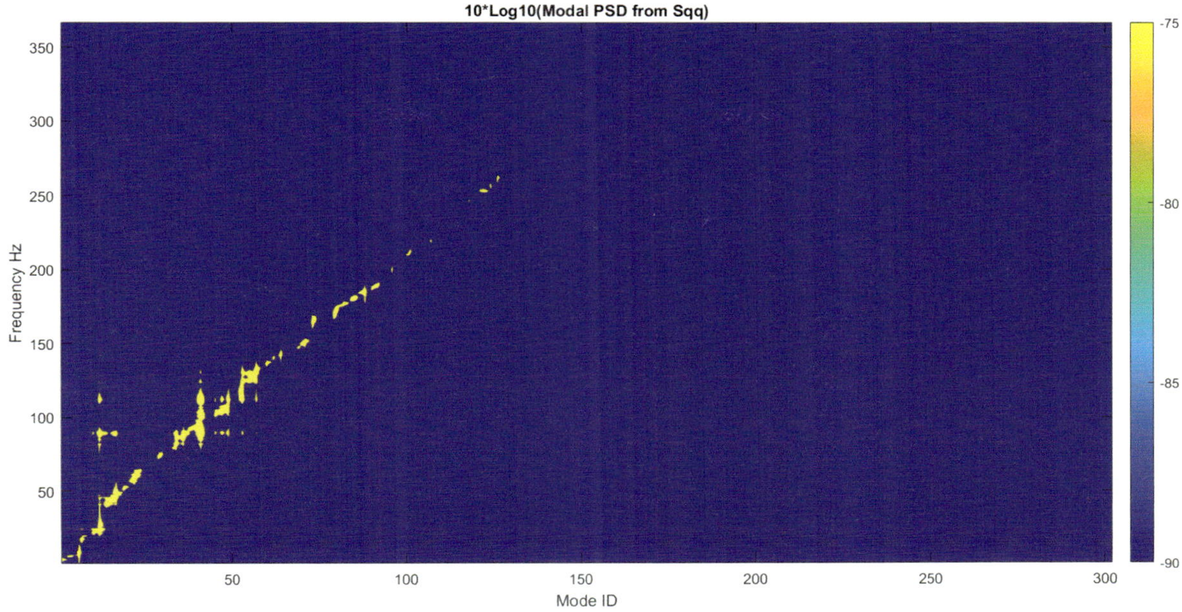

Fig. 5 Diagonal of $[S_{qq}]$ as a function of frequency.

The cross-spectral density matrix of physical responses, $[S_{yy}]$, can be calculated from $[S_{qq}]$ as

$$[S_{yy}] = [\Phi] [S_{qq}] [\Phi]^H, \tag{1}$$

where $[\Phi]$ represents the modal matrix with modal vectors organized into columns. This formulation allows recovery of any structural response for which modes can be supplied.

Test Simulation

The objective of simulating acoustic excitation is to better understand the validity of extracting modes from acoustically excited test articles. Specifically, the objective is to determine 1) which mode shapes the acoustic system should excite and 2) which apparent modes that may appear in the test data which are not actual structural modes.

For this paper, the sources are analytically defined to be equal to 1 mPa/Hz^2 over all frequencies. This differs from an acoustic test because 1) acoustic excitation sources typically roll off at frequencies below 20–30 Hz and 2) in test, the excitation levels are used to set levels certain levels over 1/n frequency bands. Future analysis efforts should also include the control algorithm used for setting exciter levels.

The matrix $[S_{yy}]$ was calculated two ways using the FRF matrices. The first way assumes that the sources are uncontrolled and constant as a function of frequency. Unfortunately, the sources cannot be measured directly, so the second way calculates it assuming that the control microphones were uncorrelated and set to 1 mPa/Hz^2. The second calculation was done by assuming the control microphone levels were set at each frequency by inverting the $[H_{cs}]$ and then postmultiplying the $[H_{ys}]$ matrix to generate an FRF matrix associated with microphones as references, such that

$$[H_{yc}] = [H_{ys}] [H_{cs}]^{-1}. \tag{2}$$

It should be noted that this is *not* how the control microphones levels are set, but performing this calculation can lead to insight into the pretest analysis. Future effort on modeling the control algorithm directly should be a priority.

The $[H_{yc}]$ matrix can be measured directly in test and was also investigated as a way to solve for modes. To do so, it was used to simulate the $[S_{yy}]$ assuming the $[S_{cc}]$ was equal to the identity matrix and then comparing it to the original $[S_{yy}]$ matrix that assumes $[S_{ff}]$ matrix was equal to the identity matrix.

Modal Extraction

The operational modal analysis technique described in [2] was used to extract modes from the simulated test data assuming $[S_{ff}]$ was equal to the identify matrix. The full 94 × 94 $[S_{yy}]$ matrix was fed into ATA's OPoly modal analysis tool and then the following procedure was performed over a series of frequency bands from 0 to 101 Hz.

1. Virtual references were calculated over small frequency bands of closely spaced modes by performing singular value decomposition of the $[S_{yy}]$ matrix.
2. The columns of the $[S_{yy}]$ matrix were reduced to these virtual references, shrinking the matrix from 94 × 94 to the number of modes in the frequency range (typically 1 to 4).
3. Real modes were solved and exported.

Once completed, the test simulated modes were compared to the original modes from NASTRAN.

The simulated test self-orthogonality matrix is presented in Table 2. Off-diagonal values are higher than what would be typical for a modal test. This is most likely due to the fact that the panels of the test article are very susceptible to the effects of air mass because they are light, flexible, and have large surface areas. Typically, the self-orthogonality matrix is used to help debug the test setup, as large off-diagonals are often associated with inaccurate modal extractions due to modes being poorly excited or not well differentiated with other closely spaced modes, or errors in the channel table. If the added air mass is not accounted for in the model, then other methods of verifying the shape extractions, such as viewing animated modes shapes or overlaying test data with simulated data synthesized from the modal parameters must be performed during an actual test.

Table 2 Simulated acoustic structural test modes – self-orthogonality matrix.

Test Self Orthogonality Table

Test Shapes

Simulated		1	2	3	4	5	6	7	8	9	10	11	12	13	14	15	16	17	18	19	20	21	22	23	24	25	26	27	28	29	30
Test Shapes		3.80	3.87	6.05	6.18	8.74	17.71	22.11	24.12	24.62	26.44	41.71	43.04	46.09	47.42	49.17	51.98	52.86	56.97	59.16	61.37	63.85	73.76	82.30	85.53	86.28	89.31	89.50	91.81	93.57	98.07
1	3.80	100																													
2	3.87		100																												
3	6.05			100																											
4	6.18				100																										
5	8.74					100																									
6	17.71						100		39	14																					
7	22.11							100		7																6	14	6			
8	24.12						39		100	25													5			7	24	7			
9	24.62						14	7	25	100														7	5	9	34	8			6
10	26.44										100																				
11	41.71											100																			
12	43.04												100																		
13	46.09													100	16								6				10				
14	47.42													16	100	5											6				
15	49.17														5	100															
16	51.98																100	20													
17	52.86																20	100													
18	56.97																		100	7											
19	59.16																		7	100	10										
20	61.37																			10	100	6					5				
21	63.85																				6	100									
22	73.76								5					6									100	7	5		5		5		
23	82.30									7													7	100	19		18				
24	85.53									5													5	19	100	29	20	35			
25	86.28							6	7	9															29	100	41	42			
26	89.31							14	24	34				10	6						5		5	18	20	41	100	52		11	6
27	89.50							6	7	8															35	42	52	100		9	
28	91.81																						5						100	29	8
29	93.57																										11	9	29	100	8
30	98.07									6																	6		8	8	100

The cross-orthogonality matrix between the simulated test modes (rows) and the NASTRAN FEM shapes (columns) is shown in Table 3. The NASTRAN modes that were not extracted are highlighted in pink. The high values in the Test CRSS columns show that each simulated test mode is a mass-weighted, linear combination of the FEM shapes. All simulated test modes are captured by the FEM shapes with the exception of mode 26, which is best mapped by a FEM mode just above 100 Hz. The CRSS rows show how much of each FEM shape is captured by the simulated test shapes. FEM modes 4, 8, 9, 26, and 27 were not extracted because the acoustic sources did not excite them adequately enough to obtain good modal parameters. Note that damping levels are almost twice the nominal value for simulated test mode 26. The differences in damping could be due to structure/air interaction that is independent of excitation source, or it could be due to the excitation source interacting with the test article.

Table 3 Acoustic structural modes using in vacuo mass matrix – baseline FEM modes cross-orthogonality matrix.

FEM/Simulated Test Cross Orthogonality Table

Simulated Test			FEM Shapes																																			Test	Test
No.	Freq Hz	Damp %crit	1	2	3	4	5	6	7	8	9	10	11	12	13	14	15	16	17	18	19	20	21	22	23	24	29	30	33	34	35	36	37	38	39	40	41	CRSS 3%	CRSS All
			3.84	3.91	6.06	6.20	6.90	8.78	17.82	19.97	20.26	23.02	25.06	27.39	27.58	42.64	44.02	47.51	48.85	50.43	53.23	54.29	58.79	61.14	62.94	65.28	75.35	76.58	80.91	84.34	87.57	87.67	90.96	93.74	95.16	99.43	100.43		
1	3.80	0.50	100																																			100	100
2	3.87	0.50		100																																		100	100
3	6.05	0.50			100																																	100	100
4	6.18	0.50				100																																100	100
5	8.74	0.50						100																														100	100
6	17.71	0.50							89				46																									89	100
7	22.11	0.50										99																										99	100
8	24.12	0.51											86	48																								86	100
9	24.62	0.49											28	90	26																							94	100
10	26.44	0.51												28	96																							100	100
11	41.71	0.51														100																						100	100
12	43.04	0.51															100																					100	100
13	46.09	0.51																98																				99	100
14	47.42	0.52																30	95																			100	100
15	49.17	0.51																		99																		99	100
16	51.98	0.51																			99																	100	100
17	52.86	0.51																				99																100	100
18	56.97	0.51																					100															100	100
19	59.16	0.52																						99														100	100
20	61.37	0.52																							99													99	100
21	63.85	0.52																								99												99	100
22	73.76	0.51																									100											100	100
23	82.30	0.55																												99								99	100
24	85.53	0.56																													37	92						99	100
25	86.28	0.52																													74	61						96	100
26	89.31	1.12												37																27		30	25				65	70	97
27	89.50	0.58																														39	90				20	90	100
28	91.81	0.60																																99				99	100
29	93.57	0.53																																26	92			96	100
30	98.07	0.52																																		95	34	98	100
CRSS	3%		100	100	100	100	1	100	89	3	3	99	100	94	96	100	100	99	99	99	100	100	100	99	99	99	100	9	7	99	96	98	93	99	96	95	68		
CRSS	All		100	100	100	100	2	100	100	4	4	100	100	100	100	100	100	100	100	100	100	100	100	100	100	100	100	16	14	100	100	100	100	100	100	99	90		

A plot of the first three singular values of the $[S_{yy}]$ matrix with red boxes around the frequencies of the unextracted modes is shown in Fig. 6. Peaks in the singular values can be seen for most of these modes, but they are not as pronounced as they are with the other modes, and the authors believe that the modes would not be accurately extracted if there were any reasonable level of noise in the test data. These results are similar to those from almost any modal test that uses modal shakers as the input source, and the solution is to perform another test in which those modes are excited directly.

The singular values of the control microphone cross spectrum matrix are shown in Fig. 7. The local minima in this matrix (indicated by the vertical cursors) can potentially lead to fictitious modes if microphones are used as references when calculating FRF. The peaks in the FRF are likely due to an acoustic node coinciding with the microphone locations at these frequencies.

An overlay of the three primary singular values for constant source input and constant microphone input are presented in Fig. 8. The two peaks near 87 and 121 Hz in the microphone-generated singular values correspond to the local minima in Fig. 7 and are not actual modes, but the mode near 110 Hz looks very similar to the apparently heavily damped peak evident in the source singular values.

One way to verify whether the changes in damping are due to the structure interacting with air or the excitation source is to excite the modes directly with a non-acoustic source. This will eliminate any damping changes due to the source.

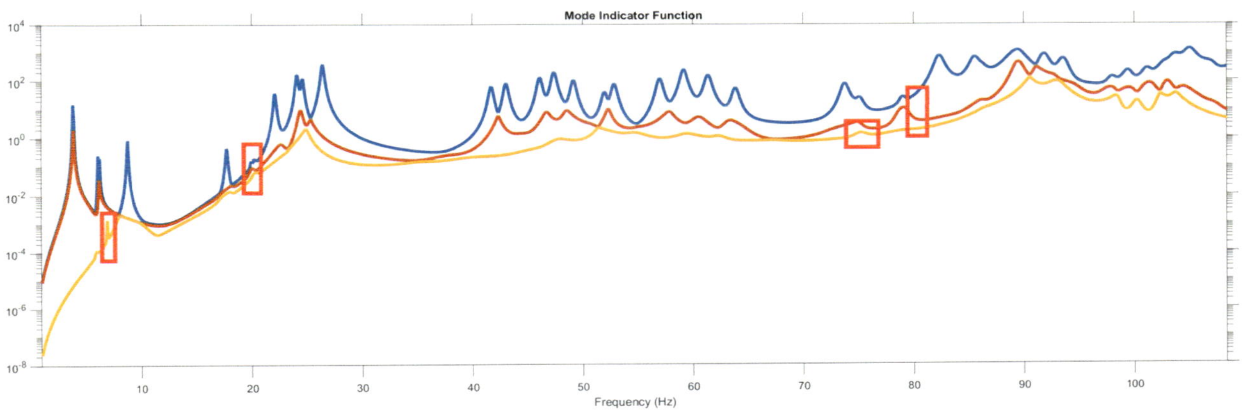

Fig. 6 Singular values of acceleration cross spectrum matrix. Acoustically insensitive modes are identified inside red boxes.

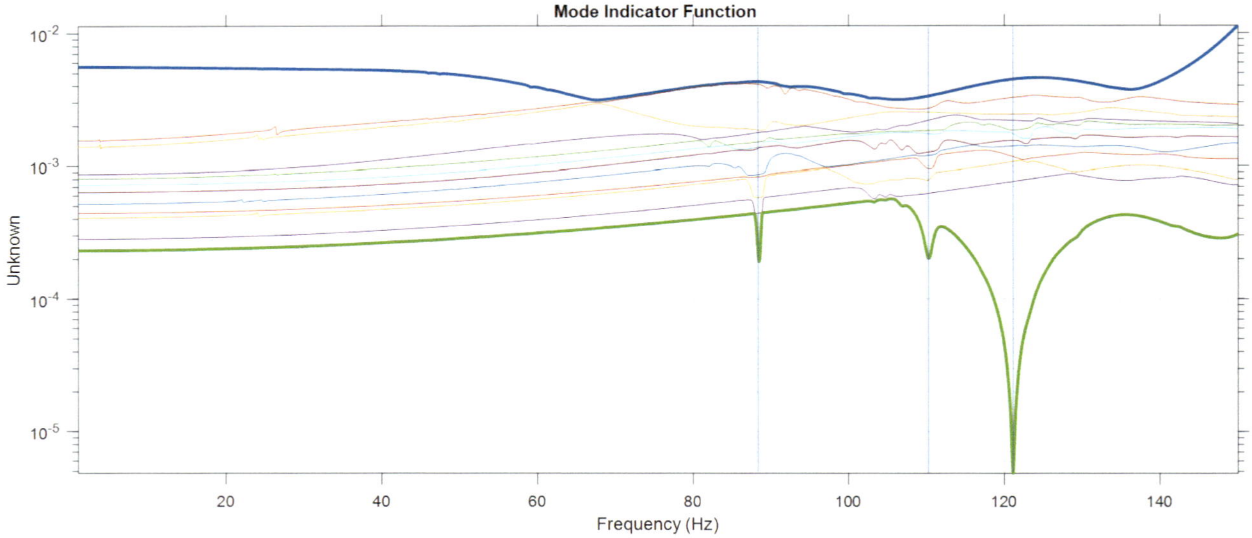

Fig. 7 Singular values of control microphone cross spectrum matrix.

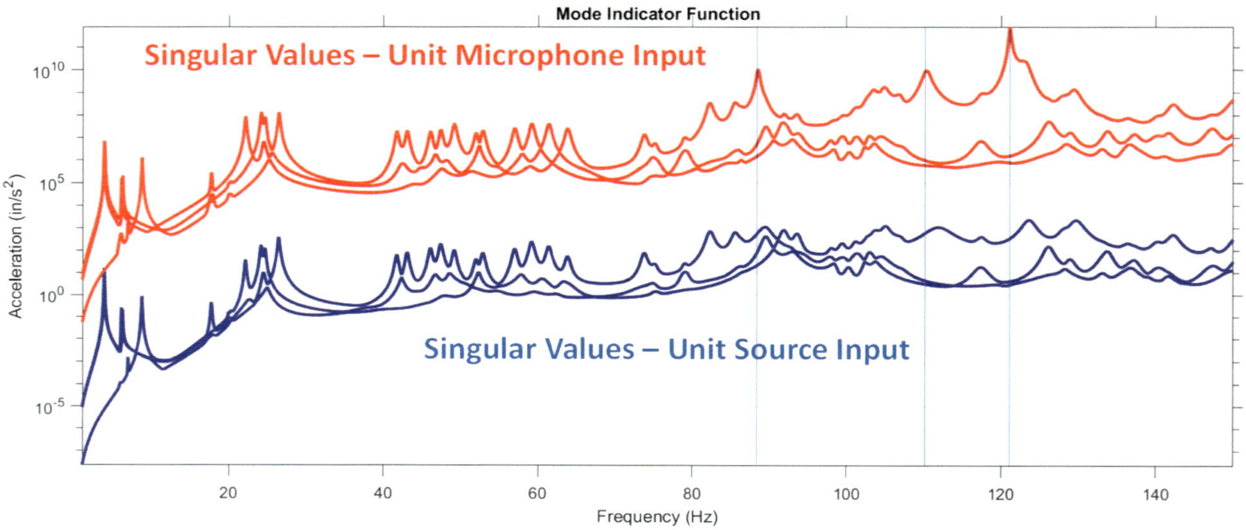

Fig. 8 Singular values of $[S_{yy}]$ due to unit source input and unit control microphone input.

Summary and Observations

The pretest analysis in this paper shows that modes can be extracted from acoustic tests. As with any modal survey test, using conventional sensor selection algorithms for placing accelerometers is sufficient even when the excitation source is acoustic. However, for acoustically sensitive structures, the effects of air mass should be included if test self-orthogonality matrices are used as a test exit criterion. That said, the baseline mass matrix should be sufficient for test-FEM cross orthogonality comparisons.

As with most modal survey tests, the input sources may not excite all of the modes of interest. In these cases, plans should be made to excite those modes by other means. Likewise, test results showing that there are duplicate modes extracted at different frequencies, likely due to zeros in the microphone/source FRF, should also be verified by exciting those modes directly by other means.

The changes in modal damping are due to either interaction between the structure and air mass or the way the source interacts with the system.

In this work, a comparison between the modal extractions from acoustic excitation and modes calculated without acoustic effects incorporations was presented. Therefore it was difficult to determine whether changes in modal parameters such as damping were due to frequency variation of the acoustic input loads or to the structure residing in fluid air. Thus, future work should include a comparison of modal extractions to the modes associated with the wet structure.

References

1. Napolitano, K., Yang, M., Friedlander, E., and Schick, D., "Mode Shape Extraction Using Direct Field Acoustic Noise Test Data," *43rd International Modal Analysis Conference*, February 10–13, 2025.
2. Flanigan, C., and Botos, D., "Automated Selection of Accelerometer Locations for Modal Survey Tests," *10th International Modal Analysis Conference*, San Diego, California, February 3–6, 1992.
3. Crowley, J.R., Klosterman, A.L., Rocklin, G.T., and Vold, H., "Direct Structural Modification Using Frequency Response Functions," *Proceedings of the Second International Modal Analysis Conference*, Orlando, Florida, February 1984, pp. 58–65.
4. Fladung, W.A., "Why Don't We Just Use the Cross Spectra for Operational Modal Analysis?" *43rd International Modal Analysis Conference*, February 10–13, 2025.

Chapter 6
Experimental Study on Measuring the Constant Off-Set in Displacement from Phase Resonance Testing of Contact-Gap Nonlinearity

Dana Dulcinea Figueroa and Benjamin Robert Pacini

Abstract Phase resonance testing is a popular technique for testing nonlinear structures where closed loop control maintains 90 degrees relative phase between the excitation force and acceleration response. Measurements from these experiments collected at many excitation levels can be used for nonlinear system identification. Typically, accelerometers are used to collect the response data. This data is integrated numerically to produce measured velocities and displacements which are then used to conduct the nonlinear system identification. However, this integration cannot recover certain components of the displacement such as the constant offset typical of contact-gap type nonlinearities. Excluding this data has been shown to produce inaccurate identification of the nonlinearity. This work seeks to demonstrate experimentally the constant offset in displacement as a first step in recovering this information from acceleration measurements. Phase resonance testing is conducted on a structure with a mode which exhibits a contact-gap nonlinearity. Acceleration measurements are acquired via accelerometers, and displacements at various locations on the structure are measured using a high-speed camera. The constant offset in the displacement is shown from the raw measured time histories as well as the error in the displacement obtained via numerical intragrain of the measured acceleration.

Keywords Force appropriation · Nonlinear · Structural dynamics · DC offset · Displacement

Introduction

System identification is an integral task in developing a finite element model and is the process of extracting dynamic properties of a structure from test. For linear structures, this is accomplished via modal testing where natural frequency, damping, and mode shapes are extracted from frequency response functions (FRFs) [1]. For nonlinear structures, system identification is still an open area of research [2]. Of particular interest in this work are asymmetric nonlinearities (such as contact-gap type behavior) where the corresponding restoring forces are not the same in magnitude for positive and negative oscillations of the displacement response. These types of nonlinearities produce constant offsets in the displacement response (referred to as DC offsets in this work) which must be captured either through direct measurement or through post processing to accurately identify the nonlinearity. Acceleration values measured during excitation can be double integrated to get displacement values if and only if the initial conditions of displacement are known. If the initial displacement values are unknown, the DC value will get lost in integration resulting in inaccurate displacement values.

This work is an initial investigation into directly measuring these DC offsets during a force appropriation experiment. Nonlinear force appropriation testing, also known as phase-resonance testing [3, 4], is a technique where closed loop control is used to maintain a structure in phase resonance [5, 6](i.e., 90 degrees relative phase between excitation force and response) as the input is slowly increased. This allows for the characterization of a single nonlinear mode of a structure from low to high energy levels and results in measurements that can be used for system identification.

Sandia National Laboratories is a multimission laboratory managed and operated by National Technology & Engineering Solutions of Sandia, LLC, a wholly owned subsidiary of Honeywell International Inc., for the U.S. Department of Energy's National Nuclear Security Administration under contract DE-NA0003525. SAND2024-1760036

Dana Dulcinea Figueroa · Benjamin Robert Pacin
Sandia National Laboratories, PO Box 5800 - MS0557
e-mail: danafigu@hotmail.com; brpacin@sandia.gov

Brandon Dilworth et al. (eds.), *Topics in Modal Analysis & Parameter Identification I, Vol. 9*, Conference Proceedings of the Society for Experimental Mechanics Series, https://doi.org/10.13052/9788743801542-6

The remainder of this paper is outlined as follows: Section 2 provides a motivating example for the importance of properly capturing the DC offset in dynamic testing. Section 3 gives a short background of the previous experimentation from which the data originated. Section 4 covers the data processing for DC extraction. Section 5 describes the processes and equations used to calculate DC offset. Section 6 provides lessons learned, future work to implement the techniques developed in this work, and a conclusion of the entire experimentation and data processing.

Motivation

To demonstrate the importance of including DC offset in the displacement, results from [7] are used where Phase-Resonance Multi-Harmonic Balance (PR-MHB) [8] was used to conduct virtual nonlinear force appropriation tests on a SDOF oscillator with a contact-gap spring element (Fig 1). PR-MHB is a method of solving nonlinear equations of motion in the frequency domain while enforcing constraints which maintain phase resonance between the excitation force and response, so the results are analogous to those produced from a nonlinear force appropriation test. The equation of motion for the contact-gap oscillator is

$$m\ddot{x}(t) + c\dot{x}(t) + kx(t) + f_{nl}\left(x\left(t\right)\right) = f(t) \tag{1}$$

where f is the excitation force and $f_{nl}\left(x\right)$ is the nonlinear restoring force given by

$$f_{nl}(x(t)) = \begin{cases} 0 & x(t) < x_g \\ k_{\mathrm{p}}\left(x(t) - x_g\right) & x(t) \geq x_g \end{cases} \tag{2}$$

The piece-wise linear penalty spring, k_{p}, activates once the displacement, x, exceeds the gap distance, x_g. Otherwise, the system behaves linearly where the modal properties are defined by mass (m), damping (c), and stiffness (k).

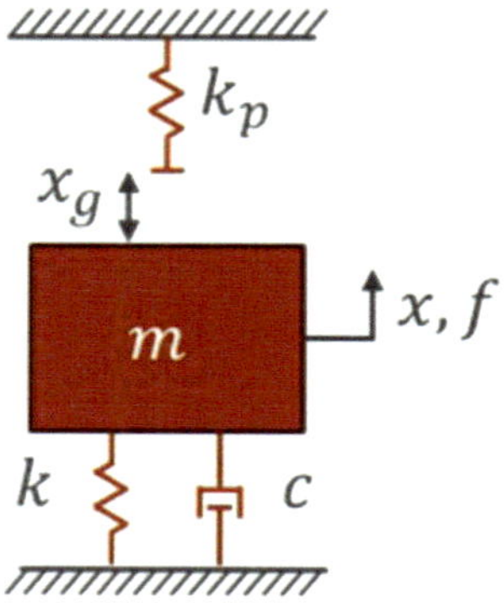

Fig. 1 contact gap oscillator.

The PR-MHB results from [7] of the contact-gap oscillator provide the Fourier Coefficients of the displacement response at the fundamental frequency and associated harmonics as well as the DC component. Thus, $x(t)$ can be reconstructed with and without the DC offset to study the resulting influences on the identification of $f_{nl}\left(x\right)$. In the system identification scenario, it is assumed that a linear modal test has been conducted so that m, c, and k are known. Additionally, the PR-MHB results provide the measured displacement and excitation force from the virtual experiment. Therefore, the "measured" $f_{nl}\left(x\right)$ can be computed by rearranging Eq (1) for cases with and without the DC component in displacement:

$$f_{nl}\left(x\left(t\right)\right) = f\left(t\right) - m\ddot{x}\left(t\right) - c\dot{x}\left(t\right) - kx(t). \tag{3}$$

As mentioned previously, $\ddot{x}\left(t\right)$ is typically the response quantity measured during a force appropriation test and is used to compute $\dot{x}(t)$ and $x\left(t\right)$ numerically via integration. However, the DC offset in displacement is not recovered in this process, so the scenario explored here where the DC offset is excluded replicates the typical measurement case. Using the Force-Response Curve (FRC) technique for system identification from [7](which is similar to approaches from [9, 10]), $f_{nl}\left(x\left(t\right)\right)$ is plotted versus $x\left(t\right)$ to construct $f_{nl}\left(x\right)$ as shown in Figure 2. Comparing these results with Eq (2), the effect of the DC offset in displacement is evident in that when the DC offset is excluded, the resulting $f_{nl}\left(x\right)$ is incorrect. Therefore, in a practical scenario where a structure exhibits similar asymmetric behavior, if the DC offset is not included in the displacement response, the resulting identification will be erroneous. This work describes initial attempts to measure the DC offset directly from nonlinear force appropriation experiments for nonlinear system identification.

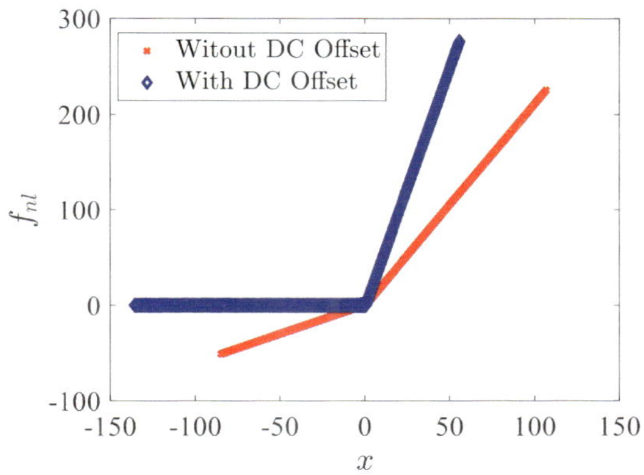

Fig. 2 Nonlinear restoring force for the contact-gap oscillator with and without including the DC offset in displacement.

Test Setup

The data used to extract the DC offset came from a previous experiment done by Alkady et.al [11] in which a half c-beam assembly (Fig 3) was investigated for nonlinear behavior. The purpose of their testing was to address the limitations of traditional sensors used in modal analysis by using full-field, high-speed, and high-fidelity Digital Image Correlation (DIC) with the addition of phase-based motion magnification (PMM)to better characterize the nonlinear response of bolted joints .

Fig. 3 Unbolted Assembly [11].

The test set up is shown in Figure 4 and consisted of the 2 c-beams (Fig 3) bolted together and suspended by bungee cords to simulate free-free boundary conditions. A speckle pattern sticker was placed at the area of interest, i.e., the joint. A shaker

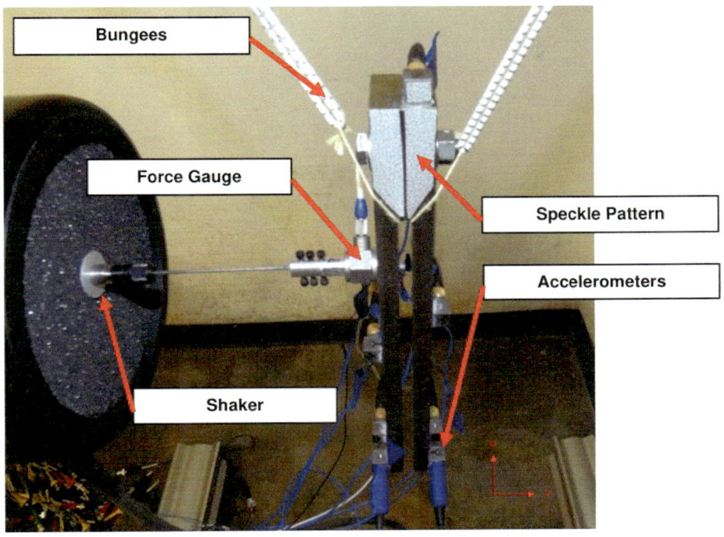

Fig. 4 Test setup [11].

was connected to a location that was optimized for exciting the out-of-phase bending mode which activates open/closing behavior of the joint. High-speed cameras were set up in stereo to get displacements in three dimensions and lights were also placed to properly illuminate the speckle pattern.

Force appropriation using a phase-locking algorithm was used at voltage amplitudes of 0.1V – 0.8V with an increment of 0.1V Before each run, a reference image of the beam was taken at rest for calculation of displacements later. The shaker is then activated at the lowest voltage at a starting frequency suspected to be the desired mode. Phase resonance is found through closed loop control from Siemens LMS. Once phase resonance is found, data is collected for 2 seconds. MatchID, an image analysis software from Siemens, was then used to extract responses from the collected frames of the tests and the displacements of the chosen subsets were calculated. Experimentation showed that as the amplitude of excitation increased, so did the height and length of the gapping along the joint interface which resulted in asymmetric nonlinear behavior.

Data Processing

MatchID was used to align the coordinate system of the beam with that of the master camera. Five sets of nodes were placed near the joint as seen in Figure 5. The *v* direction data was the focus of this analysis. The variable $v_{ij}(t)$ is the measured *v*-direction displacement time history of node ij with respect to the reference image. The relative displacement of point pairs across the joint is designated v_j (e.g., $v_5 = v_{15} - v_{25}$).

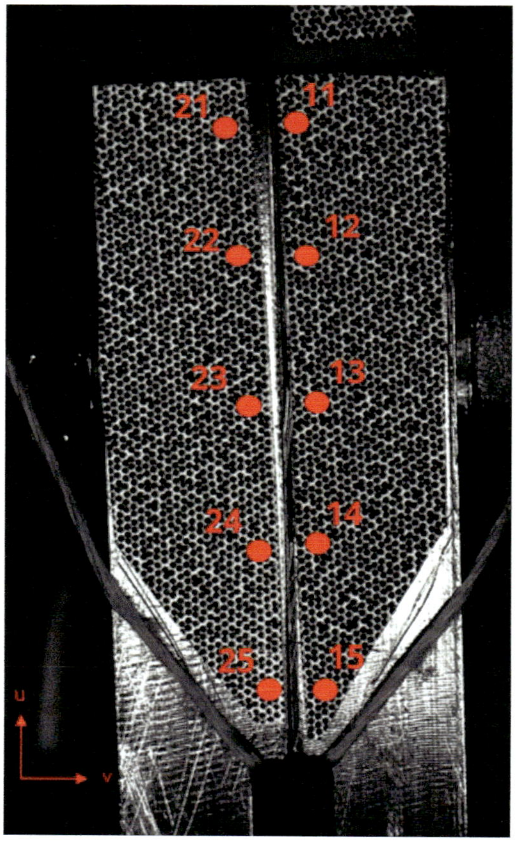

Fig. 5 Approximate point locations.

The objective of this work is to directly measure the DC offset due to nonlinearity, which means we need to extract the frequency content of v_{ij}. This was accomplished by fitting the functional form of a Fourier series (Eq (4)) to the steady state response.

$$v_{ij}(t) = B_0^{ij} + \sum_{k=1}^{N} A_k^{ij} sin(k\omega t) + B_k^{ij} cos(k\omega t) \tag{4}$$

where $v(t)$ is the time history, B_0^{ij} is the DC offset, A_k^{ij} and B_k^{ij} are the of the sine and cosine portions of the kth harmonic, ω is the frequency of the signal, and N is the number of harmonics present. When the measured response is discretized into n samples with $v_{ij}(t_m)$, where $m = 1, \ldots, j$, the following matrix can be constructed:

$$\overline{v}_{ij}(t) = \begin{bmatrix} \sin(\omega t_1) & \sin(2\omega t_1) & \cdots & \sin(N\omega t_1) & \cos(\omega t_1) & \cos(2\omega t_1) & \cdots & \cos(N\omega t_1) & 1 \\ \sin(\omega t_2) & \sin(2\omega t_2) & \cdots & \sin(N\omega t_2) & \cos(\omega t_2) & \cos(2\omega t_2) & \cdots & \cos(N\omega t_2) & 1 \\ \vdots & \vdots & \cdots & \vdots & \vdots & \vdots & \cdots & \vdots & \vdots \\ \sin(\omega t_j) & \sin(2\omega t_j) & \cdots & \sin(N\omega t_j) & \cos(\omega t_j) & \cos(2\omega t_j) & \cdots & \cos(N\omega t_j) & 1 \end{bmatrix} \begin{bmatrix} A_1 \\ A_2 \\ \vdots \\ A_N \\ B_1 \\ B_2 \\ \vdots \\ B_N \\ B_0 \end{bmatrix} = C\overline{A} \tag{5}$$

The coefficient vector, $\overline{A}$, can be solved for in a least squares sense by

$$\overline{A} = C^{+}\overline{v_{ij}}, \tag{6}$$

where C^{+} is the pseudo inverse of matrix C

These coefficients are computed for each DOF at each excitation level, so that their change can be observed from low to high response. This process allows for the extraction of B_0^{ij} from the measured time response v_{ij}. The magnitude of the other harmonics is computed using Equation (7) and is compared to B_0^{ij} to evaluate the significance of the DC offset in the measured displacement [5].

$$M_k^{ij} = \sqrt{{A_k^{ij}}^2 + {B_k^{ij}}^2}, \tag{7}$$

DC Offset Directly from DIC Measurement

Once the magnitude of the harmonics is computed for each DOF using Equation (7), they are plotted against each input voltage level. Figure 6 shows the harmonic content for each point in Figure 5 with even harmonics plotted as dotted lines, odd harmonics plotted as solid lines, and the DC (B_0) plotted as a black line.

There is a non-monotonic trend with respect to voltage in the B_0 for all points. Moreover, the B_0 is largest when the displacement (and therefore the nonlinear response) is the lowest. Since the magnitude of B_0 is commensurate with the strength of the nonlinearity, it is reasonable to expect that the largest B_0 should occur at the largest voltages. however, this is not the trend observed in Figure 6; the largest B_0 occurs at the lowest voltage. Therefore, it appears that a phenomenon is contributing to the B_0 in addition to the nonlinear physics.

It is believed that the other contributor to the measured DC offset is static, rigid translation of the beam within the camera frame. The measured DC offset (B_0) is thus the sum of the DC due to nonlinear dynamics ($B_{0,NL}$) and that due to static motion of the part within the camera frame ($B_{0,Cam}$):

$$B_0 = B_{0,cam} + B_{0,NL} \tag{8}$$

For system identification, $B_{0,NL}$ is desired and therefore $B_{0,Cam}$ needs to be determined. We hypothesize that $B_{0,cam}$ can be determined by finding the time instances when the structure is undeformed. Since the measured values of points v_{ij} are in relation to the reference image, subtracting point pairs directly across the joint from each other removes the effect of the static rigid translation of the part within the camera frame. Therefore, when this difference is equal to 0, the relative position of the point pairs is the same as their relative position in the reference image, and thus represents the time instances of the undeformed state. These time instances could then be used to adjust the measurements of v_{ij} to remove the effect of $B_{0,cam}$. This process is carried out with two point pairs ($v_{21} - v_{11} = \Delta v_1$ and $v_{25} - v_{15} = \Delta v_5$) as shown in Figure 7, where the red x's represent the time instances when Δv_i is equal to zero. It is left as a future work to use this data to adjust the measure v_{ij} to remove the effects of$B_{0,cam}$.

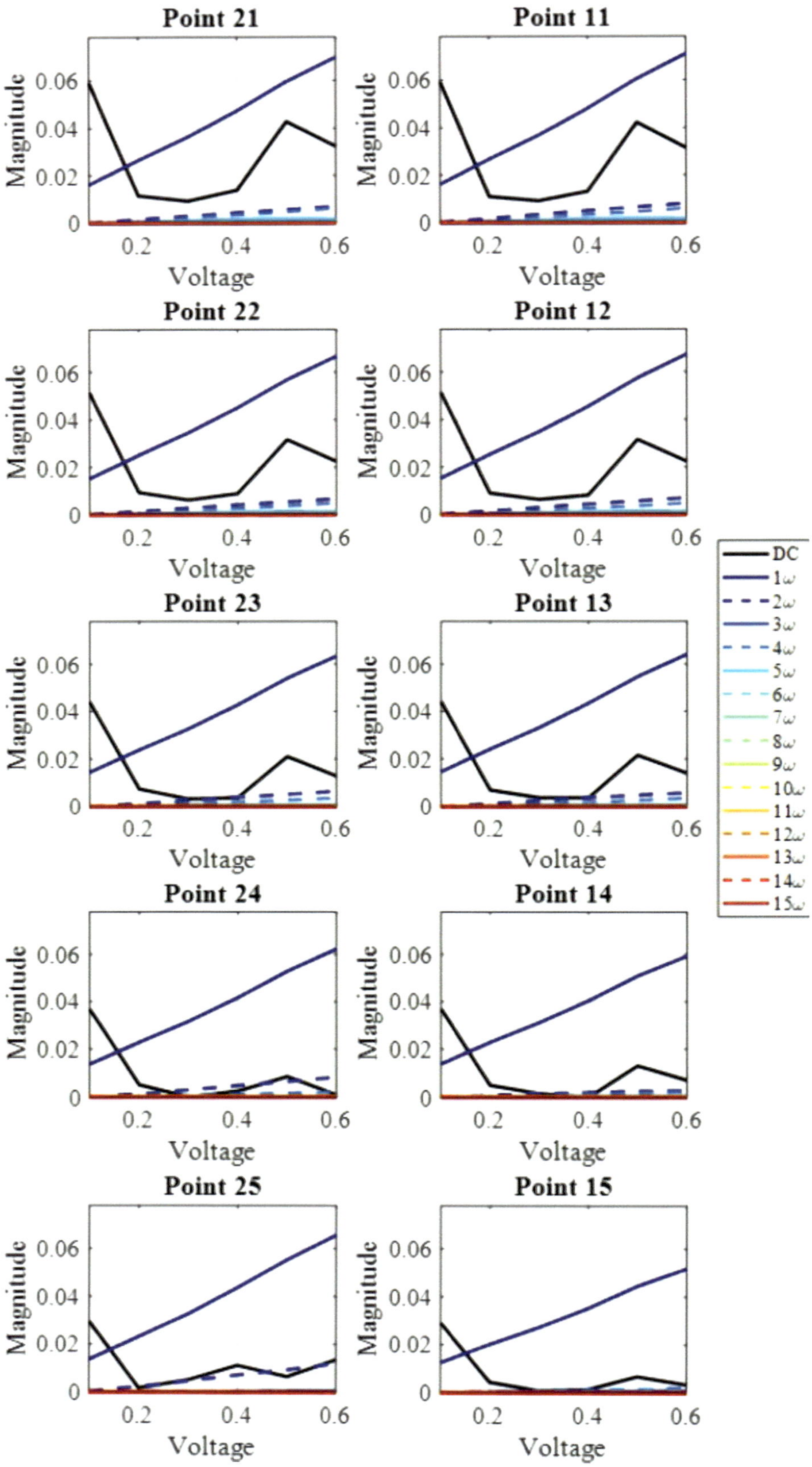

Fig. 6 Harmonic content at each point from Figure 5.

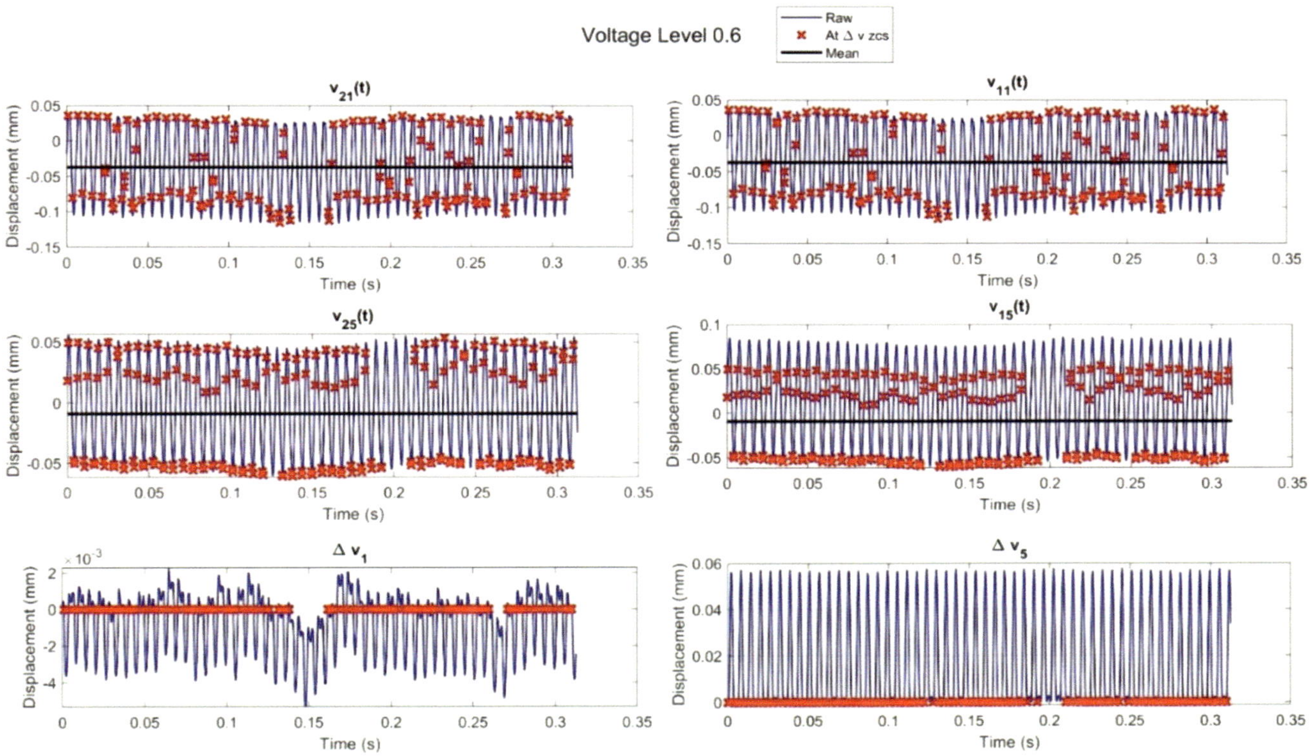

Fig. 7 Plots of the zero-crossings of point sets 1 and 5.

Conclusions

While not all efforts were discussed here, there are many lessons learned from this exploratory work. Three-dimensional displacement measurements obtained using stereo DIC measurements are required since 2D motions measured with a single camera interpret out-of-plane motion as in-plane motion. This was realized during an initial setup (separate from that from [4]) where 2D motion of six points on a full c-beam assembly were measured using a single high-speed camera. While analyzing the results, the in-plane displacements were distorted by out-of-plane motion of the c-beam, leading to the use of data from [4].

This work demonstrated that even with stereo measurements, the extraction of the DC offset due to nonlinear physics from measured response is not straightforward. Static rigid translations of the part within the camera frame contribute to the observed DC offset and must be removed to perform nonlinear system identification. A simple technique was proposed in this work which utilized differences in the displacement of point pairs directly across the joint to determine time instances of when the structure was undeformed. This information could then be used to adjust the measured displacements such that the static, rigid motion of the part within the camera frame is removed. This is left as a future work.

References

1. D. J. Ewins, Modal Testing: Theory, Practice and Application. John Wiley & Sons, 2009.
2. J. P. Noël and G. Kerschen, "Nonlinear system identification in structural dynamics: 10 more years of progress," Mech. Syst. Signal Process., vol. 83, pp. 2–35, Jan. 2017, doi:10.1016/j.ymssp.2016.07.020.
3. M. Peeters, G. Kerschen, and J. C. Golinval, "Dynamic testing of nonlinear vibrating structures using nonlinear normal modes," J. Sound Vib., vol. 330, no. 3, pp. 486–509, Jan. 2011, doi:10.1016/j.jsv.2010.08.028.
4. M. Scheel, S. Peter, R. I. Leine, and M. Krack, "A phase resonance approach for modal testing of structures with nonlinear dissipation," J. Sound Vib., vol. 435, pp. 56–73, Nov. 2018, doi:10.1016/j.jsv.2018.07.010.
5. M. Volvert and G. Kerschen, "Phase resonance nonlinear modes of mechanical systems," J. Sound Vib., vol. 511, p. 116355, Oct. 2021, doi:10.1016/j.jsv.2021.116355.

6. M. Volvert and G. Kerschen, “Resonant phase lags of a Duffing oscillator,” Int. J. Non-Linear Mech., vol. 146, p. 104150, Nov. 2022, doi:10.1016/j.ijnonlinmec.2022.104150.
7. B. R. Pacini, R. J. Kuether, and D. R. Roettgen, “Shaker-structure interaction modeling and analysis for nonlinear force appropriation testing,” Mech. Syst. Signal Process., vol. 162, p. 108000, Jan. 2022, doi:10.1016/j.ymssp.2021.108000.
8. D. Fowler, R. Kuether, and B. Pacini, “Multi-Input, Multi-Harmonic Nonlinear Phase Resonance Simulations with Harmonic Balance.,” Sandia National Lab. (SNL-NM), Albuquerque, NM (United States), SAND2021–12913C, Oct. 2021. Accessed: Sep. 10, 2024. [Online]. Available: https://www.osti.gov/biblio/1892154
9. T. Dossogne et al., “Nonlinear Ground Vibration Identification of an F-16 Aircraft - Part II Understanding Nonlinear Behaviour in Aerospace Structures Using Sine-sweep Testing,” Jun. 2015.
10. M. F. Platten, J. R. Wright, G. Dimitriadis, and J. E. Cooper, “Identification of multi-degree of freedom non-linear systems using an extended modal space model,” Mech. Syst. Signal Process., vol. 23, no. 1, pp. 8–29, Jan. 2009, doi:10.1016/j.ymssp.2007.11.016.
11. K. Alkady et al., “Full-Field Diagnostics of Bolted Joints Using High-Speed Optical Techniques”, presented at the 42nd International Modal Analysis Conference Orlando, Florida, 2024.

Chapter 7
Comparison of Data-Driven Techniques for Structural Dynamics Model Order Reduction

Celso T. do Cabo, Yujie Xi, Raymond Joshua, and Zhu Mao

Abstract The vibrational behavior of structures is oftentimes used to define their state awareness and can be further employed for damage detection and prognosis. However, most structures have a complex behavior that cannot be easily interpreted or directly applied for damage detection. While many methods can be employed to model those systems, such as finite element models (FEM), these models depend on a strong understanding of physics as prior knowledge. With the increased number of monitoring systems and data availability for structural dynamics, data-driven technologies are becoming increasingly more popular for a variety of problems. Among unsupervised learning methods, dimension reduction techniques are widely used to simplify high-dimensional datasets. In addition, for linear models, Principal Component Analysis (PCA) or Proper Orthogonal Decomposition (POD) are some of the most known methods, which consists of employing Singular Value Decomposition (SVD) or eigen decomposition in the dataset itself. Furthermore, other techniques have been developed specifically for time-series applications, such as Dynamic Mode Decomposition (DMD). This work focuses on the comparison between the performance of data-driven dimension reduction techniques, such as the ones mentioned previously, as well as other improved versions of such technologies, such as optimized DMD when applied to structural dynamics. Different techniques are implemented and compared to the context of structural vibrations, and all techniques are compared with respect to their advantages and limitations, as well as the corresponding mathematical investigation.

Keywords Model Order Reduction · Structural Dynamics · Principal Component Analysis · Dynamic Mode Decomposition

Introduction

Vibrational behavior of structures is of critical importance for a variety of applications, such as to define its state awareness which can be further employed for damage detection and prognosis. However, their dynamical behavior oftentimes has a high complexity, which makes it difficult to interpret or directly employ for damage detection. While many methods can be applied to model dynamical systems, such as finite element models (FEM), these models depend on strong understanding of the physics as prior knowledge. With the increasing in data availability for structural dynamics, data-driven technologies are becoming increasingly more popular for a variety of applications. Among unsupervised methods, Principal Component Analysis (PCA) is a very well-known dimension reduction technique, which uses Singular Value Decomposition (SVD) to decompose the dataset into a different basis and reduce its order for simplification [1, 2]. In addition, Proper Orthogonal Decomposition (POD) works in a similar manner as PCA using SVD to decompose physical measurements and are often compared on how they are computed [3–5]. Such techniques were also previously employed into vibrational systems as a manner to reduce the order of the system, as well as to decompose the original signals into different modes [6–8].

NSC-614-5662 10/2024
Unclassified Unlimited Release

Celso T. do Cabo · Yujie Xi · Zhu Mao (✉)
Department of Mechanical and Materials Engineering, Worcester Polytechnic Institute, Worcester, MA 01609
e-mail: ctdocabo@wpi.edu; yxi@wpi.edu; zmao2@wpi.edu

Raymond Joshua
Honeywell Federal Manufacturing & Technologies, LLC operates the Kansas City, National Security Campus for the United States Department of Energy / National Nuclear
Security Administration under Contract Number DE-NA0002839
e-mail: rjoshua@kcnsc.doe.gov

Brandon Dilworth et al. (eds.), *Topics in Modal Analysis & Parameter Identification I, Vol. 9*, Conference Proceedings of the Society for Experimental Mechanics Series, https://doi.org/10.13052/9788743801542-7

However, among dimension reduction techniques, more techniques have been developed specifically for physical problems, such as the Dynamic Mode Decomposition (DMD), which was developed specifically for time-series applications, initially being applied into fluid dynamics problems [9–11]. The technique uses the Koopman operator to obtain an approximate matrix which is time invariant, later applying eigen solution to the operator in order to obtain the dynamic modes [12]. This technique had several applications including controls and in vibrational systems, however, in the context of video-based sensing [13, 14]. In addition, modifications of the DMD algorithm were created, such as the optimized DMD, which uses an optimization approach to obtain the dynamic modes [15], or approaches that includes physics knowledge of the system [16].

This work proposes a comparison between different methods of order reduction using machine learning approaches, such as PCA, SVD and DMD. For that, different applications will be used such as sparse measurement obtained from accelerometers, a full-field measurement obtained from lased Doppler vibrometer (LDV) and video-based sensing.

Background

Dimension reduction techniques are usually known for machine learning applications. However, order reduction techniques can have similar procedure for other applications where the physical knowledge of the system is known. For example, modal analysis employs the eigen decomposition of the parameters of a governing equation (e.g. from a FEM) and can use a smaller number of mode shapes to describe the behavior of a structure. POD will have a similar mathematical procedure with measurements of a physical quantity. While for statistical or mathematical applications PCA and SVD will be used to decompose a set into smaller dimension. SVD for instance, can decompose an initial matrix X into two unitary matrices and a scalar as presented in Equation (1).

$$X \approx U\Sigma V^T \tag{1}$$

Where, U and V are unitary matrices and Σ is a rectangular and diagonal matrix containing the singular values. Meanwhile, PCA and POD can use either SVD for the decomposition, or it can calculate the covariance matrix of the dataset X. Since the covariance matrix will be a square matrix, then the eigen decomposition can obtain the modes and values for the variation of the data. The covariance matrix can be calculated according to Equation (2).

$$\widehat{\Sigma} = \frac{1}{n}\sum_{i=1}^{n}(x_i - \overline{x})(x_i - \overline{x})^T \tag{2}$$

Where, $\widehat{\Sigma}$ is the covariance matrix of the dataset, $\overline{x}$ is the mean of the data. After computing the covariance matrix of the normalized dataset, the principal components will be given by its eigen solution. DMD works in a similar manner to PCA and SVD. However, instead of using either the dataset itself or the covariance matrix, it will calculate an $[A]$ matrix which will be a time invariant matrix computed based on the Koopman operator as shown in Equation (3) and the process to calculate the DMD modes can be seen in Figure 1.

$$X^{'} \approx AX \tag{3}$$

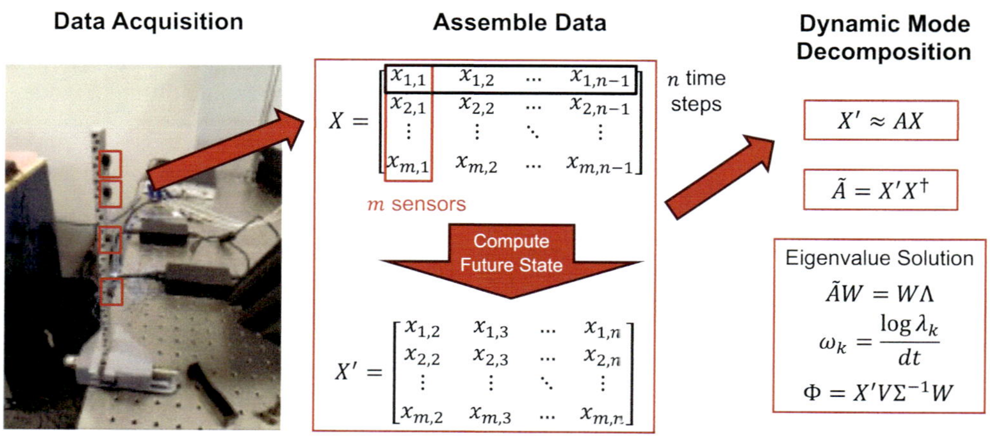

Fig. 1 Flowchart of DMD measurement and mode decomposition.

where, X' is the future state of the system, X is its current state and A the linear operator that predicts the future state based on the current state. Since DMD aims to reduce the order of the system, a low rank $\tilde{A}$ can be calculated based on the linear operator by applying SVD to the equation, as shown in Equation (4).

$$\tilde{A}{\approx}U^T AU = U^T X' V\Sigma^{-1} \tag{4}$$

After calculating the low rank matrix $\tilde{A}$, the eigen decomposition will be computed following Equation (5).

$$\tilde{A}W{=}W\Lambda \tag{5}$$

where, W are the mode shapes associated with $\tilde{A}$ and Λ its eigenvalues. Finally, the DMD modes Φ can be calculated based on Equation (6).

$$\Phi{=}X' V\Sigma^{-1}W \tag{6}$$

Later the signal reconstruction for each DMD mode is done by an exponential approximation as presented in Equation (7).

$$t_{DMD}{=}be^{\omega t} \tag{7}$$

t_{DMD} is the time reconstruction for each DMD mode, b is a scale factor based on the initial condition for each mode and sensor, and ω is the natural frequency calculated using the eigenvalue following Equation (8).

$$\omega_k{=}\frac{\log\lambda_k}{dt} \tag{8}$$

Given dt as the time-step between measurements. Finally, the time reconstruction from DMD is given by:

$$\hat{X}{\approx}\Phi \times t_{DMD} \tag{9}$$

Another existing approach for DMD is the optimized DMD. Instead of using linear algebra to calculate the DMD modes and frequencies, optimized DMD uses an iterative method by optimizing the following equation.

$$\min \|X - \Phi{\times}t_{DMD}\|_F \tag{10}$$

where $\|.\|_F$ is the Frobenius norm of a matrix and given by the square root of the matrix trace times its conjugate transposed. This approach optimizes the DMD reconstruction to the measured data, leading to a better time reconstruction if compared to the exact (original) DMD.

Experimental Setup

There were three experimental setups employed to compare the different order reduction techniques. Starting with an impact test in a cantilever beam, with a sparse measurement obtained from accelerometers. The setup can be seen in Figure 1, where four accelerometers were placed in the beam and the data collected consisted of 1,024 time-steps at 2.56kHz of sampling rate. The first two natural frequencies of the beam occurred at 48.6Hz and 435.3Hz.

For the second test, a cantilever plate was employed. For this case, the LDV scanned 133 points equally distributed thought the plate. The test collected a total of 50,000 timesteps at 100kHz of sampling rate. The excitation was a burst chirp for 50% of the testing time ranging from 100Hz to 10kHz. This testing setup meant to be employed as a full-field measurement of the structure, with higher number of measuring points, however, still with a smaller number of measured points than timesteps. The setup is presented in Figure 2a).

Finally, the last test was the same impact test from the cantilever beam, however, using a video-based measurement. No post processing was employed into the video, except for cropping the frame from a full HD resolution (1920x1080 pixels) to 400x1080 pixels. That was done to focus on the beam only and reduce the area of background. The measurement was performed at 960Hz of sampling rate and 2,000 points collected. The setup for the video-based sensing is shown in Figure 2b).

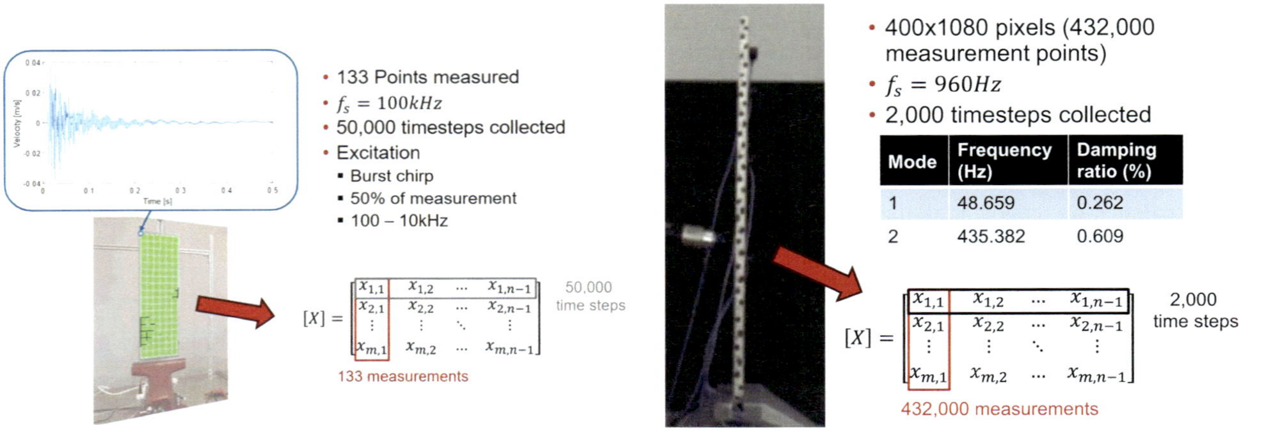

(a) (b)

Fig. 2 Experimental setup for the cantilever plate with LDV measurement (a) and cantilever beam with video-based measurement (b).

Results and Discussion

The results obtained by the reduction techniques will be presented by comparing each result of PCA, exact DMD and optimized DMD for each case. Starting with the results for the cantilever beam, which is a sparse measurement with only four accelerometers. The PCA results for the cantilever beam are presented in Figure 3 below.

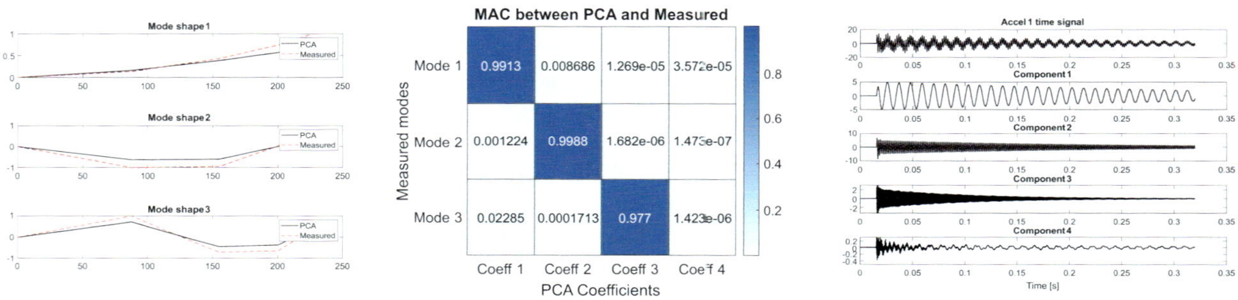

(a) (b) (c)

Fig. 3 Results of PCA to the cantilever beam, principal components compared to the mode shapes (a), MAC between the principal components and measured mode shapes (b) and time estimation for each component (c).

For the impact test, the highest variation of the data occurs based on the mode shapes of the structure, leading to a good correlation between the measured modes and principal components coefficients. As shown in Figure 3b) the MAC for the first three mode shapes are above 95% and the time estimation presented in (c) has a similar behavior, going from the low frequency sine wave to a high frequency one, with the last reconstruction having a behavior similar to noise. When applying exact DMD with sparse sensing, the mode shape estimation will also have good accuracy compared to the ones obtained by measurement for both mode shapes computed, as shown in Figure 4. However, DMD approximates the motion of the system using an exponential function. In order to obtain the oscillatory motion of the system, the eigenvalues computed will be composed of complex values. Therefore, four DMD modes can obtain only two of the real mode shapes of the beam as it can be seen in Figure 4b).

In addition, while exact DMD estimates modes well, its natural frequencies and time reconstruction have low accuracy. Figure 4c) presents each modal response, considering the small number of measurements, some of the eigenvalues obtained will be real values, leading to an exponential instead of an oscillatory behavior. Furthermore, the complex eigenvalues obtained possessed a high frequency and high damping ratio, leading to a small oscillation in the time domain, as shown in the two top plots of Figure 4c).

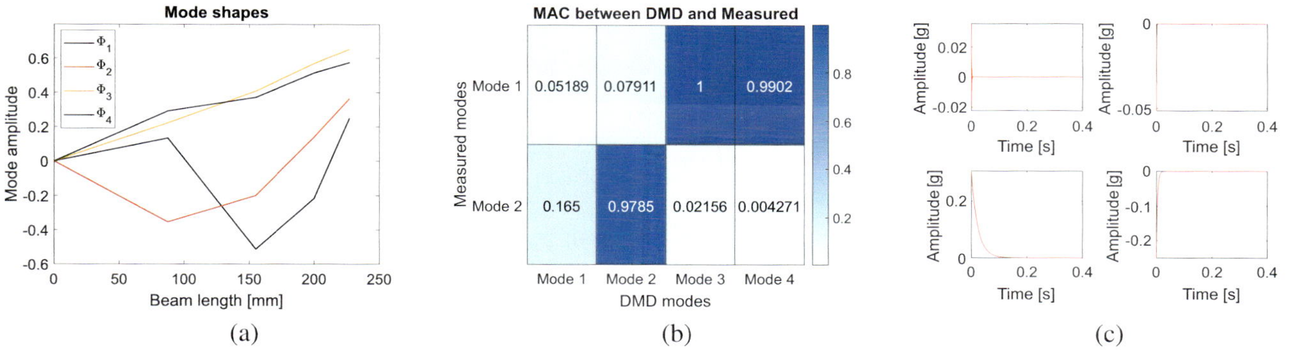

Fig. 4 Mode shape estimation (a) and MAC comparison (b) between exact DMD and measurement and time reconstruction for each mode (c).

Meanwhile, when applying optimized DMD on the dataset, the optimization algorithm focuses on the time reconstruction, as described in Equation (10). Therefore, the time estimation obtained will be better compared to the exact DMD as shown in Figure 5.

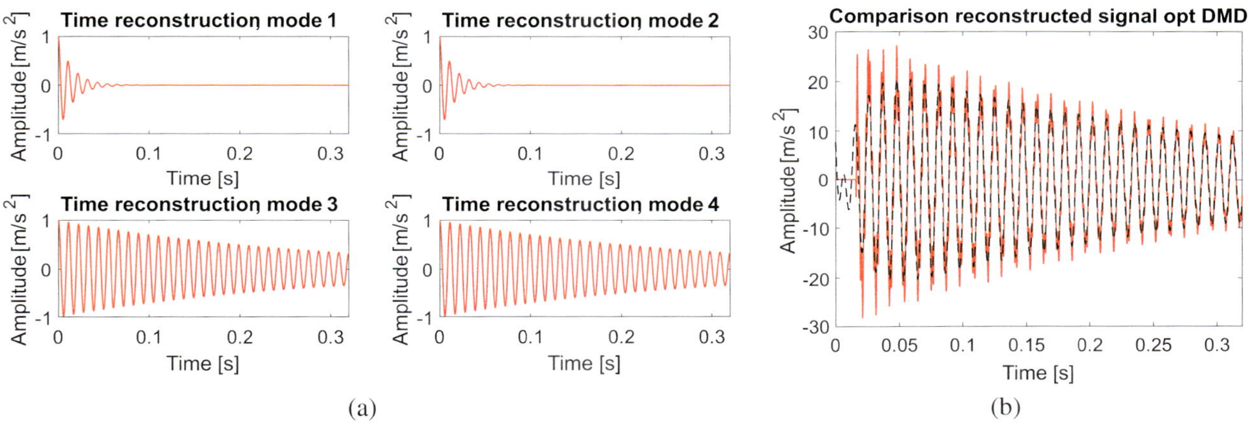

Fig. 5 Time estimation for each mode shape (a) and signal reconstruction (b) using optimized DMD.

In this case, modes 3 and 4 behave similarly to a modal response, and the signal reconstruction will have a better accuracy than the previous model. However, to obtain a good time reconstruction, the eigenvalues estimated are in a similar frequency range, as shown in Figure 6b). Since the natural frequency at 93.5Hz possesses the highest energy, the DMD estimation obtained the frequencies around the natural frequency estimation. Thus, only the first mode shape was extracted. The results of PCA applied to the cantilever plate having a full-field measurement using LDV is presented in Figure 7 as follows.

As shown in Figure 7a), most of the variation of the data happens in the first 20 components. Therefore, only 20 out of the 133 components would be able to reconstruct the original signal with a small error. However, since the forced vibration has different amplitude for different frequencies, it would be challenging to obtain the natural frequencies of the system based on the obtained parameters. In addition, since the order of the principal components are unknown, then the modes obtained can be from any natural frequency as it can be seen in (b) and (c). Meanwhile, when applying exact DMD to the plate, more mode shapes can be estimated, however, only when decomposing all 133 possible modes that some of the main natural frequencies are obtained.

Figure 8a) has the eigenvalues estimated for the plate, however, the eigenvalues are estimated from the highest frequency to the lowest and all frequencies are above 50Hz, avoiding some of the first mode shapes of the plate, such as the first bending mode at around 5$\sim$6Hz. In addition, in (b), the time reconstruction for two nodes is given. Even using more than 100 mode shapes for the estimation, the estimation does not look like the measured signal (due to the difference they could not be plotted together, and the estimated signal would be too small and not visible). Finally, (c) presents the DMD mode at 268Hz, which has a similar behavior to a high-frequency mode shape.

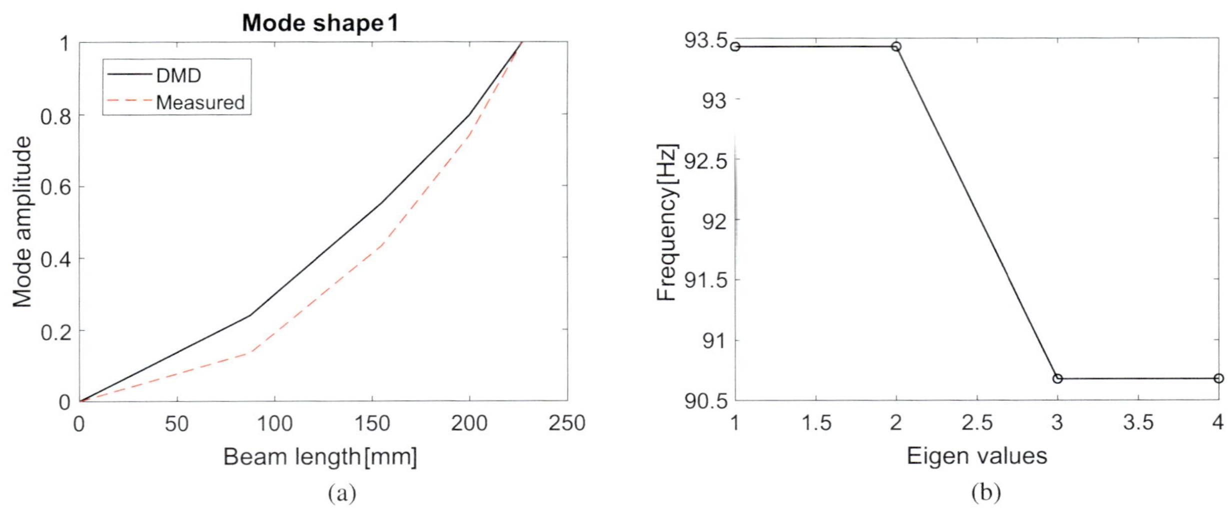

Fig. 6 Mode shape (a) and natural frequencies (b) estimations using optimized DMD.

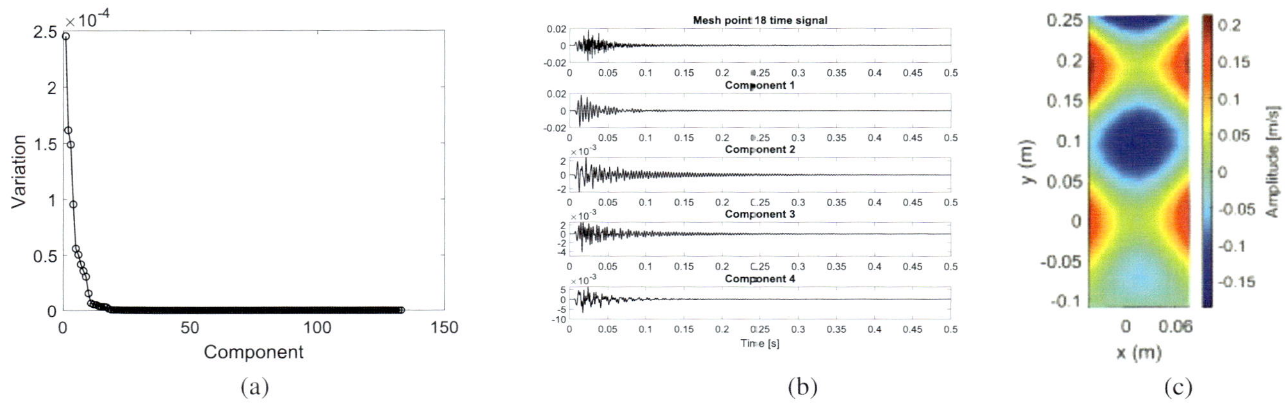

Fig. 7 Principal components (a), time reconstruction for each component (b) and first mode estimation (c) for PCA applied to the cantilever plate.

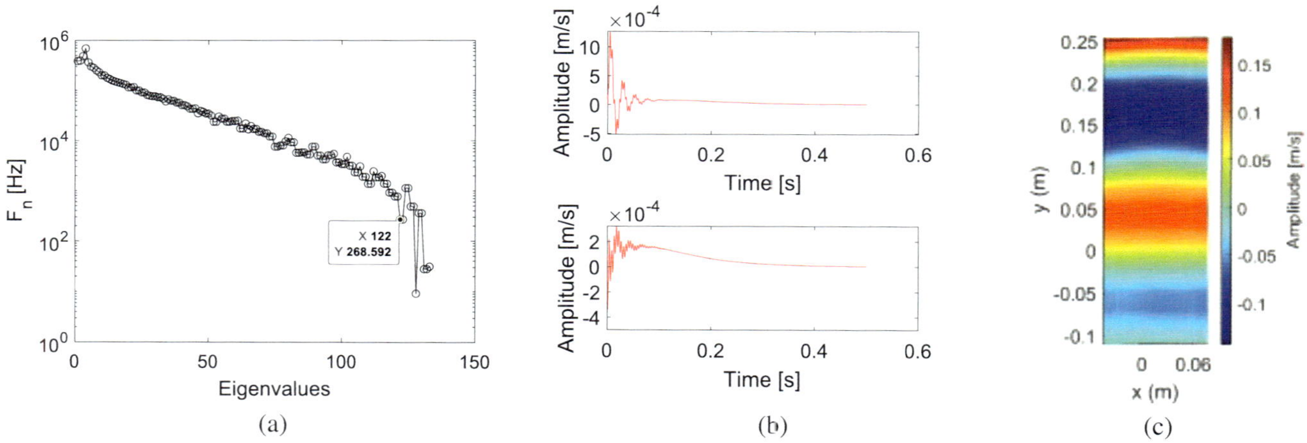

Fig. 8 Natural frequencies obtained from eigenvalues (a), time reconstruction (b) and mode shape estimation at 268Hz (c) using exact DMD.

When employing the same dataset into the optimized DMD algorithm, although the time for computing the correct answer is much higher than when using exact DMD, it requires a much lower number of eigenvalues to perform a good time reconstruction of the time signal. In Figure 9a) the estimated frequencies for the first 20 modes are presented. Similarly to the previous example, the eigenvalues are computed in pairs due to being estimated as a complex value. Using only 20 eigenvalues will give the TRAC shown in (b), in which most of the values are above 80% of signal reconstruction. The only exceptions are near the base of the plate, where the boundary condition causes low signal amplitude, and in the location where the shaker is positioned (which has around 60% reconstruction). Finally, the lowest frequency mode is presented in (c). This mode shape has a corresponding frequency of 5.6Hz which is similar to the real mode shape obtained by the LDV measurement. In addition, the first mode resembles a bending mode shape with values in the base close to zero and the highest value near the top of the plate.

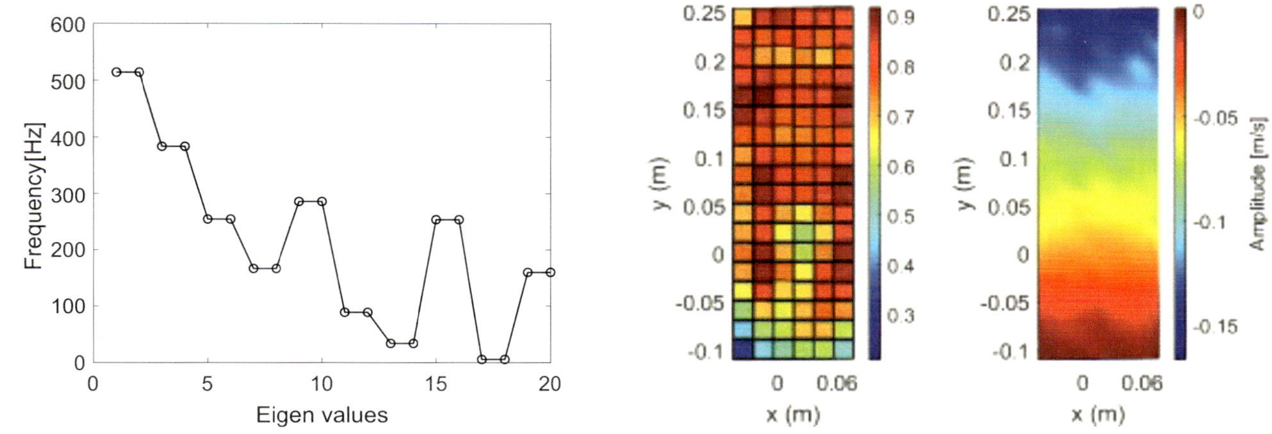

(a) (b) (c)

Fig. 9 Estimated natural frequencies (a), TRAC (b) and mode shape estimation at 5.6Hz (c) using optimized DMD.

Finally, PCA was employed for video-based datasets, for this case, the video of the cantilever beam was used, the image having 400x1080 pixels will give more than 400 thousand measure points while 2000 timesteps were recorded. For the application of PCA into the video-based data the results are presented in Figure 10 as follows.

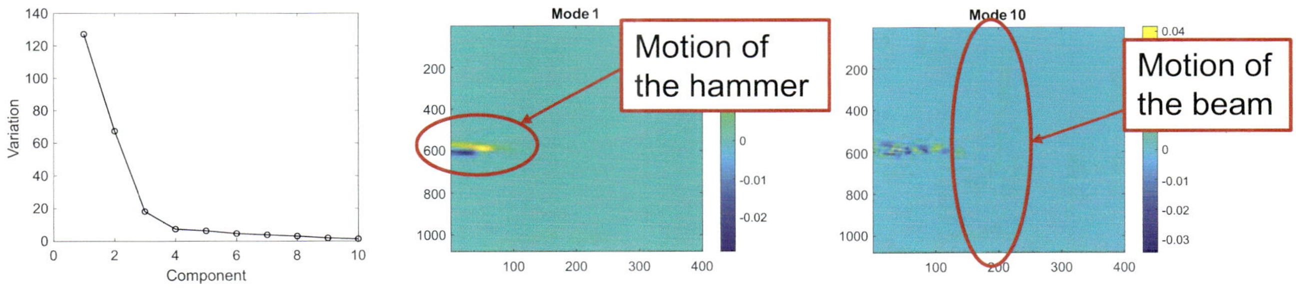

(a) (b) (c)

Fig. 10 Principal components (a), first mode reconstruction (b) and 10th mode reconstruction (c) for PCA applied to video-based data.

Similarly to the cantilever plate case, most of the variation of the data happens on the first 10 components. However, for this case, the most variation of the data occurs on the transient motion from the hammer hitting the cantilever beam. Therefore, the modes obtained are similar to the ones presented on Figure 10b) and (c) with the mode only showing the motion of the hammer. Only after 10 modes it is possible to slightly see some motion of the beam itself. However, due to the natural frequencies to be unknown it is difficult to predict which mode will have any beam behavior. In addition, after the 10th mode, the noise of the video starts to appear in the components as well, making it difficult to obtain the vibrational signal alone.

In terms of computational cost, PCA can compute all 2,000 modes from the data, having a similar time consumption from exact DMD. However, the optimized DMD has a much higher computational time required, allowing the usage of 40 dynamic modes. While, when employing exact DMD, 500 eigenvalues were computed, and the time of calculation was still considerably smaller than using optimized DMD. In addition, with 500 eigenvalues for the approximation a good time reconstruction could be performed.

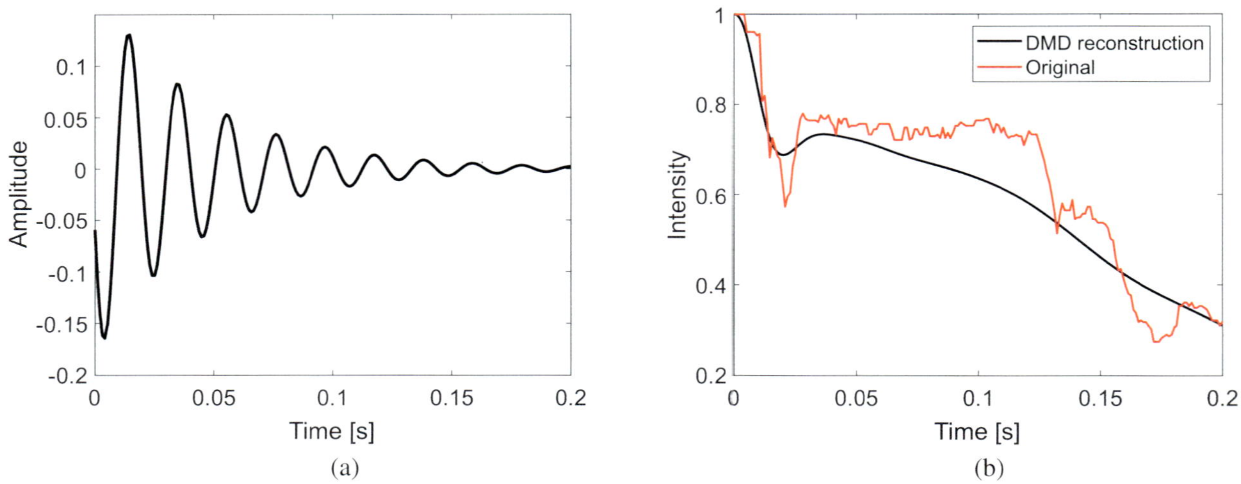

Fig. 11 Time estimation for first mode shape of the beam (a), time reconstruction for an arbitrary pixel in the video (b) using exact DMD.

Figure 11a) presents the time response of the first DMD mode of the beam, while (b) shows the time reconstruction (in blue) of an arbitrary pixel. Since the measurement is given by the pixel intensity the intensity will only have a sine wave behavior in the edges of the beam, while most of the background will have only a noisy measurement.

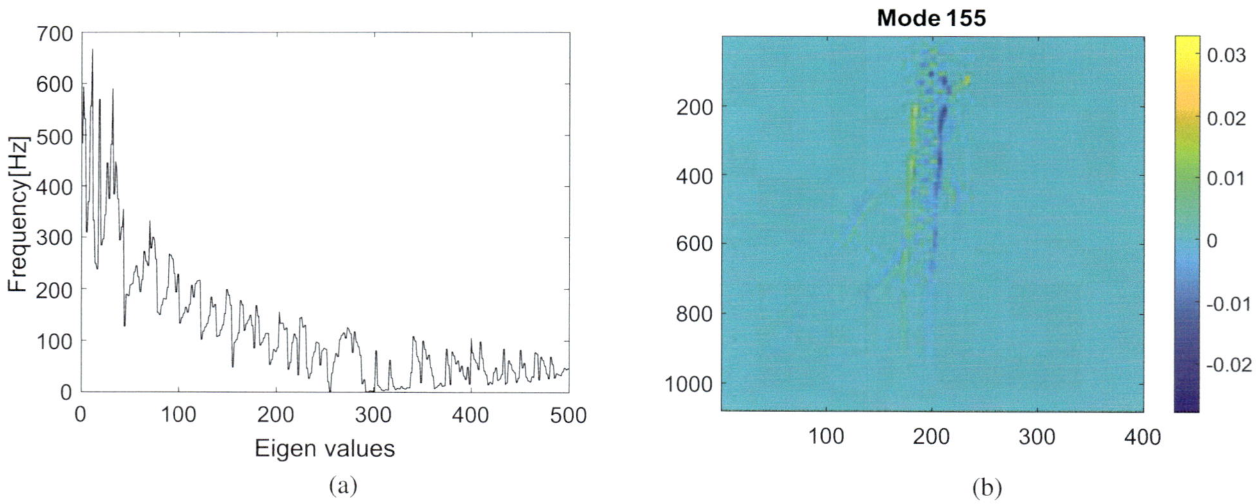

Fig. 12 Eigenvalues (a) and first mode shape (b) of the beam using exact DMD in video-based data.

Figure 12a) shows the estimated frequencies from the eigenvalues. However, most of the measurements obtained in the video will be either noise floor measurements (background) or transient motion (such as the hammer moving to hit the beam). There will be eigenvalues corresponding to many frequencies. Then only the DMD mode which is equivalent to the natural frequency of the beam will be correctly identified, as in (b).

When applying the same dataset to optimized DMD, a smaller number of eigenvalues must be used to describe the system dynamics. However, since the dataset is large due to the number of measurements, the time consumption is considerably higher. Figure 13a) shows the eigenvalues obtained from optimized DMD when solving for 40 DMD modes. Since most of the background of the video is noise measurement, then many of the eigenvalues estimated were in low frequency (20Hz and below). However, since the first bending mode of the beam has a high energy level, then using 40 components is enough to obtain the bending mode, which is presented in (b) and now is the first mode of the model.

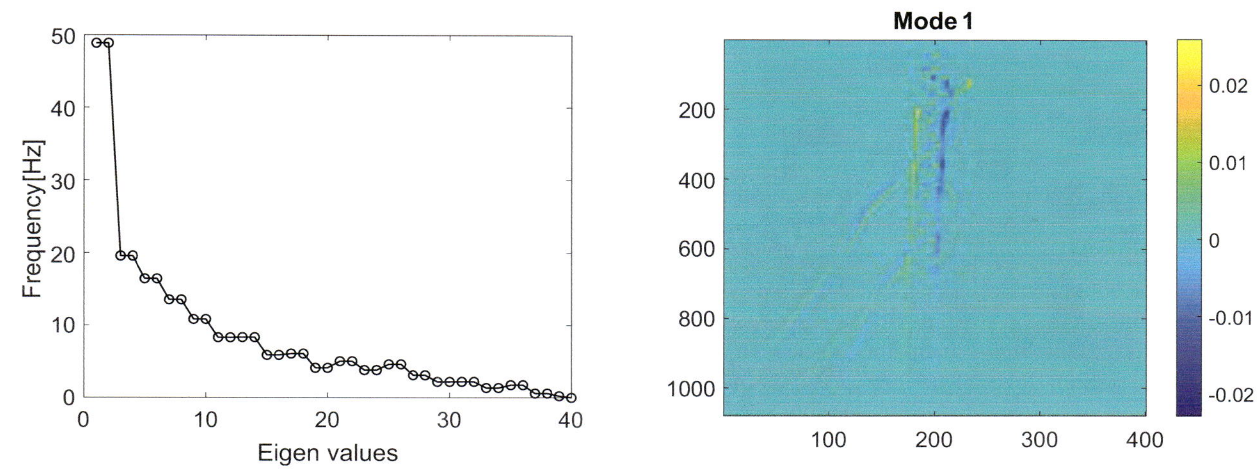

(a) (b)

Fig. 13 Eigenvalues (a) and first mode shape (b) of the beam using optimized DMD in video-based data.

When observing the time reconstruction of the original signal, Figure 14a) presents the time reconstruction for the first mode shape at 48.9Hz. While (b) shows the TRAC for all the pixels in the video. Notice that the TRAC is higher than 96% for all the pixels available, having then a very good time reconstruction for the vibration of the beam, as well as the transient motion of the hammer and the background noise.

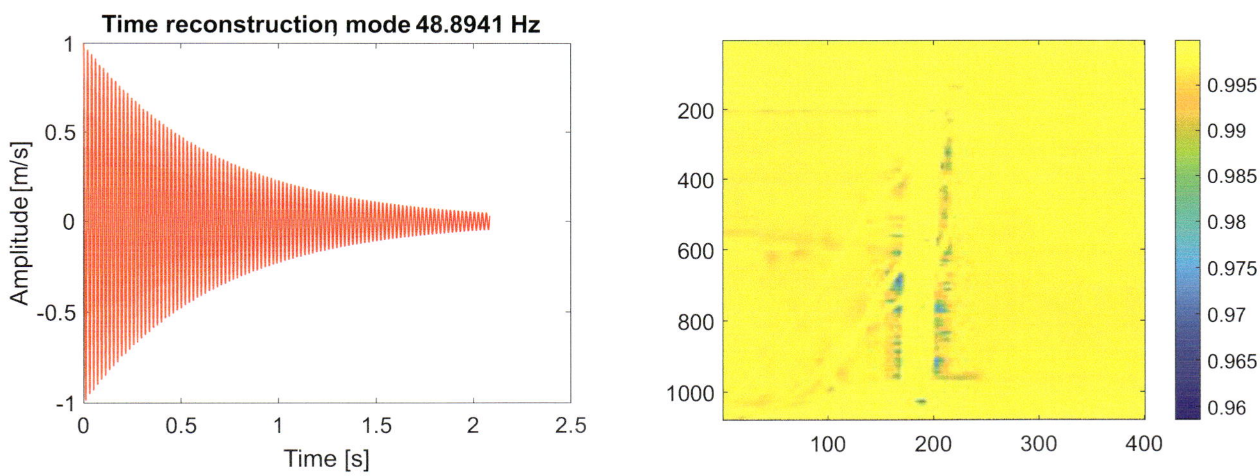

(a) (b)

Fig. 14 Response estimation for the first DMD mode (a) and TRAC for all the pixels (b).

In summary, when employing PCA for vibrational systems, it was observed that its performance gets better for time reconstruction, since it is only a transformation in the basis of the measurement. However, the mode shape reconstruction will be feasible only for simple systems where it is known that the modes of interest have the most excitation during the test. Meanwhile, it was observed that the exact DMD will perform better for high-dimensional datasets. In other words, generally for datasets that possess more measuring points than timesteps, e.g. video-based data, will lead to a better DMD implementation. For low dimensional data, such as accelerometer and LDV measurements, there will be too many real eigenvalues, which will reduce the accuracy of the signal reconstruction. Meanwhile, optimized DMD has a better time and frequency estimation for all systems, and it requires a smaller number of measurements to be effective. For instance, with 20-40 eigenvalues it was able to reproduce with good accuracy the measurements from the video data and LDV measurements, not to mention the feasibility on dealing with sparse measurements, such as accelerations at discrete locations. However, due to the limited number of sensors, it will only be able to obtain the first mode shape of the system. The limitation of exact DMD lies in the computational and time cost to perform the calculations. For example, the LDV data has a small number of sensors, but the number of timesteps was large, leading to a large computational time. Similarly, the video-based data had a small number of timesteps, but a large number of pixels, leading to a high computational cost.

Conclusion

This work presents a comparison study between different data-driven techniques used for order reduction. The applications selected were based on different measurement equipment, that can obtain sparse or full-field measurement. In addition, when performing full-field measurement, video-based data was also employed leading to a dataset with more measuring points than time-steps obtained. Optimized DMD had overall a better estimation for all applications; while having a good accuracy for signal reconstruction it also maintains the physical information of the system. However, its high computational cost, might not be feasible to high-dimensional data, such as video-based.

For future research directions, other variations of both DMD and other traditional dimension reduction techniques could be explored, such as physics-informed DMD or t-SNE. In addition, studies on subsystems and nonlinear systems could be implemented using the data-driven approaches presented.

Acknowledgments This work is supported by the Department of Energy Kansas City National Security Campus Managed by Honeywell under contract # N000510678. NSC-614-5662 10/2024. Unclassified Unlimited Release

References

1. S. Wold, K. Esbensen, and P. Geladi, "Principal component analysis," Chemometrics and intelligent laboratory systems, vol. 2, no. 1–3, pp. 37–52, 1987.
2. M. E. Wall, A. Rechtsteiner, and L. M. Rocha, "Singular value decomposition and principal component analysis," in A practical approach to microarray data analysis: Springer, 2003, pp. 91–109.
3. C. Wu, Y. Liang, W. Lin, H. Lee, and S. Lim, "A note on equivalence of proper orthogonal decomposition methods," Journal of Sound and Vibration, vol. 265, no. 5, pp. 1103–1110, 2003.
4. G. Kerschen and J.-C. Golinval, "Physical interpretation of the proper orthogonal modes using the singular value decomposition," Journal of Sound and vibration, vol. 249, no. 5, pp. 849–865, 2002.
5. P. J. Schmid, "Data-driven and operator-based tools for the analysis of turbulent flows," in Advanced Approaches in Turbulence: Elsevier, 2021, pp. 243–305.
6. E. Aoki, C. T. do Cabo, Z. Mao, Y. Ding, and S. Ozharar, "Vibration-Based Status Identification of Power Transmission Poles," IFAC-PapersOnLine, vol. 55, no. 27, pp. 214–217, 2022.
7. R. J. Allemang, A. W. Phillips, and M. R. Allemang, "Application of principal component analysis methods to experimental structural dynamics," in Structural Dynamics, Volume 3: Proceedings of the 28th IMAC, A Conference on Structural Dynamics, 2010, 2011: Springer, pp. 477–498.
8. H.-W. Ma, Y.-Z. Lin, and Z.-H. Nie, "Physical interpretation of principal component analysis for structural dynamics through string vibration," International Journal of Structural Stability and Dynamics, vol. 19, no. 09, p. 1950109, 2019.
9. P. J. Schmid, "Dynamic mode decomposition of numerical and experimental data," Journal of fluid mechanics, vol. 656, pp. 5–28, 2010.
10. J. H. Tu, "Dynamic mode decomposition: Theory and applications," Princeton University, 2013.
11. J. N. Kutz, S. L. Brunton, B. W. Brunton, and J. L. Proctor, Dynamic mode decomposition: data-driven modeling of complex systems. SIAM, 2016.
12. S. L. Brunton, "Notes on Koopman operator theory," Universität von Washington, Department of Mechanical Engineering, Zugriff, vol. 30, 2019.
13. J. L. Proctor, S. L. Brunton, and J. N. Kutz, "Dynamic mode decomposition with control," SIAM Journal on Applied Dynamical Systems, vol. 15, no. 1, pp. 142–161, 2016.
14. N. A. Valente, C. T. do Cabo, Z. Mao, and C. Niezrecki, "Dynamic Mode Decomposition for Resonant Frequency Identification of Oscillating Structures," in Society for Experimental Mechanics Annual Conference and Exposition, 2023: Springer, pp. 155–162.
15. T. Askham and J. N. Kutz, "Variable projection methods for an optimized dynamic mode decomposition," SIAM Journal on Applied Dynamical Systems, vol. 17, no. 1, pp. 380–416, 2018.
16. P. J. Baddoo, B. Herrmann, B. J. McKeon, J. Nathan Kutz, and S. L. Brunton, "Physics-informed dynamic mode decomposition," Proceedings of the Royal Society A, vol. 479, no. 2271, p. 20220576, 2023.

Chapter 8
Mock Truss-Braced Wing Ground Vibration Test using Fixed Base Correction Method

Benjamin Park, Natalie Spivey, Keerti Bhamidipati, Saketh Vegunta, and Samson Truong

Abstract A truss-braced wing pathfinder research test article was designed by the Flight Loads Laboratory (FLL) at NASA Armstrong Flight Research Center (AFRC) in Edwards, CA. The Mock Truss-Braced Wing (MTBW) is a scaled aluminum 10-ft test article that consists of a high-aspect ratio swept wing box section supported at mid-span by a main strut, and a smaller jury strut. The MTBW wing box and main strut were attached to a strongback test fixture using interface hardware designed for loads calibration testing. Given the inherent challenges of designing a fixed boundary condition ground vibration test (GVT) fixture for large high aspect ratio wings, and to help develop test techniques for similar future test articles, the Fixed Base Correction (FBC) method developed by ATA Engineering was used to decouple MTBW test article modes mounted to the loads calibration interface hardware and strongback test fixture.

Pre-test Finite Element (FE) analysis showed test article modes drastically coupled with the loads calibration interface hardware and strongback test fixture. Test article modal data was acquired using impact hammer excitation. To implement the FBC method, additional impact hammer data and driving point accelerometer data at the bolted interface locations for the wing root and main strut root were acquired to use those locations as references when computing frequency response functions (FRF). By tapping at multiple bolted interface locations in three orthogonal directions, rigid body rotations were also accounted for to numerically "fix" the test article in all six degrees of freedom. By numerically fixing the test article, the test article modes were decoupled from the rest of the assembly and correlated more closely with the FE analysis when pinning the corresponding locations in the FE model.

Keywords Mock Truss-Braced Wing · Modal test · Ground vibration test · Fixed-base correction method

Background

As a pathfinder research test article, the MTBW, was used to inform loads calibration and ground vibration testing techniques of a truss-braced wing design. The strongback and interface hardware the test article was mounted to was designed primarily for loads calibration. This interface hardware consisted of many parts because traditional methods for loads calibration on a wing do not work with the addition of a main strut as the structure becomes statically indeterminate, thus predicting reaction loads at the wing and main strut roots becomes more complicated.

The test article interface hardware consisted of strategically placed load cells for measuring the reaction loads at the wing and main strut roots. Additional load pins were integrated into the test article to measure the load share at the wing and main strut joint, and jury strut joints. The inclusion of all the load cells resulted in a relatively flexible interface hardware that affected the structural modes of the test article. In addition, the strongback and interface hardware structural modes coupled with test article modes of interest.

The Flight Loads Laboratory [1] (FLL) at NASA Armstrong Flight Research Center (AFRC) employed the fixed-base correction (FBC) method developed by ATA Engineering [2–5] to attempt to decouple the modes of the strongback and interface hardware from those of the test article. Decoupling the test article modes from the modes of the strongback and interface hardware also simplifies correlation to finite element model (FEM) predictions. The FLL previously applied the FBC method utilizing impact hammer excitation at candidate fixed-boundary points [6]. This FBC technique was once again

Benjamin Park · Natalie Spivey · Keerti Bhamidipati· Saketh Vegunta· Samson Truong
NASA Armstrong Flight Research Center, Edwards, CA 93523 USA
e-mail: benjamin.c.park@nasa.gov; natalie.d.spivey@nasa.gov; keerti.k.bhamidipati@nasa.gov; saketh.b.vegunta@nasa.gov; samson.s.truong@nasa.gov

Brandon Dilworth et al. (eds.), *Topics in Modal Analysis & Parameter Identification I, Vol. 9*, Conference Proceedings of the Society for Experimental Mechanics Series, https://doi.org/10.13052/9788743801542-8

utilized to numerically "fix" degrees of freedom (DOFs) for the MTBW test, and numerically apply different boundary conditions (BCs) to the test data.

Test Setup

The MTBW GVT was conducted in September 2024 in the NASA AFRC FLL High Bay using impact hammers to excite the test assembly. The test assembly (Strongback + Interface hardware + MTBW test article) was bolted to the floor tracks of the lab high bay at the base of the strongback. The test article was mounted upside down on the strongback for the loads calibration test so the vertical up-load could be simply simulated by hanging weights at various wing and main strut stations. Since the loads calibration test was performed just prior to the GVT, load instrumentation such as strain gage and fiber optic wires were still connected to the test article for the GVT. These additional weights were not accounted for in the pre-test FEM predictions. The FBC method allowed using the same test setup for the GVT as the loads test which significantly reduced the cost of an additional test setup.

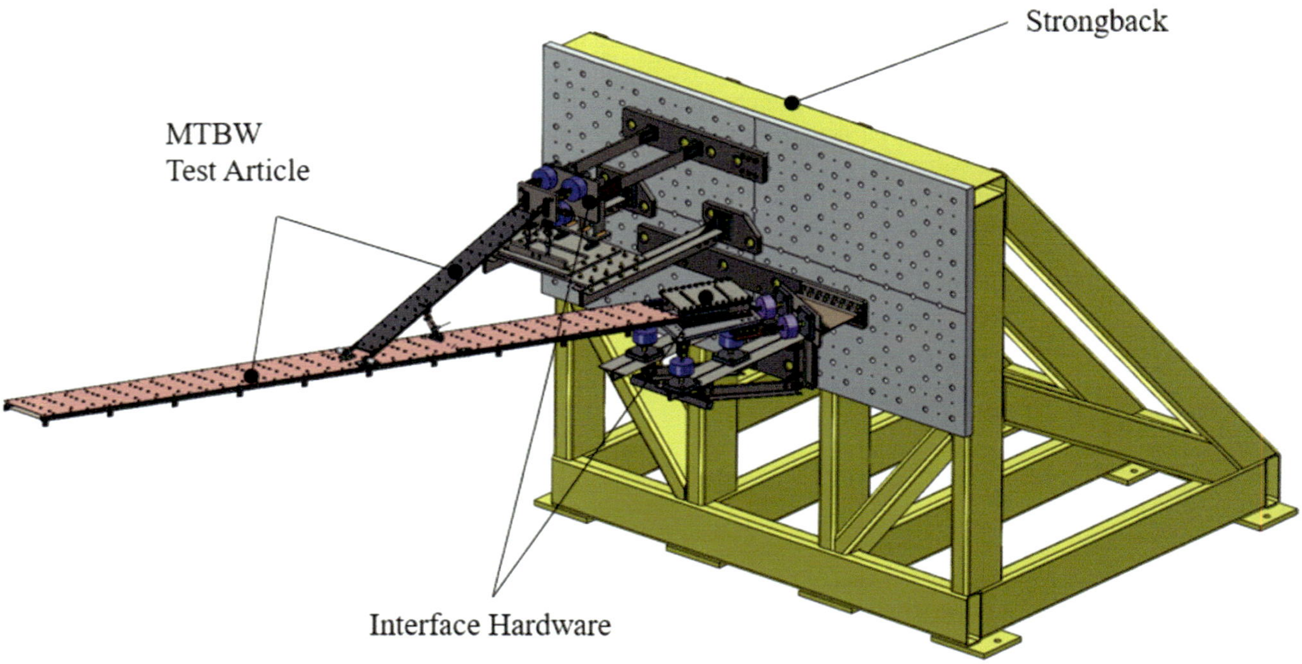

Fig. 1 MTBW GVT Test Assembly Structural Components

Test article

The test article consisted of a 10-ft, semi-span wingbox with a sweep angle of 24.7 degrees, a main strut with a dihedral of 17.2 degrees connected to the wing at an angle of 15.7 with the wing, and a jury strut connecting the wing and main strut inboard of the wing and main strut joint. The test article was fabricated using 7075-T6 aluminum. The interface hardware was fabricated using A36 steel. The test article was connected to the interface hardware at the wing root by four bolts, and at the main strut by two pins allowing the strut to rotate about the pin axis. The jury strut consisted of two in-line load cells to measure the axial load through it for the loads calibration test. During the GVT, both in-line load cells and load pins were monitored in real-time to check that the stiffness through the joints remained consistent across all test runs.

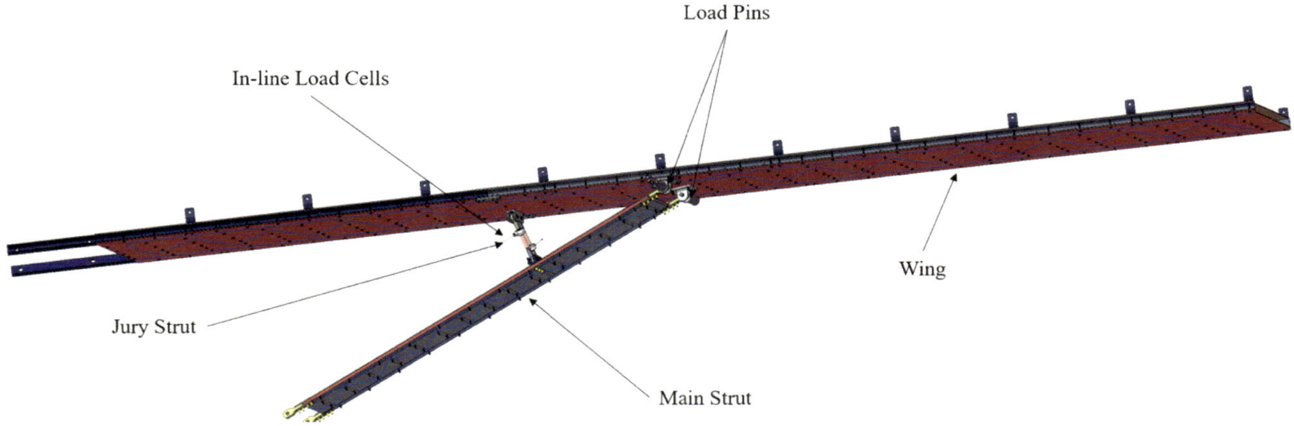

Fig. 2 MTBW Test Article Components

Instrumentation

The data acquisition system used for the test consisted of Brüel & Kjær LAN-XI hardware and BK Connect software. Several LAN-XI 3053 modules housed in two LAN-XI 3660 11-slot mainframes recorded the 200+ channels needed to acquire the impact hammer and accelerometer response data. PCB 356A16 triaxial accelerometers were used throughout the test assembly, along with 12 PCB 393B04 seismic accelerometers installed on the strongback corners to help capture lower amplitude responses from the stiffer structure. Seismic and triaxial accelerometers were co-located at the strongback corners to assess the data quality of attempting the FBC method on the strongback corners using the two different sensors sensitivities (100 mV/g vs. 1000 mV/g). Table 1 summarizes the GVT node numbering and number of accelerometers used each structural component.

Table 1 GVT Node Numbering by Structural Component and Accelerometer/Channel Count

Component	Node ID	# of Accels	# of Channels
Wing	100 series	19	57
Main Strut	200 series	10	30
Jury Strut	300 series	2	6
Interface Hardware	400 series	24	72
Strongback	500 series	12	36
Strongback Corners (Seismic)	600 series	12	12
Total Accelerometers		**79**	**213**

Excitation locations

Test article excitation was performed using a small Dytran 5850B impact hammer. A large Dytran 5802A impact hammer was used to excite the strongback corners in all three DOF's. For the FBC method, driving point FRF's are needed at DOF's to be numerically fixed, and were acquired by tapping at each candidate "fixed" location corresponding to the DOF. Due to accessibility directly at the bolts that connect the wing spars to the interface hardware, data at two sets of candidate locations to be "fixed" were gathered to attempt the FBC method at the wing root interface. Figure 3 shows the two sets of "fixed" candidate locations at the wing root: the Upper Plate (Nodes 401-404) and the Lower Plate (Nodes 405-407). Taps in each of the X, Y, Z directions were performed at each of these nodes, and triaxial accelerometers were used at each node to obtain driving point FRF's.

At the main strut root, candidate FBC locations consisted of the clevises (Nodes 416,417) and the Back Plate (Nodes 415,418,419) as shown in Figure 4. Taps in each of the X, Y, Z directions were performed at each of these nodes, and triaxial accelerometers were used to obtain driving point FRF's.

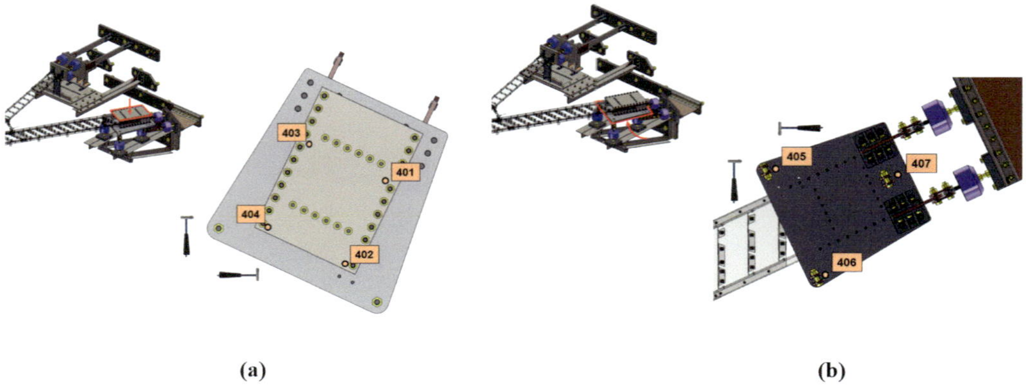

Fig. 3 Wing Root Fixed Candidate Locations: (a) Upper Plate (401-404), (b) Lower Plate (405-407)

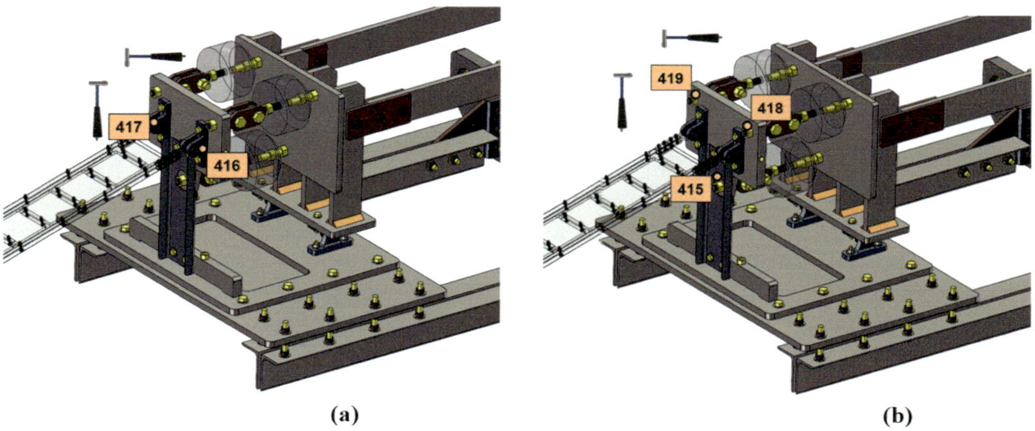

Fig. 4 Main Strut Root Fixed Candidate Locations: (a) Clevises (416,417), (b) Back Plate (415,418,419)

Results

Figure 5 shows the GVT test display model (TDM) that was used to visualize the mode shapes from the test. Each structural component is color coded for clarity. The TDM consisted of triangular elements and tracelines connecting nodal locations. Triaxial accelerometers were installed at all node locations.

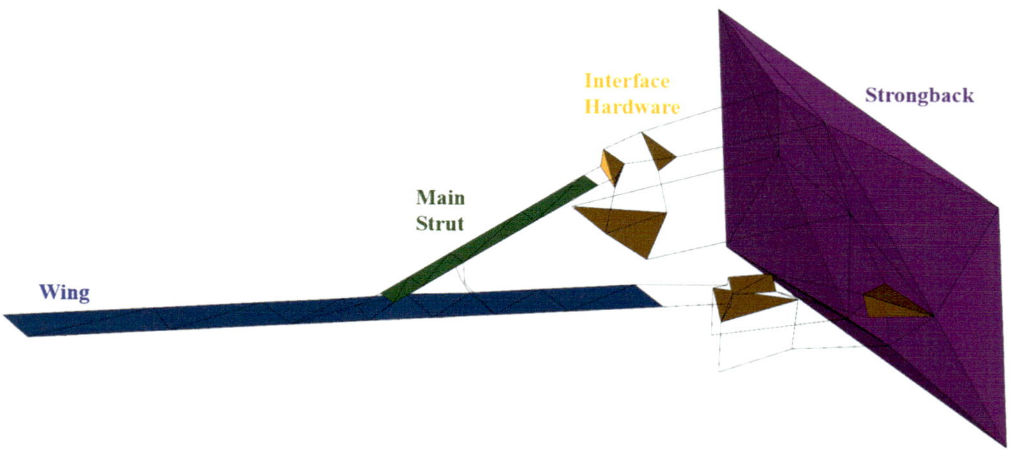

Fig. 5 GVT Test Display Model

Baseline modes

Baseline test runs, which are more traditional GVT runs, were performed with the small impact hammer at the wingtip, using excitation in both vertical and fore/aft directions. The first wing bending mode was observed at 6.3 Hz and second wing bending (with some main strut bending) was observed at 12.2 Hz. Third wing bending with strut vertical bending observed at 33 Hz. This mode is highlighted for comparison between baseline and FBC results.

The baseline test mode shape for wing third bending with strut vertical bending is shown in Figure 6. Dashed lines represent the undeformed test shape, and the solid lines represent the deformed test shape. The interface hardware substantially displaces (represented by black tracelines and yellow triangles), yielding significant modal coupling between the test article and interface hardware.

A review of ambient accelerometer data showed that for excitation at the wingtip, many accelerometer responses on the interface hardware were within or close to the noise floor up to about 20 Hz but had better separation above 20 Hz. Thus, for clarity, the mode shape at 33 Hz is used for illustration of the FBC method in the following figures.

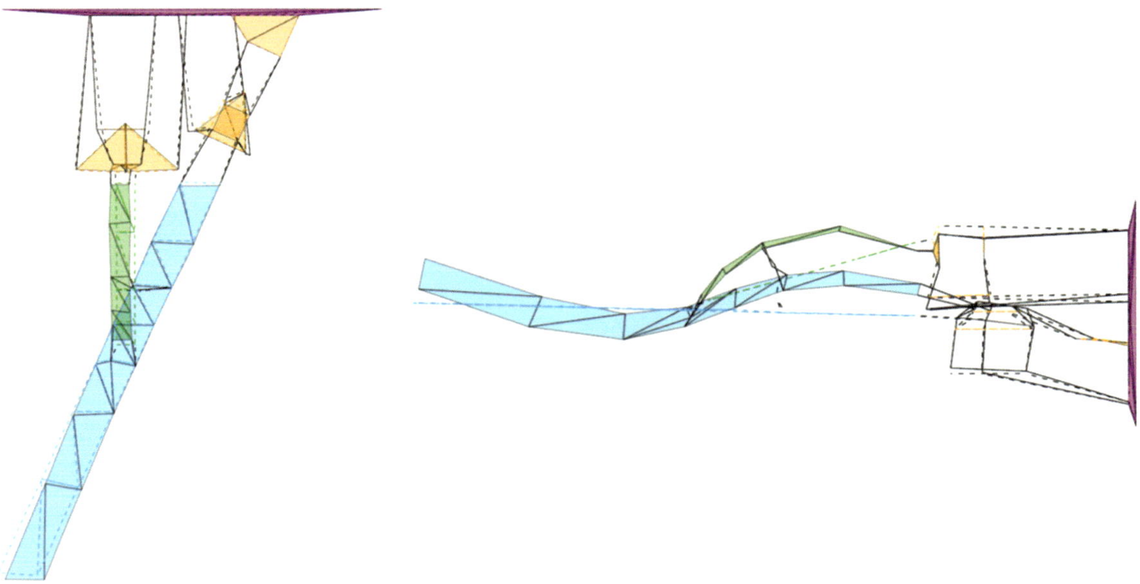

(a) (b)

Fig. 6 Baseline Wing Third Bending with Strut Vertical Bending (33 Hz) Test Mode (without FBC): (a) Top View, (b) Side View

FBC with pinned BC at strut root Clevis and fixed BC at wing root lower plate

To implement the FBC method time histories from the BK Connect software were imported into ATA Engineering's IMAT (Interface between MATLAB®, Analysis, Test) software to compute the FBC FRF's [2–5]. The FBC method was attempted at the Strut Root Clevises (Nodes 416,417) and Lower Plate (Nodes 405-407) of the wing root. This "fixed" boundary condition resulted in the smallest displacement in the interface hardware behind the fixed locations, which now appear to not be moving and modes are decoupled from the test article modes. The MTBW test article mode shape before and after applying FBC appears largely the same while mode frequency shifts down slightly from 33 to 32.3 Hz.

Figure 8 shows a Complex Mode Indicator Function (CMIF) overlay for the baseline results (red) with the FBC results (blue). The mode shape of interest shown in the previous figures is annotated in the plot. A shift in the frequency and cleaner peak is observed due to the FBC method. Curve-fitting for the lower frequency modes below 20 Hz requires further investigation as the noise in the interface hardware FRF's presents difficulty in extracting the FBC modes. Using the PCB 393B04 seismic accelerometers at this fixed location would most likely clean up the FRF data below 20 Hz, but this was not attempted for this test.

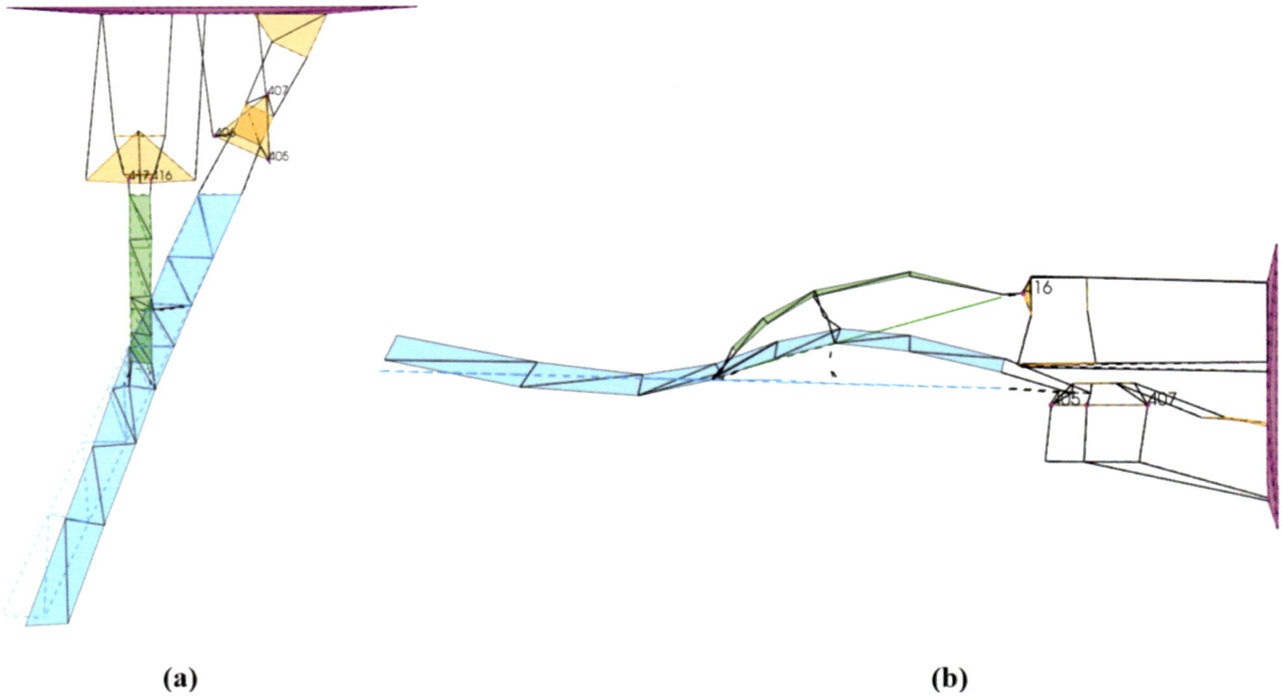

Fig. 7 Wing Third Bending with Strut Vertical Bending (32.8 Hz) Test Mode for FBC at Lower Plate: (a) Top View, (b) Side View

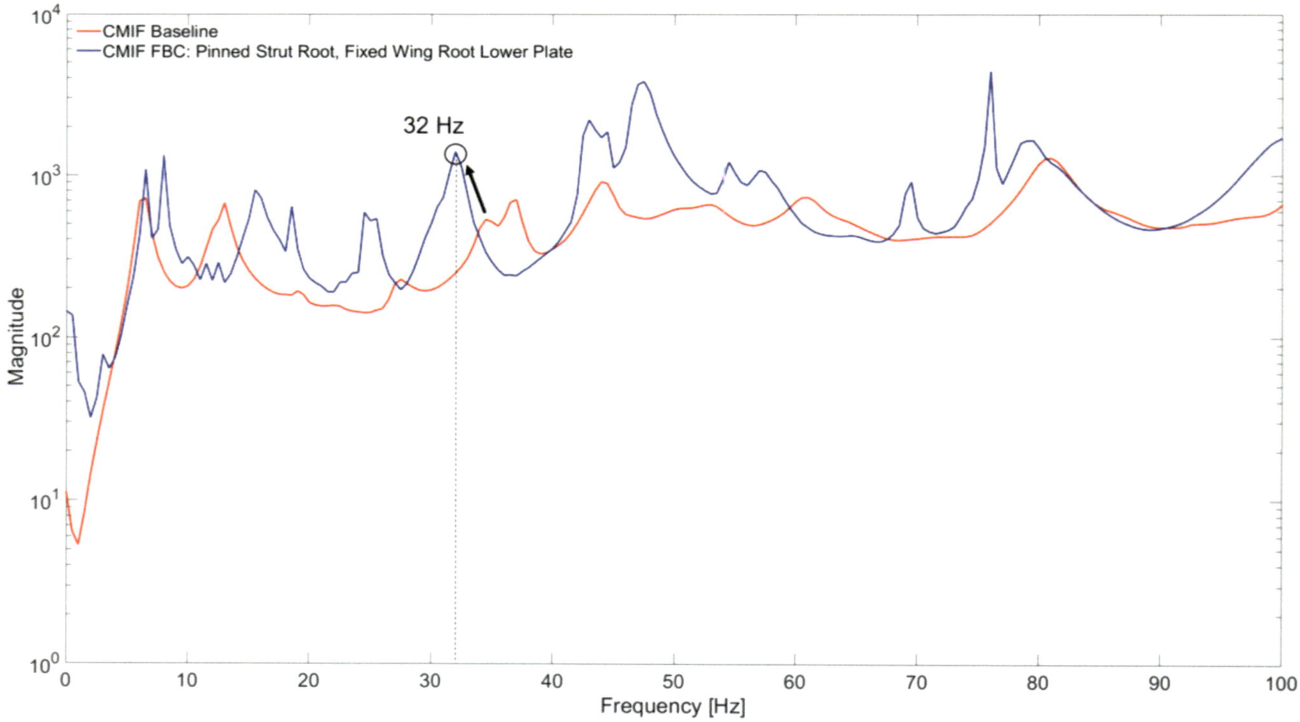

Fig. 8 CMIF Comparison between Baseline Results (Red) with FBC Results (Blue)

Conclusion

Utilizing the FBC method significantly reduced the displacement of the interface hardware by fixing the wing and strut root locations of the test article. In general, the frequencies went down from the baseline frequencies per corresponding mode shape. Some residual mode shape displacement at the interface hardware could be due to data quality or over-constraining the fixed locations. Further investigation is required to reduce the number of DOF's at the fixed locations to see if the mode shape displacements at the interface hardware decrease.

Challenges with applying the FBC method at low frequencies can be attributed to the sensitivity of accelerometers, the environment in which the test is conducted, the source of excitation etc. It can be difficult to obtain clean FRF's after applying the FBC method if there is insufficient separation in between accelerometer responses and the noise floor at the nodes where the correction is applied.

Acknowledgments The authors would like to thank Kevin Napolitano of ATA Engineering and James Winkel of NASA Langley Research Center for their guidance on applying the Fixed-Base Correction Method. The authors would also like to thank the AFRC FLL and the other AFRC Code 560 Aerostructures personnel who supported the operations to accommodate testing in the lab.

References

1. Armstrong Flight Loads Laboratory, https://www.nasa.gov/centers/armstrong/research/Facilities/FLL, accessed September 19, 2024.
2. Napolitano, Kevin L., and Nathanael C. Yoder, "Fixed Base FRF Using Boundary Measurements as References - Analytical Derivation," Proceedings of the SEM IMAC XXX Conference, Jacksonville, Florida, 2012.
3. Napolitano, Kevin L. "Fixing Degrees of Freedom of an Aluminum Beam by Using Accelerometers as References," Topics in Modal Analysis I, Volume 5, Proceedings of the SEM IMAC XXX, A Conference on Structural Dynamics, Jacksonville, Florida, pp. 309-317, 2012.
4. Spivey, N., Miller, K. Saltzman, R., and Napolitano, K., "Modal Testing of a Flexible Wing on a Dynamically Active Test Fixture Using the Fixed Base Correction Method," IFASD 2019-108, 2019.
5. Spivey, N., Saltzman, R., Wieseman, C., Napolitano, K., and Smith, B., "Passive Aeroelastic Tailored Wing Modal Test Using the Fixed Base Correction Method" Proceedings of the SEM IMAC XXXVIII Conference, Houston, Texas, 2020.
6. Bhamidipati, K., Spivey, N., Stebbins, S., Truong, S., Park, B., "X-57 Cruise Motor GVT using Fixed-Base Correction Technique" Proceedings of the SEM IMAC XLII Conference, Orlando, Florida, 2024.

Chapter 9
Model Updating Technique for Modal Shaker Modeling

Abraham Ramirez, Peter Fickenwirth, John Schultze, and Shannon Danforth

Abstract Electrodynamic shakers are commonly used in the shock and vibration testing field, but despite their commonality, a proper characterization of their dynamics is often unknown. An improved understanding of these shakers can help inform test engineers on the feasibility of achieving a test specification, which will help to reduce delays and improve selection of test equipment. The work presented here is a unique approach to numerically estimate lumped model parameters based on the system's experimental frequency response functions (FRFs). The model parameters were then optimized to reduce the normalized root mean squared error between modeled and experimental responses. The similarity between the modeled FRFs and the experimental FRFs was then presented. This updating technique provides a method to predict the experimental FRFs of the shaker given differing environments and test object masses, thus aiding test engineers in determining test feasibility.

Keywords Electrodynamic shaker · Vibration testing · Modal testing · Model Updating, Optimization

Introduction

Environmental testing is a necessary step to qualify that a system will continue to work as intended during and after it is subjected to dynamic loads that it will see throughout its lifetime. One part of this environmental testing is vibration and shock testing, which most commonly uses electrodynamic shakers. During a vibration test, the response of the device under test (DUT) is monitored and the output level of the shaker is adjusted to meet a pre-specified power spectral density (PSD) function. Historically, shakers are selected based similarity to past tests, engineering judgement, and simple calculations using Newton's second law of physics. However, the electrodynamic shaker systems used to perform these tests have complicated dynamics, and there are many variables to consider when predicting a system's capability. Having a more detailed understanding of these capabilities would allow the test engineers to predict test limitations and better utilize the equipment available.

Electrodynamic shakers can be be modeled by solving a representative multi degree of freedom (DoF) lumped parameter model. The model includes both mechanical and electrical components, and uses a coupling coefficient that serves to couple the dynamics of the mechanical system to the electrical system. A few of the model parameters can be directly measured or are provided by the shaker manufacturer, but the remaining model parameters must be estimated. Previous work has shown that this method for modeling electrodynamic shakers is promising [1], but this approach requires a large amount of manual tuning and was applied to only larger, fixed-base shakers. One suitable method for reducing the amount of manual tuning is to use experimentally identified natural frequencies and knowledge of the shaker's mode shapes. A further improvement to the model fidelity may then be achieved by using an error reduction optimization.

This paper builds on previous shaker modeling work by applying the method described above to modal shakers and improving performance in frequency ranges with poor experimental prediction accuracy. First, we provide an introduction to electrodynamic shaker construction and dynamics. Next, we introduce our model of the electrodynamics shakers used in this study and detail the methods for modal parameter identification. We then introduce an optimization algorithm that identifies frequency ranges where the model performed poorly, determines which model parameters affected performance, and varies those parameters only in the identified frequency ranges. This paper will be primarily focused on smaller modal shakers as opposed to larger fixed base shakers. Our comparison to experimental results shows that the method proposed in this paper for estimating the model parameters yielded predicted FRFs that represented the true system dynamics well.

Abraham Ramirez · Peter Fickenwirth · John Schultze · Shannon Danforth
Los Alamos National Laboratory
e-mail: ajrami@umich.edu; petefickenwirth@gmail.com; schultze@lanl.gov; sdanforth@lanl.gov

Brandon Dilworth et al. (eds.), *Topics in Modal Analysis & Parameter Identification I, Vol. 9*, Conference Proceedings of the Society for Experimental Mechanics Series, https://doi.org/10.13052/9788743801542-9

Electrodynamic Shaker Construction and Modes

The basic functionality of an electrodynamic shaker comes from a coil that is suspended in a fixed magnetic field and is passed an alternating current. When this current is passed through a coil that is wrapped around the armature, a magnetic field is created. The interaction between the fixed magnetic field and the induced electromagnetic field of the coil create axial vibrations on the armature [2].

The coil is made from heavy conductors that allows a large amount of current to flow through. The flexures comprise the suspension system that suspends the armature and coil in the magnetic field. These flexures allow axial motion and limit all other motion. The magnets create the fixed radial magnetic field. Lastly, the stinger is a thin rod that is attached to the shaker by a collet and is used to transfer excitations to a device under test (DUT). A visual representation of these parts is shown in Fig. 1, as proposed by Schultz [3].

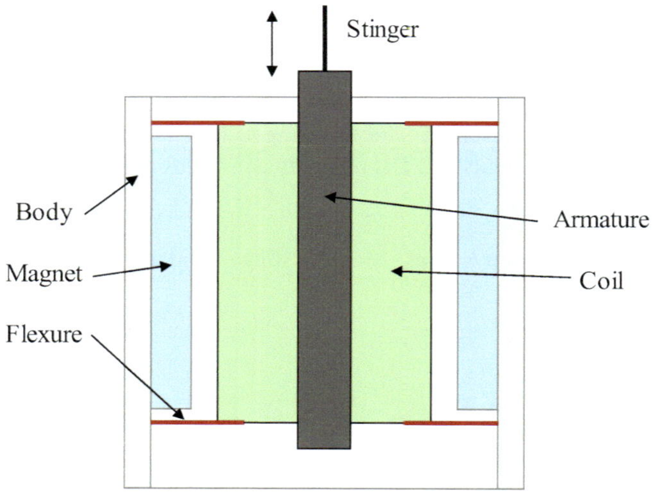

Fig. 1 Electrodynamic shaker design.

Due to this construction, shakers typically display two modes of vibration:

1. **Suspension mode**: Armature, coil and flexures move opposite the body, low frequencies (10 - 30 Hz).
2. **Stinger mode**: Stinger moves opposite the armature, high frequencies (1500 - 4500 Hz).

A depiction of the mode shapes of both modes are seen in Fig. 2 A sample stinger acceleration over current FRF of the system shows two 90° phase shifts that correspond to the two modes in Fig. 3.

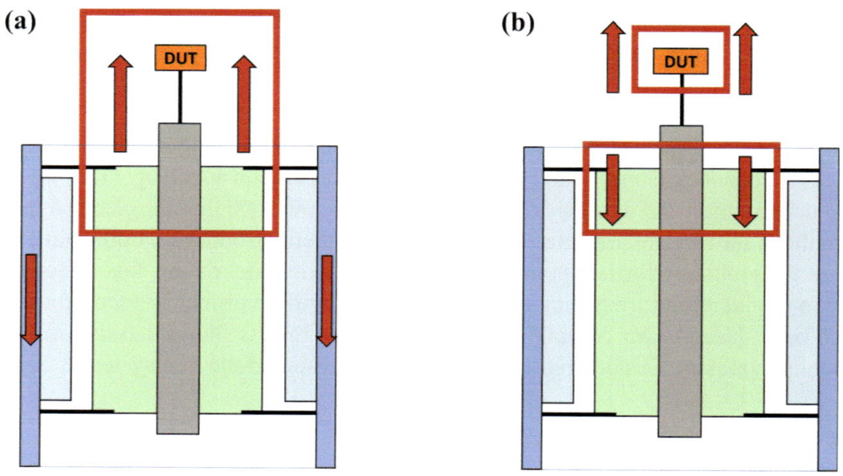

Fig. 2 Modal shakers vibration modes. (a) Suspension mode. (b) Stinger mode.

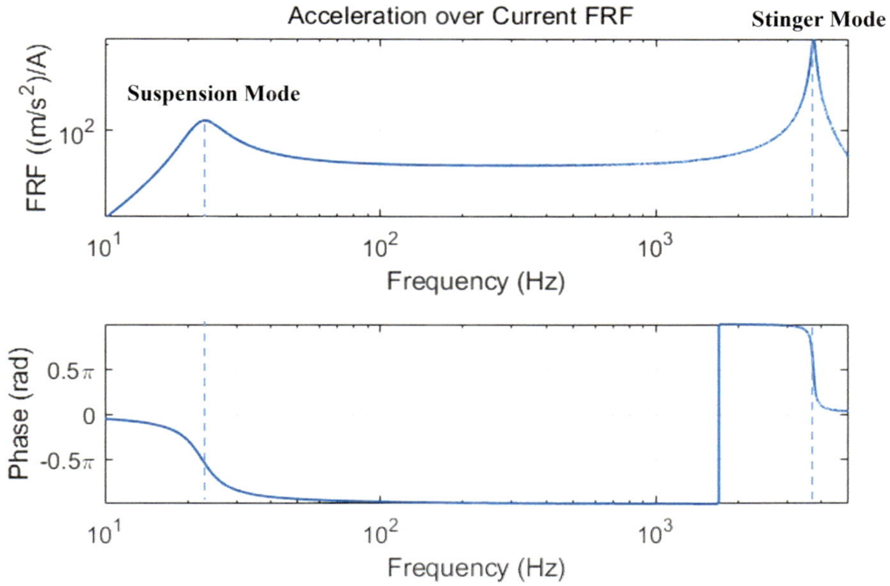

Fig. 3 Acceleration over current frequency response showing peaks and phase shifts correlating to vibration modes.

It is worth noting that at very low frequencies, there is another mode called the isolation mode. At this mode, the entire body of the shaker moves axially as a rigid body. Since it is very rare to encounter this mode in practice, it is not considered in this work.

Shaker Limitations

Shakers have differing limitations across frequency ranges that are commonly tested [2]. In general, at low frequencies the shaker is limited by the maximum stroke length and/or the maximum root mean squared (RMS) voltage of the amplifier. Then, just past the suspension mode frequency in the flat region of the acceleration over current FRF, the shaker is limited by the maximum RMS current of the amplifier. At high frequencies in the region sloping up to the coil mode, the shaker is limited mechanically by maximum armature force rating. Lastly, for anything beyond the force-limiting range, the shaker is limited again by the maximum RMS voltage capability of the amplifier. A representation of the the limitations across the frequency range can be seen in Fig. 4.

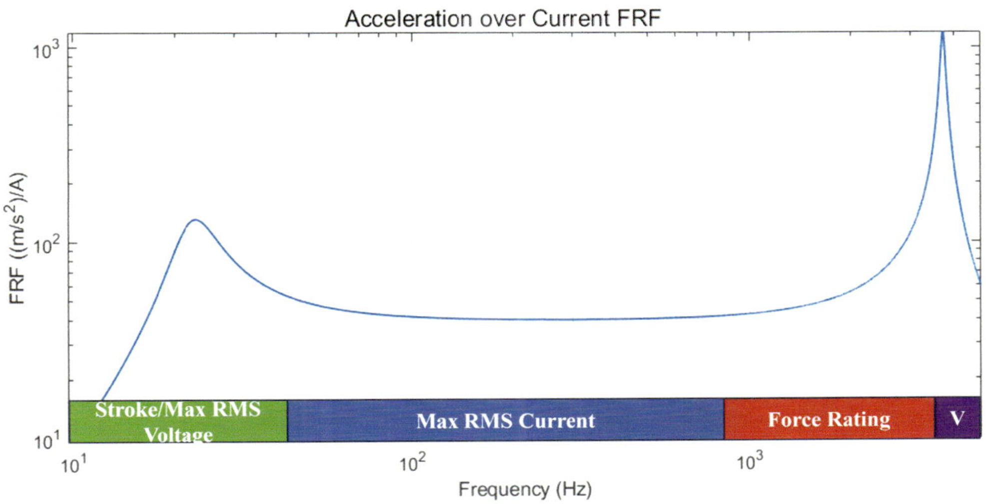

Fig. 4 Shaker limitations on frequency response magnitude plot.

The values of the shaker's natural frequencies are subject to changing test conditions. These changing conditions include the DUT mass, orientation of the shaker, stinger length, and stinger thickness. This shift in natural frequencies then changes where the aforementioned limitations occur in the frequency range. Knowledge of the shaker limitations and the frequency ranges of each limitation is valuable information for a test engineer in the planning and execution stages of a test.

Electromechanical Lumped Parameter Model

Many different ways of modeling a shaker using an equivalent lumped parameter model have been proposed. Most of the work has been focused on modeling fixed-base shakers, which have different dynamics when compared to smaller modal shakers. For fixed-base shaker modeling, Tiwari et al. laid out a framework for using an equivalent electrical (RLC) circuit and ways to reduce the corresponding impedance expression in order to numerically estimate the model parameters using experimental data [4]. Other work for modeling fixed-base shakers used an equivalent mechanical system (MCK) coupled to an electrical circuit with a coefficient that links the electrical and mechanical DoFs [1][5][6]. Schultz used a similar equivalent electromechanical model, but focused on modeling the electrical impedance of modal shakers [3]. The limitation of modeling only the impedance is that the impedance is a ratio of electrical signals, which can hide inaccurate acceleration amplitudes. Thus, only analyzing the modeled impedance may not be advantageous in providing the test engineer with a true representation of the system.

In this study, we use similar techniques to Martini, but apply the methodology to modal shakers rather than fixed base shakers. The model used in this study is a representative electromechanical model consisting of two mechanical DoFs and one electrical DoF with a coupling coefficient, as seen in Fig. 5.

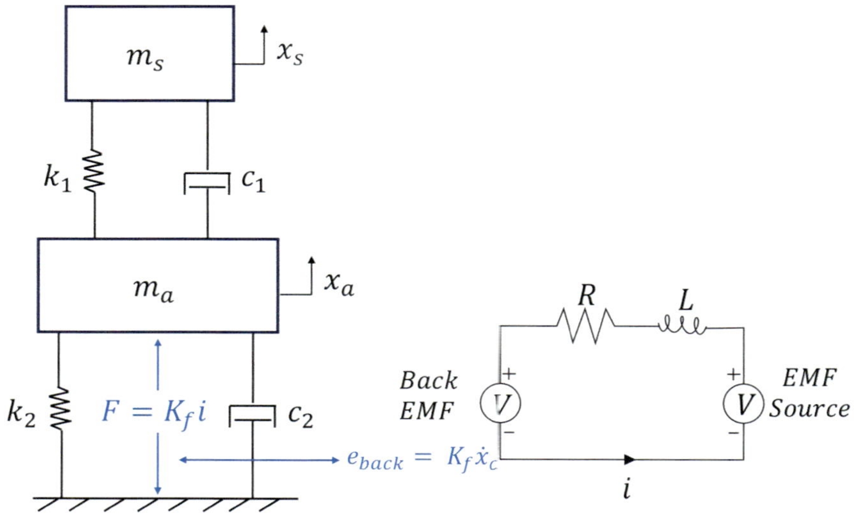

Fig. 5 Combined electromechanical lumped parameter model.

The mass m_a represents the mass of the armature, and m_s represents the mass of the stinger and relative DUT mass. The stiffness and damping of the flexures are represented by k_2 and c_2, respectively. Similarly, the stiffness and damping of the stinger are represented by k_1 and c_1, respectively.

The electrical system is represented by a voltage source, resistor, and inductor all in series. There is another voltage source that is representative of the back electromotive force (EMF). This back EMF is a voltage that is generated by the relative velocity of the coil within the magnetic field. The back EMF subtracts from the voltage generated by the amplifier and is greatest at lower frequencies when the coil has higher displacements. At high frequencies, the motion of the coil is negligible and the back EMF is therefore also negligible. This coupling is represented by the coefficient K_f, which is equal to the magnetic field strength, B, multiplied by the total coil length, l. This coefficient couples the current in the electrical domain to the motion of the coil in the mechanical domain. A visual of this coupling may be seen in Fig. 6 as depicted in the H560 shaker manual by Unholtz-Dickie Corporation [7].

From this model, a set of equations of motions may be formed. Each DoF has its own equation, meaning that there are two mechanical equations of motion and one electrical equation of motion. A block matrix representation is shown below:

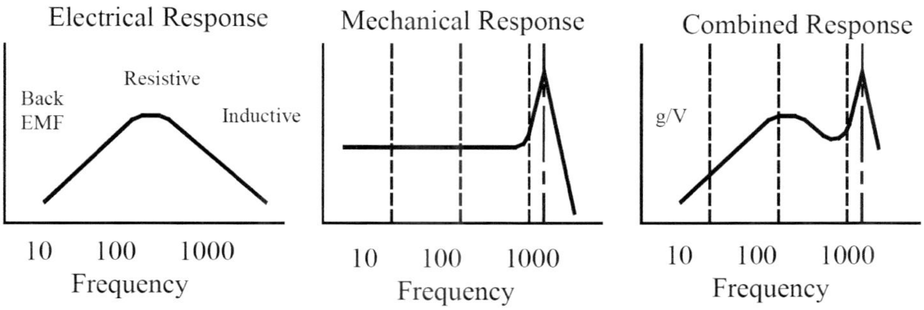

Fig. 6 Visual of the coupling between the electrical and mechanical systems.

$$\begin{bmatrix} m_s & 0 & 0 \\ 0 & m_a & 0 \\ 0 & 0 & 0 \end{bmatrix} \begin{Bmatrix} \ddot{x}_s \\ \ddot{x}_a \\ \ddot{i} \end{Bmatrix} + \begin{bmatrix} c_1 & -c_1 & 0 \\ -c_1 & c_1 + c_2 & 0 \\ 0 & -K_f & L \end{bmatrix} \begin{Bmatrix} \dot{x}_s \\ \dot{x}_a \\ \dot{i} \end{Bmatrix} + \begin{bmatrix} k_1 & -k_1 & 0 \\ -k_1 & k_1 + k_2 & K_f \\ 0 & 0 & R \end{bmatrix} \begin{Bmatrix} x_s \\ x_a \\ i \end{Bmatrix} = \begin{Bmatrix} 0 \\ 0 \\ E \end{Bmatrix}$$

Lumped Model Parameter Identification

As mentioned previously, only a few of these parameters are provided or are easily measurable. The masses may be found by either information provided in the shaker manual (m_a) or by measurement (m_s). A method to determine the remaining mechanical parameters is to utilize knowledge of the shaker modes to make simplified transfer functions. Using these simplified transfer functions the experimentally identified natural frequencies and magnitudes may be used to estimate the stiffness, damping, and coupling coefficient values.

The transfer function of the whole mechanical system is identified by taking the Laplace transform of both equations of motion, eliminating x_a by substitution, and rearranging in the form of stinger acceleration over current. This equation can be seen below:

$$H_{x_s,i} = \frac{X_s s^2}{I} = \frac{K_f(k_1 + c_1 s)s^2}{s^4(m_s m_a) + s^3(m_s(c_1 + c_2) + m_a c_1) + s^2(m_s(k_1 + k_2) + m_a k_1 + c_1 c_2) + s(k_1 c_2 + k_2 c_1) + k_1 k_2} \tag{1}$$

Coupling Coefficient Estimation

We estimate the coupling coefficient, K_f, by inspecting the magnitude of experimental stinger acceleration over current frequency response away from any influence of the suspension or stinger modes. We chose to analyze the magnitude of the response at 10x the suspension mode. The simplified transfer function for this case is given by

$$H_{x_s,i}(10 * f_{Sus.m}) = \frac{K_f}{m_a + m_s}. \tag{2}$$

Rearranging to solve for K_f gives

$$K_f = (m_a + m_s) \mid H_{x_s,i}(10 * f_{Sus.m}) \mid . \tag{3}$$

Low Frequency Simplifications

As discussed in the Electrodynamic Shaker Construction and Modes section, the transfer function may be simplified by leveraging knowledge of the shaker's modes. At low frequencies near the suspension mode, the armature and stinger move as one rigid mass. Thus, the model may be simplified to a one DoF system as seen in Fig. 7.

The stinger acceleration over current transfer function at low frequencies then becomes

$$H_{x_s,i_{LF}} = \frac{K_f s^2}{s^2(m_a + m_s) + sc_2 + k_2}. \tag{4}$$

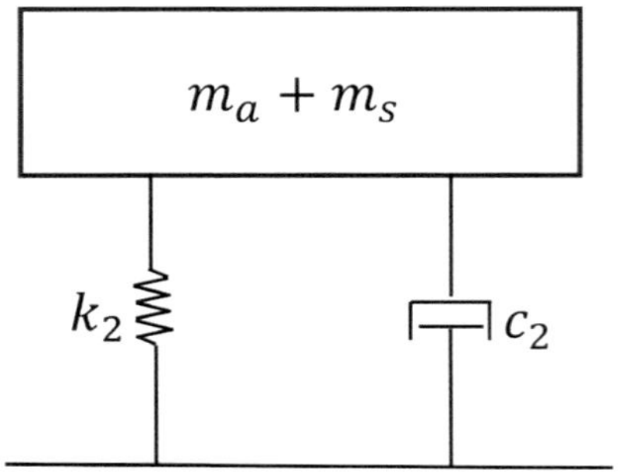

Fig. 7 Low frequency simplified mechanical model.

We can then use Eq. 4 to solve for the system's natural frequency near the suspension mode, given by

$$f_{Sus.M} = \frac{1}{2\pi}\sqrt{\frac{k_2}{m_a + m_s}}. \tag{5}$$

From Eq. 5, the flexure stiffness, k_2, can be solved for by using the experimentally identified suspension mode natural frequency and the known masses

$$k_2 = (2\pi * f_{Sus.M})^2(m_a + m_s). \tag{6}$$

Now, to solve for the flexure damping, c_2, Eq. 4 may be used. It is known that at a natural frequency the sum of the real parts of the frequency response approach zero. So the transfer function turns into to

$$H_{x_s,i_{LF}} = \frac{K_f s}{c_2}. \tag{7}$$

Rearranging Eq. 7 gives the following expression for flexure damping,

$$c_2 = \frac{K_f s}{\mid H_{x_s,i}(f_{Sus.M}) \mid} = \frac{K_f(2\pi * f_{Sus.M})}{\mid H_{x_s,i}(f_{Sus.M}) \mid}. \tag{8}$$

High Frequency Simplifications

Similar to the low-frequency simplifications, we simplify the model at high frequencies based on knowledge of the behavior of the stinger mode. At high frequencies, the flexures have very little influence on the response of the shaker. Therefore, we reduce the model such that the armature mass and stinger mass are connected to each other only by k_1 and c_1. This assumption then reduces the model to the two DoF model that is shown in Fig. 8.

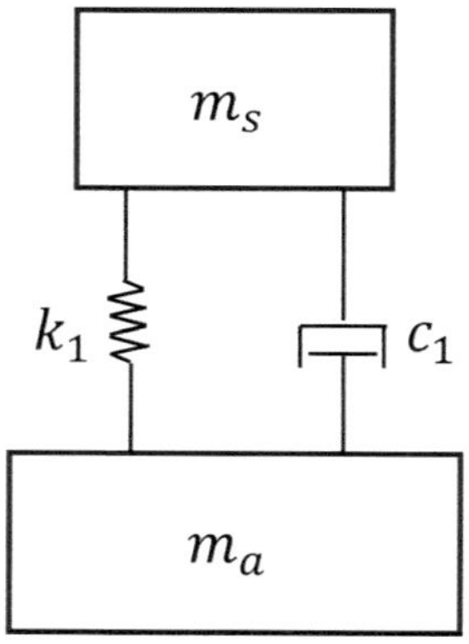

Fig. 8 High frequency simplified mechanical model.

Based on this model, the stinger acceleration over current transfer function at high frequencies may be represented as

$$H_{x_s,i_{HF}} = \frac{K_f(k_1 + c_1 s)}{s^2(m_a m_s) + s(c_1(m_s + m_a)) + k_1(m_s + m_a)}. \tag{9}$$

From Eq. 9, the natural frequency of the system may be represented as

$$f_{St.M} = \frac{1}{2\pi}\sqrt{\frac{k_1(m_s + m_a)}{m_a m_s}}. \tag{10}$$

Now, from Eq. 10 the stinger stiffness, k_1, may be solved for using the experimentally identified stinger mode frequency and the known masses

$$k_1 = (2\pi * f_{St.M})^2 \frac{m_s m_a}{m_s + m_a}. \tag{11}$$

Similar to the low-frequency case, to solve for the stinger damping, c_1, the high-frequency transfer function is reduced to

$$H_{x_s, i_{HF}} = \frac{K_f(c_1 s + k_1)}{s(c_1(m_s + m_a))}. \tag{12}$$

In order to isolate c_1, the fraction in Eq. 12 may be broken up to

$$H_{x_s, i_{HF}} = \frac{K_f c_1 s}{s(c_1(m_s + m_a))} + \frac{K_f k_1}{s(c_1(m_s + m_a))}. \tag{13}$$

From here, the $c_1 s$ in the first fraction of Eq. 13 may be cancelled and leaves

$$H_{x_s, i_{HF}} = \frac{K_f}{m_s + m_a} + \frac{K_f k_1}{s(c_1(m_s + m_a))}. \tag{14}$$

Lastly, because it is known that $k_1 >> K_f$, the term with the k_1 term will dominate the response. Thus for simplicity, the first fraction in Eq. 14 with K_f in the numerator is considered to be negligible. Then the equation can be reduced and used to solve for c_1 using

$$c_1 = \frac{K_f k_1}{(m_s + m_a)s \mid H_{x_s,i}(f_{St.M}) \mid} = \frac{K_f k_1}{(m_s + m_a)(2\pi * f_{St.M}) \mid H_{x_s,i}(f_{St.M}) \mid}. \tag{15}$$

Electrical Parameters

The two remaining parameters to be identified are the two electrical parameters; R and L. The resistance is given nominally in the shaker manual as approximately 1 ohm. This resistance value was then verified experimentally. As for the inductance, an initial value was simply estimated and tuned manually until the model closely matched the experimental data.

Optimization of Model Parameters

It is important to note that the Lumped Model Parameter Identification section lays out a methodology for *estimating* the model parameters. The reason it is only an estimation is because the previously simplified lumped parameter model was further reduced using knowledge of the shaker's modes. These simplifications were made so it was possible to mathematically solve for the model parameters. To further improve the model, an optimization of the parameters may be performed to reduce the model error. To do this, we inspect model predictions and experimental results while investigating the model's sensitivity to different experimental parameters. To understand the model parameter sensitivities, we plotted the stinger acceleration over current and stinger acceleration over voltage FRFs with each parameter at the estimated value, 0.5x estimated, and 2x estimated. Figure 9 shows a sample parameter sensitivity plot where k_2 was varied.

Recall one of the goals of this work was create a methodology for optimizing the modeled FRFs to improve the model in frequency ranges where it previously performed poorly. Therefore, the most important information to pull from the parameter sensitivity study is where in the frequency range a certain parameter affects the model. A summary of all the model parameter sensitivities can be seen in Table 1. This is so that when building the optimization, parameters are only varied in the frequency range in which they affect the model. This aids in minimizing parameters conflicting with one another during the optimization. As a result, a more accurate representation may be found and the overall optimization time is decreased.

The objective function used in this optimization is a normalized RMS error between the model and experimental data, similar to what was presented previously by Fickenwirth [1]. The normalization is done because the magnitude of the current driven response is much higher than the voltage driven response, thus the current driven response would dominate the error.

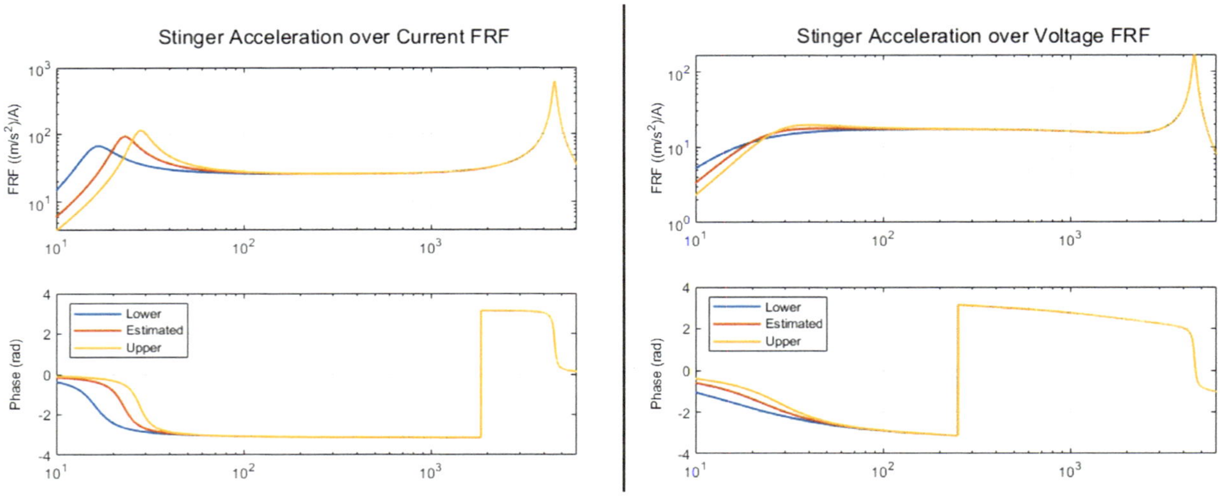

Fig. 9 Model sensitivity to flexure stiffness. Acceleration over current (left) and acceleration over voltage (right).

Table 1 Summary of parameter sensitivities

Parameter	**Effect of Increasing the Estimate on Acceleration over Voltage FRF**	**Effect of Increasing the Estimate on Acceleration over Current FRF**
m_s - Stinger mass	Decreases stinger mode frequency	Decreases stinger mode frequency
m_a - Armature mass	Decreases suspension and stinger mode frequencies, decreases overall amplitude	Decreases suspension and stinger mode frequencies, decreases overall amplitude
c_1- Stinger damping	Decreases coil mode amplitude	Decreases coil mode amplitude
c_2 - Flexure damping	Decreases suspension mode amplitude	Decreases suspension mode amplitude
k_1 - Stinger stiffness	Increases stinger mode frequency	Increases stinger mode frequency
k_2 - Flexure stiffness	Increases suspension mode frequency	Increases suspension mode frequency
K_f - Coupling coeff.	Increases overall amplitude	Increases overall amplitude
R - Resistance	Decreases overall amplitude	No effect
L - Inductance	Decreases amplitude near stinger mode	No effect

This magnitude difference is because the voltage driven response is heavily effected by the electromagnetic damping from the cross-coupling term, and the current driven response is not. The equation for the RMS error is

$$RMSE_{FRF} = \sqrt{\frac{\sum_{n=1}^{N} \sum(real(h_{n,model}) - real(h_{n,measured}))^2}{N}}. \tag{16}$$

In Eq. 16, h_n is the value of the frequency response at the nth frequency line and N is the total number of spectral lines. There are a few different ways to normalize RMS error [8]:

1. **mean**: $NRMSE = \frac{RMSE}{\bar{y}}$
2. **range**: $NRMSE = \frac{RMSE}{y_{max} - y_{min}}$
3. **standard deviation**: $NRMSE = \frac{RMSE}{\sigma}$

For the purpose of this work the mean normalization was used. Then the total error is then represented as

$$error = NRMSE_{Accel/Voltage} + NRMSE_{Accel/Current}. \tag{17}$$

This objective function is then minimized using MATLAB's fmincon algorithm. Fmincon is a constrained nonlinear optimizer that finds the minimum of a scalar function starting at an initial estimate.

Experiment and Results

As described in section 4, we conduct the estimation using the natural frequency peaks from the acceleration over current FRF. In order to get these measurements, we threaded an impedance head onto the end of the stinger to measure acceleration. We monitored current from the amplifier's built in current monitor and measured the voltage supplied to and from the amplifier. These measurements were taken to be used later in calculating the acceleration over voltage FRF, which is used for further model comparison. The acceleration over voltage FRF was also used in the objective function for the optimization. For this work, the 2060E shaker from The Modal Shop was used. The test was a continuous random vibration test from 10-6000 Hz. Figure 10 shows the test setup.

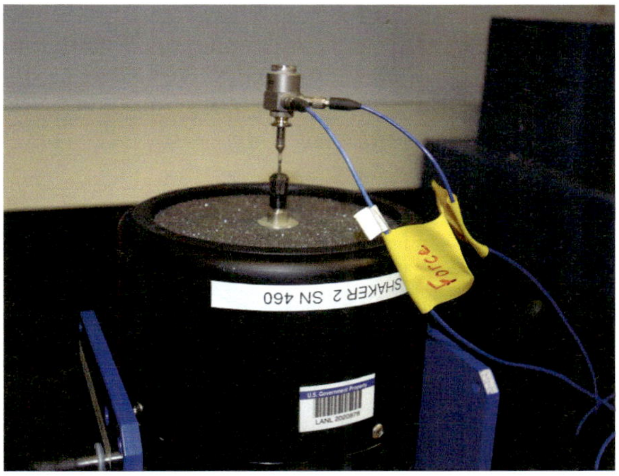

Fig. 10 Experimental test setup.

Initial Estimates of Model Parameters

Using the collected experimental data, we calculated the frequency responses and identified the natural frequencies corresponding to the suspension mode and stinger mode, as shown in Fig. 11. These natural frequencies are listed in Table 2.

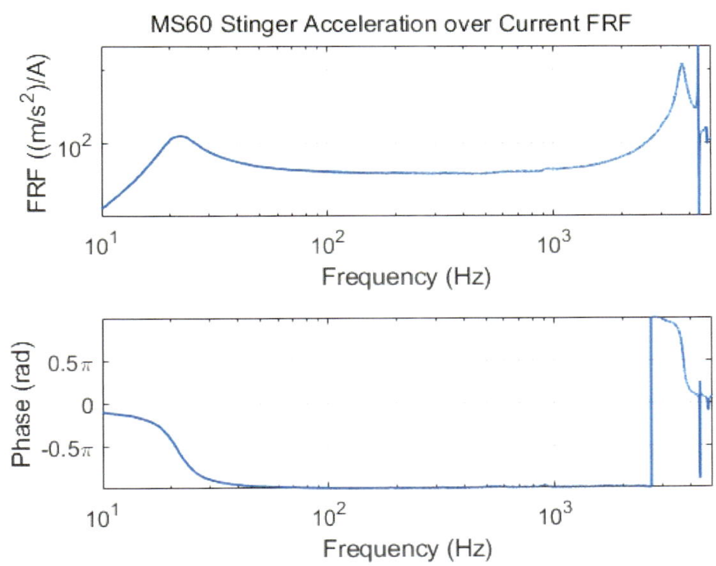

Fig. 11 Experimental acceleration over current FRF.

Table 2 Experimentally identified natural frequencies.

Mode	Symbol	Frequency (Hz)
Suspension	$f_{Sus.M}$	22.5
Stinger	$f_{St.M}$	3731.5

We then used the two natural frequencies to estimate the model parameters using the equations from section 4. The estimated model parameters are shown in Table 3. These estimated parameters are then plugged into the block matrix representation of the system and the direct frequency response method is used to calculate the modeled FRFs. [1].

Table 3 Estimated model parameters.

Model Parameter	Symbol	Initial Estimate	Unit
Stinger stack mass	m_s	0.038	kg
Armature mass	m_a	0.27	kg
Stinger damping	c_1	25.6	N/(m/s)
Armature Damping	c_2	13.4	N/(m/s)
Stinger stiffness	k_1	1.92E7	N/m
Armature Stiffness	k_2	6.16E3	N/m
Coupling Coefficient	K_f	12.2	-
Resistance	R	2	Ohms
Inductance	L	1e-4 - 1i*9e-7	Henry

$$H = (-\omega^2[M] + j\omega[C] + [K])^{-1} \tag{18}$$

Eq. 18 is calculated at each frequency line and forms the frequency response matrix, H, which is a $3x3xn$ matrix where n is the number of frequency lines. As described in section 3, the only force acting on the system is the applied voltage from the amplifier. This means that only the last column, which are the responses to a voltage reference, are needed to compare the model to the experimental results. The stinger acceleration over voltage FRF data is found in row 1 and the current over voltage FRF data is found in row 3. The modeled acceleration over current FRF is found by taking the reciprocal of the current over voltage FRF (also called the impedance) and multiplying by the acceleration over voltage FRF. The comparison of the estimated model (prior to any optimization) to the experimental results are shown in Fig. 12 and Fig. 13.

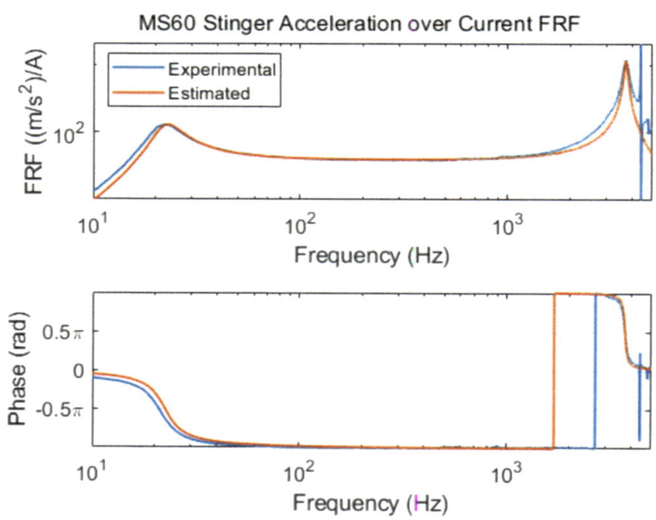

Fig. 12 Comparison for estimated model vs experimental acceleration over current FRFs.

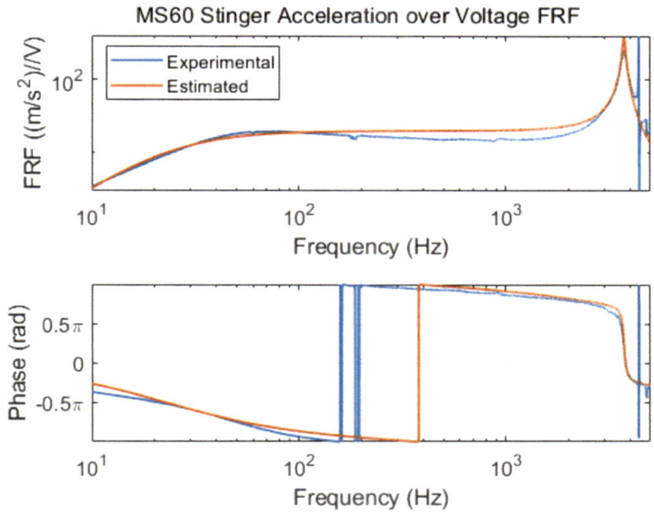

Fig. 13 Comparison for estimated model vs experimental acceleration over voltage FRFs.

Optimizing Model Parameters

Using the initial estimates as initial values, the optimization described in section 5 was formulated by: (1) Following the order of operations laid out by Schultz [3] and (2) Identifying the frequency range in which each variable is most effective, using the parameter sensitivity study as a starting point. The following shows the order of operations mentioned prior:

1. Optimize k_2 and k_1 to match the frequencies of the suspension and stinger modes, respectively.
2. Optimize L to match the curvature of the experimental acceleration over voltage FRF.
3. Optimize c_2 and c_1 to match the amplitudes of the suspension and stinger modes, respectively.
4. Optimize K_f to match the amplitude in the region between the two modes in the acceleration over current FRF.

Then by inspection of the FRF comparisons, each variable was given a specific frequency range in which it was most effective. For example, it is known from the parameter sensitivity study that the suspension stiffness, k_2, affects the model most near the suspension mode. Thus, k_2 was varied by only minimizing the error calculated between 10-30 Hz. A similar process was then followed for the rest of the variables. Table 4 shows how the optimization changed the model parameters. It should be noted that the masses were not varied.

Table 4 Comparison of estimated vs optimized variables.

Model Parameter	Symbol	Initial Estimate	Optimized	Unit
Stinger stack mass	m_s	0.038	0.038	kg
Armature mass	m_a	0.27	0.27	kg
Stinger damping	c_1	25.6	28.9	N/(m/s)
Armature damping	c_2	13.4	12.4	N/(m/s)
Stinger stiffness	k_1	1.92E7	1.92E7	N/m
Armature stiffness	k_2	6.16E3	5.55E3	N/m
Coupling coeff.	K_f	12.2	12.2	-
Resistance	R	2	2.15	Ohms
Inductance	L	1E-4 - 1i*9E-7	1.37E-4 - 1i*2.56E-5	Henry

Figures 14 and 15 shows a visual comparison between the initial estimated values and the optimized values to the experimental values.

A quantitative analysis of the similarity between the experimental and the estimated and optimized respectively was performed by calculating the RMS value of the decibel (dB) error at every frequency line [9]. This metric was chosen because it is calculated on a log scale, meaning that it weighs each point equally. Other metrics such as % RMS error favor

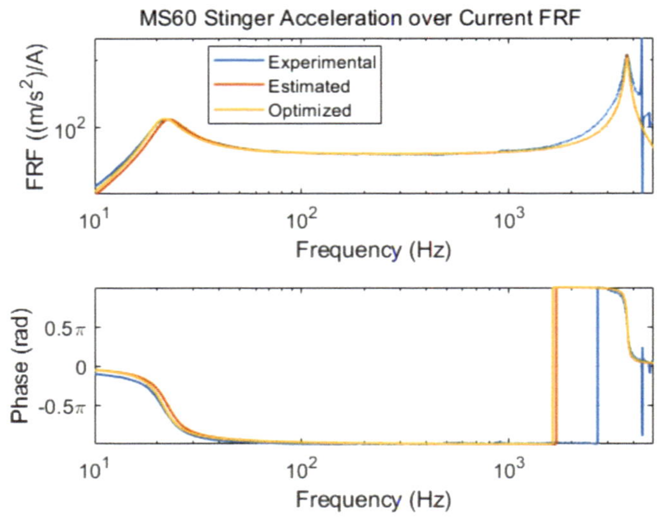

Fig. 14 Comparison of estimated vs optimized parameters for the acceleration over current FRF.

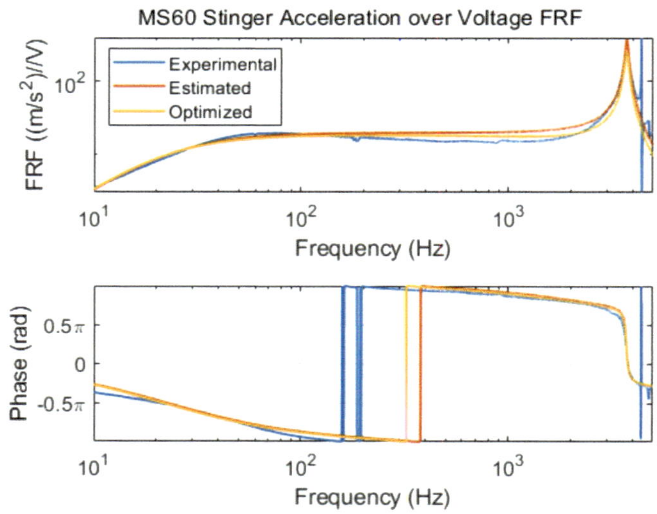

Fig. 15 Comparison of estimated vs optimized parameters for the acceleration over voltage FRF.

error at higher magnitudes more than low magnitude error, which can skew the total error. The formula for the RMS dB error metric is

$$RMSdB : \delta = \sqrt{\frac{1}{nf}\sum_{i=1}^{nf}\frac{1}{na}\sum_{k=1}^{na}[[log_{10}\beta_A(\omega)] - [log_{10}\beta_B(\omega)]]^2}. \tag{19}$$

$\beta_A(\omega)$ = Signal 1
$\beta_B(\omega)$ = Signal 2
nf = number of frequencies
na = number of channels
δ = error scalar

The results of the RMS dB error calculations are shown in table 5. These values are meant to compare the relative similarity between the modeled FRFs and the experimental FRFs. These calculations are single data comparisons for the acceleration over current FRFs and the acceleration over voltage FRFs, respectively.

Table 5 Model RMSdB error values of estimated values and optimized values.

	Initial Estimates	Optimized
A/C FRF RMS dB Error	26.864	27.785
A/V FRF RMS dB Error	12.210	10.416

Discussion

Overall it is seen that the lumped parameter model is highly representative of the real system. The initial values that used the acceleration over current FRF to estimate the parameters performed well. Due to this performance of the initial estimate, the optimization improvements are slight. This improvement can be observed qualitatively by inspection of figures 14 and 15 and by looking at the RMS dB error values in table 5. The two main areas of improvement are: (1) an improved alignment of the suspension mode frequency in the acceleration over current FRF, (2) overall improved amplitude prediction at the stinger mode for both FRFs. Elaborating more on the stinger mode amplitude improvement, Fig. 16 shows a zoomed in comparison for the stinger mode peak on both acceleration over current and acceleration over voltage FRFs.

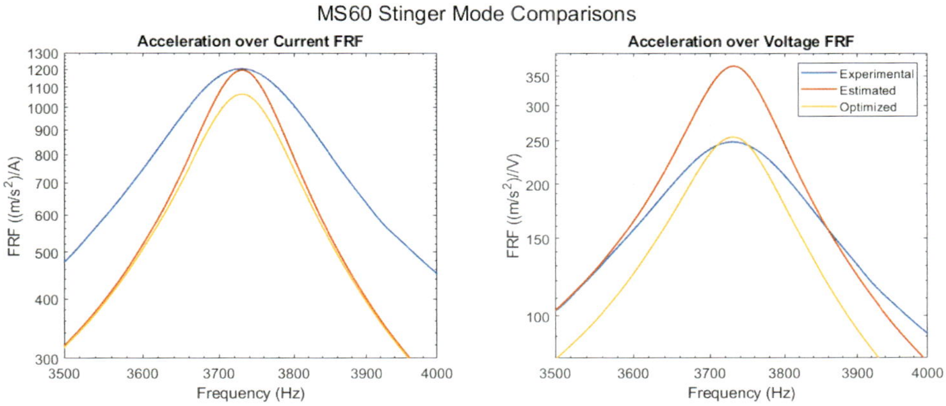

Fig. 16 Zoomed in view of stinger mode on both acceleration over current and acceleration over voltage FRFs.

Due to the initial estimate being done using the experimental acceleration over current FRF, it is reasonable that the model aligns at the stinger mode peak for the acceleration over current FRF prior to optimization. As a result, the acceleration over voltage FRF is over-predicting the stinger mode peak. Thus, the optimization resulted in the acceleration over current FRF increasing in error near the stinger mode peak and decreasing the error near the stinger mode peak for the acceleration over voltage FRF. The quantitative similarity comparison agrees with this visual observation. As the acceleration over voltage FRF's RMS dB error decreased due to the optimization, the acceleration over curent FRF's RMS dB error was increased. It should be noted that the RMS dB error was only calculated from 10-4000 Hz because the experimental data had an unusual sharp peak around 4100 Hz that is likely not a mechanical response but rather an error in the measurement for the electrical signals.

Conclusions

The aim of this study was to formulate an approach to estimate lumped model parameters that are representative of modal shakers. Overall, the proposed methods require only a small data set that yields a highly representative model. This approach may also be applied to many other modal shakers that share a similar construction to the one used for the experimental work used in this paper. Although the methods were shown to be successful, further improvements may still be made. Modal shakers dynamics are highly dependent on changing test conditions. These conditions include stinger length, stinger thickness, mass loading, boundary conditions, and orientation. For example, changing the stinger length will tend to decrease the stinger stiffness and will shift the stinger mode natural frequency down as a result. The methods described in this paper are not highly robust to these changing test conditions. This means that the shaker model estimations will need to be made using data that comes from a shaker in similar conditions to what the test engineers believes it will be used in the real test.

The improved shaker modeling method described in this paper can be used in dynamic substructuring to couple the shaker's dynamics to the dynamics of a device under test. This coupled model can then predict test feasibility by obtaining the required electrical inputs from the amplifier, which makes up a large portion of the shaker's limitations as described in Shaker Limitations section. Having this information that aids in determining test feasibility will ultimately help to reduce delays and improve the overall efficiency of ground environmental test series.

Acknowledgments This work was funded by the Delivery Environments program at Los Alamos National Laboratory, under the Office of Engineering and Technology Maturation. LA-UR-24-30342.

References

1. Fickenwirth, P. (2023). Electrodynamic Shaker Capability Estimation Through Experimental Dynamic Substructuring [Thesis]. https://doi.org/10.2172/1958984
2. Lang, G. F., and Snyder, D. (2001). Understanding the physics of electrodynamic shaker performance. Sound and vibration, 35(10), 24-33.
3. Schultz, R. (2019). Calibration of shaker Electro-Mechanical models. Proceedings of the 38th IMAC, https://www.osti.gov/biblio/1642863
4. Tiwari, N., Puri, A., and Saraswat, A. (2017). Lumped parameter modelling and methodology for extraction of model parameters for an electrodynamic shaker. Journal of Low Frequency Noise, Vibration and Active Control, 36(2), 99-115.
5. Martini, Luca. (2016). Real-time control of an Electrodynamic Shaker. Master's thesis, Alma Mater Studiorum - Università di Bologna,. http://amslaurea.unibo.it/10080/.
6. Adam, Caroline. (2022) Virtual Shaker Testing: Modelling, vibration analysis, and experimental validation of an electrodynamic shaker model coupled to a test specimen[BR]- Integration Internship. MatheO - Master Thesis Online matheo.uliege.be/handle/2268.2/14589.
7. Unholtz-Dickie Corporation (2018). H560 Operating and Maintenance Manual.
8. How to normalize the RMSE. (2019, January 7). https://www.marinedatascience.co/blog/2019/01/07/normalizing-the-rmse/
9. Tuman, M.J., Behling, M., Allen, M.S. et al. (2024). Balancing Impedance and Controllability in Response Reconstruction with TS-IMMAT. Exp Tech 48, 51–68. https://doi.org/10.1007/s40799-023-00645-1

Chapter 10
Combining Waves Propagation Theory, Modal Analysis and Dynamic Response to Assess the Condition of Fluid-Filled Pipes

Sebastien Perrier, Marshal D. Kafle, Gurvinder Mundi, Elia Rizkalla, and Cameron White

Abstract Water distribution networks, conveying water through thousands of miles of pipes, are critical infrastructures subjected to various structural and environmental degradation mechanisms. Timely, non-invasive, and non-destructive assessments are crucial in preventing breaks and leaks and managing the loss of these valuable resources, thereby avoiding extensive damage and repair costs. This paper explores the application of the vibroacoustic method combined with modal analysis and dynamic response techniques in evaluating the structural health of pipelines. The method includes deploying sensors to capture vibrational data that can be spaced as far as 2,000ft, applying finite element modelling to simulate pipeline behavior, and using advanced signal processing techniques to interpret the data. Until now, the technology has been tested on water mains of various pipe materials such as HDPE, PVC, Steel, Cast Iron, Ductile Iron, Asbestos Cement and Concrete for diameters ranging from 3 to 72 inches. The level of resolution acquired is typically between 6 and 15ft and varies with pipe type and diameter, as well as the distance between the sensors.

Keywords Pipeline Condition Assessment · Coupled Waves · Vibro-Acoustics · Dynamic / Modal Response Analysis

Introduction

Pipes are vital to modern society for transporting and distributing drinking water and wastewater. Capital budget constraints, pipe age, and other environmental factors have all contributed to pipe degradation, and between 2012 and 2018, the overall water main break rates increased by 27% [1]. Acoustic methods in fluid-filled pipes have been widely used for decades to acoustically monitor leaks [2]. For condition assessment, starting in the early 2000s, the Moens-Korteweg equation [2] has also been applied to fluid-filled pipes, such as watermains, to model the relationship between wave speed and the elasticity of the wall, allowing to assess the average degradation of pipes, typically over 300 to 600ft. While this approach has provided valuable information to pipeline owners and asset managers, there is a need for more granular information to make the right decision in terms of repair, rehabilitation or replacement of these 20 to 40-foot-long buried assets. This paper discusses the combination of modal analysis and dynamic response techniques with the vibroacoustic wave theory to evaluate the condition of the fluid-filled pipes and generate that finer resolution, which is otherwise incredibly challenging if using wave speed-based methods only.

Results from experimental case studies demonstrate the efficacy of this integrated approach in detecting and localizing damage within pipeline structures. The findings suggest that combining modal analysis and dynamic response techniques can significantly enhance the early detection of faults, thus reducing the risk of catastrophic failures and extending the operational lifespan of pipelines. This technology underscores the potential of non-destructive evaluation methods as robust tools for proactively managing pipeline infrastructure.

Sebastien Perrier · Marshal D. Kafle · Gurvinder Mundi · Elia Rizkalla · Cameron White
KenWave Solutions Inc., 7080 Derrycrest Drive, Mississauga, ON L5W 0G5, CA
e-mail: sperrier@kenwavesolutions.com; mkafle@kenwavesolutions.com; gmundi@kenwavesolutions.com; erizkalla@kenwavesolutions.com; cwhite@kenwavesolutions.com

Brandon Dilworth et al. (eds.), *Topics in Modal Analysis & Parameter Identification I, Vol. 9*, Conference Proceedings of the Society for Experimental Mechanics Series, https://doi.org/10.13052/9788743801542-10

Background

The coupled wave equation of motion governs the propagation of acoustic waves through a material medium that interacts with the structure, such as a viscoelastic pipe containing fluid. In this case, both the medium and the mechanical properties of the pipe play a role in how the wave propagates. The coupled eigenfrequencies are the frequencies at which the fluid-structure system resonates and are crucial pieces of information in the assessment of the pipe condition.

The modal analysis determines the pipe's eigenfrequencies and mode shapes. From the baseline from the undamaged pipes, the deviation in dynamic properties or indicators, such as shifts in natural frequency and mode shapes, suggests deterioration in pipes. The thinning walls are more flexible due to decreases in the stiffness of the pipe, leading to lower eigenfrequencies and increased vibrational energy. For simplicity, the pipe can be modeled as a cylindrical beam, and the eigenfrequency f_n of the mode n can be expressed as [3]:

$$f_n = \frac{\lambda_n^2}{2\pi L^2}\sqrt{\frac{EI}{\rho A}}$$

where, λ is mode shape constant, L is the length of the pipe, E is the Young's modulus, I is the moment of inertia, ρ is the density of the material and A is the cross-sectional area of the pipe. The combined fluid-structure interaction (FSI) is more complex and involves solving the wave equation for both the pipe wall and the fluid. In such cases, the eigenfrequencies can be obtained via experimental modal analysis or modeling the pipe numerically.

The dynamic response technique involves measuring the response of the pipeline using accelerometers when subjected to dynamic loads; the loads are generated using an external device. For a simple harmonic excitation $F(t) = F_0 \sin(\omega t)$, the dynamic response at frequency ω is [4]:

$$X(\omega) = \frac{F_0}{\sqrt{(k - m\omega^2)^2 + (c\omega)^2}}$$

where, $X(\omega)$ is the response at frequency ω, F_0 is the magnitude of external force, m, k, c are mass, stiffness and damping of the system which are functions of the pipe wall thickness.

The response can be fed into the signal processing tools, which give the dominant frequencies at which the pipeline is dynamically responding. Comparing and matching the response with the eigenfrequencies helps access the indicators to quantify the level of degradation.

Analysis of Eigenfrequencies using COMSOL

For numerical estimation of the eigenfrequencies of a coupled wave, an FSI analysis is carried out using a COMSOL platform. The study comprises a 3 m (10 ft) ductile iron pipe with a nominal bore diameter of 300 mm (12 in) as well as a 2D model with the same diameter and a parametric sweep of the wall thickness between 8 and 13 mm (1/3 and 1/2 in) with 1 mm (3/64 in) increments. The vibroacoustic-structure interfaces ensure a proper connection between acoustic pressure and the displacement of elastic material. The radial mode shape for a pipe with a wall thickness of 13 mm (1/2 in) is shown in Fig. 1.

The frequency shift for a radial mode as the wall thickness is reduced is observed in a 2D model (shown in Fig. 2(a)), with the results from the 3D case overlapping nicely. A similar trend is observed in the average of 8 modes for the 3D case. This reinforces the theory explained in the background section that the deviation in indicators such as eigenfrequencies can be analyzed and compared with the baseline (undamaged) to assess the level of pipe wall degradation. This result is further matched with the experimentally measured response, to obtain further interpretation of the data.

Field Result – Case Study

The City of Gresham, Oregon, with a population of 110,000 people, manages over 240 miles of water mains through a proactive, risk-based approach to maintain reliable service. As part of its long-term strategy, the City plans to restart its pipe replacement program in 2026. To prioritize pipeline replacements, Gresham assigns a Likelihood of Failure score to water mains that haven't been inspected, based on pipeline age, material, and leak/break history.

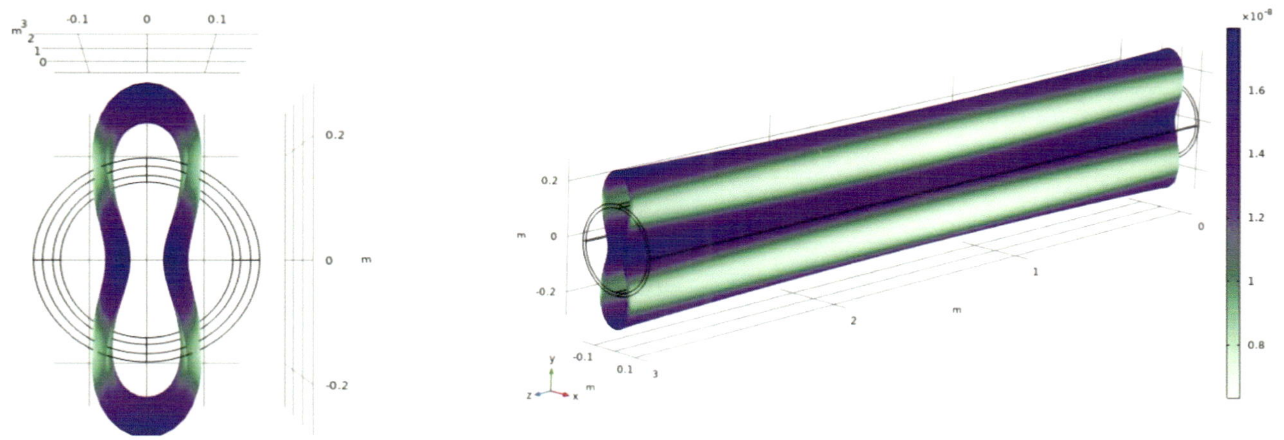

Fig. 1 Schematic of a radial mode occurring at 259 Hz.

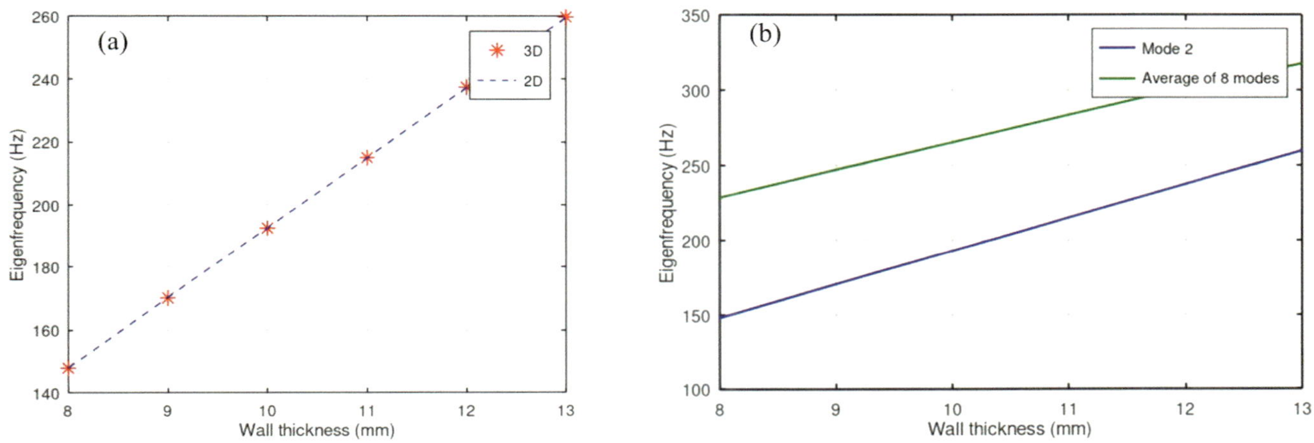

Fig. 2 The comparison of eigenfrequencies vs wall thickness: (a) between 2D and 3D model for a radial mode; (b) for mode 2 and average of 8 modes for a 3D model.

To improve decision-making and extend the life of its water mains, the City conducts condition assessments on pipelines installed before 1980. For the inspected pipes, the Likelihood of Failure score is based on estimates of Remaining Useful Life and historical leak/break data. This helps the City focus on replacing or repairing the most critical sections while keeping older but still functional segments in use.

In line with this strategy, Gresham engaged KenWave Solutions to assess four cast iron and ductile iron pipelines, ranging from 6 to 10 inches in diameter and spanning a total of 3,528 feet. KenWave's non-invasive Dynamic Response Imaging^{TM} (DRI^{TM}) technology provided detailed residual wall thickness measurements with 6-foot resolution, enabling the City to identify both healthy areas and sections showing signs of increased degradation.

The DRI results identified localized changes in wall thickness between access points, enabling the City to prioritize areas requiring immediate attention. To verify these findings, Gresham excavated seven locations and used an ultrasonic gauge to scan the pipe as a general accuracy check. Additionally, two sections of pipe were removed from the most deteriorated areas and examined. The results and comparison between DRI and ultrasonic measurements are presented in the Table below.

Table 1 Validation Results

Pipeline	Pipe Type	Pipe Size (In)	Nominal Stiffness Lost (%)	DRI Residual Wall Thickness (in)	Validation Method	Measured Minimum Avg Hoop Thickness (in)
NE 5th St	Cast	6	**19%**	0.30	Slice	0.32
NE 5th St	Cast	6	**33%**	0.25	Pipe Stick	0.27
NE 5th St	Cast	6	**3%**	0.34	Slice	0.36
SE 10th Dr	Ductile	6	**0%**	0.25	Slice	0.24
SE 10th Dr	Ductile	6	**24%**	0.19	Pipe Stick	0.19
NE 23rd St	Cast	8	**10%**	0.40	Slice	0.40
NE 23rd St	Cast	8	**3%**	0.42	Slice	0.41

This process confirmed that the predicted wall thickness data was accurate.

KenWave's assessment data is now helping Gresham predict the remaining useful life of its pipelines and update the Likelihood of Failure scores for inspected sections. This information is crucial for planning future pipe replacements, ensuring efficient resource allocation and minimizing service interruptions.

Conclusion

The methodology combining waves propagation theory, modal analysis and dynamic response of watermains can provide granular longitudinal information regarding pipe wall thickness with a resolution of 2 m (6 linear feet). Comparison of changes in the wall thickness from the measured dynamic response of the pipes agreed with the validation performed on metallic distribution mains, confirming that the predicted localized wall thickness data was accurate.

Specifically, results from experimental case studies demonstrate the efficacy of this integrated approach in detecting and localizing damage within pipeline structures. The findings suggest that combining modal analysis and dynamic response techniques can significantly enhance the early detection of faults, thus reducing the risk of catastrophic failures and extending the operational lifespan of pipelines.

More projects are ongoing with several utilities worldwide with different levels of validation on various pipe materials such as HDPE, PVC, Steel, Cast Iron, Ductile Iron, Asbestos Cement and Concrete for diameters ranging from 3 to 72 inches.

This technology underscores the potential of non-destructive evaluation methods as robust tools for proactively managing pipeline infrastructure.

Acknowledgments The authors and KenWave Solutions Inc. want to acknowledge the support for this project provided by the City of Gresham.

References

1. Folkman, Steven. "Water main break rates in the USA and Canada: A comprehensive study." (2018).
2. Muggleton, J. M., M. J. Brennan, and P. W. Linford. "Axisymmetric wave propagation in fluid-filled pipes: wavenumber measurements in in vacuo and buried pipes." *Journal of Sound and Vibration* 270.1-2 (2004): 171-190.
3. Xu, M-R., S-P. Xu, and H-Y. Guo. "Determination of natural frequencies of fluid-conveying pipes using homotopy perturbation method." *Computers & Mathematics with Applications* 60.3 (2010): 520-527.
4. Chopra, Anil K. *Dynamics of structures*. Pearson Education India, 2007.

Chapter 11
Analysis of Acoustic-Structure Interaction Case, Modelling and Possible Validation

Daniele Fabbri, Carlo Rosso, and Fabio Bruzzone

Abstract This paper presents the analysis of the interaction between sound and an elastic plate in the air domain. Both numerical and experimental methods will be employed to investigate the acoustic field that results from the interaction of a thin flexible structure with an incident acoustic wave. The two domains are discretized using the Finite Element Method, and the Helmholtz equation together with the elastic equation are numerically solved. In order to study the level of coupling between the two domains different types of analysis are carried out. Initially, the structure is considered rigid and a hard wall boundary condition is used for the acoustic problem solution, the second analysis included the study of the thin plate displacement when it is stressed by the acoustic pressure. Finally, a multiphysics analysis is performed to consider the movement of the thin plate caused by an incident acoustic wave, which in turn induced new sound waves in the air. To ensure a precise simulation it is necessary to have a full bidirectional coupling between the acoustic field and the structure domain. A possible setup for the experimental validation is presented in the last section of the paper

Keywords Multiphysics, Acoustic, Structure, Acoustic structure interaction, Finite element analysis (FEA)

Introduction

The willingness to study more physics in the same simulation has been a challenge in recent years. A fascinating and old example is the study of the interaction between a fluid and a structure, one of the most intriguing areas in multiphysics, yet it remains broad, complex, and not fully understood.

Fluid-Structure Interaction (FSI) has a lot of different fields of application as biomechanics [1], which focuses on developing and verifying novel algorithms for accurately predicting hemodynamics in major arteries. Finite element (FE) simulations are used to model the interaction between blood flow and the deformation of arterial walls, especially in a healthy aorta. The interaction between the vehicle's body and the fluid volume within its interior is typically studied as a noise vibration harshness (NVH) problem. In [2] an analysis of different methods used to solve the FE model has been carried out. The methods taken into account are Direct, Automated Multilevel Substructuring, AMLS, and Lanczos. They were compared using mesh refinement and the frequency of analysis investigation. Other FSI applications are: Battery Thermal Management[3], particle motion in an incompressible fluid [4]and magneto-hydrodynamics [5].

The aim of this paper is to describe a numerical model that represents acoustic structure interaction (ASI), a branch of FSI, which describes what happens when sound waves travel through a medium, such as air or water, and encounter a structure, such as a wall, diaphragm, or membrane. As explained in [6], a wave is the movement in a medium of a disturbance from one point to another and it takes place at a finite speed. A sound wave is a way of propagating energy by alternating compressed and rarefied particles, the distance between two consecutive points of the same phase is called wavelength and it is inversely proportional to its frequency. When a wave comes into contact with a structure, it causes a vibration by exerting pressure on it, the structural response can then modify the propagation of the sound waves, creating a continuous interaction between the two fields. At certain frequencies, the structure can resonate, amplifying specific sound waves, while at other frequencies, it can absorb or reflect the sound, changing its characteristics.

Some studies have been carried out in the same field. The eigenmodes and the vibro-acoustic response of the coupled system composed of a box and acoustic cavities were predicted by *Shi et al.* in [7] using an energy principle and Fourier series. They studied the dynamic behavior of the entire system and demonstrated how certain acoustic modes have a significant

Daniele Fabbri · Carlo Rosso · Fabio Bruzzone
Department of Mechanical Engineering, Politecnico di Torino, TO 10129
e-mail: daniele.fabbri@polito.it; carlo.rosso@polito.it; fabio.bruzzone@polito.it

Brandon Dilworth et al. (eds.), *Topics in Modal Analysis & Parameter Identification I, Vol. 9*, Conference Proceedings of the Society for Experimental Mechanics Series, https://doi.org/10.13052/9788743801542-11

impact on the structure's mode. Their work was based on [8], in which a modal coupling analysis was done to demonstrate that if two modes shapes of the uncoupled systems are well matched the difference between their resonance frequencies determines the rate of energy transfer. *Pan et Al.* demonstrate also that the resonance frequency of the coupled system differs from the corresponding acoustic mode, in particular, a structural mode with a specific resonance frequency will tend to "push away" the cavity mode with which it interacts. The same coupled system was investigated in [9] by changing the plate material, starting with elastic isotropic materials, such as steel and aluminum, and then with composite material. The effects of material, ply angle, and number of layers on the coupled vibro-acoustic characteristics of composite plate-cavity systems have been examined. The results highlighted that: the coupled fundamental frequencies were higher than the corresponding structural and acoustical frequencies for all materials, the aluminum plate-cavity system was more affected by the coupling than the steel case, and the composite plate-cavity systems are highly affected by the coupling compared to isotropic plate systems, with the increase in ply angle having a positive effect on the fundamental coupled frequencies.

Two main approaches can be used to solve a multiphysics problem: monolithic and partitioned. The first method treats fluid and solid domains as a single integrated system, which results in a system of equations that can be solved simultaneously with mesh movement. Instead, the partitioned considers the fluid and solid as separate systems linked through an interface. In [10] *Felippa and Park* explained the advantages of partitioned solution procedures, focusing also on their stability. They explained that the main cause of instability was the delayed feedback of fluid radiation damping energy from the fluid equation to the structural equation. To improve the convergence and stability of the partial solver an additional iteration loop can be used. This leads to a strongly coupled partitioned solution [11]. The partitioned approach presents two potentially significant advantages. It requires relatively few modifications to single-field analyzers, and this modularity is valuable given the current costs associated with software development, modification, and maintenance. The computational efficiency is also improved as the cost per time step of the staggered solution is approximately the same as processing the component fields separately. The staggered approach is economical advantageous when time step size restrictions are not an issue. Instead, in case of strong interaction, a monolithic approach ensures convergence and stability of the coupled solution. It consists of simultaneous procedures that solve in a single iteration loop the entire coupled system. Newton's method [12] is typically used to solve a unique system of equations, but consolidating multiple equations into a single system can lead to ill-conditioned system matrices, which can sometimes have zero entries on the diagonal. The work done by *Heil et Al.* [13] compares the two approaches in different test cases. It turns out that monolithic solvers are competitive in CPU time, even in cases with weak interaction. Instead for strongly coupled systems, the monolithic approach must be used as the partitioned tends to diverge. Nevertheless, in the case of large-scale problems, especially in three dimensions, maximizing the utility of monolithic solvers requires the availability of efficient preconditioners.

In this paper, a formulation that coupled pressure and displacement in the two physical domains and their FEM discretization is summarised in the background section. The multiphysics model and results are presented in the Analysis Section. Finally, a brief summary of the results and possible experimental setup is presented in the Conclusion.

Background

The governing equation for the pressure in an acoustic medium in the frequency domain is the Helmholtz equation:

$$\nabla^2 P + \frac{\omega^2}{c_a^2} P = -i\rho_a \omega q \qquad in\ \Omega_a \tag{1}$$

where: P, ρ_a and c_a are the pressure the density of the acoustic domain, and the speed of sound, in the analysis domain Ω_a. The angular frequency and the wavenumber are denoted by ω and k, respectively. The Helmholtz equation can be solved using the appropriate boundary conditions, in this paper the following boundary conditions will be used:

- Sound Hard Wall Boundary condition

$$n\ \nabla P = 0 \tag{2}$$

- Imposed normal Impedance

$$P = \frac{iZ}{\rho_a \omega} \frac{\partial P}{\partial n} \tag{3}$$

where n is the outward unit normal to the fluid medium and Z is the acoustic impedance.

In the structural domain Ω_s Newton's second law in the frequency domain can be described as follows:

$$\nabla \sigma = -\omega^2 \rho_s u \qquad in\ \Omega_s \tag{4}$$

In (4) σ is the stress tensor, ρ_s the structural mass density and u the displacement vector while the body forces are not taken into account. Classic Neumann and Dirichlet boundary conditions are applied on the structural domain. As the paper is focused on a multiphysics model solved with a monolithic approach, for the sake of brevity the interface condition applied to Ω_s and Ω_a in the segregated approach will not be presented. However, to understand how it is possible to obtain a system of equations in the monolithic approach, a formulation called mixed displacement/pressure finite element will be explained. As this method is well described in [14] and [15] only some equations are reported.

The governing equations of this mixed formulation are: the relationship between stress and strain (5), the pressure and volumetric strain relationship (6) and the 2D definition of deviatoric (7) and volumetric strain (8):

$$\sigma = K\epsilon_v\delta + 2Ge \tag{5}$$

$$P = -K\epsilon_v \tag{6}$$

$$e = \epsilon - \frac{\epsilon_v}{2}\delta \tag{7}$$

$$\epsilon_v = \frac{\Delta V}{V} \tag{8}$$

With K , G and ρ are the bulk modulus, the shear modulus, the mass density, three material properties, which should be used alternatively between the acoustic Ω_a and the structural domain Ω_s, instead δ is Kronecker's operator. The basic approach of mixed displacement/pressure finite element formulations is to interpolate the displacements and pressure simultaneously. This requires that the principle of virtual work must be expressed using the independent variables u and P:

$$\int_\Omega \delta e^T C\boldsymbol{e}\, d\Omega - \int_\Omega P\delta\epsilon_v\, d\Omega = \int_\Omega -\omega^2\rho\delta\boldsymbol{u}^T\boldsymbol{u}\, d\Omega \tag{9}$$

$$\int_\Omega (p/K + \epsilon_v\delta P)\, d\Omega = 0 \tag{10}$$

Where the virtual displacement, the virtual deviatoric strain, the virtual strain are denoted by δu, δe, $\delta\epsilon$ respectively, C is the stress–strain matrix for the deviatoric stress and strain component which must satisfy the following equation:

$$(\sigma + P\delta) = C(\epsilon - \frac{1}{2}\epsilon_V\delta) \tag{11}$$

The discretization with finite element of both acoustic domain [16], [17], [18] and structural domain [19] is well known and widely reported, so it is only explained how to apply FEM to this mixed displacement/pressure formulation. The starting point is writing displacement u using the standard shape functions matrix N_d and Pressure P using matrix N_p:

$$\hat{u} = \sum_{i=1}^{n_d} \mathbf{N_d}u_i \qquad \hat{P} = \sum_{j=1}^{n_p} \mathbf{N_p}P_j \qquad i = 1...n_d \qquad j = 1...n_p \tag{12}$$

Where n_p and n_d are the number of prescribed shape functions for pressure and displacement. It is also possible to interpolate the the deviatoric strain e and the volumetric strain ϵ_V using matrices B_d and B_v as reported below:

$$e = \mathbf{B_d}\{u_i\} \qquad \epsilon_V = \mathbf{B_v}\{u_i\} \qquad i = 1...n_d \tag{13}$$

The standard discretization of Equations 9 and 10 yields to the following linear system to be solved:

$$\begin{bmatrix} \mathbf{K_{uu}} - \omega^2\mathbf{M_{uu}} & \mathbf{K_{up}} \\ \mathbf{K_{up}}^T & \mathbf{K_{pp}} \end{bmatrix} \begin{Bmatrix} U \\ P \end{Bmatrix} = \begin{Bmatrix} F_a \\ P_a \end{Bmatrix} \tag{14}$$

where the structural displacement and pressure vectors are denoted by U and P, respectively. The stiffness matrices for displacement and pressure, the mass matrix, and the external force vectors are denoted by $\mathbf{K_{uu}}$, $\mathbf{K_{pp}}$, $\mathbf{M_{uu}}$, F_a, P_a respectively, instead the coupling matrix $\mathbf{K_{up}}$ is defined as [15]

$$\mathbf{K_{up}} = \mathbf{K_{pu}^T} = -\int_V \mathbf{B_v}^T\mathbf{N_p}dV \tag{15}$$

Solving the linear system of equations using a specific solver like MUMPS [20] or PARDISO [21] it is possible to find the unknown vectors U , P for each frequency. In the following section the design of a multiphysics model representing acoustic structure interaction will be presented, based on the theoretical bases established.

Analysis

The 2D axisymmetric multiphysics model presented in this section simulates the behavior of an aluminum plate, modeled as a shell, when it is excited by an incident acoustic wave generated by a loudspeaker in the air domain. The acoustic source is located at one end of a steel tube, which has a length such that the waves incident on the plate are plane, as specified by EN ISO 10534 [22]. At the other end of the pipe, a sound-absorbing material (Melamine Foam) is placed to absorb waves that might reflect at the end of the tube, thus minimizing the reflection coefficient. Eight evenly spaced flanges are welded onto the tube to secure it to mechanical supports. These flanges also need to prevent any mechanical modes of the tube within the frequency range of the plate's first natural frequency.

The purpose of this numerical model is to determine the amount of acoustic pressure transmitted when a structure is excited by an acoustic source, focusing on the range near its first natural frequency and the behavior of the transmitted pressure behind the structure. To ensure that the structure is excited by a planar wave, the pipe is designed according to the same standards used for impedance tubes, creating a controlled and consistent environment.Three different numerical models were created to determine if studying both fluid-structure interaction and acoustic behavior together is necessary. The first model, called *"1_A.S.I."* , takes into account the interaction between the structure and the acoustic field, in a fully coupled model.The second model simplifies the system by assuming the plate as rigid, isolating the acoustic response without structural dynamics and understanding the acoustic modes of the tube, it is called *"2_Plate_rigid"*. In *"3_Plate_displacement"*, third and last model the acoustic source has been turned off and a prescribed displacement to the plate has been assigned, the prescribed movement of the plate derived from the acoustic-structure interaction results of the first case. This step It aids in comparing how each approach influences the transmitted pressure and evaluating the need for coupling both physics in future analyses. In Figure 1 the geometric 2D axisymmetric model built on Comsol Multiphysics is shown, the geometric dimension of the components are presented in table 1.

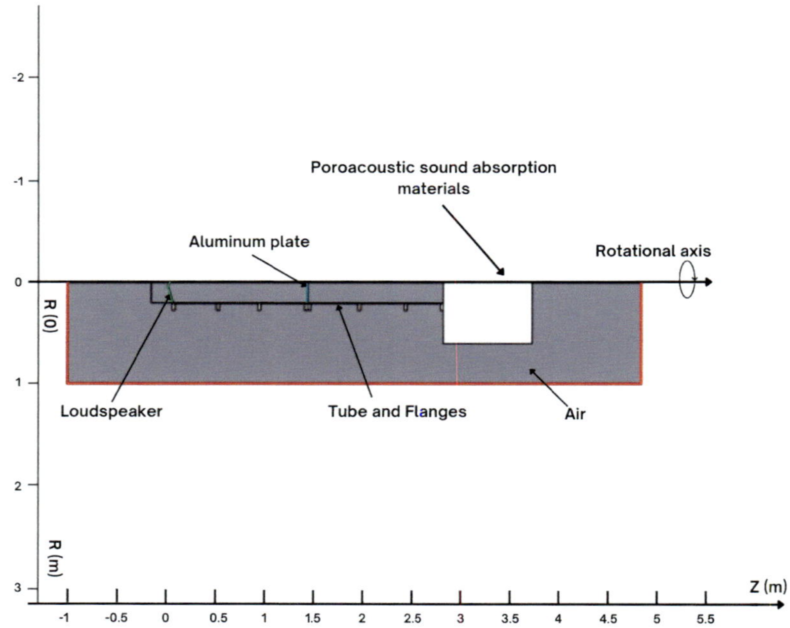

Fig. 1 Geometric 2D axisymmetric model

The boundaries of the air domain indicated in red in Figure 1 have been assigned a perfectly matched layer boundary condition to simulate an infinite domain in which the sound waves do not reflect. An high thickness layer of melamine foam is located at one end of the pipe to limit the reflection of the wave. To accurately simulate the behavior of the poroacosutic material, a dedicated domain has been created, using the poroacoustics domain features of the Pressure Acoustics interface. The Johnson-Champoux-Allard model with a rigid frame has been selected for this purpose. This model represents an equivalent fluid model for a rigid frame porous material [23]. The melamine foam material parameters are indicated as follow: The acoustic source, a loudspeaker, is modelled as lumped system, geometrically is represented as boundary indicated in green in figure 1. This model represents a moving-coil loudspeaker, where a lumped parameter analogy is used to describe the behavior of both the electrical and mechanical components of the speaker. The coupling with the pressure acoustic

Table 1 Geometric dimension of the model

Symbol	Value	Description
R_1	$198.2\ [mm]$	Inner Tube radius
R_2	$203.2\ [mm]$	Outer tube radius and inner flange radius
R_3	$270\ [mm]$	Outer flange radius and plate radius
R_4	$600\ [mm]$	Melamine Foam for insulating Box radius
R_5	$190\ [mm]$	Loudspeaker membrane radius
T_1	$2\ [mm]$	Thickness of the aluminum plate
Z_1	$850\ [mm]$	Length of Melamine Foam for insulating Box
Z_2	$2600\ [mm]$	Length of the tube
Z_2	$1300\ [mm]$	Position of the aluminum plate

Table 2 Melamine foam material parameters

Symbol	Value	Description
ϵ_p	0.995	Porosity
R_f	$10500\ [Pa * s/m^2]$	Flow resistivity
s	$0.49\ [mm]$	Viscous characteristic length parameter
L_{th}	$470\ [\mu m]$	Thermal characteristic length
L_v	$240\ [\mu m]$	Viscous characteristic length
τ	1.0059	Tortuosity factor

environment is achieved using the built-in Interior Lumped Speaker Boundary feature. The loudspeaker is modeled with an open back volume. These electric circuit models have been employed successfully for many years. The parameters that characterize a loudspeaker's low-frequency performance are commonly referred to as the Thiele-Small or small-signal parameters [24]. All parameters are constants, as they are given within the model's low-frequency limit, in table 3 the parameters associated to a commercial loudspeaker are listed.

Table 3 Small signal parameters

Symbol	Value	Description
M_{MD}	$56.1\ [g]$	Moving mass (voice coil and diaphragm)
C_{MS}	$180e-6\ [m/N]$	Suspension compliance
R_{MS}	$2.16\ [N * s/m]$	Suspension mechanical losses
BL	$22.4\ [T * m]$	Force factor
R_E	$5.9\ [\Omega]$	Voice coil resistance
L_E	$0.48\ [mH]$	Voice coil inductance
a	$19\ [cm]$	Equivalent piston radius of driver

The interaction between the two domains occurs in the part of the plate corresponding to the pipe's internal cross-section, indicated in blue in Figure 1. The aluminum plate, modeled as a shell with a thickness of 2 mm, is constrained along the entire edge, being positioned between two series of flanges which are connected by a threaded connection.

As described in [22], for an impedance tube, an upper limit, denoted as f_u, is calculated to avoid the occurrence of non-plane wave mode propagation, considering the dimensions of the pipe represents in the model, this value is $428.8\ Hz$. To ensure that the plate has its first natural frequency within this range, modal analysis has been conducted, the first natural frequency is at $127.93\ Hz$.

All the analyses were studied in the $50 - 450\ Hz$ frequency range to be inside the plane wave region, the geometry was meshed with a 2D Finite element whose max size was 5 times smaller than the max wavelength λ to provide enough resolution to represent the sound field accurately. The results will be presented regarding plate displacement and acoustic pressure measured in these points inside the tube:

- $(R = 0\ m,\ Z = 0\ m),\ \ (R = R_1,\ Z = 0\ m)$ to measure the acoustic pressure at the speaker output
- $(R = 0\ m,\ Z = 1.2\ m),\ \ (R = R_1,\ Z = 1.2\ m)$ to measure the acoustic pressure before the plate in a region where the non-planar waves generated by the speaker are dissipated.

- $(R = 0\ m,\ Z = 2.6\ m)$, $(R = R_1,\ Z = 2.6\ m)$ to measure the acoustic pressure before the end of the pipe
- The Z-component displacement of the plate is measured at the center of the plate $(R = 0\ m,\ Z = 1.3\ m)$

Figure 2 shows the plate displacement in the 1_A.S.I. analysis, the structural response is at 120 Hz which differs from the plate resonant frequency by more than 7 Hz, this behavior seems similar to the one described in [9] where the natural frequencies of the structure in a coupled system with a fluid cavity changes.

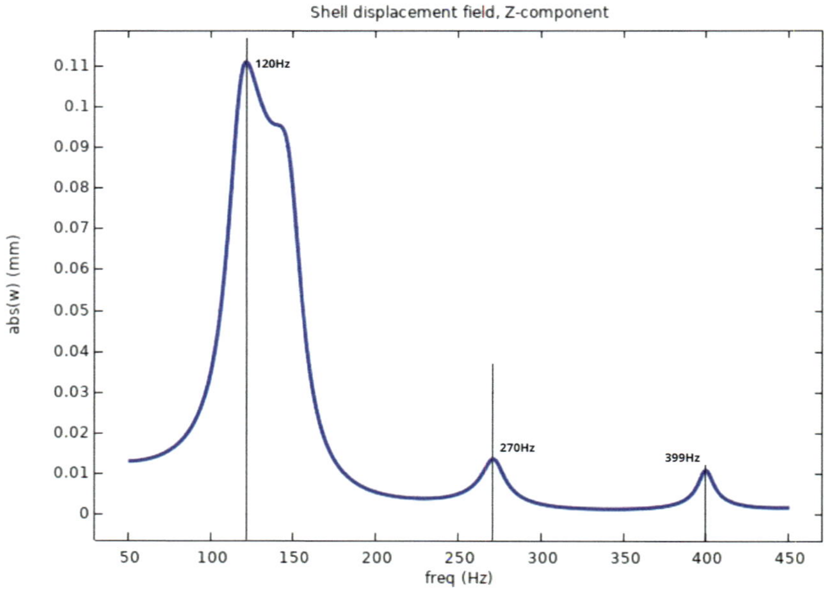

Fig. 2 Plate displacement in 1_A.S.I.

In addition to the response at the first natural frequency, there are two distinct spikes that can be explained using the acoustic pressure graphs. In figure 3 is presented the acoustic pressure measured at the speaker output $Z = 0\ m$ at the center of the tube and the inner radius.

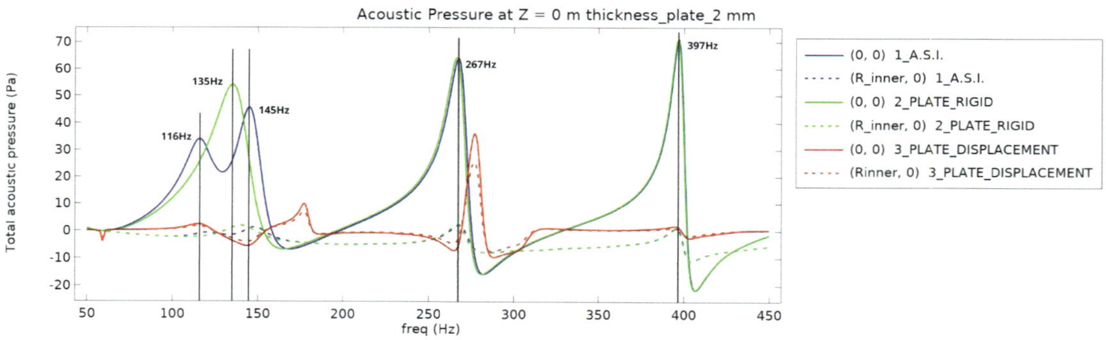

Fig. 3 Acoustic pressure inside the tube at Z = 0 m, thickness of the shell 2 mm

The continuous lines represent the points at $R = 0$ and the dotted at $R = R_1$, as mentioned before the waves generated by the speaker are not immediately planar, for this reason the curves do not match. Moreover, in the figure 3, it is possible to notice a difference between the first two analyses, for the first case, in which the acoustic structure interaction has been studied, two spikes of pressure in the range $[115 - 150\ Hz]$ are present, the same trend is not replicated in the second analysis shown in green. The first peak of pressure at 116 Hz highlights the interaction between the two physics given by the movement of the plate near its coupled natural frequency which affects the acoustic field. In the rigid plate case, three peaks of pressure occur at frequencies: $135\ Hz$, $267\ \ Hz$, and $397\ Hz$, to which are associated wavelengths of $2.6\ m$, $1.3\ m$, $0.87\ m$. These peaks are related to the loudspeaker, which excites the air inside the impedance tube, at certain frequencies which coincide with the tube resonant frequencies. These resonant frequencies are determined by the tube length , $1.3\ m$, and correspond to wavelengths that fit integer multiples of half-wavelengths within the tube. The resulting standing waves occur due to the constructive and destructive interference of the incident and reflected waves within the tube. Peaks in acoustic pressure indicate locations of antinodes, where constructive interference occurs, while nodes represent points where pressure remains zero due to destructive interference. The red lines are associated with the case in which the loudspeaker is turned off and the displacement is imposed as a boundary condition to the structure, in this case, no distinct trend can be observed comparable to the other two cases.

Figure 4 reports the acoustic pressure at $Z = 1.2\ m$, since the case *"3_Plate_displacement"* did not show any significant trend, in this graph, for the sake of clarity, only the first two analyses are displayed. This figure highlights areas of low

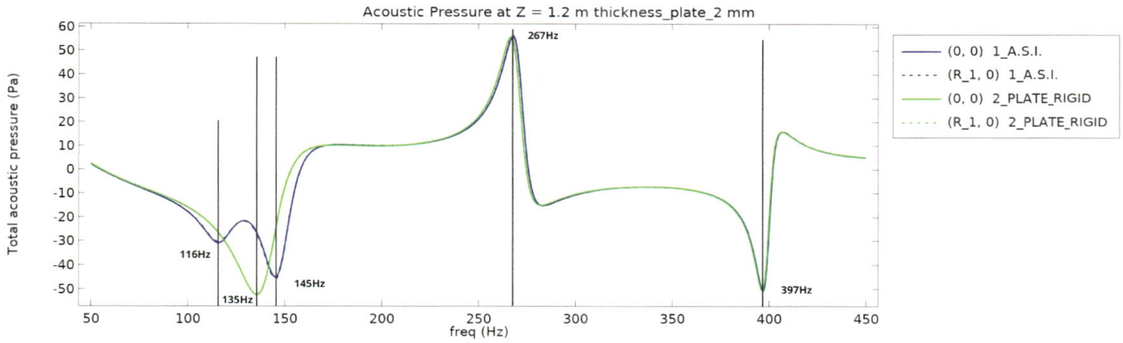

Fig. 4 Acoustic pressure inside the tube at Z = 1.2 m, thickness of the shell 2 mm

pressure near the first and third acoustic resonant frequencies of the tube, also, in this case, the influence the interaction between the structure and the acoustic field is quite clear, with a similar trend to $Z = 0\ m$, however, the curves corresponding to different radii are now superimposed because the waves have become planar.

In figure 5 is presented the case at $Z = 2.6\ m$, all three analyses are displayed:

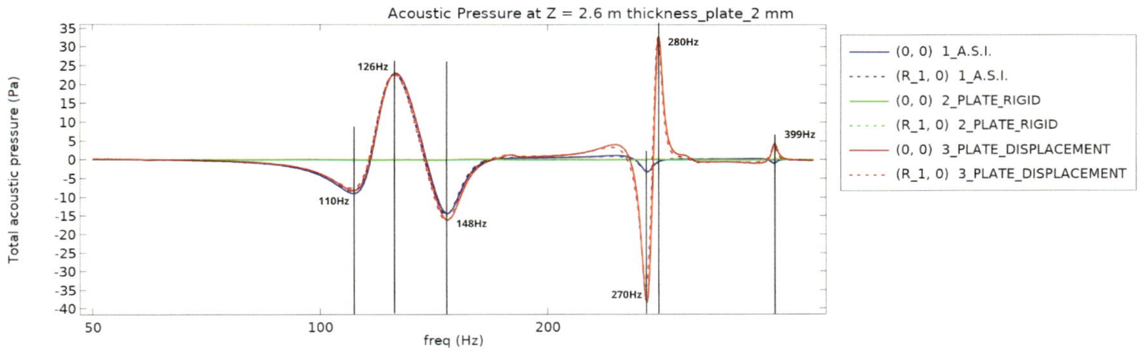

Fig. 5 Acoustic pressure inside the tube at Z = 2.6 m, thickness of the shell 2 mm

It is possible to notice that in the frequency range associated with the first mode of the plate, the acoustic pressure transmitted over the tube reaches a value bigger than $20\ Pa$, given by the coupled presence of the plate and tube resonant frequency, this is confirmed by the behavior at the other tube resonant frequencies, here high-pressure peaks do not occur. The *2_Plate_rigid* case shows an acoustic pressure value equal to $0\ Pa$ at all frequencies. The plate-imposed displacement case, despite a slight difference of around $2\ Pa$, reconstructs the pressure curve in the plate resonance frequency range. However, at the tube acoustic resonant frequencies, the model produces very high values of pressure, which indicates how this analysis should be revised in more detail.

To replicate this experiment, a possible setup has been created. The dimensions are the same as those used in the multiphysics model. In the geometric model, mechanical carriers are present, even though numerically they are considered as boundary constraints. The speaker is inside the aluminum box, but as a preliminary simulation showed some numerical errors, it will be decided in the future whether to use it with open air behind or use melamine foam inside the box to ensure proper sound insulation. The CAD model is presented in figure 6, however, there are no microphones for recording pressure, similar to those used in impedance tests, and the optical sensor for measuring plate displacement.

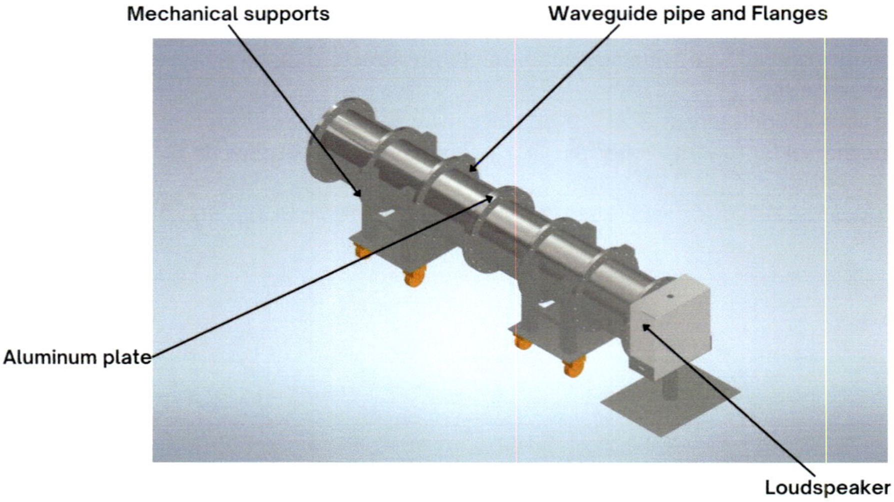

Fig. 6 Possible experimental set-up

Conclusion

The results of this study demonstrate the significant impact of interactions between different physical domains. The acoustic-structure interaction case shows that when a structure is excited by an acoustic source at its resonance frequency, a substantial amount of pressure is transmitted downstream of the plate, especially when the mechanical resonance frequency of the structure and the acoustic resonance frequency of the pipe are similar. The three analyses presented examined the possibility of avoiding the need for modelling multiphysics coupling. It was discovered that deviating from a multiphysics approach produced noticeable differences, however further investigations are required to fully evaluate this possibility. Furthermore, to strengthen the validity of the numerical model presented in this study, future experimental tests using the setup outlined in the last section are necessary. The purpose of these tests is to compare numerical predictions with real measurements, which will lead to a more robust framework for understanding acoustic-structure interactions and improving the model accuracy.

Acknowledgments This publication is part of the project PNRR-NGEU which has received funding from the MUR – DM 117/2023.

References

1. Crosetto, Reymon, Deparis, Kontaxakis, Stergiopulos, and Quarteroni. "Fluid–structure interaction simulation of aortic blood flow". *Computers & Fluids*, 43(1):46–57 (2011)
2. Kropp and Heiserer. "Efficient broadband vibro-acoustic analysis of passenger car bodies using an fe-based component mode synthesis approach". *Journal of Computational Acoustics*, 11(2):139–157 (2003)
3. Liao, Y., Xu, H., Huang, S.X., Taishuo, and Hu, Z. "Modeling of fluid-structure interaction to enhance battery thermal management in electric vehicles". pages 14–29 (2023)
4. Koshizuka, S. and Oka, Y. "Moving-particle semi-implicit method for fragmentation of incompressible fluid". *Nuclear Science and Engineering*, 123(3):421–434 (1996)
5. MÜCK, B., GÜNTHER, C., MÜLLER, U., and BÜHLER, L. "Three-dimensional mhd flows in rectangular ducts with internal obstacles". *Journal of Fluid Mechanics*, 418:265–295 (2000)
6. Blackstock, D.T. *Fundamentals of physical acoustics / David T. Blackstock.* Wiley (2000)

7. Shi, S., Wang, J., Liu, K., Jin, G., and Xiao, B. "Vibro-acoustic modelling of the box structural–acoustic coupling system". *Results in Physics*, 31:104915 (2021)
8. Pan, J. and Bies, D.A. "The effect of fluid–structural coupling on sound waves in an enclosure—Theoretical part". *The Journal of the Acoustical Society of America*, 87(2):691–707 (1990)
9. Sarıgül, A.S. and Karagözlü, E. "Vibro-acoustic coupling in composite plate-cavity systems". *Journal of Vibration and Control*, 24(11):2274–2283 (2018)
10. Felippa, C. and Park, K. "Staggered transient analysis procedures for coupled mechanical systems: Formulation," *Computer Methods in Applied Mechanics and Engineering*, 24:61–111 (1980)
11. Tallec, P.L., Gerbeau, J.F., Hauret, P., and Vidrascu, M. "Fluid structure interaction problems in large deformation,". *Comptes Rendus Mécanique,*, 33:910–922 (2005)
12. Galantai, A. "The theory of newton's method". *Journal of Computational and Applied Mathematics*, 124:25–44 (2000)
13. Heil, M., Hazel, A., and Boyle, J. "Solvers for large-displacement fluid–structure interaction problems: segregated versus monolithic approaches". *Computational Mechanics*, 43:91–101 (2008)
14. Yoon, G., Jensen, J., and Sigmund, O. "Topology optimization of acoustic–structure interaction problems using a mixed finite element formulation". *International Journal for Numerical Methods in Engineering*, 70:1049 – 1075 (2007)
15. Bathe, K. *Finite Element Procedures*. Prentice Hall (2006)
16. Desmet, W. and Vandepitte, D. "Finite element method in acoustics" (1999)
17. Ihlenburg, F. and Babuška, I. "Finite element solution of the helmholtz equation with high wave number part i: The h-version of the fem". *Computers & Mathematics with Applications*, 30(9):9–37 (1995)
18. Prinn, A.G. "A review of finite element methods for room acoustics". *Acoustics*, 5(2):367–395 (2023)
19. Macneal, R.H. *Finite Elements: Their Design and Performance*. DEKKER, 270, Madison Avenue, New York (1994)
20. Amestoy, P., Duff, I., and L'Excellent, J.Y. "Multifrontal parallel distributed symmetric and unsymmetric solvers". *Computer Methods in Applied Mechanics and Engineering*, 184:501–520 (2000)
21. Schenk, O. and Gärtner, K. *PARDISO*. Springer US, Boston, MA (2011)
22. International Organization for Standardization. "Iso 10534-2:2023 - acoustics — determination of acoustic properties in impedance tubes-part 2: Two-microphone technique for normal sound absorption coefficient and normal surface impedance" (2023)
23. Cao, L., Fu, Q., Si, Y., Ding, B., and Yu, J. "Porous materials for sound absorption". *Composites Communications*, 10:25–35 (2018)
24. Falaize, A. and Hélie, T. "Passive modelling of the electrodynamic loudspeaker: from the thiele–small model to nonlinear port-hamiltonian systems". *Acta Acustica*, 4:1 (2020)

Chapter 12
Mechanical Property Characterization of Small Granular Materials with Laser Doppler Vibrometry and Resonant Ultrasound Spectroscopy

Joshua Bartlett, Caleb Fryer, Dr. Pablo Tarazaga, and Dr. TJ Ulrich

Abstract Resonant Ultrasound Spectroscopy (RUS) is a reliable, non-destructive measurement technique used to investigate the elastic properties and internal structure of various specimens. Widely used in the fields of material science, geophysics, and engineering, it is has become an increasingly popular characterization method due to its high precision, sensitivity, and versatility in measuring both single crystal structures and complex composites. Despite its advancements over the last forty years, RUS is still afflicted by challenging sample preparation, insensitivity to small-scale defects and inhomogeneities, and limitations in soft or highly damped materials. While recent efforts have succeeded in resolving some of these issues using finite element models, these versions of RUS are computationally expensive and slow. This study attempts to develop an alternative, efficient approach for RUS by incorporating interferometric detection, allowing for rapid data collection, reduced material preparation, and increased measurement sensitivity. To accomplish this, a series of modal vibration tests are conducted using a laser doppler vibrometer (LDV) and adjustable scanning mirrors. The test specimen is initially placed in contact with a piezoelectric disk within an acoustically dead platform and excited using a series of swept periodic sinusoidal signals. The recorded measurements are then processed to identify the natural frequencies and vibrational modes of the specimen, where a comparison is formulated against an idealized model. Utilizing initially predicted independent elastic constants; the general eigenvalue problem is iteratively solved using the Levenberg-Marquart minimization scheme to determine the elastic tensor of the test specimen. Understanding the mechanical properties of granular materials allows for quantification of its functionality and longevity, and accurate determination of physical changes over time. Additionally, this study addresses the difficulties of enhancing this technique and explores the potential for its application within structural health monitoring and quality control in high efficiency manufacturing.

Keywords Resonant Ultrasound Spectroscopy · Interferometric Detection · Data Collection · Material Preparation

Introduction & Background

Resonant Ultrasound Spectroscopy (RUS) is a frequency analysis technique capable of determining the mechanical properties of a material sample in a non-destructive manner. By utilizing the normal modes or mechanical resonances of a solid, homogeneous object, it is possible to identify the independent elastic constants C_{ij} that corresponds to its unique geometry, anisotropy, and density.

Before running a RUS test, the sample should follow certain assumptions. It should be a homogenous material with an equally distributed density. The sample should also fall under the umbrella of symmetries as the symmetry of a sample influences the number of independent elastic constants. When conducting the experiment, a sample is placed between an actuator and a receiver. Typically, individual piezoelectric transducers are used for each role. However, a laser vibrometer can be used as a receiver. As the natural frequencies of the samples are actuated across a bandwidth, the receiver can calculate the sample's displacement, velocity, or acceleration from the voltage response produced by the laser effected

Joshua Bartlett · Caleb Fryer · Dr. Pablo Tarazaga
Fusion of Analysis, Simulations and Testing Laboratory (FAST), J. Mike Walker '66 Department of Mechanical Engineering, Texas A&M University, College Station, TX, USA
e-mail: jbartlett21@tamu.edu; cifryer@tamu.edu; ptarazaga@tamu.edu

Dr. TJ Ulrich
ALDW Division, Los Alamos National Laboratory, Los Alamos, NM, USA
e-mail: tju@lanl.gov

Brandon Dilworth et al. (eds.), *Topics in Modal Analysis & Parameter Identification I, Vol. 9*, Conference Proceedings of the Society for Experimental Mechanics Series, https://doi.org/10.13052/9788743801542-12

doppler effect. Using this measured response as the dependent variable and the frequency as the independent variable, a Fast Fourier Transform (FFT) can be developed. With the FFT, the modal frequencies can be extracted.

To identify the independent elastic constants of a sample, the factor of error between experimental modal frequencies and theoretical modal frequencies can be calculated through a derivation of the linear elastic Lagrangian energy equation as,

$$L = \int_V (E_k - E_p)\, dV = \int_V \left(\frac{1}{2} \sum_i \rho \omega^2 u_i^2 - \frac{1}{2} \sum_{i,j,k,l} c_{ijkl} \frac{\partial u_i}{\partial x_j} \frac{\partial u_k}{\partial x_l} \right) dV, \tag{1}$$

where the equation takes the integral of the difference between the kinetic energy density, E_k, and the potential energy density, E_p, with respect to the volume of the sample, V. In this case, E_k is determined using the density ρ, angular frequency ω, and i^{th} displacement factor u_i. E_p is determined from the elastic stiffness tensor c_{ijkl} multiplied by partial derivatives of the displacement vectors with respect to their particular Cartesian coordinate, marked by the subscripts i, j, k, and l. After expanding the Lagrangian by using a displacement field, deriving it under stationary conditions, and exploiting symmetries related to the elastic properties, the equation can be simplified into the following eigenvalue matrix equation,

$$\omega^2 \boldsymbol{E} \boldsymbol{a} = \boldsymbol{\Gamma} \boldsymbol{a}, \tag{2}$$

where $\boldsymbol{E}$ is the kinetic term, ω is the frequency, a is the approximate motion, and $\boldsymbol{\Gamma}$ is the elastic energy term. To better understand how this simplification is made, refer to the derivation provided by Visscher et al. [1].

To effectively calculate the theoretical frequencies, the mass, dimensions, symmetry condition, and estimated independent elastic properties must be used to numerically converge to a solution using a set of basis functions (i.e., Rayleigh-Ritz Method). With these, the calculated frequencies, ω_C, can be compared with the experimental frequencies, ω_E, using the residual error equation.

$$F = \sum_{n=1}^{N} w_n (\omega_E - \omega_C)^2 \tag{3}$$

The weighted variable, w_n, is set to one for measured frequencies and zero for missed frequencies. Frequencies that were not captured experimentally can be identified through models or predicted frequencies and should be included if there are experimental frequencies missing inside the measured bandwidth. With the error function, the Levenberg-Marquardt algorithm is used to minimize the factor of error by iteratively adjusting the elastic constants until the predicted frequencies closely match with the experimental frequencies.

Due to RUS's high accuracy and efficiency, it has become particularly useful for identifying the independent elastic constants for advanced or complex materials that cannot be traditionally evaluated through standard destructive methods. However, it does require an initial guess on the independent elastic constants. Additionally, collecting optimal frequency responses requires the sample actuated under free boundary conditions with the assumption that it is symmetric and linearly elastic.

Experimental Design & Experimental Data Collection

Collecting experimental data through RUS requires an impact or frequency sweep to actuate a sample's resonance frequencies. To capture the sample's response, a transducer is typically used. However, based on the work from Adebisi et al. [2], the apparatus for collecting the frequency response of the sample was the VibroFlex QTec laser from Polytec. When developing the experimental setup, there were three major factors that were considered with respect to this laser: the orientation of the laser with respect to the sample, a means of controlling the laser, and designing a suitable sample mount.

For laser-based RUS to work effectively, not only does the laser have to shine on the sample, but the reflection must also be clearly registered by the infrared sensor. For the laser doppler vibrometer to work effectively, the laser should point at a location on the sample that yields the most resonance frequencies while the signal received is still normal to the receiver of the laser [3]. Inspiration was drawn from the work of Beardslee et al. [4] by implementing the use of external controllable mirrors that can redirect the laser orthogonally. This allows the laser to rest at a horizontal orientation while still pointing the beam onto the sample from a vertical orientation. The schematics of the test setup with the laser configuration can be seen in Figure 1. The same could be obtained with a scanning laser vibrometer and a stationary mirror aimed at the sample.

There are two subset configurations to this experimental setup: The data acquisition system and excitation system. The data acquisition system includes a computer that utilizes the Resonance Inspection Techniques and Analysis (RITA©) software which serves as the signal processing system and the means of controlling the conditions for the RUS experiment [5].

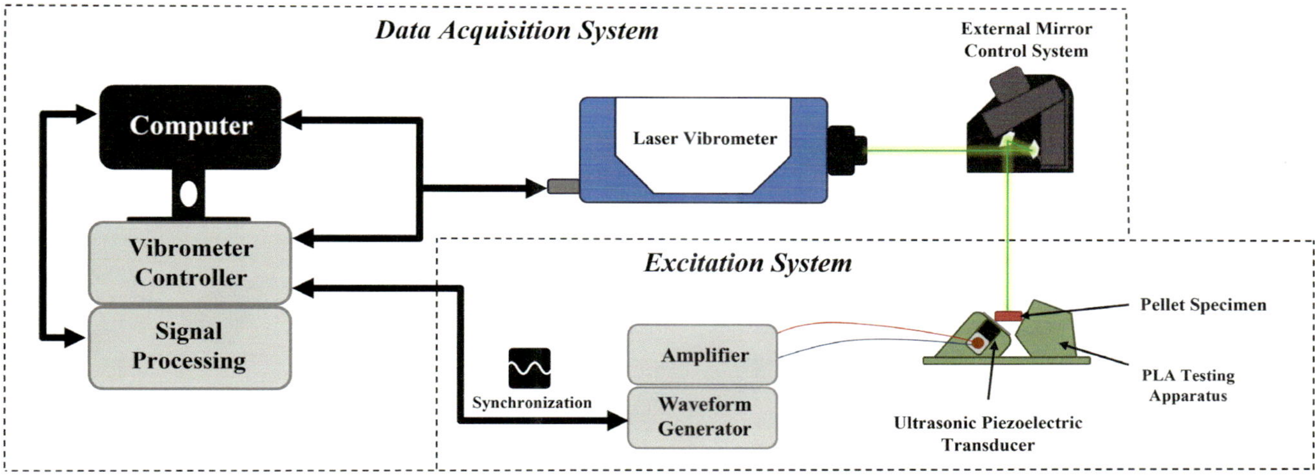

Fig. 1 Diagram of experimental setup for measuring experimental response of a pellet specimen.

From this, a waveform is generated across the desired bandwidth and is amplified by a Tegam high-voltage amplifier, model 2350, with a gain of 50 volts. Granulated aspirin pellets are used as the samples for this experiment and a 1 MHz V103-RM Olympus piezoelectric transducer was used to adequately drive the resonant peaks for the sample's modal responses. This ultrasonic transducer was chosen as the excitation response is flat or vibrationally unresponsive within the measured bandwidth, making it useful for capturing the FRF without interference.

The sample mount was designed specifically for this experiment to hold the sample in an assumed unconstrained boundary condition. There are three contact points with the sample attempting to minimize points of contact on the sample. First is the piezoelectric transducer, the other two are 3D printed fins. As seen in Figure 1, the transducer and fins form a profile like a chuck. The distance between transducer and fin decreases, allowing for samples of various diameters to neatly fit into the sample holder. With this design, samples between 4mm and 13mm diameters fit into the holder while contacting the piezoelectric transducer. For this experiment, samples measured were compressed, finely-granulated aspirin pellets with a diameter of 10.15mm and a thickness of about 2.37mm.

With the help of the external mirror control system the laser can be directed onto any point on the top face of the sample and, with the aid of a python code, it can also be systematically used to quickly scan the surface of a sample. The surface scan can be compiled into a raster image of the operation deflection shape (ODS). This, in turn, can then be used in a modal assurance criteria (MAC) function to confirm the mode shapes of the sample with respect to their resonance frequencies.

Integration of Mode Shape Identification & Automation

The identification of eigenmodes within the analysis of a RUS inversion is not a particularly novel concept. Studies have been conducted to determine the elastic constants of geometrically complex materials with multi-axis scanning [3], incorporate optimal measurement point locations [5], and improve the error minimization function [6, 7]. While these proposed techniques show potential in improving the accuracy and processing time of RUS, they still require manual interpretation by an experimentalist and do not directly attempt to analyze any potential modes that are absent or swapped for a provided test sample. This section presents a new method for systematically identifying and sorting the modes of a material specimen by comparing its operational deflection shapes to numerically approximated resonant modes through the modal assurance criterion.

When conducting a basic experimental measurement using RUS, four standard steps are typically completed to achieve the desired elastic constants: measure the sample behavior to a presented excitation, compute the frequency response function, isolate the natural frequencies, and conduct the RUS inversion algorithm. This process is effective but can only be easily automated for the second and third steps using frequency response function calculators and rational function approximations. Assuming that the experimental design for the system is sufficient to allow for the operational deflection shape to accurately represent the resonant modes (i.e., well separated modes), a new fifth step can be implemented into this process to automate the input parameter for the RUS algorithm. The procedure this identification process would follow is shown in Figure 2.

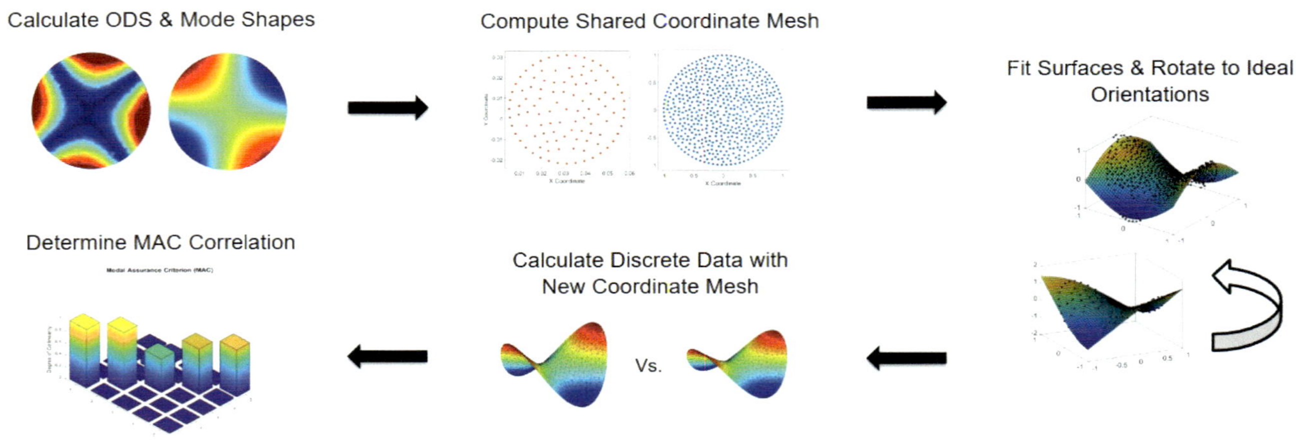

Fig. 2 Representative flowchart of automatic MAC identification process for one natural frequency.

As seen in Figure 2, a fast-scanning raster image of the material specimens' surface was taken for each identified natural frequency. The operational deflection shapes were then computed within the frequency domain and rotated to match the same orientation of an analytically approximated mode shape using the Rayleigh-Ritz numerical method. A new shared discrete mesh was then applied to each surface to produce a common set of discrete positional coordinates. The colinearly of the out-of-plane displacement for each mode was then calculated using the modal assurance criterion function in Equation (4).

$$MAC\left(\{\varphi_E\},\ \{\varphi_A\}\right) = \frac{\left|\{\varphi_E\}^T\{\varphi_A\}\right|^2}{\left(\{\varphi_E\}^T\{\varphi_E\}\right)\left(\{\varphi_A\}^T\{\varphi_A\}\right)}, \tag{4}$$

where this function is a normalized inner product of the surface vectors of the experimental operational deflection shapes, φ_E, and the analytical mode shapes, φ_A, at each common nodal mesh point.

Results & Discussion

The measured material specimen locations produced the average vibrational response seen in Figure 3. Six natural frequencies were identified at 43.7, 69.2, 85.4, 94.6, 121.7, and 129.5 kHz. Note that the fourth natural frequency was determined to be a measured in-plane response and was not included due to concerns about reliability from our experimental design.

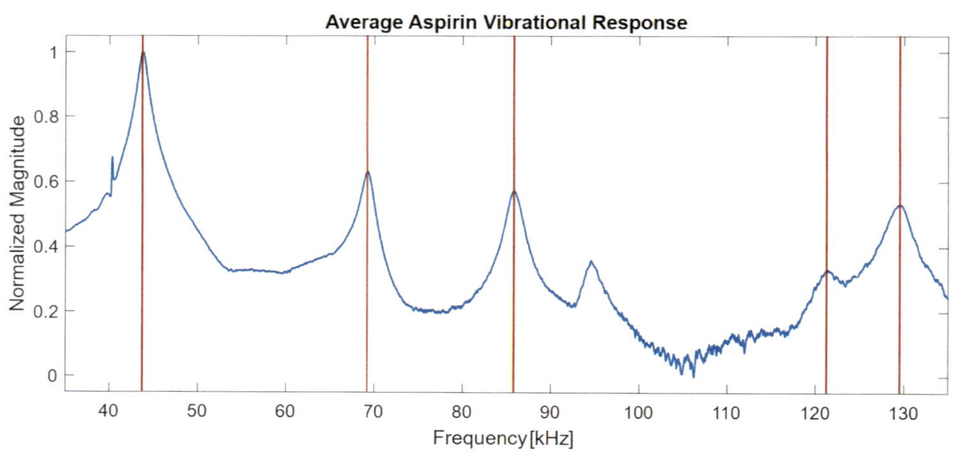

Fig. 3 Frequency response function and first five out-of-plane natural frequencies of aspirin pellets.

Using these values the new modal assurance identification process was conducted, producing Figure 4. The five operational deflection shapes were determined to have a degree of collinearity of 98.2, 87.8, 75.3, 2.4, and 90.1 percent. This correlation was found to be logical as the first, second, third, and fifth natural resonances were well-defined. The fourth operational deflection shape had minimal correlation to its expected mode due to its high degree of coupling. This comparison can be visually confirmed when reviewing the compared operational deflection shapes and analytical modes found within the appendix. Additionally, it was found that no mode swapping was present and that only the second experimental operational deflection shape was non-degenerate.

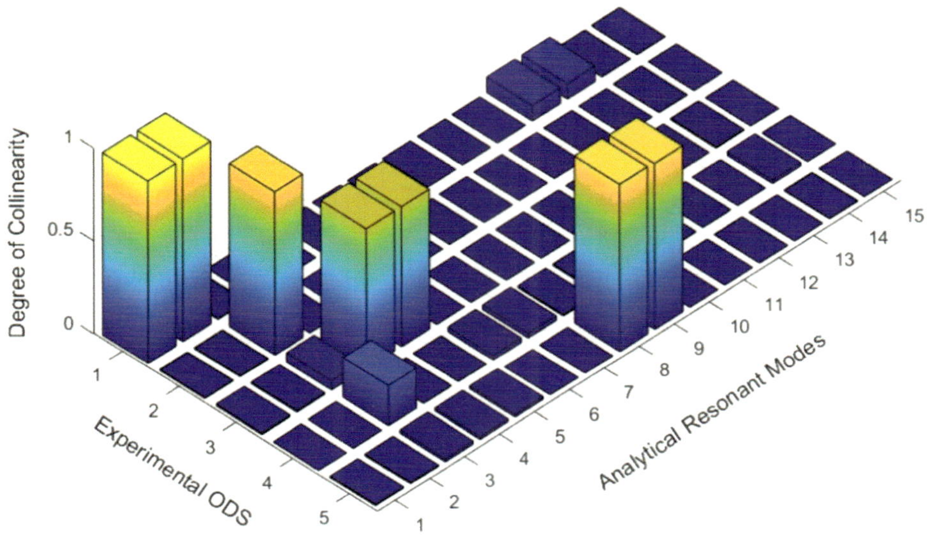

Fig. 4 Bar chart comparison of experimental ODS & numerical modes of aspirin pellets.

Considering these observations, only four measured natural frequencies are reliable for usage within the RUS algorithm. Since the general rule of thumb for RUS states that a total of ten unique modes are required to properly define the elastic tensor solution surface for an isotropic material [8], the elastic properties for this data set cannot reliably be determined. Nevertheless, the proposed identification techinique using modal assurance criterion was successful and shows promise for automating the RUS inversion process.

Challenges and Future Work

Several challenges arose during this research, with one key difficulty being the precise alignment of the laser with the external mirror control unit. Due to the weight of the external mirrors, drooping occurred throughout the experiment and led to the laser doppler vibrometer becoming misaligned. This affected the accuracy of the measurements and introduced error through the introduction of a laser incidence angle. Additionally, material samples composed of a larger granular size proved to be more difficult in scanning during the raster imaging process because of increased surface irregularities and texturing, scattering the reflection of the laser and disrupting the signal quality.

Future work will focus on the further optimization and automation of this process by reducing the total measurement and computational time. Enhancing the precision of the laser alignment with the external mirror control unit and ensuring the measurement efficacy for material samples will be prioritized. There is also potential for the integration of continuous scanning laser doppler vibrometer (CLSDV) or machine learning algorithms to rapidly extract ODS and generate the proper indexing of modes for automated comparison to the model. This will allow for more accurate, generalized surface scanning that is not dependent on specified measurement locations and reduced mathematical complexity when determining the degree of collinearity between the experiment and numerical model. Finally, implementing an optical lens to adjust the laser's incidence angle would allow for the increased recognition of in-plane operational deflection shapes. These advancements would enhance the overall reliability and versatility of the experimental system for future applications.

Conclusions

This research successfully identified the operational deflection shapes of compressed, granular aspirin samples and accurately correlated them with a numerical model, providing a robust validation of the experimental data used with RUS when determining a material's elastic properties. By addressing the issues of mode swapping and missing modes, this study eliminates significant challenges in analyzing the vibrational behavior of a system and the uncertainty of a material specimen's response. Furthermore, the use of modal assurance criterion values creates a more efficient and streamlined workflow, allowing for the automation of the RUS inversion process and reduction of potential errors in manual input. These advancements contribute to a more precise and confident modal analysis as well as improve the reproducibility of a RUS experiment. While this proposed method was demonstrated to be viable for isotropic samples of cylindrical geometry, further development is necessary to successfully obtain enough vibrational information to conduct a RUS inversion for samples of large damping.

Acknowledgments The authors would like to express their gratitude towards Los Alamos National Laboratory for providing the necessary resources and funding that made this research possible. The authors would also like to thank Dr. Paul Geimer for his invaluable technical expertise in operational deflection shape measurement and Dr. Marcia Cooper for her assistance in granular sample preparation and manufacturing. Dr. Tarazaga would like to thank the support of the James J. Cain '51 Faculty Fellowship.

Declaration of Competing Interests The authors have no conflicts to disclose regarding to any known financial interests or personal relationships that could influence this paper.

Data Availability The supporting data to this study is available upon request.

References

1. Visscher, Migliori, Bell, Reinert, "On the Normal Modes of Free Vibration of Inhomogeneous and Anisotropic Elastic Objects.", The Journal of the Acoustical Society of America., vol. 90, pp. 2154-2162, 1991.
2. Adebisi, Lesthaeghe, Cherry, Sathish, Shade, "Development of a LASER-based resonant ultrasound spectroscopy and a framework for error propagation in the estimated elastic moduli," Presented at 44th Annual Review of Progress in Quantitative Nondestructive Evaluation, vol 37, pp. 170002.
3. Beardslee, Shokouhi, and Ulrich, "Optimal Measurement Point Selection for Resonant Ultrasound Spectroscopy of Complex-Shaped Specimens Using Principal Component Analysis," NDT & E International, vol. 141, 2024.
4. Paya, Ulrich, Le Bas, Saleh, Guimaraes, "Quantitative linear and nonlinear resonance inspection techniques and analysis for material characterization: Application to concrete thermal damage". The Journal of the Acoustical Society of America, 136, 537-546, 2014
5. Yamamoto and Sakuda, "Determination of Elastic Constants in Complex-Shaped Materials through Vibration-Mode-Pattern-Matching-Assisted Resonant Ultrasound Spectroscopy.", Journal of Applied Physics, vol. 135, no. 20, 2024.
6. Ogi, Sato, Asada, Hirao, "Complete Mode Identification for Resonance Ultrasound Spectroscopy", The Journal of the Acoustical Society of America, vol, 112, no. 6, pp. 2553-2557, 2002.
7. Reese, Telschow, Lillo, Hurley, "On the Establishment of a Method for Characterization of Material Microstructure through Laser-Based Resonant Ultrasound Spectroscopy.", IEEE Transactions on Ultrasonics, Ferroelectrics, and Frequency Control, vol. 55, no. 4, pp. 770-777, 2008.
8. Migliori, Darling, Baiardo, Freibert, "Resonant Ultrasound Spectroscopy (RUS)", Experimental Methods in the Physical Sciences, vol. 39, pp. 189-220, 2001.

Appendix

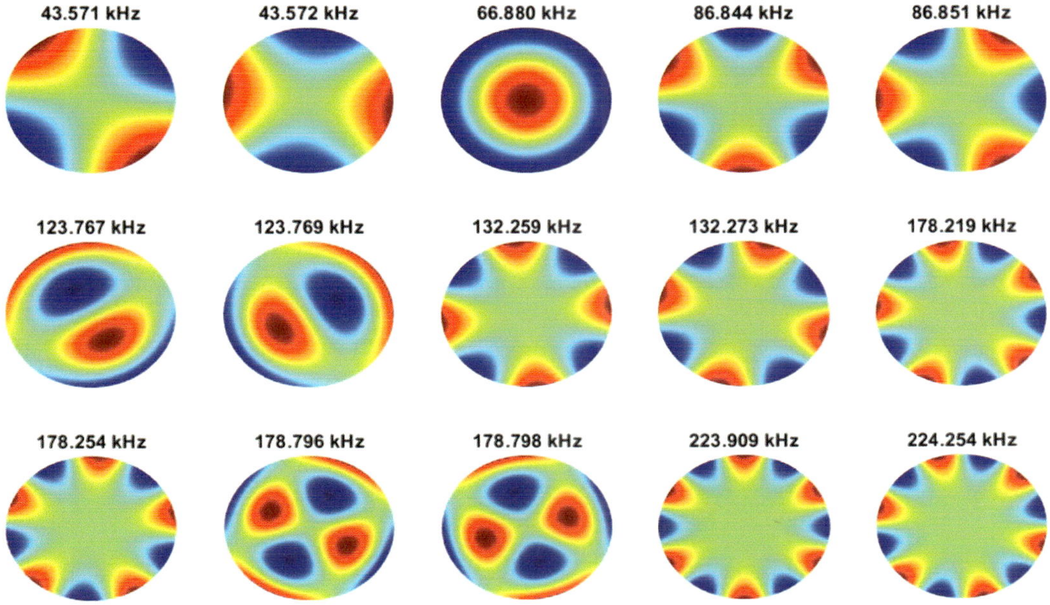

Fig. A First ten out-of-plane analytical modes of aspirin pellets.

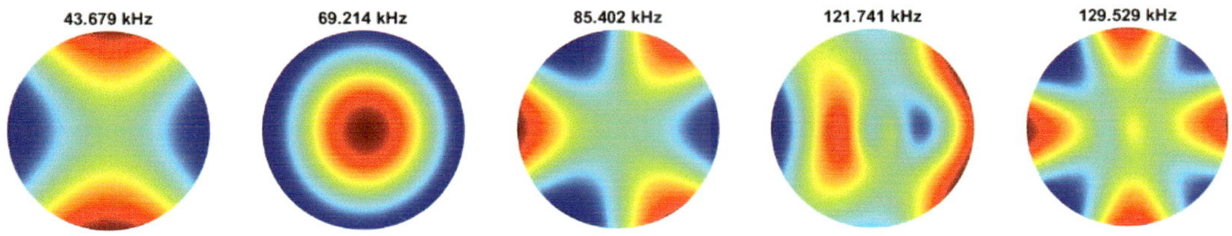

Fig. B Five experimentally measured operational deflection shapes.

Chapter 13
Identification of Dominant Modes for Cavitating Flows using Spectral Proper Orthogonal Decomposition

Grigorios Hatzissawidis, Moritz Sieber, and Peter F. Pelz

Abstract Cavitating flows exhibit complex, chaotic, multimodal, and intermittent behaviour. The dominant flow patterns are often hidden to the naked eye. Classical methods such as Proper Orthogonal Decomposition (POD) or Dynamic Mode Decomposition/Discrete Fourier Transformation (DMD/DFT) often fail to decompose the flow field into physically meaningful modes. To overcome this problem, we apply Spectral Proper Orthogonal Decomposition (SPOD). Using this method, it is possible to continuously shift between POD and DFT by varying a single parameter called filter size which is applied to the correlation matrix between individual snapshots. In this paper, SPOD is applied to high-speed images of cloud cavitation in the top and side view. We demonstrate that by appropriately varying the filter size, it is possible to decompose the data into the physical meaningful dominant modes. The intrinsic feature of SPOD to conduct a transient analysis through the time coefficients facilitates the understanding of the physical mechanisms corresponding to a specific mode. We show how the filter size affects the SPOD results and demonstrate how SPOD provides a more meaningful basis for modal representation of the images than POD and DMD/DFT. We perform a transient analysis to capture the intermittent flow behaviour, characterised by switching between two dominant modes as well as the presence of higher harmonics. Furthermore, extended SPOD (eSPOD) is applied to simultaneously captured pressure data along with the high-speed imaging, providing the correlation between the SPOD time coefficients and the pressure data.

Keywords Modal decomposition · Reduced-order modelling · Fluid mechanics · Cloud cavitation · Image processing

Introduction

Cloud cavitation is among the most severe forms of cavitation, commonly occurring in pumps, ship propellers, and mechanical heart valves [1]. It exhibits periodic behaviour, characterised by: (i) the formation and growth of a cavity sheet until it reaches an asymptotic length, (ii) the triggering of shedding by either re-entrant flow beneath the sheet, [2, 3], or an upstream-propagating condensation shockwave, [3, 4], and (iii) the formation of a cloud that is advected downstream due to the bulk flow. The subsequent collapse of this cloud may result in noise, vibration, erosion, efficiency drop etc.

The fundamental dynamics of cloud cavitation are not always immediately apparent to the naked eye. While it may appear unimodal, exhibiting a single shedding mode with a corresponding frequency, multimodal and intermittent behaviour can also occur, [5–7]. Multiple modes can occur simultaneously or exclusively. To gain deeper insights into the underlying physics, modal analysis tools have become increasingly prevalent in fluid mechanics problems [8]. These methods are typically applied to velocity fields obtained from simulations or Particle Image Velocimetry (PIV). However, in cavitation studies, experimental velocity fields are scarce, and high-speed imaging is more commonly employed. Consequently, modal analysis techniques are often applied to high-speed images to break down the flow field into physically meaningful modes.

Among these techniques, the most widely used are Proper Orthogonal Decomposition (POD), introduced by [9, 10], and Dynamic Mode Decomposition (DMD), introduced by [11]. POD ranks modes based on their variance, which corresponds to the turbulent kinetic energy when the snapshots represent velocity fields. DMD generates modes that are characterised by distinct frequencies and associated growth or decay rates.

Grigorios Hatzissawidis · Peter F. Pelz
Chair of Fluid Systems, Technische Universität Darmstadt, 64287 Darmstadt, Germany
e-mail: grigorios.hatzissawidis@tu-darmstadt.de; peter.pelz@tu-darmstadt.de

Moritz Sieber
Laboratory for Flow Instabilities and Dynamics, Technische Universität Berlin, 10623 Berlin, Germany
e-mail: m.sieber@fdx.de

Brandon Dilworth et al. (eds.), *Topics in Modal Analysis & Parameter Identification I, Vol. 9*, Conference Proceedings of the Society for Experimental Mechanics Series, https://doi.org/10.13052/9788743801542-13

However, these methods have certain limitations: POD modes may not clearly decompose specific underlying physical phenomena, as the dynamics of different modes can be mixed, i.e., the temporal coefficients contain more than one frequency. In contrast, DMD assigns a single frequency to each mode, which does not account for subtle cycle-to-cycle variations. If the frequency undergoes slight changes, the mode shifts to neighbouring frequencies, limiting the method's ability to capture gradual frequency variations. Moreover, determining which modes hold physical significance is challenging, as DMD does not inherently provide a ranking of modes. To address these challenges, Spectral Proper Orthogonal Decomposition (SPOD) is used [12, 13]. This method enables a continuous transition between POD and DFT by applying a filter to the correlation matrix of individual snapshots, thereby providing a more flexible decomposition. The only parameter that requires adjustment is the filter size, which must be carefully selected based on the specifics of the underlying problem. The intrinsic capability of SPOD to perform transient analysis through its time coefficients is crucial for data analysis, as modes in cavitating flows may occur intermittently.

To demonstrate the method, we apply SPOD to high-speed images of cloud cavitation. We extend our study in [13], conducting a more detailed analysis. Specifically, we examine the impact of filter size and illustrate how two distinct physical modes can be decomposed. Following this, a transient analysis is conducted, revealing that the modes occur exclusively and providing evidence of higher harmonics. Finally, we employ extended SPOD (eSPOD), [14, 15], allowing us to correlate data from other sources with the SPOD results.

Experimental overview

Experiments were performed at the water cavitation tunnel at the Technische Universität Darmstadt. The test section has a rectangular cross-sectional area with a height H of $70\,\mathrm{mm}$, a depth b of $25\,\mathrm{mm}$, and a length of $462\,\mathrm{mm}$. The test model is a two-dimensional NACA0015 hydrofoil having a chord length L of $46\,\mathrm{mm}$, positioned along the centreline of the test section and spanning its full depth. A schematic view of the test section is provided in Figure 1. For more details regarding the test rig, we refer to [13]. The data used in this study is the same as in [13]. The operation point is defined with the chord-based Reynolds number, $Re := U_\infty\, L/\nu$, and the cavitation number $\sigma := 2\,(p_\infty - p_\mathrm{v})\,/\,\left(\varrho U_\infty^2\right)$, where U_∞ and p_∞ represents the reference free-stream velocity and pressure and p_v, ϱ and ν denote the fluid's vapour pressure, density and kinematic viscosity, respectively.

The experiment in this study is performed at a fixed Reynolds number of $Re = 8 \times 10^5$, a cavitation number of $\sigma = 2$ and an incidence α of $12°$. This operating point was selected because it exhibits intermittent and multimodal behaviour, making it suitable for the analysis of complex cavitation dynamics. All uncertainties were quantified in accordance with the ISO Guide to the Expression of Uncertainty in Measurement (GUM), [16]. To characterise the inflow, Laser Doppler Velocimetry (LDV) measurements were performed. The flow uniformity was found to deviate by no more than 3% at its maximum, [13]. High-speed imaging was conducted using a dual-camera system, consisting of a Photron FASTCAM NOVA S12 for the top view and an IDT MotionPro Y7 S3 for the side view. Both cameras operated at a frame rate of $18\,\mathrm{kHz}$, with spatial resolutions of $0.078\,\mathrm{mm/px}$ and $0.035\,\mathrm{mm/px}$ using a Carl Zeiss Makro-Planar T* 2/50 mm ZF lens and Carl Zeiss Distagon 1.4/35 mm lens, respectively. Illumination was provided by two triggered Veritas Constellation 120 LED lights and one IDT 19-LED.

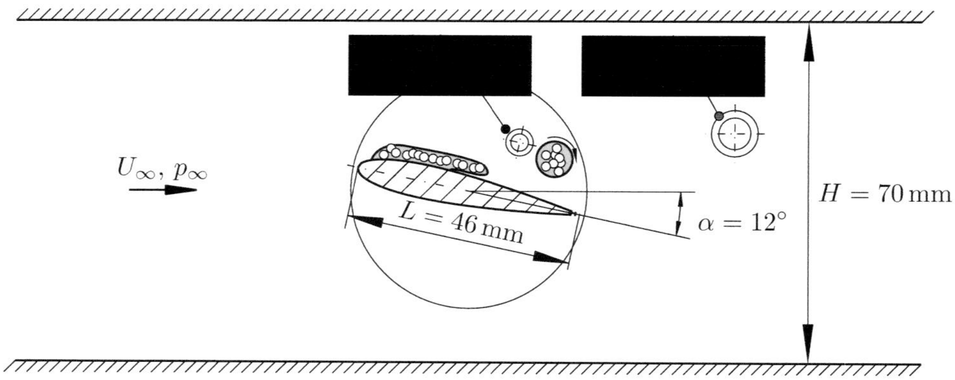

Fig. 1 A schematic representation of the hydrofoil within the test section is shown. The model is a two-dimensional NACA0015 hydrofoil with a chord length of $46\,\mathrm{mm}$ and a span of $25\,\mathrm{mm}$. A cavity sheet forms near the hydrofoil's leading edge and periodically sheds cavitation clouds. The flow direction is from left to right.

Unsteady pressure measurements were simultaneously acquired using two piezoelectric transducers: a Kistler type 601CAB with an eigenfrequency of $215\,\mathrm{kHz}$, and a Kistler type 701A with an eigenfrequency of $70\,\mathrm{kHz}$, both connected to Kistler 5018A single-channel charge amplifiers, cf. Figure 1. The first transducer is flush-mounted $8\,\mathrm{mm}$ downstream and $8\,\mathrm{mm}$ above the rotational axis of the hydrofoil and rotates along with it. The second transducer is flush-mounted $54\,\mathrm{mm}$ downstream and $12\,\mathrm{mm}$ above the rotational axis. The recorded pressure signals are denoted as $\tilde{p}_1(t)$ and $\tilde{p}_2(t)$, respectively.

Modal analysis using SPOD and extended SPOD

Spectral Proper Orthogonal Decomposition, developed by Sieber et al. [12], is applied to the time-varying pixel intensities $I(\mathbf{x}, t)$ of high-speed images to extract the dominant coherent structures in cloud cavitation and their corresponding frequencies as it is conducted in [13]. The following provides a brief overview of the SPOD calculation, while a detailed description of the SPOD algorithm can be found in [12]. The procedure follows the method of snapshots approach [10]. We seperate our data into a mean and fluctuating components, $I(\mathbf{x}, t) = \overline{I}(\mathbf{x}) + I'(\mathbf{x}, t)$ and decompose only the fluctuating part into N SPOD spatial modes $\Psi_i(\mathbf{x})$ and temporal coefficients $b_i(t)$:

$$I'(\mathbf{x}, t) = \sum_{i=1}^{N} b_i(t)\Psi_i(\mathbf{x}), \tag{1}$$

where N is the number of time-resolved snapshots. The core concept of SPOD involves applying a filter to the correlation matrix of the individual snapshots $R_{i,j} = 1/N \langle I'(\mathbf{x}, t_i), I'(\mathbf{x}, t_j)\rangle$. The eigendecomposition of the filtered correlation matrix $\mathbf{S}$ yields the temporal coefficients $\mathbf{b}_i$ and the corresponding mode energies μ_i through the eigenvalue decomposition $\mathbf{S}\mathbf{b}_i = \mu_i \mathbf{b}_i$. To clarify, the mode energies in the case of intensity values do not represent physical energies; rather, they correspond to variances in a more general sense. The spatial modes are obtained by projecting the snapshots onto the temporal coefficients, cf. [12]. Once the modes are identified, it is necessary to establish mode pairs, similar to the sine and cosine components in the Fourier Transform, [13]. This pairing is achieved by evaluating the harmonic correlation between individual modes.

The key parameter of SPOD to be adjusted is the filter size N_f. For no filter or $N_\mathrm{f} = 0$, the method simplifies to the classic POD. When the filter encompasses the entire correlation matrix or $N_\mathrm{f} = N$, we obtain a DFT. While a true DFT corresponds to an infinite filter size, the outcome remains nearly unchanged for $N_\mathrm{f} > N$. The filter size must be tailored to the underlying problem. An appropriate filter size is achieved when the results remain stable and unaffected by variations around the selected filter size.

The primary advantage of SPOD lies in its inherent capability to perform transient analysis using the time coefficients. From the complex time coefficients $\tilde{b}_i(t) = b_j(t) + \mathrm{i}\, b_k(t)$, where the time coefficients j and k constitute mode i and are identified through the harmonic correlation, both amplitude and phase can be extracted, $\tilde{b}_i(t) = |\tilde{b}_i(t)| \exp[\mathrm{i}\, \varphi(t)]$. The derivative of the phase $\partial\varphi(t)/\partial t$ equals the time-resolved angular frequency $\omega(t)$, where the frequency in Hz can be calculated as $f(t) = \omega(t)/(2\pi)$ and the Strouhal number as $St(t) = f(t)\, L/U_\infty$, enabling a detailed frequency-time analysis.

We applied the extended POD (ePOD), once again utilising the time coefficients. Originally introduced by Borée, [14], for classical POD, ePOD can be seamlessly extended to SPOD through the use of its time coefficients, a method referred to as extended SPOD, cf. [15]. eSPOD enables the modal representation of additional quantities that are recorded simultaneously with the decomposed data or snapshots. It is possible to use entire fields, such as pressure fields or intensities of OH*-chemiluminescence, as demonstrated in [15, 17]. In this study, we employ the two unsteady one-dimensional pressure signals from the two piezo-electric transducers, Figure 1. The formulation of eSPOD is analogous to the Pearson correlation coefficient between the ith complex time coefficient $\tilde{b}_i(t)$ and the unsteady pressure signal $\tilde{p}_k(t)$, expressed as

$$r_{\tilde{b}_i(t), \tilde{p}_k(t)} := \frac{1}{N\, \sigma\left[\tilde{b}_i(t)\right] \sigma[\tilde{p}'_k(t)]} \sum_{j=1}^{N} \tilde{b}_i(t_j)\, \tilde{p}'_k(t_j), \tag{2}$$

with $\tilde{p}'_k(t)$ being the fluctuating part of $\tilde{p}_k(t)$, $k = 1, 2$. The absolute value of the complex Pearson correlation coefficient can range between 0 and 1, indicating no correlation and perfect correlation, respectively.

In the present study, a total of $N = 8001$ high-speed images are used and downscaled to 50% of their original size. A mask is applied to cover the location of the piezoelectric transducer and the hydrofoil in the side view. The image edges are handled by applying periodic boundary conditions.

Results & Discussion

The SPOD spectrum for a filter size N_f of 300, corresponding to 3.58 periods of the first mode with $f_1 = 215\,\text{Hz}$ or $St_1 = 0.61$, is shown Figure 2. The Power Spectral Density (PSD) calculated using the Welch method, [18], of the unsteady pressure signals $\tilde{p}_1$ and $\tilde{p}_2$, is also included in the same spectrogram for comparison. The two peaks extracted from these signals are indicated by vertical dotted lines in the spectrogram, corresponding to $St_1 = 0.61$, $St_2 = 0.14$ or $f_1 = 215\,\text{Hz}$, $f_2 = 50\,\text{Hz}$. The first two modes identified by the SPOD correspond to these two frequency peaks. The blade pass frequency of the main pump is also represented as a vertical line in the spectrogram. The SPOD spectrum from the high-speed images does not reveal any modes at this frequency, indicating that no fluctuations at the blade-pass frequency are influencing the cavitation behaviour.

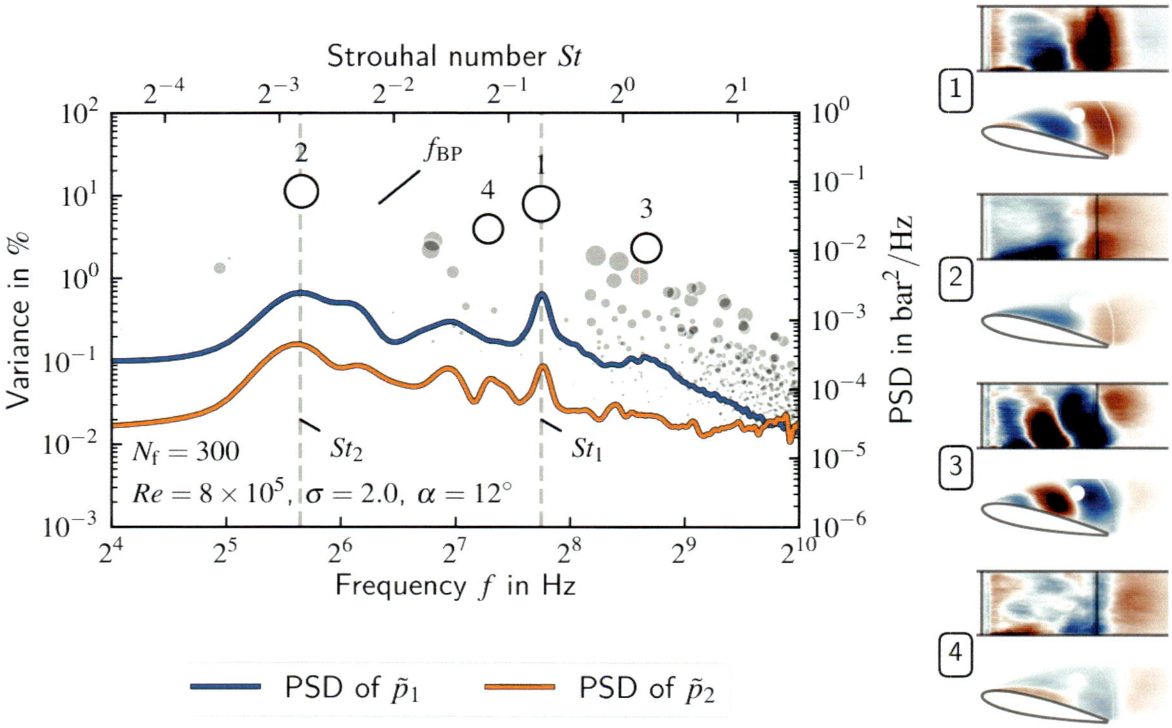

Fig. 2 SPOD spectrum for a filter size of $N_f = 300$. The modes are organized according to their harmonic correlation, which is visually represented by the size of the dots. The first four modes are highlighted. The frequencies St_1 and St_2, corresponding to the two dominant peaks extracted from the piezoelectric transducer, align with the first two dominant modes identified by SPOD. At the right-hand side, the real part of the first four spatial modes in the side and top view are plotted.

At the right-hand side, the real parts of the four spatial modes Ψ_i are plotted. Mode 1 has a slightly smaller wavelength in the flow direction than mode 2. These modes correspond to the periodic cloud cavitation occurring at higher and lower frequencies, respectively. Mode 3 has a smaller wavelength than Modes 1 and 2 and approximately double the frequency of Mode 1, with $f_3 = 406\,\text{Hz}$ or $St_3 = 1.15$. It contains components of higher harmonics of Mode 1, as will be shown later. It is not obvious which physical, coherent structure mode 3 corresponds to, although this frequency is prominent in the PSD of $\tilde{p}_2$, while it is absent in $\tilde{p}_1$.

The influence of the filter size on the identification of the dominant modes is shown, Figure 3. The horizontal lines for St_1 and St_2 are the frequencies extracted from the PSD from pressure signals $\tilde{p}_1$ and $\tilde{p}_2$. As the filter size N_f increases, the relative variance (or energy, in the case of a velocity field) decreases, which is denoted by the size of the dot. It is distributed across additional weaker modes, thereby increasing the noise component. An appropriate filter size is one where the decomposition remains stable and does not strongly depend on slight variations in the filter size. We find that a filter size of $N_f = 300$ is suitable, as it captures the dominant features without losing too much variance. This dependency is also discussed in [19]. It is noteworthy that, depending on the filter size, the ordering of the modes – based on harmonic correlation – varies.

It can also be observed that with smaller filter sizes, approaching the behaviour of POD, the mode with the frequency St_1 is not detected. On the other hand, in the extreme case approaching the DFT, the two peaks detected align with St_1 and St_2; however, the other modes become indistinct, and the variance is dispersed into weaker, less significant modes.

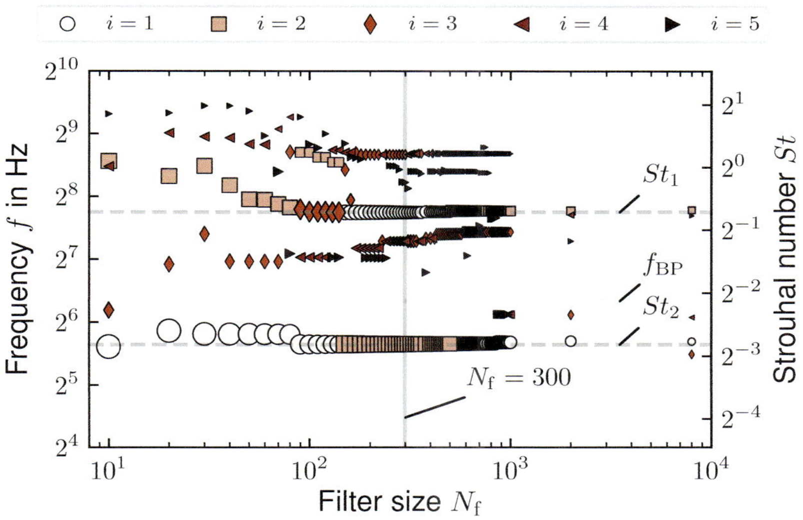

Fig. 3 The frequencies of the identified ith modes are plotted against the filter size N_f. The size of the dots represents the relative variance of the individual modes, decreasing with higher filter size. The vertical line denotes the filter size at 300 which was selected for further analysis. The horizontal lines represent the frequencies extracted from the PSD of the pressure signals. The blade pass frequency is also plotted, demonstrating that no modes are identified at this frequency for any filter size.

This behaviour becomes more evident when examining the PSD of the time coefficients across different filter sizes, cf. Figure 4. For a sensible comparison, we take the modes for each filter size, which corresponds to the frequency St_1 and St_2, respectively. Again, the vertical lines are the frequencies from the peaks of the piezoelectric transducers. Figure 4 (a) illustrates the filter coefficients associated with St_1, while Figure 4 (b) presents those corresponding to St_2. With a filter size of 50, the two modes are not distinctly separated, as evidenced by the two broad peaks around St_1 and St_2. Consequently, the dynamics of these modes become intertwined. As the filter size increases to 400, the peaks become narrower, while the spectral content diminishes at higher frequencies in Figure 4 (b) and at both lower and higher frequencies in Figure 4 (a). An effective approach for selecting the appropriate filter size is to choose the smallest value at which no spectral content from other flow structures is apparent in the spectrum, [20]. For a filter size of 300, this condition is satisfied, keeping in mind that the scale is logarithmic. In the DFT case, with $N_f = 8001$, the peaks are well identified; however, the variance is dispersed across other frequencies, and variations in both frequency and amplitude cannot be detected.

In contrast, SPOD is well-suited for transient analysis. The real and complex components of the time coefficients for modes 1 and 2 are shown in Figure 5. Figure 5 (a) to (d) reveals that the modes are not consistently present over time. Between $t' = 100$ and 140, mode 2 becomes dominant, while mode 1 weakens, indicating that these modes occur exclusively. This variation in amplitude demonstrates that the modes occur intermittently. The Probability Density Function (PDF) of the Strouhal number at the right hand side of Figure 5 (b) and (d) shows the slight modulation in frequency. The corresponding amplitude-weighted mean and standard deviation is also given.

The tendency of the modes 1 and 2 to occur exclusively becomes particularly evident when plotting the real part of the time coefficient of mode 1, $\Re(\tilde{b}_1)$, against the absolute value of the time coefficient of mode 2, $|\tilde{b}_2|$, as shown in Figure 6. When mode 2 is weak, indicated by a low amplitude $|\tilde{b}_2|$, mode 1 exhibits strong fluctuations, as reflected by the real part of the time coefficient $\Re(\tilde{b}_1)$. These fluctuations tend to diminish as $|\tilde{b}_2|$ increases.

We now analyse the correlation between mode 1 and mode 3. Given that the latter has approximately half the wavelength, as shown in Figure 2, and exhibits twice the frequency, with $St_1 = 0.61$ and $St_3 = 1.15$, this suggests that mode 3 could be a harmonic of mode 1. The Lissajous figure, real part of the time coefficient $\tilde{b}_1$ against the real part of the time coefficient $\tilde{b}_3$, exhibit an eight-shape, indicating that there is a phase relation between mode 1 and 3, see Figure 7 (b). However, without the red averaged curve over the cycles, this relationship would not be immediately apparent to the unaided eye. For completeness, the real and imaginary parts of $\tilde{b}_1$ are plotted to illustrate the shrinking and growing cycles, highlighting the intermittent behaviour of mode 1, see Figure 7 (a).

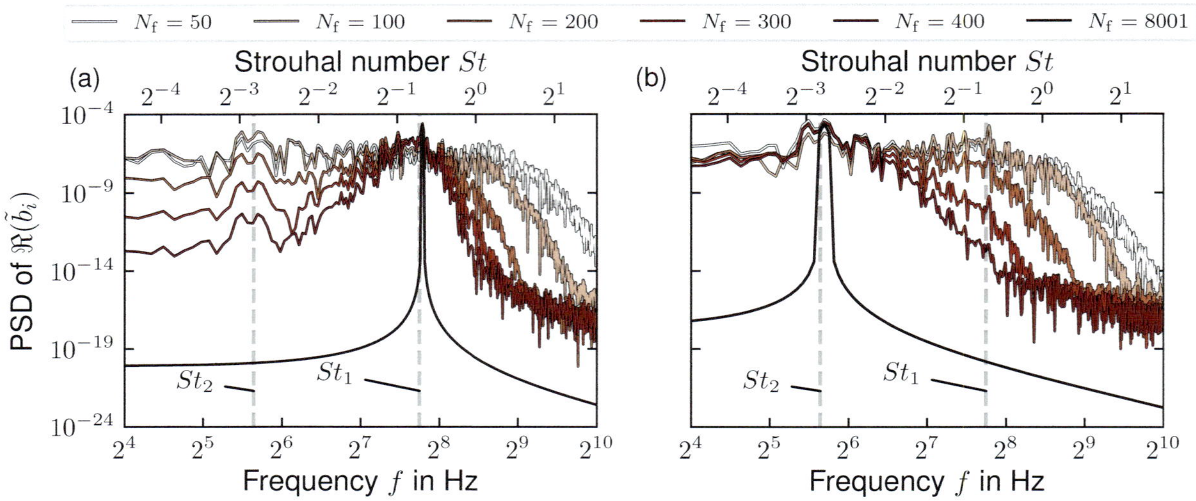

Fig. 4 The PSD of the real part of the time coefficients for varying filter size. For a sensible comparison, the modes corresponding to St_1 and St_2 from the piezoelectric transducers are taken, since the order of the modes for varying filter sizes changes.

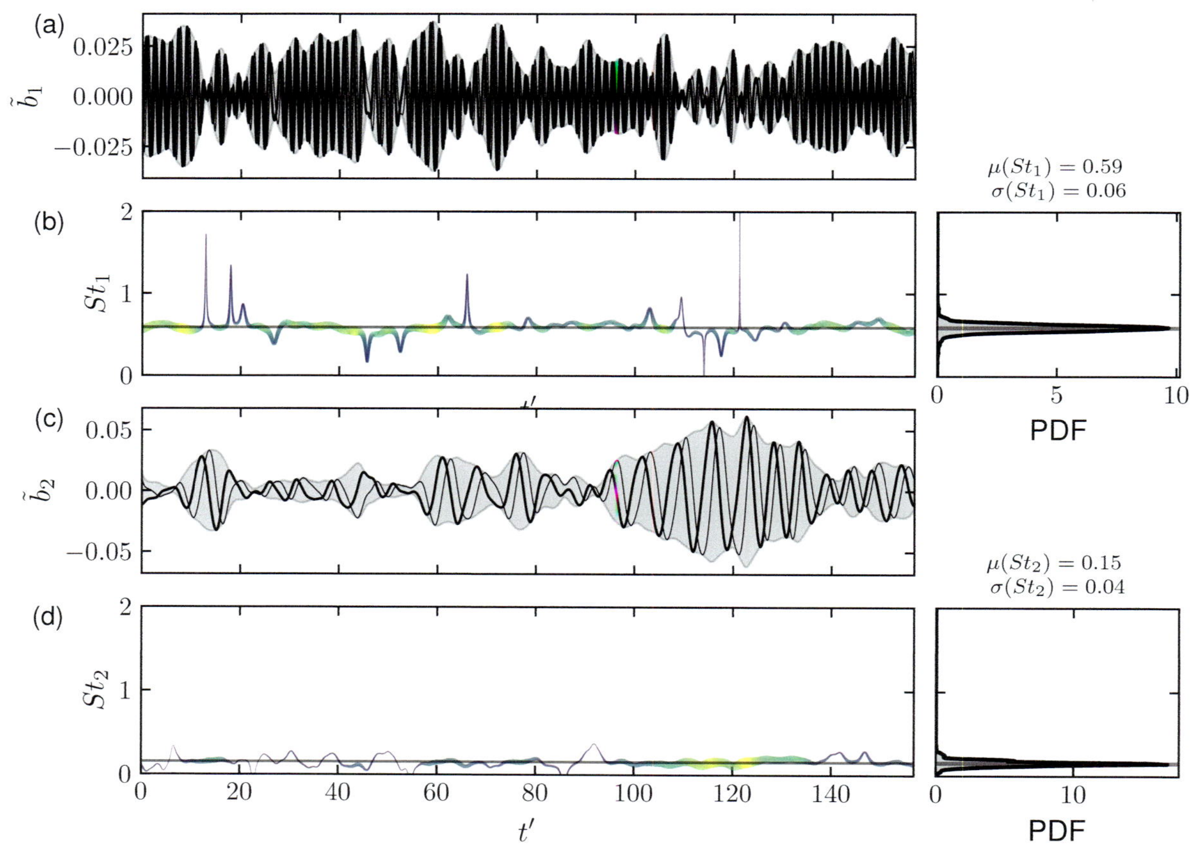

Fig. 5 (a) and (c) Complex time coefficients for mode 1 and 2 for a filter size of $N_f = 300$ and (b) and (d) the Strouhal numbers for mode 1 and 2 over time calculated from the complex time coefficients, respectively. The colourmap indicates the absolute value or the amplitude. The grey-filled area is the envelope of the real and complex part of the time coefficient, which equals the amplitude. The Probability Density Function (PDF) is calculated from the time-varying Strouhal number. $\mu(St_i)$ and $\sigma(St_i)$ are the weighted mean and the weighted standard deviation, respectively.

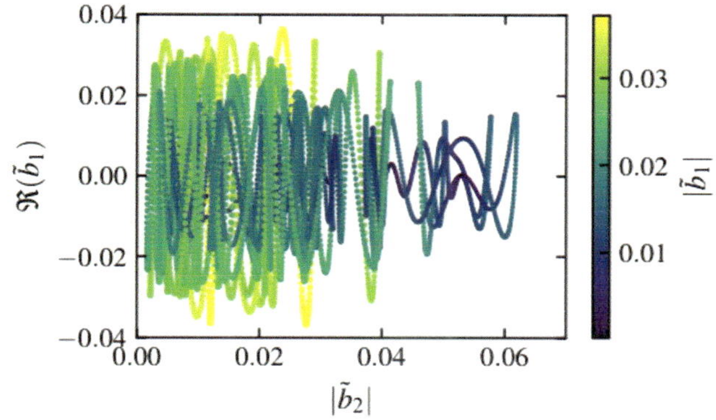

Fig. 6 The real part of the time coefficient of mode 1, $\Re(\tilde{b}_1)$, plotted against the absolute value of the time coefficient of mode 2, $|\tilde{b}_2|$, highlights their intermittent behaviour. The colourbar represents the absolute value of $|\tilde{b}_1|$ to enhance visualisation.

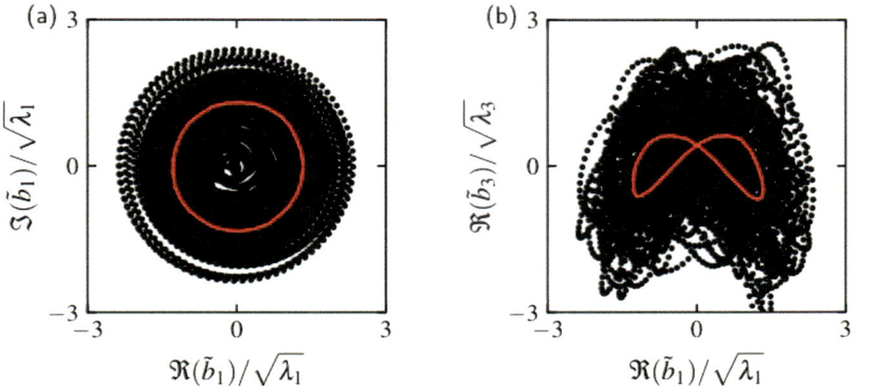

Fig. 7 The Lissajous figure of the real part of the time coefficient $\tilde{b}_1$ for mode 1 is plotted against (a) its imaginary part, and (b) the real part of the time coefficient $\tilde{b}_3$ for mode 3. The time coefficients are normalised by their variance. The red lines are the phase-average over the cycles.

Further analysis following the procedure in [20] confirms that modes 3 is a harmonic of mode 1. We plot the phase angles of mode 1 and mode 3, $\varphi_1 = \arg(\tilde{b}_1)$ and $\varphi_3 = \arg(\tilde{b}_3)$, respectively, against each other in Figure 8 (a), and display the histogram of the phase difference $2\varphi_1 - \varphi_3$ as a density plot in Figure 8 (b). Since these modes are harmonics, the phase angle dots for φ_1 and φ_3 are arranged along three primary diagonals, as seen in Figure 8 (b), and the histogram

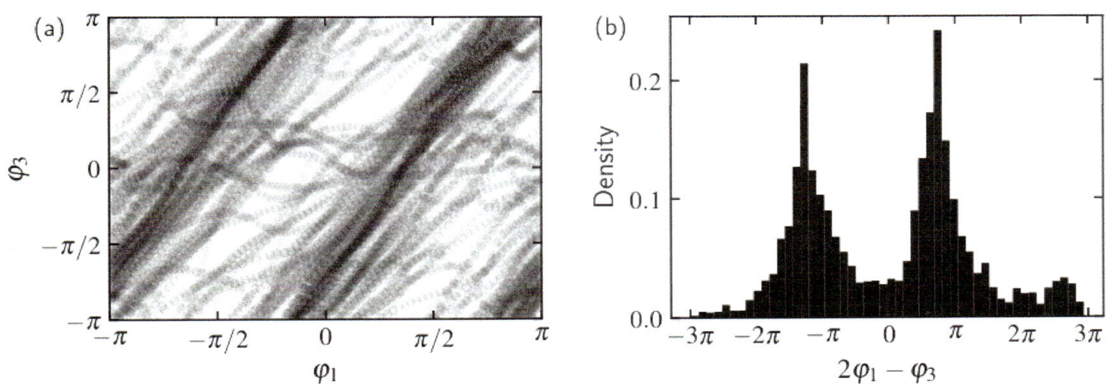

Fig. 8 Correlation between the phase angle of mode 1 and mode 3. (a) Phase angle φ_3 against φ_1, (b) histogram of the phase difference between mode 1 and 3.

exhibits distinct peaks, indicating a clear phase relationship between the two modes. Given that this trend is not consistently observed, it can be concluded that modes 1 and 3 are not perfectly coupled. It is possible that the harmonic lags behind or exhibits an ill-defined phase difference. Due to the highly transient nature of the flow, the coupling between these modes remains weak.

We proceed by applying extended SPOD (eSPOD) using the pressure data from the piezoelectric transducers. The correlation, as defined in eq. (2), between the time coefficients of modes 1 to 10 and $\tilde{p}_1$ and $\tilde{p}_2$ is shown in Figure 9 (a) and Figure 9 (b), respectively. Since the high-speed imaging is conducted at a lower frequency than the pressure measurements, the time coefficients must be upscaled accordingly. The pressure signal $\tilde{p}_1$ shows a stronger correlation with the time coefficient of mode 2, $\tilde{b}_2$, compared to its correlation with $\tilde{p}_2$. To visualise this, we plot the time curve of $\Re(\tilde{b}_2)$ alongside $\tilde{p}_1$, where mode 2 exhibits a strong presence, as indicated by a high amplitude $|\tilde{b}_2|$, specifically in the range $t' = 90$ to 150, as shown in Figure 10. The prime symbol $(\cdot)'$ in Figure 10 denotes that a signal $y(t)$ is normalised according to $[y(t)]' = \{y(t) - \mu[y(t)]\}/\sigma[y(t)]$, where μ and σ represent the mean value and standard deviation, respectively. Dividing the complex time coefficient of mode 2, $\tilde{b}_2$, by the Pearson correlation coefficient $r_{\tilde{b}_2,\tilde{p}_1}$, yields the phase-shifted time coefficient, as illustrated by the blue line in Figure 10 (a). It becomes evident that the time coefficient closely follows the same trend as the pressure signal.

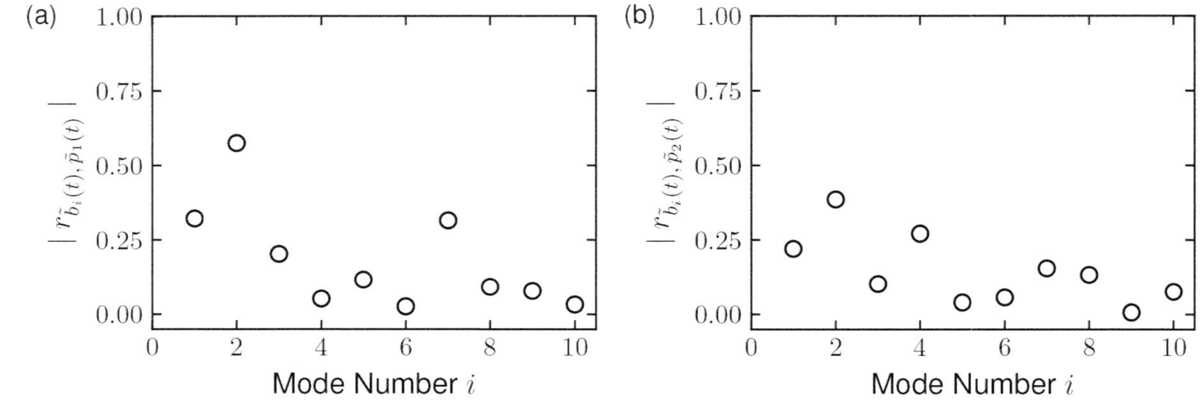

Fig. 9 Results of the eSPOD. The absolute value of Pearson correlation coefficient between the time coefficients and (a) the pressure data $\tilde{p}_1(t)$ and (b) the pressure data $\tilde{p}_2(t)$.

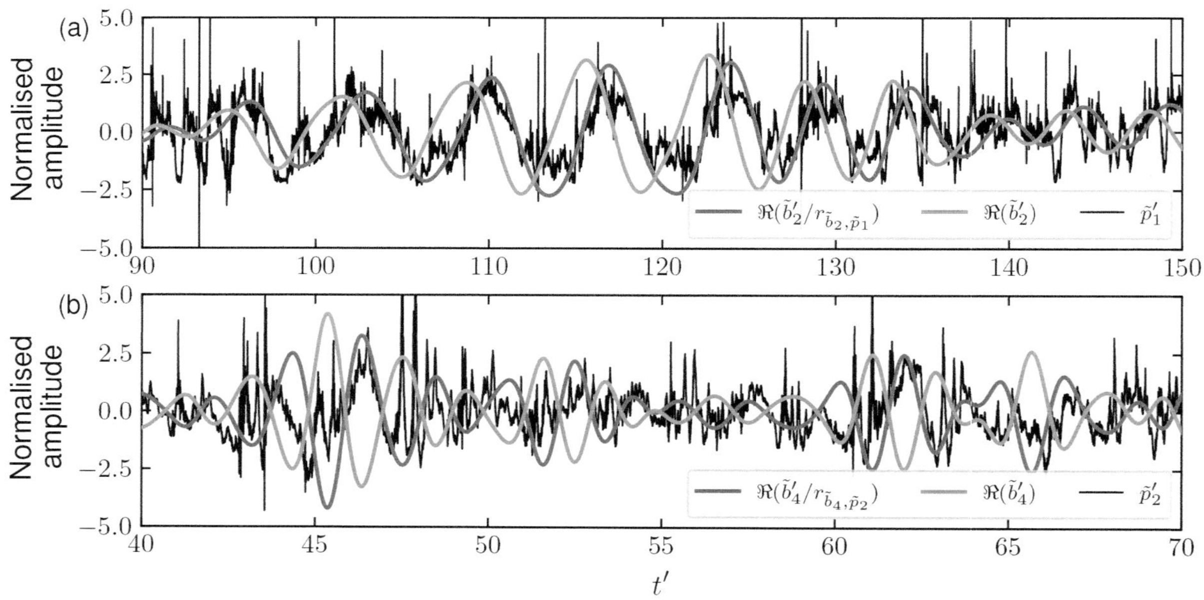

Fig. 10 The pressure signal and the real part of the time coefficient, as well as the phase-shifted time coefficient using Pearson correlation coefficient for (a) mode 2 and $\tilde{p}_1$, and (b) mode 4 and $\tilde{p}_2$. It is evident that the time coefficient follows the trend of the pressure signals.

Applying the same procedure using the time coefficient of mode 4, $\tilde{b}_4$, and $\tilde{p}_2$, we observe that mode 4 follows the trend of $\tilde{p}_2$. However, mode 4 alone is insufficient to fully reconstruct the signal. The results from the eSPOD analysis are consistent with the observations from the SPOD spectrogram and the pressure data's PSD, as shown in Figure 2. The frequency at which mode 4 appears is not evident in $\tilde{p}_1$ but is clearly visible in $\tilde{p}_2$, explaining the stronger correlation of $\tilde{b}_4$ with $\tilde{p}_2$ rather than with $\tilde{p}_1$. It should be noted that the high-frequency components, observed in the pressure signals as peaks and rapid variations, cannot be reconstructed using the time coefficients, as the high-speed data are recorded at a lower sampling frequency. These peaks are caused by condensation shocks occurring during cavitation. However, the low-frequency variations, such as cloud shedding, can still be detected.

Conclusions

Spectral Proper Orthogonal Decomposition was applied to decompose time-resolved high-speed images and identify the dominant coherent spatial structures and their corresponding frequencies. The chosen operating point exhibited intermittent and multi-modal behaviour. SPOD successfully identified the two dominant shedding modes from the high-speed recordings, whereas classical methods like POD and DFT failed. We demonstrated this by varying the filter size, allowing a continuous transition between POD and DFT. Setting the filter size appropriately is crucial, as it requires balancing the loss of variance (or turbulent kinetic energy in the case of velocity data) with the need to effectively decompose individual physical modes.

A key advantage of SPOD is its ability to conduct transient analysis, unlike other methods that require more data to capture the dominant structures. SPOD is particularly well-suited for transient analysis, as it does not demand large datasets but rather requires the inclusion of relevant dynamics. The transient analysis revealed that the two dominant modes, with higher and lower frequencies, $St_1 = 0.61$ and $St_2 = 0.14$, occur exclusively. This was further validated by examining the time coefficients and plotting them against each other. Additionally, a high-frequency mode 3 was identified as a higher harmonic of mode 1 through the use of Lissajous figures and phase analysis.

We further applied extended SPOD to incorporate pressure data from two piezoelectric transducers. This allowed for the modal representation of additional quantities that were recorded simultaneously with the decomposed data, equivalent to the Pearson correlation coefficient. It was evident from the time curves that, when strong correlations exist between the pressure data and the time coefficients, their trends closely follow each other.

Both SPOD and eSPOD provide a robust framework for physically meaningful data decomposition, aiding in the understanding of the underlying physical mechanisms.

Acknowledgments We kindly acknowledge the financial support by the Deutsche Forschungsgemeinschaft (DFG, German Research Foundation) —Project-ID 265191195—Collaborative Research Center 1194 (CRC 1194) "Interaction between Transport and Wetting Processes", project C06. The authors also gratefully acknowledge the support of the Federal Ministry for Economic Affairs and Climate Action (BMWK). The authors also thank Mr Udo Trometer and Mr Andreas Schuler for the technical support and manufacturing of the specimens.

References

1. Lee, H. and Taenaka, Y. "Characteristics of Mechanical Heart Valve Cavitation in a Pneumatic Ventricular Assist Device". *Artificial Organs*, 32(6):453–460 (2008).
2. Pelz, P.F., Keil, T., and Groß, T.F. "The transition from sheet to cloud cavitation". *Journal of Fluid Mechanics*, 817:439–454 (2017).
3. Hatzissawidis, G., Kuhr, M.M., and Pelz, P.F. "The transition from re-entrant flow-driven to shockwave-driven cloud cavitation". *Journal of Fluid Mechanics*, 1004:A13 (2025).
4. Ganesh, H., Mäkiharju, S.A., and Ceccio, S.L. "Bubbly shock propagation as a mechanism of shedding in separated cavitating flows". *Journal of Hydrodynamics, Ser. B*, 29(6):907–916 (2017).
5. Wu, J., Ganesh, H., and Ceccio, S. "Multimodal partial cavity shedding on a two-dimensional hydrofoil and its relation to the presence of bubbly shocks". *Experiments in Fluids*, 60(4):66 (2019).
6. Smith, S.M., Venning, J.A., Pearce, B.W., Young, Y.L., and Brandner, P.A. "The influence of fluid–structure interaction on cloud cavitation about a stiff hydrofoil. Part 1.". *Journal of Fluid Mechanics*, 896:A1 (2020).
7. Venning, J.A., Pearce, B.W., and Brandner, P.A. "Nucleation effects on cloud cavitation about a hydrofoil". *Journal of Fluid Mechanics*, 947:A1 (2022).
8. Taira, K., Brunton, S.L., Dawson, S.T., Rowley, C.W., Colonius, T., McKeon, B.J., Schmidt, O.T., Gordeyev, S., Theofilis, V., and Ukeiley, L.S. "Modal analysis of fluid flows: An overview". *AIAA Journal*, 55(12):4013–4041 (2017).
9. Lumley, J.L. *Stochastic Tools in Turbulence*. Academic Press (1970).
10. Sirovich, L. "Turbulence and the dynamics of coherent structures. I. Coherent structures". *Quarterly of Applied Mathematics*, 45(3):561–571 (1987).

11. Schmid, P.J. "Dynamic mode decomposition of numerical and experimental data". *Journal of Fluid Mechanics*, 656:5–28 (2010).
12. Sieber, M., Paschereit, C.O., and Oberleithner, K. "Spectral proper orthogonal decomposition". *Journal of Fluid Mechanics*, 792:798–828 (2016).
13. Hatzissawidis, G., Sieber, M., Oberleithner, K., and Pelz, P.F. "Data-driven spatiotemporal analysis of cloud cavitation by means of spectral proper orthogonal decomposition". *Experiments in Fluids*, 66(5):104 (2025).
14. Borée, J. "Extended proper orthogonal decomposition: A tool to analyse correlated events in turbulent flows". *Experiments in Fluids*, 35(2):188–192 (2003).
15. Sieber, M., Paschereit, C.O., and Oberleithner, K. "Advanced Identification of Coherent Structures in Swirl-Stabilized Combustors". *Journal of Engineering for Gas Turbines and Power*, 139(2):021503 (2017).
16. International Organization for Standardization. "ISO/IEC Guide 98-3:2008: Uncertainty of measurement – Part 3: Guide to the expression of uncertainty in measurement (GUM:1995)" (2008).
17. Verdoya, J., Dellacasagrande, M., Lengani, D., Simoni, D., and Ubaldi, M. "Inspection of structures interaction in laminar separation bubbles with extended proper orthogonal decomposition applied to multi-plane particle image velocimetry data". *Physics of Fluids*, 33(4):043607 (2021).
18. Welch, P.D. "The Use of Fast Fourier Transform for the Estimation of Power Spectra: A Method Based on Time Averaging Over Short, Modified Periodograms". *IEEE Transactions on Audio and Electroacoustics*, 15(2):70–73 (1967).
19. Mohammadi, A., Morton, C., and Martinuzzi, R.J. "Benefits of FIR-based spectral proper orthogonal decomposition in separation of flow dynamics in the wake of a cantilevered square cylinder". *International Journal of Heat and Fluid Flow*, 104:109224 (2023).
20. Vanierschot, M., Muller, J.S., Sieber, M., Percin, M., Van Oudheusden, B.W., and Oberleithner, K. "Single- and double-helix vortex breakdown as two dominant global modes in turbulent swirling jet flow". *Journal of Fluid Mechanics*, 883:A31 (2020).

Chapter 14
Crack Detection and Localization in Thermoelectric Wafers using Vibroacoustic Excitation

Thomas C. Magee, Angel F. Bravo, Sterling B. Rawls, John J. Greenhall, Nicholas A. J. Lieven, Milo G. Prisbrey, and Neel Shah

Abstract Thermoelectric materials convert electrical energy to thermal energy and vice versa via the Peltier and Seebeck effects. These thermoelectric wafers have applications such as radioisotope thermoelectric generators (RTGs) in spacecraft and solid state refrigeration systems. However, thermoelectric wafers are brittle and thus susceptible to microscopic cracking during manufacturing, which compromises the thermoelectric conversion efficiency and the structural integrity of the material in service. Cracks in the wafers are traditionally detected and localized via manual human-inspection (i.e. via microscopy), which is time intensive and prone to human error. Alternatively, acoustic resonance can be employed to detect cracks, which affect the natural resonance modes of the wafer. In these techniques, crack detection involves measuring the vibration amplitude at a single location on the wafer surface across a range of ultrasonic excitation frequencies. High vibration amplitudes corresponding with resonance modes that are dependent on each sample's geometry, and thus change if cracks are present. In this work, we extend the capabilities of previous acoustic resonance techniques to include crack localization capabilities while reducing scan times by identifying and measuring the mode shape for a small number of resonance frequencies. When a crack is present near an antinode of a resonance mode, where the vibration amplitude is maximum, a sharp discontinuity is present in the measured mode. We present a method to automate the crack detection and localization process using image processing methods to detect the discontinuities within the measured modes. We demonstrate the technique experimentally on thermoelectric wafers (N=31), for which we achieve a detection accuracy of 90.3% and localization error of 2.2%. Additionally, the new technique enabled measuring crack length with 17.8% error, compared to manually inspected microscope scans.

Keywords thermoelectric · vibroacoustic · crack · detection · localization · frequency response

Introduction

Thermoelectric materials (TEMs) have wide ranging applications in solid-state electronics. Thermoelectric compounds, such as Bismuth Telluride (Bi_2Te_3), are capable of the interconversion of electrical and thermal energy via the Peltier and Seebeck

Thomas C. Magee
Department of Physics & Astronomy, Department of Aerospace Engineering, Texas A&M University, College Station, TX 77843
e-mail: tmagee@lanl.gov

Angel F. Bravo
Department of Mechanical and Aerospace Engineering, The University of Texas at El Paso, El Paso, TX 79968
e-mail: afbravo@lanl.gov

Sterling B. Rawls
Department of Structural Engineering, University of California San Diego, La Jolla, CA 92093
e-mail: srawls@lanl.gov

John J. Greenhall · Milo G. Prisbrey · Neel Shah
Los Alamos National Laboratory, Los Alamos, NM 87545
e-mail: jgreenhall@lanl.gov; mprisbrey@lanl.gov

Nicholas A. J. Lieven
University of Bristol, Bristol BS8 1TH, UK
e-mail: Nick.Lieven@bristol.ac.uk

Brandon Dilworth et al. (eds.), *Topics in Modal Analysis & Parameter Identification I, Vol. 9*, Conference Proceedings of the Society for Experimental Mechanics Series, https://doi.org/10.13052/9788743801542-14

effects [1]. As a result, thermoelectric wafers are found in numerous applications ranging from microprocessor coolers and medical devices to solid-state refrigeration systems and radioisotope thermoelectric generators (RTGs) in spacecraft [1], [2].

TEMs such as the Bi_2Te_3 samples discussed in this paper are initially manufactured as thin wafers (roughly 0.5mm thick) that are sectioned into smaller constituents to match the scale and operational parameters of different thermoelectric modules. Due to the manufacturing process and intrinsic characteristics of TEMs (especially Bi_2Te_3), the wafers are brittle and are susceptible to cracking. The presence of cracks in TEMs greatly reduces the efficiency of the electrical-thermal interconversion by preventing optimal current and thermal flux across the wafer [1]. However, processing cracked TEMs to the point at which the current and thermal flux can be measured would result in substantial losses in terms of cost and production time. Thus, it is paramount that cracks are detected in TEMs early in the production process so the wafer can be discarded or undamaged sections can be salvaged.

Current state-of-the-art methods for detecting cracks in the wafers include inspection via optical microscopy [3], X-ray micro computed tomography (micro-CT) [4], and single point ultrasound assessment [5], [6]. In optical microscopy examination, each wafer is examined manually in the search of cracks and surface defects. However, it is time intensive and subject to errors due to various lighting conditions and surface defects or variance in operator skill. While advancements have been made in the automation of microscopic examination and analysis [7], the process is still limited in application to thermoelectric wafers due to the aforementioned reasons. X-ray micro-CT is capable of detecting cracks where density of air within the crack is much lower than that of the wafer. It, however, has limited scanning resolution of 50-100 μm, which can result in cracks smaller than this limit being missed. It also requires excessive scanning time (often $>$24 hrs) and expensive equipment [4]. Alternatively, ultrasound has been used to detect microcracks based on changes in the measured frequency response [6], [8]. When cracks are excited, the wafers exhibit Contact Acoustic Nonlinearity (CAN) wherein the vibrations cause the cracks to periodically open and close, resulting in nonlinear artifacts in the measured frequency response.

Frequency response analysis of a single-point ultrasonic excitation can inform whether or not a crack is present in the wafer but cannot localize cracks. To localize the cracks, the vibrational modes must be measured by scanning over the surface of the wafer. This can be achieved by exciting the wafer over a range of frequencies via chirp burst or frequency-sweep. The frequency response across the wafer surface is measured one location at a time using a laser Doppler vibrometer (LDV), which uses either a mechanical stage to scan the wafer or mirrors to adjust the laser position. This results in a measurement of the frequency response across the entire wafer over a range of user-specified frequencies. Scanning times for this process are dependent on the resolution and range for both frequency and spatial dimensions, but tend to be on the order of 1-2 hrs for the measurement parameters necessary to detect cracks in TEM wafers. As a result, crack localization using traditional LDV methods is infeasible for the production rates needed in an industrial manufacturing setting. Greenhall et al. employed the ultrasonic frequency-sweep method with a mechanical stage to detect cracks in thermoelectric wafers [6]. Results from Greenhall's method, which will be referred to as the mechanical scan method for the remainder of this paper, were used to develop the foundations of the presented crack detection and localization technique.

To implement ultrasonic crack detection and localization with reasonable scanning times for production-scale quality control, we present a new scanning method, wherein we use an LDV to perform spatial sweeps over the sample excited at a small number of preselected resonant frequencies. This significantly reduces the amount of time that the LDV needs to measure each point on the wafer. In doing so we are able to scan over wafers in minutes instead of hours or days. Additionally, we have developed an algorithm employing image processing methods to detect and characterize any present cracks with respect to location and size. A more complete description of this scanning technique, along with the methods applied to determine the critical excitation frequencies for each sample and subsequent post processing, is further described in § 2. Results of this novel technique are presented in § 3 and concluding remarks are presented in § 4.

Methods

When a wafer is excited at a resonance frequency, the resonance mode, i.e. vibration pattern of the wafer, can be recorded by measuring the vibrations across the surface of the wafer with a scanning LDV. When a crack is present near an antinode, where the vibration amplitude is maximum, discontinuities are observed in the measured vibrational response at the crack location. This discontinuity can be exploited in image processing to detect and localize cracks. To determine the full length of a propagated crack this technique requires high vibration amplitude at all positions where cracks may be present. To detect cracks throughout the wafer, multiple resonant frequencies must be measured to obtain a variety of mode shapes, so that all areas of the wafer will contain an antinode for at least one resonance mode. This could be completed using previously mentioned ultrasonic methods, which excite a broad range of frequencies, but these incur long measurement times. Additionally, these methods measure responses between resonance frequencies, resulting in extreme datasets of mostly low response. Thus, we present a measurement method that only measures responses at select resonance frequencies, which drastically reduces the required measurement time. This technique builds off of Los Alamos National Lab's Acoustic Steady-State Excitation Spatial Spectroscopy (ASSESS) used for structural health monitoring and thickness estimations in a variety of materials and geometries [9].

This section will describe the setup and execution of the spatial scan process referred to as rapid resonance mode scanning. It will then explain how the chosen excitation frequencies of the wafer are determined via reduced-scan single point ultrasound assessment. With an understanding of how the new experimental data are obtained, this section will then describe the image processing techniques applied to the resonance mode scan data to isolate, detect, and locate any cracks present on each analyzed thermoelectric wafer.

Rapid resonance mode scanning

In rapid resonance mode scanning, a thermoelectric wafer is excited at a single resonance frequency and the LDV scans over a rectangular region extending past the wafer's edges as to measure a single resonance mode shape. For each wafer, we repeat this process at four resonance frequencies, resulting in four resonance mode shapes. An example collection of mode shapes at each frequency is shown in Fig. 2. Here, the four resonance frequencies are selected to ensure that all potential crack locations are sufficiently close to an antinode so that they will be excited by at least one resonance mode, while also keeping the number of excited resonance frequencies low to reduce the scan time (see § 2.2 for details).

From the four resonance mode shapes in Fig. 2, we observe discontinuities in the upper- and lower-left corners, which correspond to known crack locations. We also observe that each frequency used produces different mode shapes through the wafer that highlight cracking in different locations on the wafer. This qualitatively illustrates how ultrasound mode shape imaging enables crack detection and localization (see § 2.3 for details).

Selection of excitation frequencies

Before a wafer's resonance mode shapes are measured, the resonance frequencies are experimentally determined for each sample. The selection of various resonant frequencies ensure that the every location on wafer is sufficiently close to an antinode of at least one resonance mode to ensure detection of cracks anywhere on the wafer. To measure the resonance frequencies of the wafer, we average the frequency response measured over a range of frequencies at three locations along the wafer diagonal, as shown in Fig. 3. Here, we excite the frequency range from 6kHz to 40kHz, which was empirically selected because it was found to contain resonances with antinodes that were sufficiently distributed across the sample geometry.

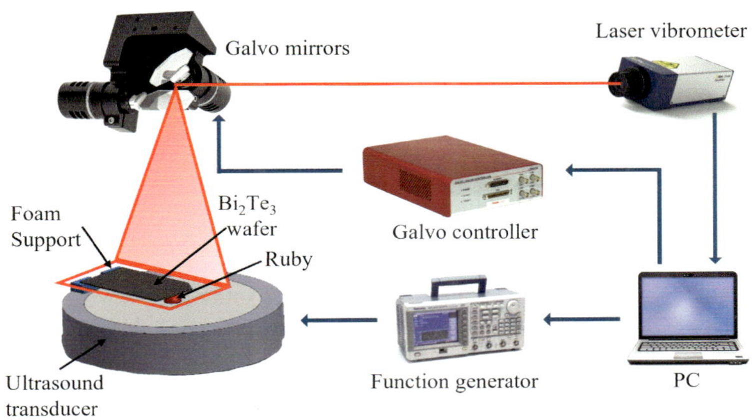

Fig. 1 Schematic of the experimental setup used in the rapid resonance mode scanning technique. A thermoelectric wafer (Bi_2Te_3) is placed in point-contact on an ultrasound transducer, balanced by foam supports. An LDV scans over the wafer surface using a set of galvo mirrors driven by a galvo controller. A function generator is used to excite the transducer at each resonance frequency, one at a time. A single computer controls the instruments and simultaneously records data obtained from the LDV.

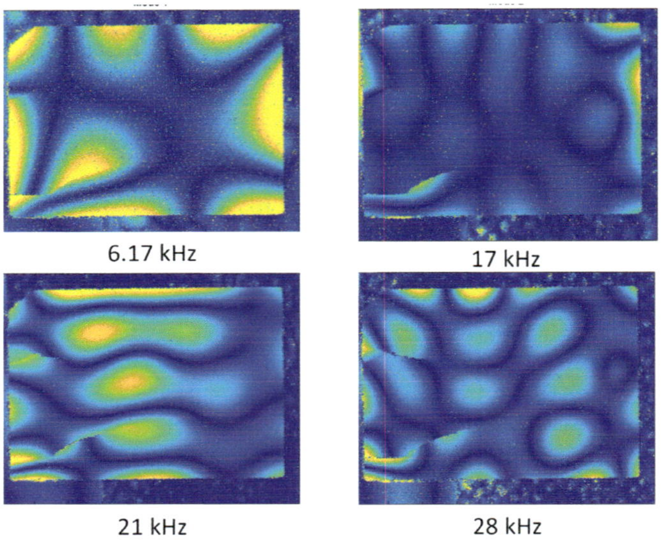

Fig. 2 Sample results of the rapid resonance mode scanning process. LDV scan outputs of a wafer scanned at four distinct resonant frequencies with modulated intensity to normalize the response amplitude. The varied mode shapes are selected to excite the full length of any possible defects in the wafer, which are present in the upper and lower left portions of the sample.

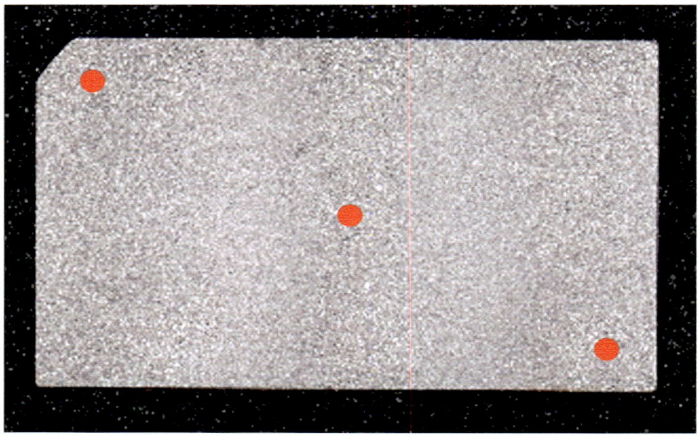

Fig. 3 Microscopic image of a sample with an overlay of 3 point locations along the diagonal. The three points along the diagonal are assessed using the LDV to obtain resonance peaks in an approximate frequency response.

The three measurement locations were selected to accurately measure the true resonance frequencies with a minimal number of measurement locations to reduce the overall measurement time. To determine the specific locations, the frequency spectrum was measured from 6 kHz to 40 kHz across the entire wafer surface for multiple wafers using chirp excitation and mechanical scanning. An example of this scan at a single frequency is shown in Fig. 4, where a cracked wafer is shown at a specific resonance frequency (28kHz). By averaging over all scan locations, we are able to obtain the frequency spectrum for the wafer, as shown in Fig. 5. Averaging is done here to ensure that all resonances are detected, even if they are missed by a measurement at a single location, i.e. if that location contains a resonance mode node. However, averaging over a scan of the entire wafer results in long data collection times (often > 2 hours), which would reduce the applicability of the technique.

To obtain a sufficiently accurate approximation of the mean wafer behavior without scanning the entire wafer, we identify a small number of locations whose average frequency spectrum matches that of the overall wafer spectrum. Previously collected mechanical scans were analyzed to determine which points in the wafer geometry most accurately represent the mean wafer response across the full excitation spectrum. This was done by comparing the frequency response at each location to the total mean wafer response via Mean-Square Error (MSE). The total wafer response was calculated by spatially averaging each pixel's frequency response over the entire sample. The MSE process can be described as

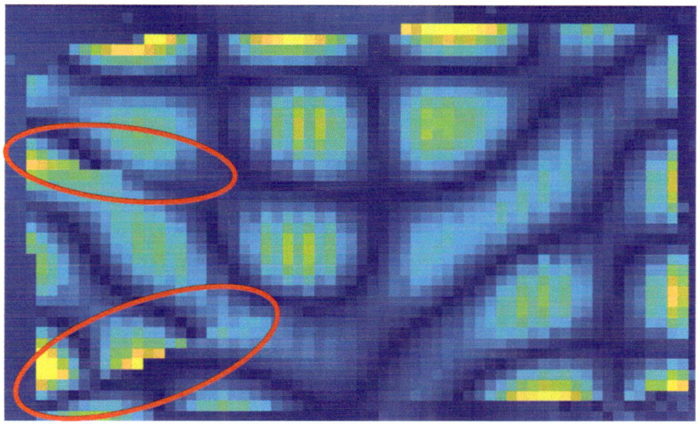

Fig. 4 Example of scan produced from the previous mechanical scanning technique on a cracked wafer at 28kHz. The assessment at the resonant frequency results in greater discontinuities at the edges of the wafer and regions of the cracks near anti-nodes. The presented scan was collected over a period of 2 hours.

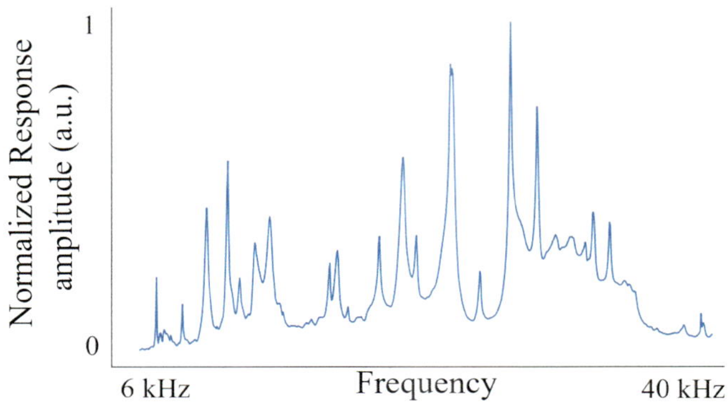

Fig. 5 Normalized frequency response of the full sample scan shown in Fig. 4. The normalization process performs a spatial average of the frequency response while incorporating scan data taken from the ultrasonic transducer below the wafer (on the outer bounds of the scan).

$$\tilde{a} = \frac{1}{N}\sum_{i=1}^{N}(a_i - \bar{a})^2, \tag{1}$$

where $\tilde{a}$ is the MSE, N is the total sample size, a_i is the frequency response at location i, and $\bar{a}$ is the spatially averaged frequency response of the analyzed sample. Equation 1 was applied to frequency responses of 13 previously analyzed wafers. From this analysis it was determined that points along the diagonal of the wafer geometry, presented in Fig. 3, most accurately represented the mean response.

Figure 6 shows an example mean response spectrum (blue) from the entire wafer compared to the combined response (red) from the three locations shown in Fig. 3. We observe that using three measurement locations results in dominant resonance frequencies that are equivalent to those of the entire wafer. From the approximated response using three measurement locations, excitation frequencies for the rapid resonance mode scans can be selected.

We use the mean frequency response to identify the resonance excitation frequencies used to measure the resonance mode shapes. We select resonance frequencies that will produce high vibration amplitudes throughout the wafer to ensure that cracks anywhere on the wafer will be detected. It is known that a response maximum is observed at a resonance frequency, but performing scans at resonance frequencies relatively close to each other (eg. peaks at 28kHz and 29.5kHz) have similar mode shapes and will therefore interrogate the same regions of the wafer. Selection criteria for the specific modes are based on spacing, prominence, and amplitude of the resonance peaks to ensure interrogation along the full length of any present defects.

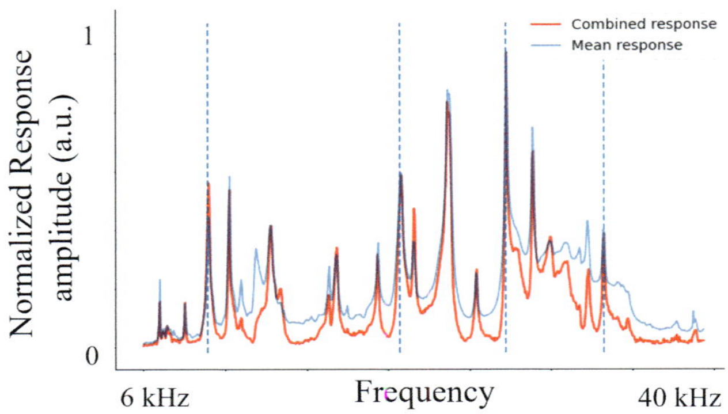

Fig. 6 Normalized frequency response of the full sample (blue) compared to the normalized approximate response from three points along the wafer's diagonal (red). In the approximate response, resonance peak behavior is conserved. Selected excitation frequencies for the rapid resonance mode scan (blue-dashed) are selected under spacing, prominence, and amplitude criteria.

The approximate mean response obtained from the three-point ultrasound assessment is used to select excitation frequencies for rapid resonance mode scanning. The selection of the assessment points used to create the approximate mean response is bolstered by MSE analysis of data collected using the mechanical scanning technique and is used to obtain wafer response characteristics in a fraction of the collection time previously required. The series of rapid resonance mode scans are performed at the selected excitation frequencies and image processing techniques are applied to detect, localize, and measure crack length and location on the resultant composite scan.

Image processing and crack localization

Following the spatial scanning process resulting in the scans presented in Fig. 2, each sample's scans undergo a series of image processing techniques to analyze the wafer and isolate any defects present on the sample. By searching for discontinuities in the samples response amplitude, the edges of the wafer and any cracks are qualitatively observed. An edge detection algorithm is applied to mask the edges of the wafer. This process isolates any defects present within the bounds of the wafer so that the discontinuities due to the edges of the wafer are not classified as cracks later on in the process. After masking the edges and detecting existing cracks on the wafer, the processed image then undergoes a series of quantification measures that automatically locate the centroid of the detected crack and calculate its length.

Prior to applying any form of image processing, a series of quality checks are performed on each of the four mode shape measurements to ensure that no detrimental artifacts are present that would reduce the accuracy of the processed scan. Quality checked scans then go through a series of edge and crack detection processes that enable the isolation, localization and quantification of any cracks.

Scan pre-processing

A common form of artifacting present in non-intrusive ultrasonic assessment with an LDV is classified as "chatter". Chatter can occur in both cracked and uncracked wafers when high excitation amplitudes from the ultrasonic transducer result in intermittent contact between the sample and transducer [6]. When present, chatter results in a high level of noise in the spatial scans and a distinct set of nonlinear response characteristics. When performing the spatial scans, the transducers excitation amplitude was tuned to maximize response amplitude without inducing chatter.

Another form of artifacting that occurred during this scan process was induced by scan speed limitations in the rapid-scan setup. If spatial scans were performed to quickly, horizontal artifacting would present on the resulting scan. The speed induced artifacting caused high response gradients that would be detected as cracks in the detection process and therefore limited the scan speed of the setup.

While there are other forms and causes of scan quality depreciation, those previously mentioned were most commonly addressed in the scanning process. Each recorded spatial scan was manually inspected for quality prior to being sent through the crack detection and localization process. The use of high quality scans in the crack detection process is necessary for accurate detection and localization of sample defects.

Edge detection and masking

Following the pre-processing quality check of the four scans preformed for each sample, an edge detection algorithm is applied to each scan. Based on mode shapes in the response, some of the images emphasize the edge of the wafer while others emphasize the crack present in the sample. This algorithm sums the four scans and returns a composite image with the combination of the modes where we can now see both the edges of the wafer and the cracks, as shown in Fig. 7.

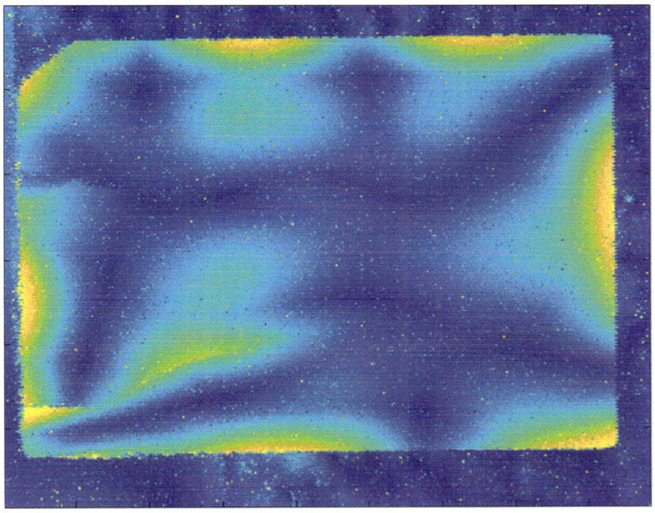

Fig. 7 Combined image of different modes extracted from the tests.

A bilateral filter is then applied to the composite image. The bilateral filter applies a Gaussian blurring to the image while preserving high gradient discontinuities [10]. Presented in Fig. 8, this process reduces any leftover artifacting while preserving the edges of the wafer and any present defects.

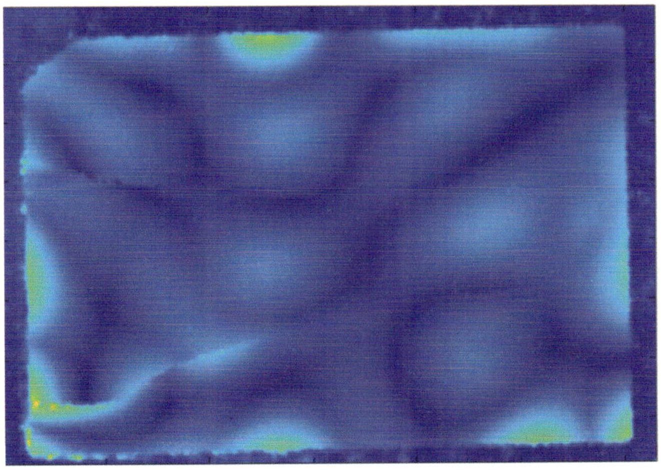

Fig. 8 Combined image with the bilateral filter applied.

A Canny edge detection function is then applied to the filtered image. The edge detection function serves to mark the edges of the wafer by returning a binary image of the high gradient regions of the input image [11]. Gaps were present in the edges of the sample after applying the Canny edge detection function at regions where the scan discontinuity at the edge was below the specified parameter. If the parameter was lowered past a critical value, mode shapes as those shown in Fig. 8 would be detected as edges. To accommodate the gaps left from the Canny edge detection, a convex hull was applied to the binary image.

Convex hull is an image processing technique that connects the outermost points in a binary image to enclose an area of interest [12]. In this specific application, the convex hull is applied to define the geometry bounded by the wafer's edges.

A perimeter detection algorithm is then applied to the binary image produced by the convex hull. This process isolates the outermost pixels of the wafer geometry leaving only the edges of the wafer. The result of the convex hull and perimeter isolation is presented in Fig. 9. This perimeter is then used to mask the edges of the wafer in the crack detection and quantification process.

Fig. 9 Perimeter of the wafer obtained after applying convex hull and perimeter detection to the combined image after bilateral filtering is applied.

Crack detection and quantification

The edge detection and masking process serves to produce a bilateral image that enables the isolation of cracks present on the wafer sample. Before this image can be used, a series of processes need to be applied to the original spatial scans before the cracks can be isolated. The four spatial scans of the sample will each go through the bilateral filtering and Canny edge detection process to emphasize both the edges of the wafer and any present defects [10] [11]. For this process, each of the filtered images will go though the Canny edge detection with varied thresholds. The independent selection of thresholds for the four resonant scans enables the user to select the threshold that best shows the edges and defects on the wafer. Different thresholds will result in different produced crack lengths. Each resonance mode scan is put through the varied threshold edge detection process independently and the four resulting binary images are combined to a single composite that produces a full image of the cracks and edges. The result the composite binary image is shown in Fig. 10.

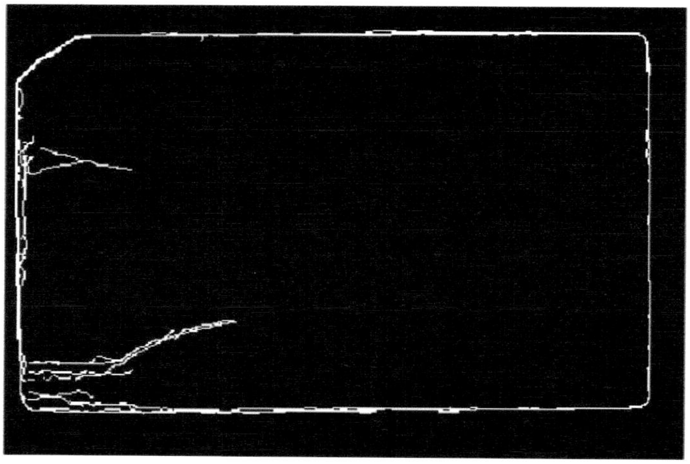

Fig. 10 Composite binary image of a wafer with cracks displaying both wafer edges and cracks present within the bounding geometry. This image is produced by applying Canny edge detection to each resonance mode scan independently and combining the resultant images.

The composite binary image produced from the four mode shape measurements will then have the edges of the wafer masked to isolate the cracks within the bounding geometry. The binary perimeter of the wafer shown in Fig. 9 is subtracted from the composite image of the full wafer. A morphological close function is applied the internal defects of the wafer remaining on the resulting binary image. The morphological close function serves to enclose the fine regions outlined by the bounds of detected cracks, essentially adding mass to their shape in the image [13]. The resulting binary image, depicted in Fig. 11, isolates the cracks and depicts the centroid locations of the detected defects.

With the internal defects of the wafer isolated and weighted in the binary image, the cracks can be quantified in both location and size with respect to the wafer geometry. The centroids are defined at the center of mass for each crack detected by the algorithm. coordinate locations of each centroid are recorded. Crack size is measured by calculating the distance between the end points of each detected crack.

Fig. 11 Binary image of the detected cracks on a sample after the edge masking and morphological filters are applied. The centroids of the detected cracks are calculated and shown as red stars.

By applying this series of image processing filters and techniques, cracks detected on scanned wafer samples are isolated and measured in both location and size. To verify the validity and accuracy of this technique, results are compared to a ground truth of manually assessed microscopic data.

Error quantification

To calculate the error of the algorithm, LDV scans of the new technique were compared to microscope scans for each wafer tested. The automatically detected cracks found in the LDV scans were compared in lenght andlocation to microscope scans that were manually mapped to find each crack and centroid coordinate location. By scaling the dimensions of the high resolution microscope scan to that of the LDV scanning technique, the centroid location determined by the image processing algorithm on the ultrasound can be compared to the centroid location of the scaled microscope scan. Centroid localization error is calculated as the distance between the two centroid locations as a percentage of the wafer length. The calculation of localization error percentage, δr, can be described as

$$\delta r = \frac{|\vec{C}_L - \vec{C}_m|}{L_w} \cdot 100\%, \tag{2}$$

where $\vec{C}_L$ and $\vec{C}_m$ are the centroid locations of the cracks found, and L_w is the measured length of the wafer. Similarly, the percent error associated with the detected crack length can be written as δl described by Eq. 3

$$\delta l = \frac{|\Delta l|}{L_w} \cdot 100\%, \tag{3}$$

where Δl is the difference in scalar length of the cracks from endpoint to end point in comparison to the microscopic assessment.

Results and Discussion

Performing these calculations on 31 scanned samples of Bismuth Telluride wafers, the new scanning technique correctly identified 28 cracked wafers resulting in a 90.3% accuracy. Of the remaining wafers there was 1 false positive and 2 false negatives.

Of the 28 correctly identified wafers, the scanning technique located the centroids of each crack with a 2.2% discrepancy between centroid location detected using traditional microscope scanning. Centroid location error is calculated using Eqn. 2. Furthermore, the scanning technique yielded 17.8% error in detected crack length with respect to analyzed microscope imaging. Crack length error is calculated using Eqn. 3. The new technique was also less susceptible to incorrect characterization caused by surface defects.

The time required to obtain a full response profile of individual samples was recorded at an average 15 minutes per wafer. This time includes the initial setup of the sample and scanning equipment, point scan and resonance frequency determination, and finally the rapid resonance mode scanning at steady state excitation. This scanning time can be further reduced by implementing an automated process to determine the resonant frequencies and input them into the resonance mode scanning algorithm.

Upon further inspection of the scans yielding false negative results, both cracks are observed to exist close to the edge of the wafer (<0.25 mm) and propagate parallel to the edge. It is hypothesized that the processes applied to detect and mask the edge currently limit the accuracy of the algorithm to regions inside the bounds of the masking area.

The methods used to determine the assumed ground truth could also contribute to the 17.8% error in detected crack length. The assessment of wafer samples via composite microscopic imaging is still subject to error by surface defects and user experience. To increase confidence in the ground truth, more robust methods such as the micro-CT can be employed to verify true crack length on chosen samples.

Concluding Remarks

This paper presents a rapid non-intrusive crack detection and localization technique for thermoelectric wafers. The technique builds on recent developments of vibroacoustic excitation for crack detection using a laser Doppler vibrometer to assess vibration responses at various resonant modes. To reduce scan times at increased resolutions, this method employs a galvo mirror controlled LDV beam to perform rapid resonance mode scanning at steady state excitation frequencies. These scanning frequencies are determined by constructing an approximate mean response of each sample by inspecting the frequency response of individual points across the wafer geometry when excited by an ultrasonic chirp signal (6kHz - 40kHz). After performing rapid resonance mode scans at four resonance frequencies selected from the approximate mean response, a series of image processing techniques isolate detected cracks and quantify the location and length with respect to the wafer geometry. While this process can be further developed to increase automation in image processing and scanning frequency selection, this technique has proven to detect and locate cracks with significant accuracy while reducing reliance on more labor intensive and time consuming processes.

References

1. S. Twaha, J. Zhu, Y. Yan, and B. Li, "A comprehensive review of thermoelectric technology: Materials, applications, modelling and performance improvement," pp. 698–726, 11 2016.
2. M. A. Zoui, S. Bentouba, J. G. Stocholm, and M. Bourouis, "A review on thermoelectric generators: Progress and applications," 7 2020.
3. A. Mohan and S. Poobal, "Crack detection using image processing: A critical review and analysis," *Alexandria Engineering Journal*, vol. 57, pp. 787–798, 6 2018.
4. P. J. Schilling, B. P. R. Karedla, A. K. Tatiparthi, M. A. Verges, and P. D. Herrington, "X-ray computed microtomography of internal damage in fiber reinforced polymer matrix composites," *Composites Science and Technology*, vol. 65, pp. 2071–2078, 11 2005.
5. A. Novak, M. Bentahar, V. Tournat, R. E. Guerjouma, and L. Simon, "Nonlinear acoustic characterization of micro-damaged materials through higher harmonic resonance analysis," *NDT and E International*, vol. 45, pp. 1–8, 2012.
6. J. Greenhall, S. Grutzik, A. Graham, D. Sinha, and C. Pantea, "Nonlinear acoustic crack detection in thermoelectric wafers," *Mechanical Systems and Signal Processing*, vol. 139, p. 106598, 2020. [Online]. Available: https://www.sciencedirect.com/science/article/pii/S0888327019308192
7. A. Arena, C. Delle Piane, and J. Sarout, "A new computational approach to cracks quantification from 2d image analysis: Application to micro-cracks description in rocks," *Computers Geosciences*, vol. 66, pp. 106–120, 2014. [Online]. Available: https://www.sciencedirect.com/science/article/pii/S0098300414000107

8. T. H. Lee and K. Y. Jhang, "Experimental investigation of nonlinear acoustic effect at crack," *NDT E International*, vol. 42, no. 8, pp. 757–764, 2009. [Online]. Available: https://www.sciencedirect.com/science/article/pii/S0963869509001169
9. I. T. Cummings, "Acoustic steady-state excitation spatial spectroscopy (assess)," Los Alamos National Laboratory (LANL), Los Alamos, NM (United States), Tech. Rep., 06 2021. [Online]. Available: https://www.osti.gov/biblio/1798098
10. J. T. Sylvain Paris, Pierre Kornprobst and F. Durand, "Bilateral filtering: Theory and applications," *Foundations and Trends in Computer Graphics and Vision*, vol. 4, no. 1, pp. 1–10, 2009. [Online]. Available: https://www.cse.iitd.ac.in/~pkalra/col783-2017/bilateral-filtering.pdf
11. P.-Z. Tian-Shi Liu, Rui-Xiang Liu and S.-W. Pan, "Improved canny algorithm for edge detection of core image," *Open Automation and Control Systems Journal*, vol. 7, 2014. [Online]. Available: https://benthamopen.com/contents/pdf/TOAUTOCJ/TOAUTOCJ-6-426.pdf
12. X. Zhang, Z. Tang, J. Yu, M. Guo, and L. Jiang, "Convex hull properties and algorithms," *Applied Mathematics and Computation*, vol. 216, no. 11, pp. 3209–3218, 2010. [Online]. Available: https://www.sciencedirect.com/science/article/pii/S0096300310004728
13. P. Maragos, "Chapter 13 - morphological filtering," in *The Essential Guide to Image Processing*, A. Bovik, Ed. Boston: Academic Press, 2009, pp. 293–321. [Online]. Available: https://www.sciencedirect.com/science/article/pii/B9780123744579000135

Chapter 15
Investigating Repeatability of Complex Dynamic Structures with Stochastic Joints

Casey Whitworth, Nicholas Pomianek, Enrique Gutierrez-Wing, Trevor Jerome, and J. Gregory McDaniel

Abstract Understanding and modeling the interfacial dynamics of bolted joints has been the subject of many studies in previous years. However, the effects of increasing the number of bolted joints in a structure on its repeatability and variability has been far less explored. This study investigated these effects utilizing two long beams with a varying number of shorter beams joining them together. The cross-sections of all beams were L-shaped. Two structures with varying geometries and numbers of bolted joints were constructed and tested. Each structure was re-assembled and tested three times. To assess repeatability of more than two transfer functions, a Normalized Standard Deviation Metric (NSDM) is proposed and used to quantify the frequency-dependent similarities of multiple transfer functions. Based on this metric, it was found that a structure with twenty joints is more repeatable, and thus more predictable, than a structure with four joints when they are constructed of the same commercially available parts.

Keywords Joint mechanics · Repeatability · Variability

Introduction

The goal of this work is to investigate the relationship between the number of mechanical joints and the repeatability of measurements for multiple assemblies of the same parts. This goal is motivated by previous work [1] showing that measured transfer functions for multiple assemblies of a structure with a single joint exhibit random variations over reasonably large frequency ranges. These stochastic joints defy deterministic models and are thus unpredictable. However, it is possible that the presence of several stochastic joints might make measured transfer functions more repeatable by effectively averaging over the stochastic joints and therefore converging to a mean value.

For a relatively recent introduction to the field of joint mechanics, see [2]. One goal of research in joint mechanics is given in the beginning of [2] as "... the development of a predictive model for the interfacial dissipation and stiffness of a joint." Overviews of research on jointed structures are given in [3] and [4]. The former includes perspectives on the need for research on joint mechanics and presents several challenges. Of these challenges, the present work pursues "advancements in physics for predictive capabilities" and "advancements in numerical and stochastic techniques." Experimental approaches and issues for mechanical joints are discussed extensively in [5]. Future work in this area is explored in [6], including a discussion of the repeatability question pursued in the present work.

Three specific areas of research are of relevance to the present work, so previous work in these areas will now be reviewed. The first of these is the design of test structures used in experiments with the goal of increasing our understanding of joint mechanics. A variety of test structures have been proposed, fabricated, and experimentally studied to understand various phenomena occurring in the dynamic excitation of mechanical joints. Six test structures are presented in [7] . One of them is the Brake Reuß Beam [1], which is a lap joint with square beam members joined by three bolts on the beam axis. Zaman *et alia* [8] also presented test structures composed of beams and plates bolted together. The beam structure consisted of two beams connected by strips running parallel to the beams which were attached with two bolts. These test structures

Casey Whitworth · Nicholas Pomianek · Enrique Gutierrez-Wing · J. Gregory McDaniel
Department of Mechanical Engineering, Boston University, Boston, MA 02215
e-mail: caseyw12@bu.edu; pomianek@bu.edu; esgw@bu.edu; jgm@bu.edu

Trevor Jerome
Naval Surface Warfare Center, Carderock Division, West Bethesda, MD 20817
e-mail: trevor.w.jerome.civ@us.navy.mil

Brandon Dilworth et al. (eds.), *Topics in Modal Analysis & Parameter Identification I, Vol. 9*, Conference Proceedings of the Society for Experimental Mechanics Series, https://doi.org/10.13052/9788743801542-15

feature a smaller numbers of joints. However, the test structures presented in [9] feature a relatively large number of joints. That work was concerned with understanding the damping due to the joints. It concluded that slip between interfaces at the joint does not generally occur within operational excitations of the joint. For a test structure consisting of a chain of beams connected by joints, it was found that damping in the joints was on the same level as material damping.

The second relevant research area is the repeatability of measurements on mechanical joints. Specifically, this area of research is concerned with changes in measured transfer functions if the test structure is disassembled, reassembled, and retested. The primary work in this area is by Brake and Reuß [1]. They presented a comprehensive study of three test structures with identical shapes but varying construction. The first was a monolithic beam with no joints or bolts. The second was a monolithic beam drilled with three holes and having three bolts secured with washers and nuts. The third test structure was composed of two beams connected by a lap joint with three bolts secured with washers and nuts. The bolt holes, bolts, washers, and nuts of the second and third test structures were identically placed. Measurements of transfer functions showed that the first two test systems experienced a great deal of repeatability over a fairly broad frequency range. When the third test structure was disassembled and reassembled, the transfer functions changed considerably. The transfer functions also changed when the order of bolt tightening was changed. Cooper *et alia* [10] investigated the degree to which the far-field properties of the structure affect the joint dynamics. The third and final relevant research area is the comparison of transfer functions to quantify similarity. Although much work has been done on assessing the similarities of two transfer functions [11, 12], it is less clear how to compare an ensemble of more than two transfer functions.

Test Structure

The test structure was constructed by attaching two long beams, each $6\,\mathrm{ft}$ long, to each other using a varying number of 1-foot long beams. All beams used in the structure had the same cross-section and came with arrays of holes for fastening. A schematic of the test structure and test equipment is shown in Figure 3. A photo of the four-joint test structure is shown in Figure 1 and a photo of the twenty-joint structure is shown in Figure 2. Commercially available parts used in the design are listed in Table 1. The test structure was designed using commercially available parts that would typically be used by engineers in construction so that the results could be immediately applicable to engineering practice and the structures could be easily replicated by other researchers at a relatively low cost. The beams, nuts, washers, and bolts were all chosen from a standard catalog of parts without any special machining or surface treatments. The L-shaped cross-section was chosen to introduce complexity. The walls of the L-shaped beams were $0.188\,\mathrm{cm}$ thick. Each test structure used washers between the head of the screw and frame and between the nut and frame. Joints were tightened with an instrumented torque wrench set to a torque of $4\,\mathrm{N}-\mathrm{m}$. The accelerometer used was a PCB Model Y352C66 with a sensitivity of $100\,\mathrm{mv/g}$. The instrumented hammer was Dytran Model 5800B2 with a sensitivity of $98\,\mathrm{mV/lbf}$. The accelerometer was attached to the beam using an adhesive mounting base.

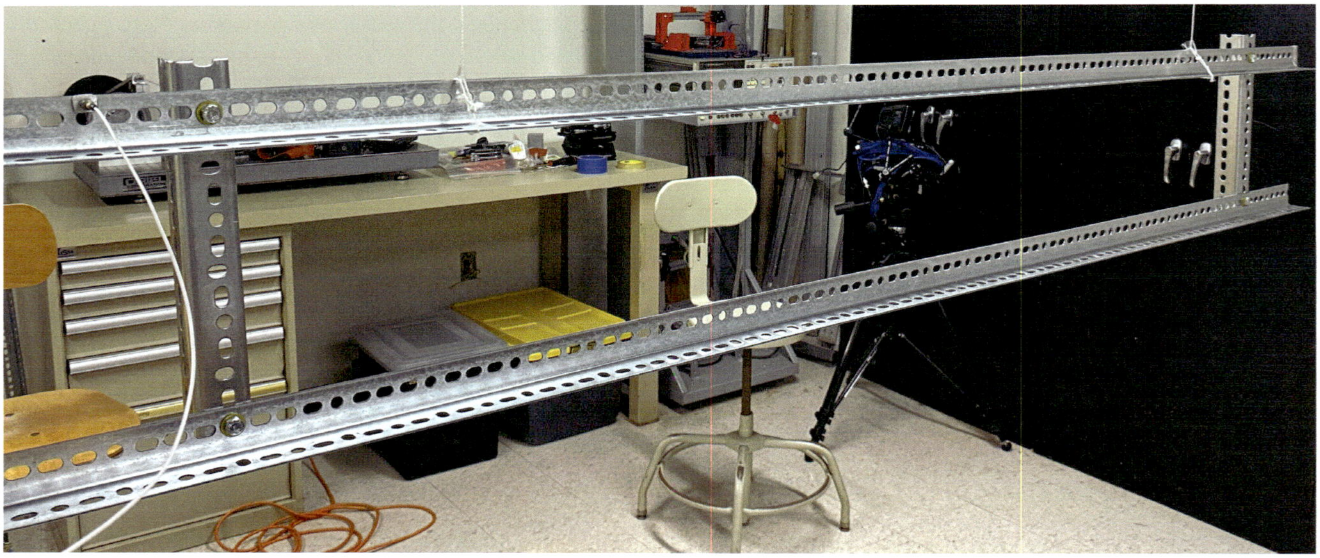

Fig. 1 Photograph of the 4 joint test structure used in this study.

Fig. 2 Photograph of the 20 joint test structure used in this study.

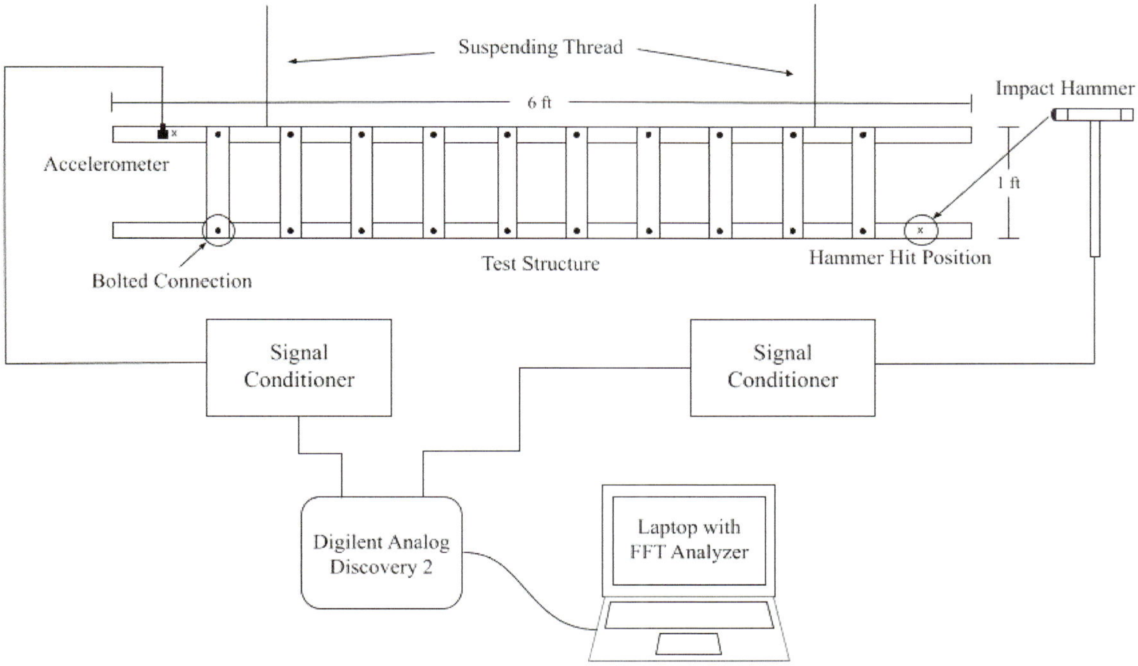

Fig. 3 Schematic of the experiments. The two impact locations marked by the symbol **x** very near the accelerometer.

Table 1 Table of components used to construct test structure

Part	Material	Dimensions
Bolt-Together Framing, L-Shaped Rail	Zinc-Plated Steel	$1 - 1/2$ inches $\times$ $1 - 1/2$ inches $\times$ 6 ft
Bolt-Together Framing, L-Shaped Rail	Zinc-Plated Steel	$1 - 1/2$ inches $\times$ $1 - 1/2$ inches $\times$ 1 ft
Hex Head Screw	Zinc-Plated Steel	$5/16$ inches-18 $\times$ $3/4$ inches
Hex Nut Grade 2	Zinc-Plated Steel	$5/16$ inches-18
Grade 9 Steel Washer	Zinc Yellow-Chromate Plated Steel	$5/16$ inches Screw Size $\times$ 0.703 inches OD

Test Procedure

Vibration tests were conducted as follows:

1. One of the two structures shown in Figures 1 and 2 was chosen.
2. One of the two impact locations shown in Figure 3 was chosen.

3. Five impacts were applied at that location, each impact being near the corner of the L-shaped cross section.
4. A new assembly was obtained by loosening and re-tightening all bolted joints to $4\,\mathrm{N-m}$.
5. Steps 3 and 4 were repeated three times for each structure and each hit location.

Two impact locations were chosen because the resulting accelerances were expected to be affected by different propagation paths of vibration. For the location near the accelerometer, the accelerance was expected to be a strong function of the local dynamics. For the impact location far away from the accelerometer, the accelerance was expected to be a strong function of the very long propagation path through most of the structure. It is understood that the two structures will have different dynamics such as natural frequencies and mode shapes. However, both structures had many natural frequencies that were excited over the frequency range of interest, therefore general conclusions about repeatability are valid as they did not require identical modal properties.

Post Processing

The acceleration and force were measured over a period of $10\,\mathrm{s}$ with a sampling frequency of $12\,\mathrm{kHz}$, which was sufficiently long that the acceleration signal had decayed to the noise floor by the end of the measurement. For each impact, a time window of duration $12\,\mathrm{ms}$ was applied to the measured force with the window centered around the impact. An FFT of the time signals was then applied to yield the frequency-domain acceleration $\tilde{a}(f)$ and force $\tilde{F}(f)$. In what follows, the subscript m shall refer to an assembly (1–3) and the subscript n shall refer to an impact (1–5). Accelerance for assembly m and impact n was computed by

$$A_{mn}(f) = \tilde{a}_{mn}(f)/\tilde{F}_{mn}(f), \tag{1}$$

The average accelerance over all five impacts for assembly m was computed by

$$\alpha_m(f) = \frac{1}{5}\sum_{n=1}^{5} A_{mn}(f). \tag{2}$$

An average over all three assemblies was computed by

$$\mu(f) = \frac{1}{3}\sum_{m=1}^{3} \alpha_m(f). \tag{3}$$

Deviation of the real and imaginary parts from their means was computed by

$$\sigma_r(f) = \sqrt{\frac{1}{3}\sum_{m=1}^{3} \left(\mathrm{Re}\left\{\alpha_m(f)\right\} - \mathrm{Re}\left\{\mu(f)\right\}\right)^2}, \tag{4}$$

$$\sigma_i(f) = \sqrt{\frac{1}{3}\sum_{m=1}^{3} \left(\mathrm{Im}\left\{\alpha_m(f)\right\} - \mathrm{Im}\left\{\mu(f)\right\}\right)^2}. \tag{5}$$

The magnitude of the complex-valued standard deviation was computed as a frequency-dependent assessment of repeatability,

$$\sigma(f) = \sqrt{\sigma_r^2(f) + \sigma_i^2(f)}. \tag{6}$$

Equations (4) and (5) are recognized as the standard deviation formula used in statistics, however those equations were used here for a very different purpose. While it is understood that the standard deviation in statistics requires an appropriately large number of realizations to be meaningful, we only used the formula as a metric of repeatability that increases with less repeatability. It is therefore a suitable metric even when the number of transfer functions is small, such as the three accelerances (for varying assemblies) used here. A mean value μ_0 of the accelerance magnitude was computed over all frequencies and assemblies and used to normalize the standard deviation. The normalized standard deviation (NSDM) is

$$\alpha(f) = \sigma(f)/\mu_0. \tag{7}$$

Results

A central question was whether a sufficient amount of non-repeatability was present in the data to allow for comparisons between the two structures. This question is addressed in Figures 4 – 6, Figure 4 shows five impacts while Figure 5 shows three assemblies. Visual comparison indicates that the repeatability between impacts was greater than the repeatability between assemblies. This observation is confirmed in Figure 6, where two differences in accelerance are plotted. The first accelerance

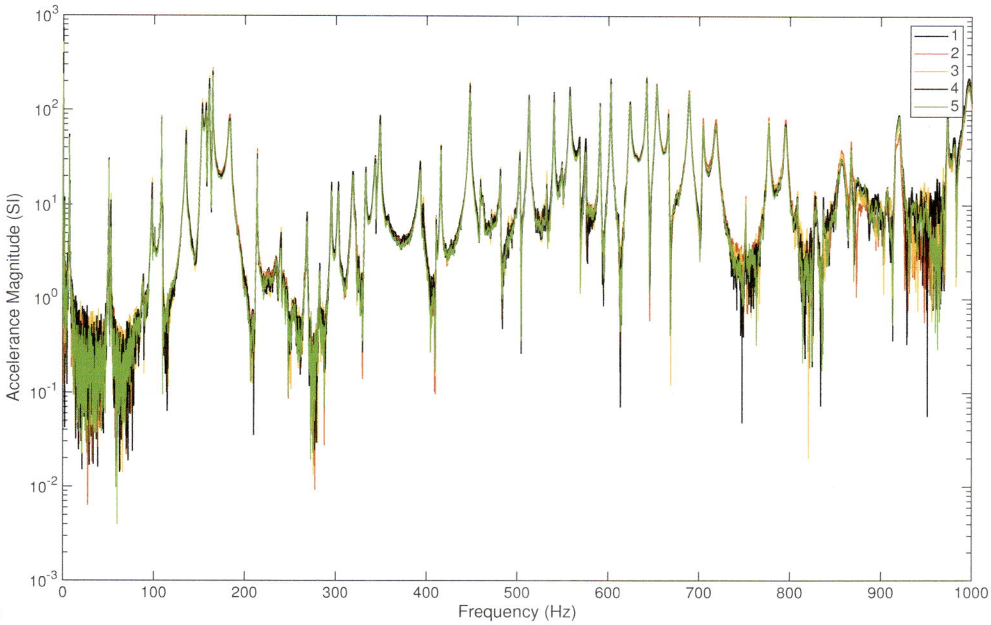

4

Fig. 4 Plots of accelerance for five impacts. The numbers 1-5 denote different impacts. The impacts were at the same spot near the accelerometer for the four-joint structure.

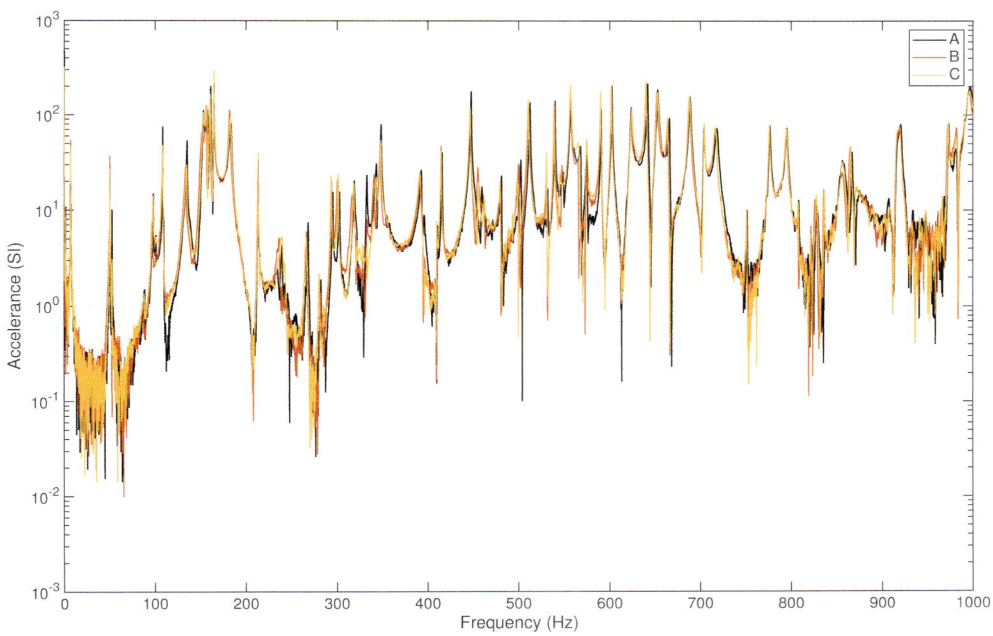

Fig. 5 Plots of accelerance for three different assemblies, where each assembly accelerance has been averaged over five impacts.The letters A, B, and C denote different assemblies. The impacts were at the same spot near the accelerometer for the four-joint structure.

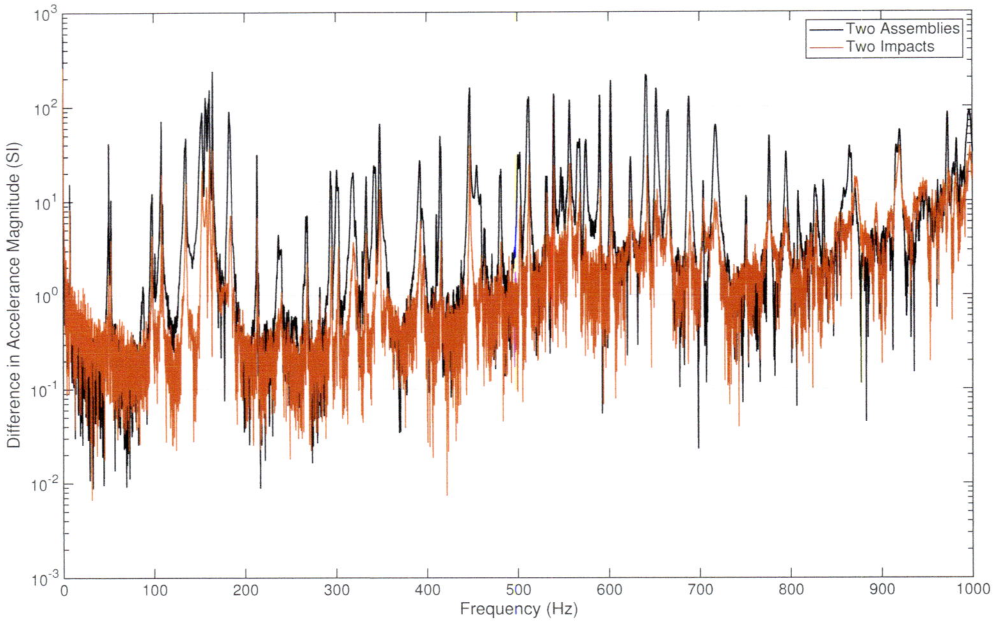

Fig. 6 Plots of the differences between accelerances. The data labeled "Two Assemblies" is the difference between two accelerances measured for two assemblies. The data labeled "Two Impacts" is the difference between two accelerances measured for two impacts. The impacts were at the same spot near the accelerometer for the four-joint structure.

difference is between two assemblies, each averaged over five impacts and the second accelerance difference is between two impacts of the same assembly. It is clear from this figure that that there was significantly more repeatability between impacts than there is between assemblies, thus justifying the use of this data to compare repeatability for the four-joint and 20-joint structures.

Figures 7 and 8 show the normalized standard deviation for the two-joint and four-joint structures. Figure 7 is for the impact near the accelerometer and Figure 8 is for the impact far away from the accelerometer. While there is no clear difference

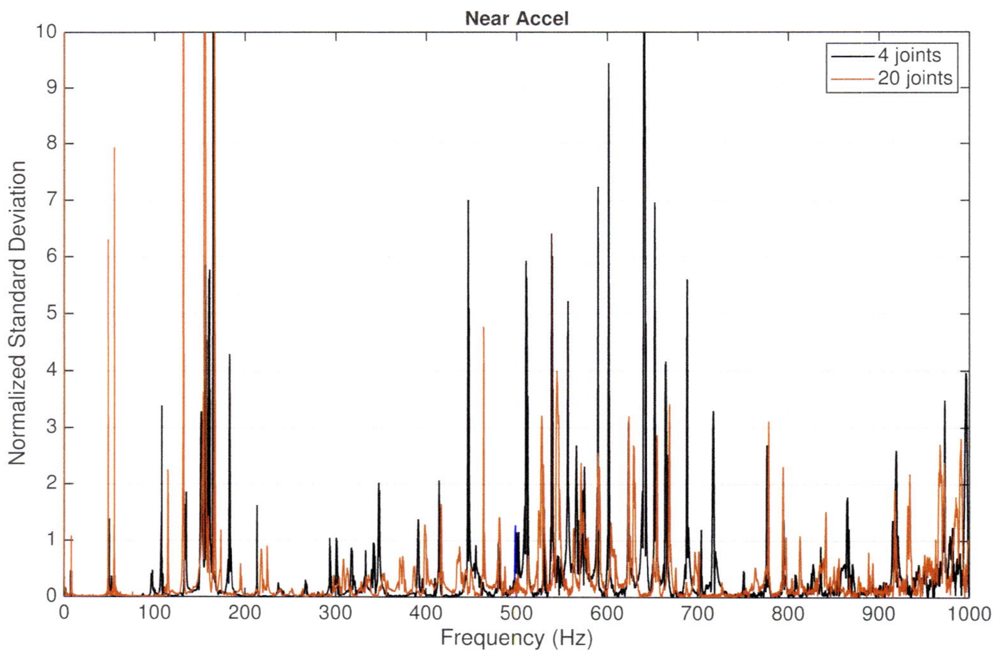

Fig. 7 Normalized standard deviation metric, $\alpha(f)$, versus frequency for an impact near the accelerometer.

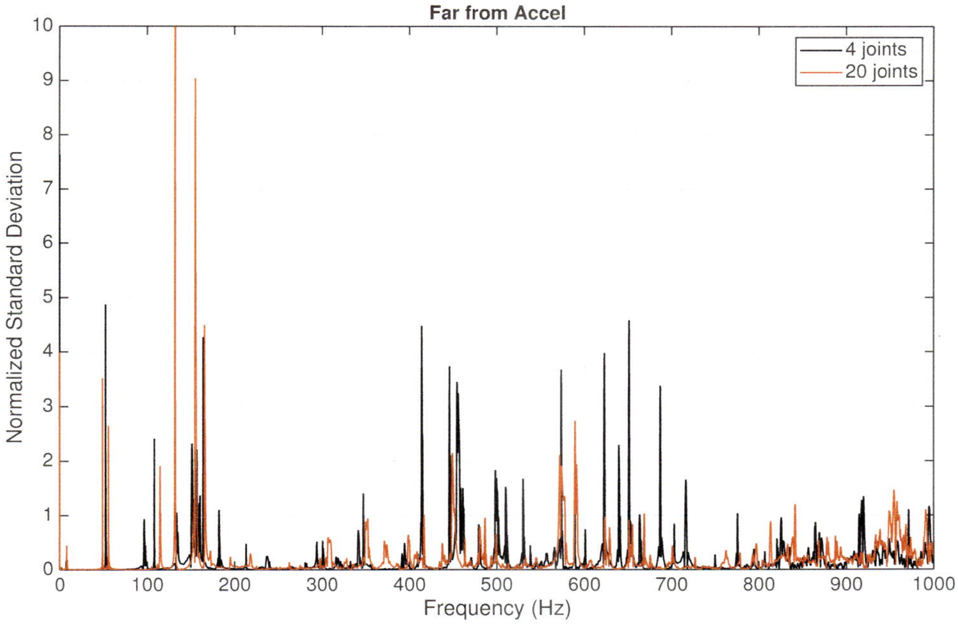

Fig. 8 Normalized standard deviation metric, $\alpha(f)$ versus frequency for an impact far away from the accelerometer.

over the frequency range 0 Hz to 300 Hz, the four-joint structure generally has higher normalized standard deviation than the twenty-joint structure over the range 300 Hz to 1000 Hz. A greater number of joints in the structure has made its dynamics more repeatable and thus predictable. No significant difference is observed between the two impact locations shown in the two figures.

Conclusions

It was experimentally demonstrated that the repeatability of a twenty-joint structure is higher than that of a four-joint structure. More work is necessary to determine if this result may be generalized to conclude that increasing the number of joints results in an increase in repeatability. If so, one could approximately assess the repeatability of a structure *a priori* and have a reasonable hope that a deterministic model will accurately predict its dynamics.

Comparison of our results to those of [13] suggests an interesting avenue of future research. The Brake Reuß Beam that was studied in [13] consisted of two beams attached by a lap joint. The metal beams had a 2.5 cm square cross-section and were attached to each other over a 12 cm region with M8 bolts. By comparison, the relatively thin L-shaped beams used in the present study had walls that were 0.188 cm thick, making them 0.075 times the thickness of the Brake Reuß beam. In comparison to the L-angle beams used in the present work, the beams in the the Brake Reuß paper were orders of magnitude stiffer. The dynamics of the structure in the present work were significantly more repeatable than the dynamics of the Brake Reuß beam. This may be due to differences in the relative stiffnesses of beams and bolts as well as the area of overlap. For example, stiff bolts connecting flexible structures may be more repeatable than flexible bolts connecting stiff structures because the former case produces a more consistent joint from one assembly to the next. Future work may investigate this question by studying a collection of structures in which these properties are varied in a systematic way.

Acknowledgments We gratefully acknowledge the support of the Navel Engineering Education Consortium through Grant Number N00174-22-1-0015.

References

1. Brake, M.R.W. and Reuß, P. "The Brake-Reuß beams: A system designed for the measurements and modeling of variability and repeatability of jointed structures with frictional interfaces". In Brake, M.R.W., editor, *The Mechanics of Jointed Structures: Recent Research and Open Challenges for Developing Predictive Models for Structural Dynamics*, pages 99–107. Springer International Publishing, Cham (2018)

2. Brake, M.R.W. "Introduction to research on the mechanics of jointed structures". In Brake, M.R.W., editor, *The Mechanics of Jointed Structures: Recent Research and Open Challenges for Developing Predictive Models for Structural Dynamics*, pages 3–10. Springer International Publishing, Cham (2018)
3. Brake, M.R.W. "An overview of the analysis of jointed structures". In Brake, M.R.W., editor, *The Mechanics of Jointed Structures: Recent Research and Open Challenges for Developing Predictive Models for Structural Dynamics*, pages 11–23. Springer International Publishing, Cham (2018)
4. Ibrahim, R.A. and Pettit, C.L. "Uncertainties and dynamic problems of bolted joints and other fasteners". *Journal of Sound and Vibration*, 279(3):857–936 (2005)
5. Smith, S.A., Catalfamo, S., Bilbao-Ludena, J.C., Brake, M.R.W., Reuß, P., and Schwingshackl, C.W. "Considerations for measurements of jointed structures". In Brake, M.R.W., editor, *The Mechanics of Jointed Structures: Recent Research and Open Challenges for Developing Predictive Models for Structural Dynamics*, pages 109–133. Springer International Publishing, Cham (2018)
6. Brake, M.R.W. "The next generation of joints research". In Brake, M.R.W., editor, *The Mechanics of Jointed Structures: Recent Research and Open Challenges for Developing Predictive Models for Structural Dynamics*, pages 675–689. Springer International Publishing, Cham (2018)
7. Brake, M.R.W. "Round Robin systems". In Brake, M.R.W., editor, *The Mechanics of Jointed Structures: Recent Research and Open Challenges for Developing Predictive Models for Structural Dynamics*, pages 45–58. Springer International Publishing, Cham (2018)
8. Zaman, I., Khalid, A., Manshoor, B., Araby, S., and Ghazali, M.I. "The effects of bolted joints on dynamic response of structures". *IOP Conference Series: Materials Science and Engineering*, 50(1):012018 (2013)
9. Goyder, H.G.D. "Damping due to joints in built-up structures". In Brake, M.R.W., editor, *The Mechanics of Jointed Structures: Recent Research and Open Challenges for Developing Predictive Models for Structural Dynamics*, pages 135–147. Springer International Publishing, Cham (2018)
10. Cooper, S.B., Rosatello, M., Mathis, A.T., Johnson, K., Brake, M.R.W., Allen, M.S., Ferri, A.A., Roettgen, D.R., Pacini, B.R., and Mayes, R.L. "Effect of far-field structure on joint properties". In Allen, M.S., Mayes, R.L., and Rixen, D.J., editors, *Dynamics of Coupled Structures, Volume 4*, pages 63–77, Cham (2017) Springer International Publishing.
11. Marinone, T. and Moya, A. "Comparison of FRF correlation techniques". In Atamturktur, H.S., Moaveni, B., Papadimitriou, C., and Schoenherr, T., editors, *Model Validation and Uncertainty Quantification, Volume 3*, pages 299–309. Springer International Publishing, Cham (2015)
12. Kramer, H.R., Manring, L.H., Schultze, J.F., Zimmerman, S.J., and Mann, B.P. "Strategies for improving the comparison of frequency response functions with similarity metrics". In Brake, M.R., Renson, L., Kuether, R.J., and Tiso, P., editors, *Nonlinear Structures & Systems, Volume 1*, pages 101–109. Springer Nature Switzerland, Cham (2024)
13. Brake, M., Schwingshackl, C., and Reuß, P. "Observations of variability and repeatability in jointed structures". *Mechanical Systems and Signal Processing*, 129:282–307 (2019)

Chapter 16
Experimental Fluid-Structure Interaction of Airflow Over a Cylinder with an Attached Cantilever Plate in a Wind Tunnel

D. T. Will and W. D. Zhu

Abstract The aim of this fluid-structure interaction work is to explore the vibration response of a stiff cantilever plate attached to a cylinder in an AEROLAB Educational Wind Tunnel under an airflow excitation. An accelerometer-based experimental modal analysis is first used to determine the first three out-of-plane natural frequencies and mode shapes of the experimental structure within a frequency band of 0-400 Hz. Using constant temperature anemometry with a wind tunnel free-stream velocity of 10 m/s and a Reynolds number on the order of $2.1\text{x}10^4$, a single-channel hot-wire anemometer probe is roved throughout the flow-field. The velocity variations in the airflow over the cylinder and cantilever plate are measured and the data is processed to observe the mean airflow velocity around the structure. Then, the structure's response to a free-stream velocity of 10 m/s, yielding a maximum measured Strouhal vortex shedding frequency of approximately 40.3 Hz, is measured using an accelerometer-based operational modal analysis to capture the first two natural frequencies and mode shapes within a frequency band of 0-400 Hz.

Keywords Fluid-structure interaction · Modal analysis

INTRODUCTION

Fluid-structure interaction (FSI) can be defined as the dynamics of a structure's response to an input caused by a working fluid, such as air or water, coupled by the subsequent effects the structure has on that working fluid [1]. In the literature, various test and numerical simulation configurations have been studied, including attached [2] or detached [3] splitter plates, rigid or flexible splitter plates [4], and splitter plates placed either in front of [5] or behind [6] a circular cylinder. Other cases studied include flow past a square prism [7], a cantilever plate with no cylinder [8], flexible wings in transverse gusts [9], and shock-wave/boundary-layer interaction in supersonic flow [10]. Typical fluid mediums tested or simulated include air, water, and other incompressible fluids such as glycerin [11]. For air, the range of Reynolds numbers examined was from $3.83\text{x}10^4$ to $3.9\text{x}10^7\ \text{m}^{-1}$, while for water and other incompressible fluids, the range of Reynolds numbers examined was from 100 to $9.5\text{x}10^5$. Most FSI research in the literature focuses on large, nonlinear deformation of a structure, while the current work examines small vortex-induced vibrations that are not visible to the naked eye. This work seeks to expand upon the current research by studying the vibration of a rigid cantilever plate attached to a rigid cylinder using the measurement techniques of experimental modal analysis (EMA) with roving impact hammer excitation and operational modal analysis (OMA) with airflow excitation and a roving accelerometer. Further, the flow field around the cylinder and cantilever plate will be examined using constant temperature anemometry (CTA), or hot-wire anemometry, to understand the mechanism by which vortex shedding excites the test specimen.

Background

The design for the experimental setup was developed given size constraints for the experiment in an AEROLAB Educational Wind Tunnel (EWT) where the test section is 304.8 mm wide, 304.8 mm tall, and 609.6 mm long [12]. The cylinder diameter selection was determined by a tradeoff between manufacturability and vortex shedding frequency. The frequency, *f*, of vortex

D. T. Will · W. D. Zhu
Department of Mechanical Engineering, University of Maryland, Baltimore County, 1000 Hilltop Circle, Baltimore, MD 21250
e-mail: dwill1@umbc.edu; wzhu@umbc.edu

Brandon Dilworth et al. (eds.), *Topics in Modal Analysis & Parameter Identification I, Vol. 9*, Conference Proceedings of the Society for Experimental Mechanics Series, https://doi.org/10.13052/9788743801542-16

shedding over a cylinder is calculated using the Strouhal number, *St*, [1]

$$f = \frac{St \times V}{D} \tag{1}$$

where *V* is the airflow velocity, *D* is the diameter of the cylinder, and the Strouhal number is given by Massey and Ward-Smith [13]

$$St = 0.198\left(1 - \frac{19.7}{Re}\right), 250 < Re < 2 \times 10^5 \tag{2}$$

or by Modarres-Sadeghi [1] as $St = 0.2,\ 300 < Re < 300{,}000$. The Reynolds number, *Re*, is defined by [14]

$$Re = \frac{\rho V D}{\mu} \tag{3}$$

where $\rho = 1.204\ \frac{kg}{m^3}$ and $\mu = 1.825 \times 10^{-5}\ \frac{kg}{m \cdot s}$ for air at normal temperature and pressure, i.e., air at 20°C and 101,325 Pa. The Reynolds number of air over a cylinder plotted as a function of the air velocity for various cylinder diameters is shown in Fig. 1 and the vortex shedding frequency of air over a cylinder plotted as a function of the air velocity for various cylinder diameters is shown in Fig. 2. A cylinder diameter of 31.8 mm was chosen, which yields a vortex shedding frequency of 28 Hz to 402 Hz over the wind tunnel velocity range of 4.5 m/s to 64.5 m/s.

EMA Setup and Results

An experimental structure was designed, machined, and assembled as described in Will and Zhu [12]. A modification to the upper mounting bracket was made to accommodate the use of a newer manufactured AEROLAB EWT where the upper mounting configuration was different from the older manufactured AEROLAB EWT used in Will and Zhu [12]. The new upper mounting bracket was 517.5 mm in length and the location of the mounting hole used to fasten the cylinder was shifted to accommodate the newer manufactured AEROLAB EWT. The experimental setup mounted inside the newer manufactured AEROLAB EWT is shown in Fig. 3.

Due to the different boundary conditions from the modified upper mounting bracket between the older manufactured EWT in Will and Zhu [12] and the newer manufactured EWT, an EMA was performed to determine the experimental setup's first three out-of-plane natural frequencies and mode shapes. One PCB Piezotronics, Inc. 352C66 single-axis accelerometer was placed on the far-side of the cylinder, cantilever plate, and upper and lower mounting brackets, where the far side is defined as the side of each component facing into the page in Fig. 3(a) and the near side is defined as the side of each component facing out of the page in Fig. 3(a). Additionally, a PCB Piezotronics, Inc. 086C01 modally tuned impact hammer with a nylon tip, four PCB Piezotronics, Inc. 080A15 adhesive mounting bases, PCB Piezotronics, Inc. 080A109 adhesive

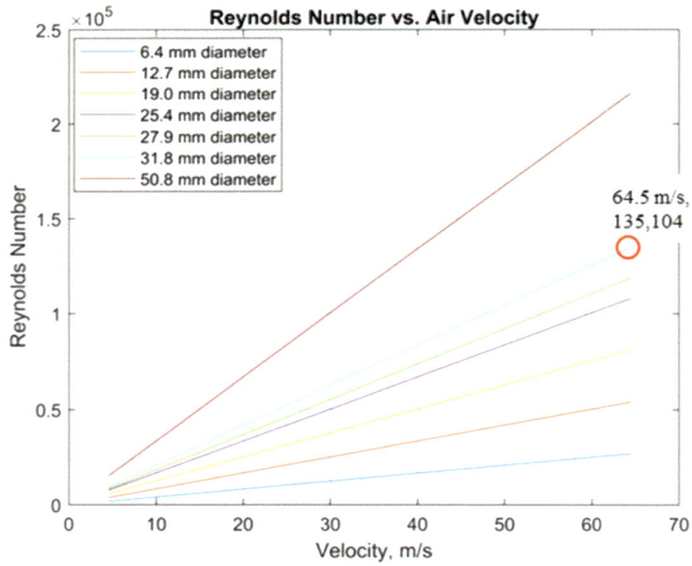

Fig. 1 A plot of the Reynolds number versus the airflow velocity for various cylinder diameters. The red circle indicates the maximum Reynolds number at the highest airflow velocity for the selected cylinder diameter of 31.8 mm.

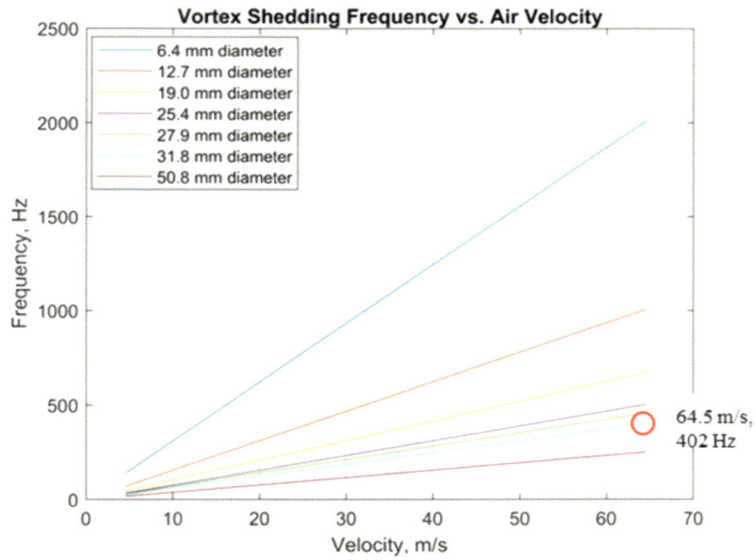

Fig. 2 A plot of the vortex shedding frequency versus the airflow velocity for various cylinder diameters. The red circle indicates the maximum vortex shedding frequency at the highest airflow velocity for the selected cylinder diameter of 31.8 mm.

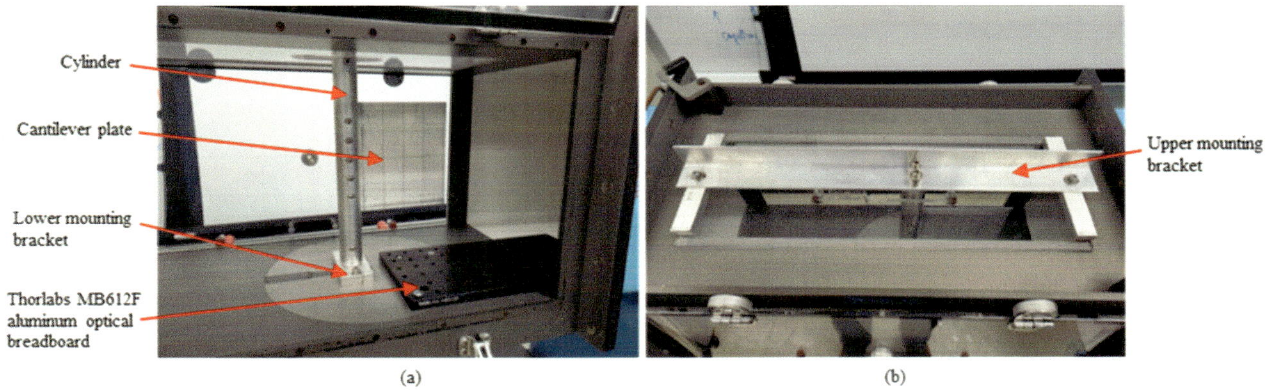

Fig. 3 Experimental setup inside the AEROLAB EWT including the (a) cylinder, cantilever plate, lower mounting bracket, Thorlabs MB612F aluminum optical breadboard, and (b) the upper mounting bracket.

wax, a Siemens Signal Conditioning and Data Acquisition System (SCADAS) Mobile SCM2E02V, and Siemens Testlab Version 2306 software were used to perform the EMA. The setup and equipment used for the EMA is shown in Fig. 4. A roving hammer test was performed using 37 impact locations, or nodes, where 4 nodes were used on the cylinder, 25 nodes were used on the cantilever plate, 5 nodes were used on the upper mounting bracket, and 3 nodes were used on the lower mounting bracket. Each node was impacted three times to compute an average of three frequency response functions (FRFs) for a total of 111 hammer impacts on the structure. The model of the experimental structure generated using Testlab is shown in Fig. 5, where the gray boxes indicate the node or impact locations, and the red circles indicate the locations of the reference accelerometers placed on the far side of the experimental structure.

After the roving hammer testing was completed, Testlab's PolyMAX algorithm was used to curve fit the FRFs using a curve fitting model size of 25 modes. The first three stable modes and their corresponding mode shapes were selected within a frequency band of 0-400 Hz, as shown in Figs. 6 and 7, respectively. As indicated in Fig. 7, mode 1 is the first bending mode of the cantilever plate, mode 2 is the first torsional mode of the cantilever plate, and mode 3 is an out-of-plane bending mode of the cylinder with minor out-of-plane bending of the cantilever plate. The modal assurance criterion (MAC) values are presented in Table 1, where values close to 0 indicate low correlation between mode shapes and values close to 1 indicate

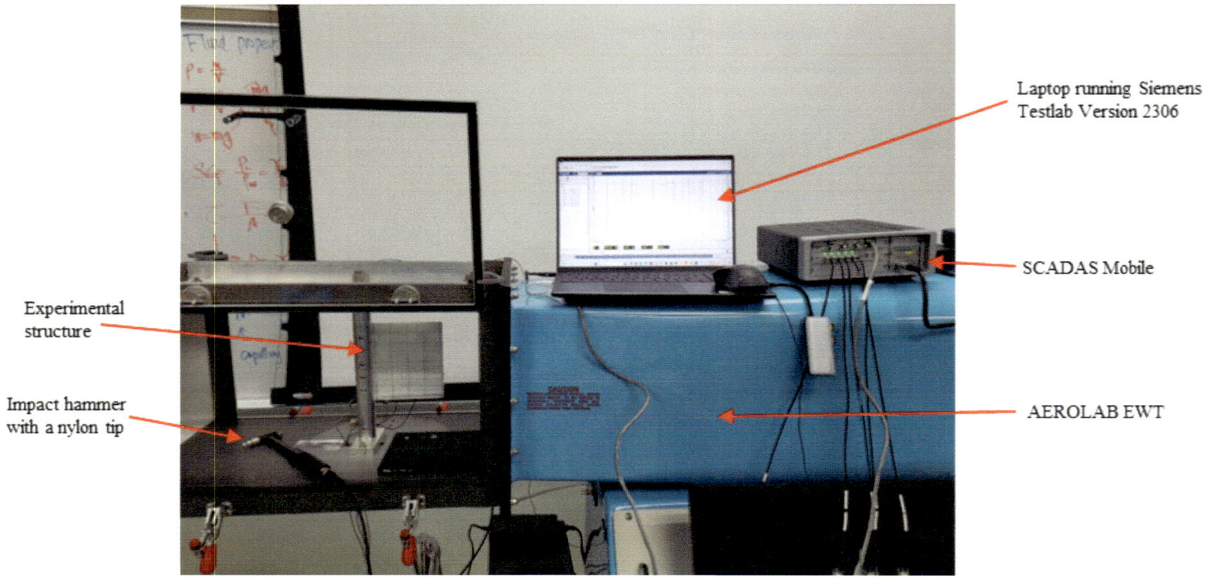

Fig. 4 Setup and test equipment used for the EMA including the AEROLAB EWT, experimental structure, impact hammer with a nylon tip, laptop running Siemens Testlab Version 2306, and SCADAS Mobile.

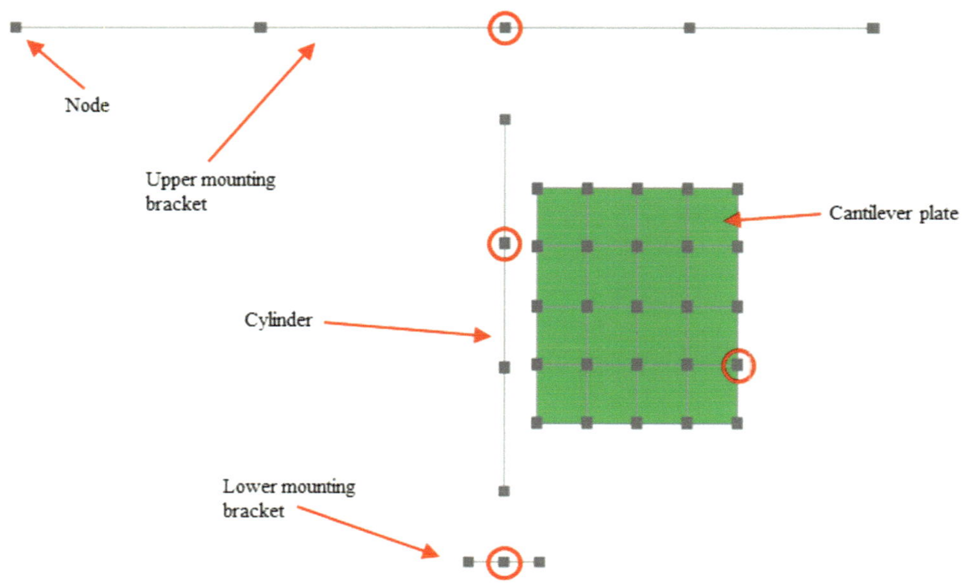

Fig. 5 Model of the experimental structure developed in Siemens Testlab Version 2306 software, where the nodes are indicated by the gray boxes and the red circles indicate the locations of the reference accelerometers placed on the far side of the experimental structure.

high correlation between mode shapes. The mode shapes in Fig. 7 and the MAC values in Table 1 indicate that modes 1 and 2 are unique, with a MAC value of 0.001, modes 1 and 3 share some similarities in cantilever plate bending, yielding a MAC value of 0.241, and modes 2 and 3 are unique, with a MAC value of 0.055.

CTA Setup and Results

A CTA experiment was performed using a Dantec Dynamics MiniCTA 54T42, 55P16 hot-wire probe, hot-wire calibrator, laptop running StreamWare Basic V7.00 software, and a National Instruments NI-9215 data acquisition board for capturing the measurements from the MiniCTA 54T42 at 10 kHz. Additionally, a hot-wire probe holder was designed and a machined,

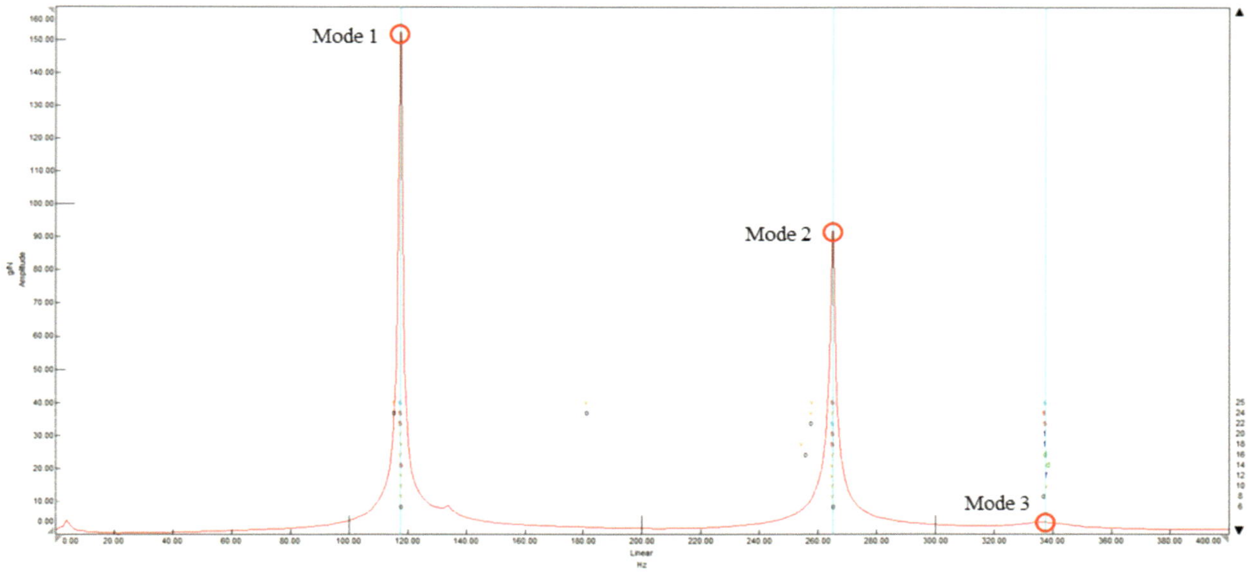

Fig. 6 Stabilization diagram using a curve fitting model size of 25 modes, where the first three stable modes between a frequency band of 0-400 Hz are indicated by red circles.

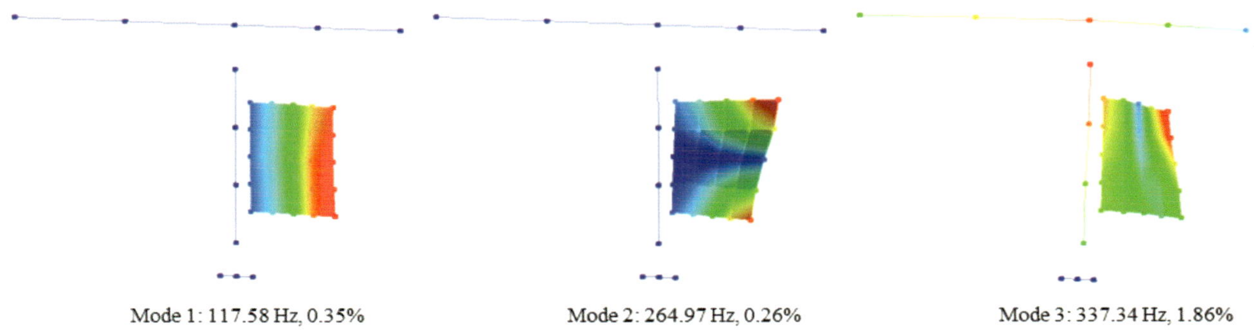

Fig. 7 First three stable mode shapes and their corresponding frequency and damping values within a frequency band of 0-400 Hz.

Table 1 MAC values for the EMA mode shapes.

EMA \ EMA	**Mode 1** (117.58 Hz)	**Mode 2** (264.97 Hz)	**Mode 3** (337.34 Hz)
Mode 1 (117.58 Hz)	1.000	0.001	0.241
Mode 2 (264.97 Hz)	0.001	1.000	0.055
Mode 3 (337.34 Hz)	0.241	0.055	1.000

which was mounted to a Thorlabs XYR1 translation and rotation stage for correct positioning of the probe during the experiment. Prior to performing the CTA experiment, a calibration of the hot-wire probe was performed. The 55P16 probe was installed onto the hot-wire calibrator and a steady flow of filtered air was supplied through the calibrator. A calibrated Traceable 38RJ43 digital barometer was used to measure the ambient pressure and a Klein Tools multimeter was used to measure the hot-wire calibrator's thermistor resistance for entry into the calibration software. After completion of the calibration procedure, the StreamWare Basic v7.00 software generated a calibration curve for accurately converting the measured voltages to airflow velocities. The complete CTA setup and equipment used for measuring the airflow velocities and the CTA calibration setup and equipment is shown in Figs. 8 and 9, respectively.

After calibration, the translation and rotation stage, hot-wire probe holder, and hot-wire probe were installed into the AEROLAB EWT, as shown in Figs. 10 and 11. Using the optical breadboard and the translation and rotation stage, the hot-

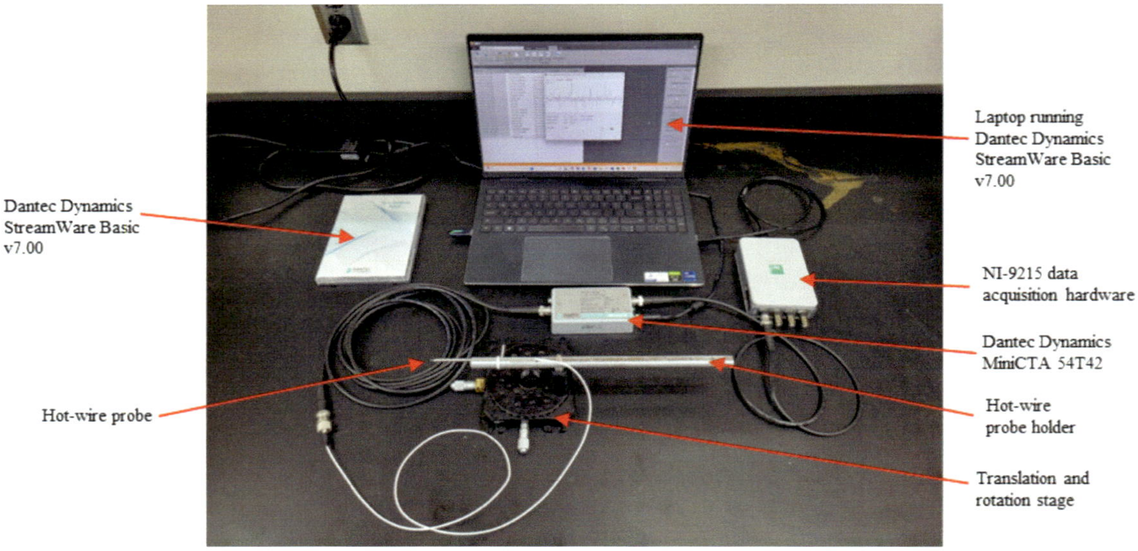

Fig. 8 CTA setup and equipment used to measure the airflow velocities around the cylinder and cantilever plate including the Dantec Dynamics MiniCTA 54T42, hot-wire probe, hot-wire probe holder, NI-9215 data acquisition hardware, laptop running Dantec Dynamics StreamWare Basic v7.00, and translation and rotation stage.

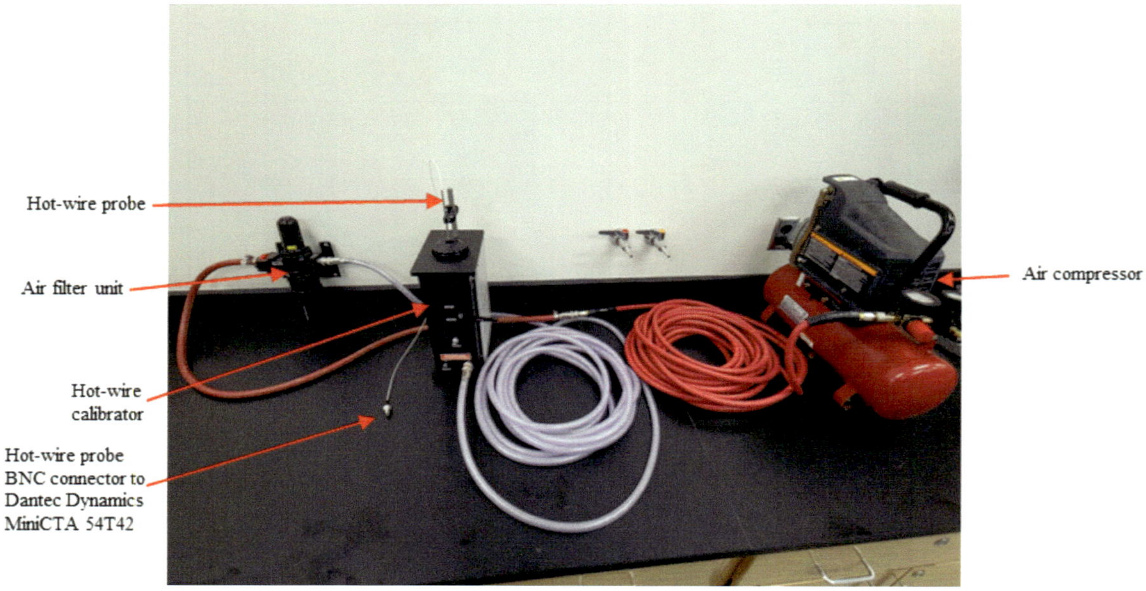

Fig. 9 CTA calibration setup and equipment including the hot-wire probe, hot-wire calibrator, air filter unit, and air compressor.

wire probe was roved through 120 points around the cylinder and cantilever plate. Referencing the origin of the coordinate axes in Fig. 11, the hot-wire probe was roved through each combination of the following positions:

- X: 0 mm, 25.39 mm, 50.79 mm, 76.19 mm, 101.60 mm, 127.00 mm, 152.40 mm, 177.80 mm
- Y: -6.34 mm, -31.75 mm, -57.15 mm, -82.55 mm, -107.90 mm
- Z: 12.69 mm, 25.39 mm, 38.09 mm

The wind tunnel free-stream velocity was set to 10 m/s and 10 s of data were collected at each of the 120 points.

After the CTA experiment was completed, the voltage data were converted into airflow velocities using the calibration curve and the mean airflow velocities at each of the 16 measurement planes were plotted. Planes along the X-axis, Y-axis, and Z-axis are shown in Figs. 12, 13, and 14, respectively.

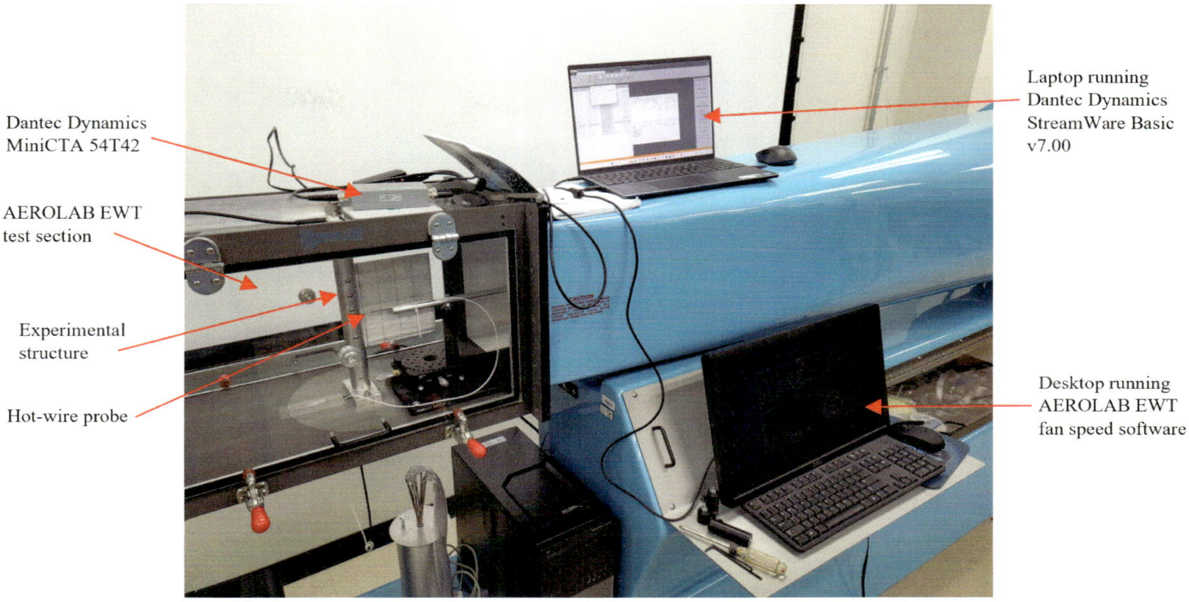

Fig. 10 Setup and test equipment used for the CTA experiment including the AEROLAB EWT with desktop computer and software for controlling the fan speed, experimental structure, hot-wire probe, Dantec Dynamics MiniCTA 54T42, and laptop running Dantec Dynamics StreamWare Basic v7.00.

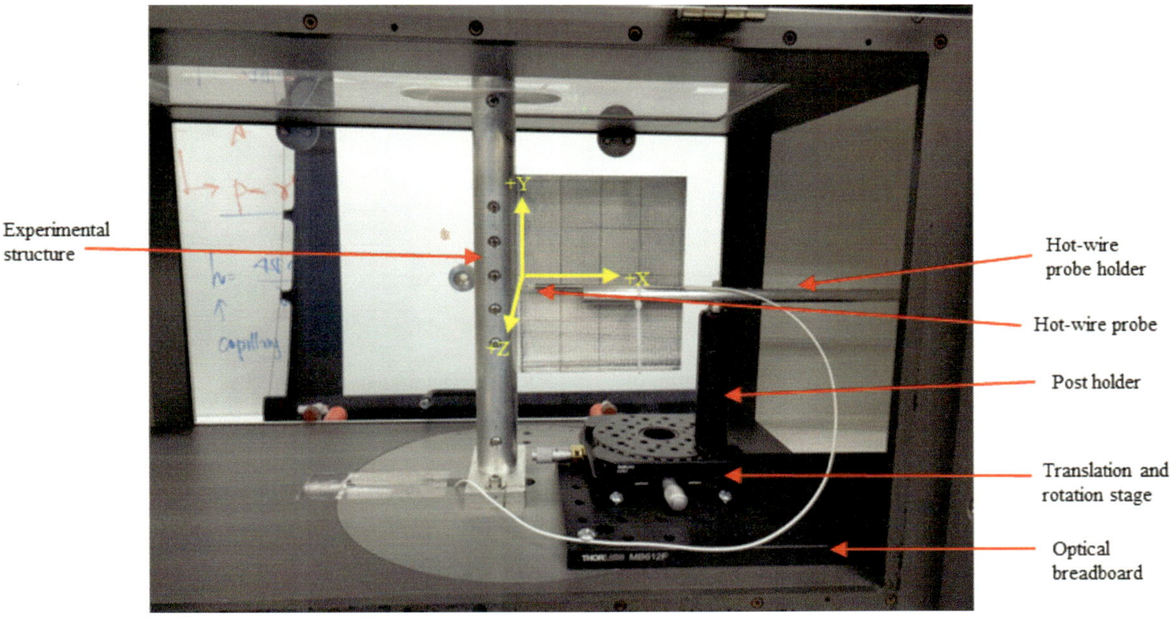

Fig. 11 Setup and test equipment used for the CTA inside the EWT test section including the experimental structure, hot-wire probe, hot-wire probe holder, post holder, translation and rotation stage, and optical breadboard. The coordinate axes defining the CTA coordinate directions used in the experiment are also depicted.

OMA Setup and Results

An OMA experiment was performed in the AEROLAB EWT using the CTA equipment as well as the SCADAS Mobile, a single roving accelerometer, four fixed reference accelerometers, and a laptop running both Siemens Testlab Version 2306 and Dantec Dynamics StreamWare Basic v7.00. Prior to conducting the experiment, a calibration of the hot-wire probe was performed and a calibration curve was obtained. During the experiment, the wind tunnel was set to a free-stream velocity of 10 m/s and the hot-wire probe was kept in a constant position at X = 127.00 mm, Y = -31.75 mm, and Z = 25.39 mm, while

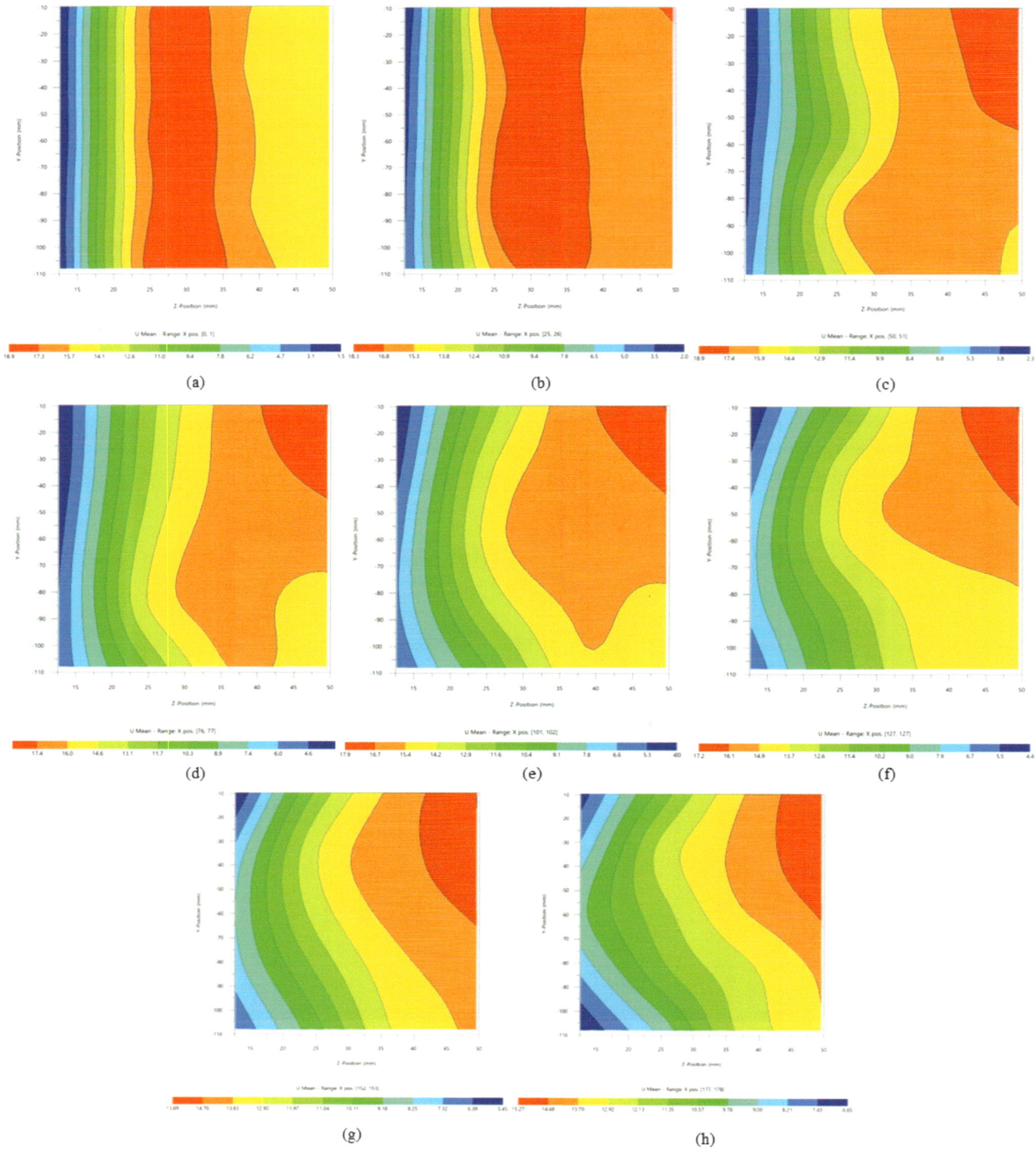

Fig. 12 Mean airflow velocity around the cylinder and cantilever plate at planes (a) X = 0 mm, (b) X = 25.39 mm, (c) X = 50.79 mm, (d) X = 76.19 mm, (e) X = 101.60 mm, (f) X = 127.00 mm, (g) X = 152.40 mm, and (h) X = 177.80 mm captured using CTA measurements at a wind tunnel free-stream velocity of 10 m/s.

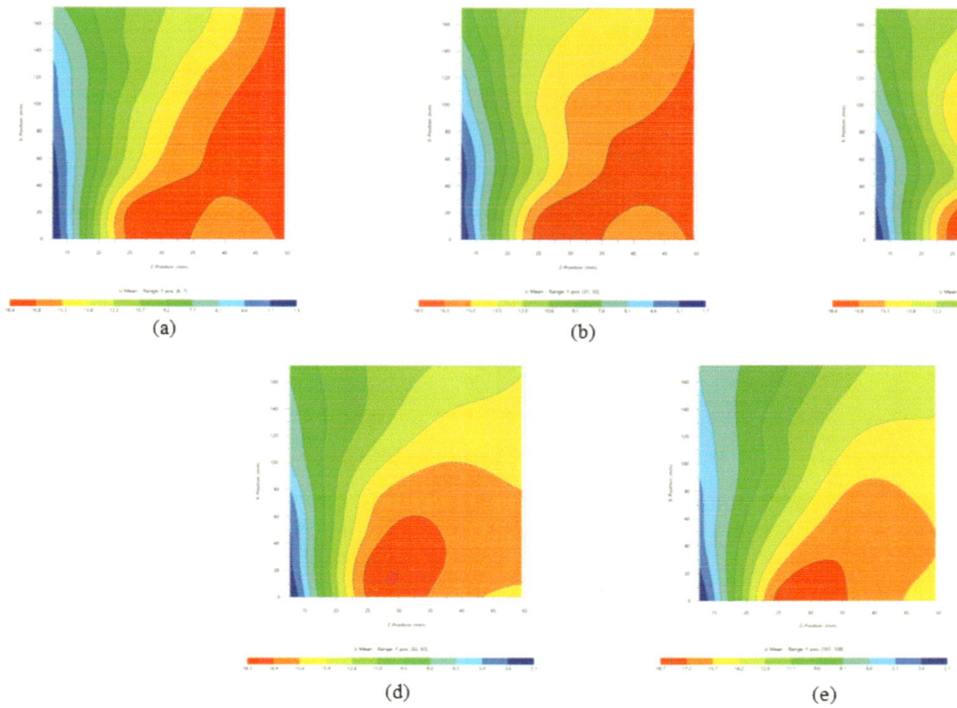

Fig. 13 Mean airflow velocity around the cylinder and cantilever plate at planes (a) Y = -6.34 mm, (b) Y = -31.75 mm, (c) Y = -57.15 mm, (d) Y = -82.55 mm, and (e) Y = -107.90 mm captured using CTA measurements at a wind tunnel free-stream velocity of 10 m/s.

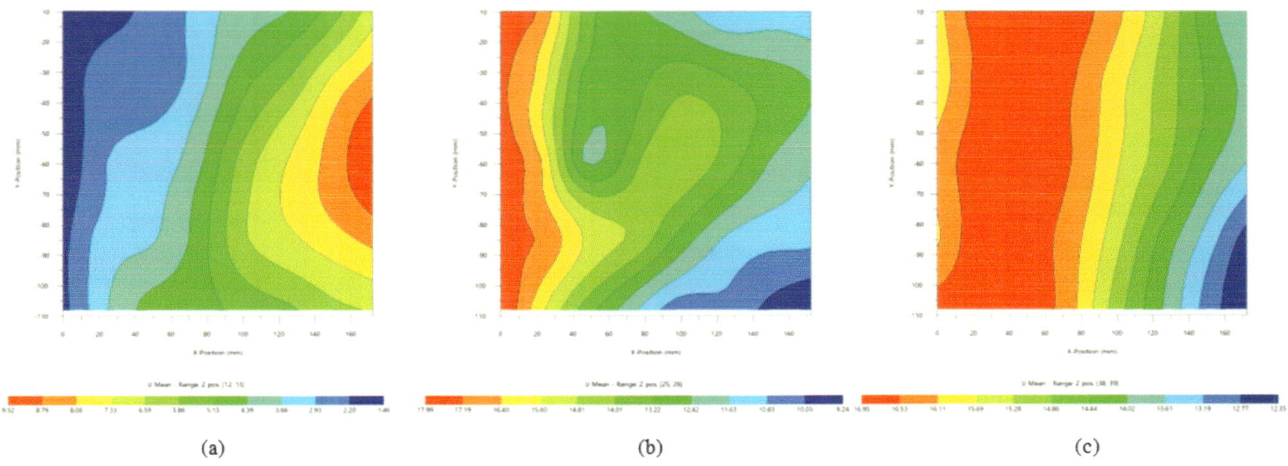

Fig. 14 Mean airflow velocity around the cylinder and cantilever plate at planes (a) Z = 12.69 mm, (b) Z = 25.39 mm, and (c) Z = 38.09 mm captured using CTA measurements at a wind tunnel free-stream velocity of 10 m/s.

the roving accelerometer was roved through each of the 37 nodes shown in Fig. 5. At each node, 30 s of accelerometer data and 35 s of CTA data were captured. The reference accelerometers were in the same positions as those of the EMA test as indicated by the red circles in Fig. 5. Siemens Testlab Version 2306 was used to perform the OMA, including data acquisition and curve fitting using the PolyMAX algorithm. The OMA experimental setup and equipment is shown in Figs. 15 and 16.

After completion of the OMA experiment, a CTA plot of the voltage versus time signal was plotted for the run in which the roving accelerometer was placed on the left-most node of the lower mounting bracket, as depicted in Fig. 5. Then, the

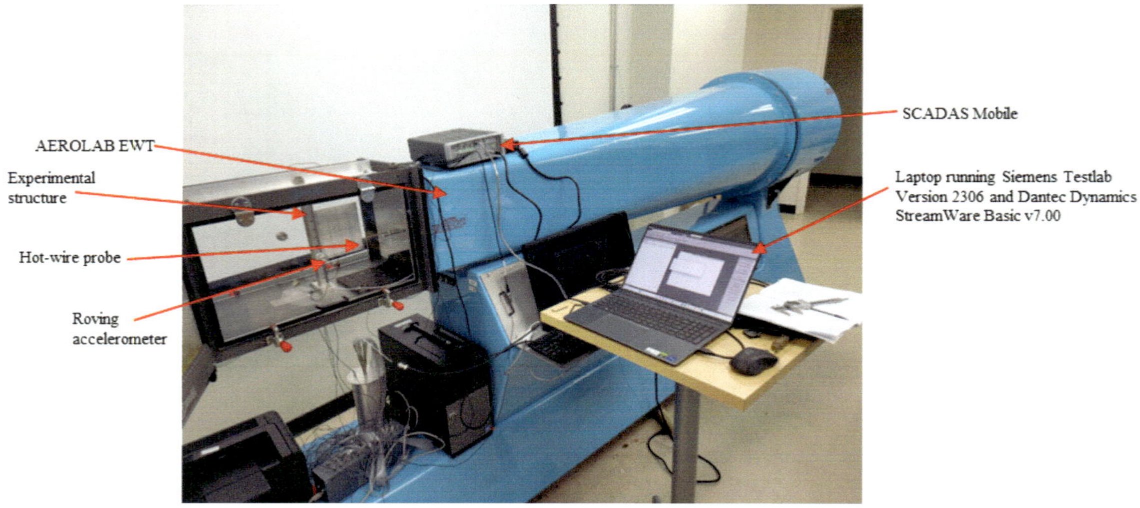

Fig. 15 OMA experimental setup and equipment including the AEROLAB EWT, experimental structure, hot-wire probe, roving accelerometer, SCADAS Mobile, and laptop running Siemens Testlab Version 2306 and Dantec Dynamics StreamWare Basic v7.00.

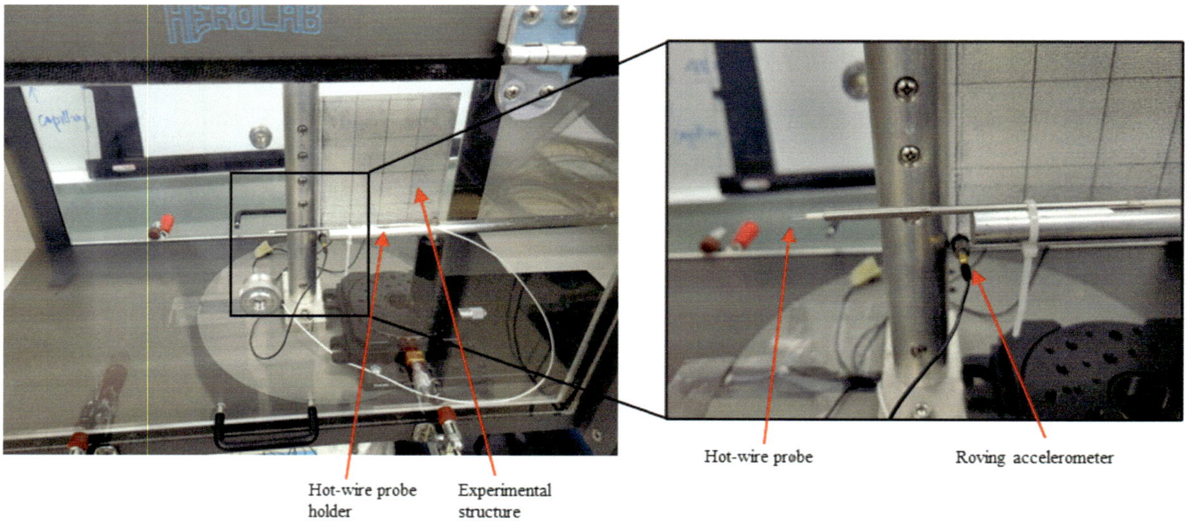

Fig. 16 OMA experimental setup inside the EWT test section showing the experimental structure, hot-wire probe, hot-wire probe holder, and roving accelerometer. The hot-wire probe is pictured in a position forward of the cylinder and cantilever plate for setting the wind tunnel free-stream velocity to 10 m/s.

power spectrum of the voltage versus time signal was calculated and plotted, where the power spectrum was calculated after applying a Hamming window and using 4096 bins with 75% overlap, yielding an uncertainty of 5.44%. The voltage versus time signal and the power spectrum are shown in Figs. 17 and 18, respectively. The peaks in Fig. 18 are specified by red circles, indicating the frequency content of the airflow at the hot-wire probe location. From the results shown in Fig. 18, the vortex shedding frequencies observed are 2.4 Hz, 18.3 Hz, and 40.3 Hz.

Testlab's PolyMAX algorithm was used to curve fit the cross-power functions that were derived from the accelerometer data captured during the OMA experiment using a curve fitting model size of 32 modes. The first two stable operational modes and their corresponding operational mode shapes were selected within a frequency band of 0-400 Hz, as shown in Figs. 19 and 20, respectively. As indicated in Fig. 20, mode 1 is the first bending mode of the cantilever plate and mode 2 is the first torsional mode of the cantilever plate.

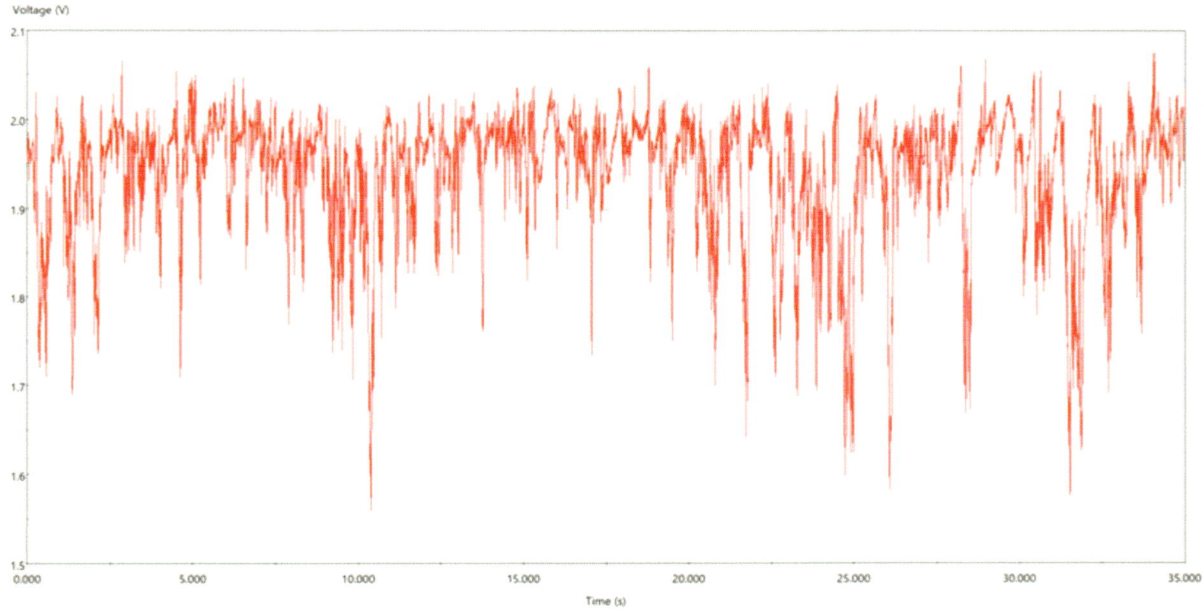

Fig. 17 CTA plot of the voltage versus time signal.

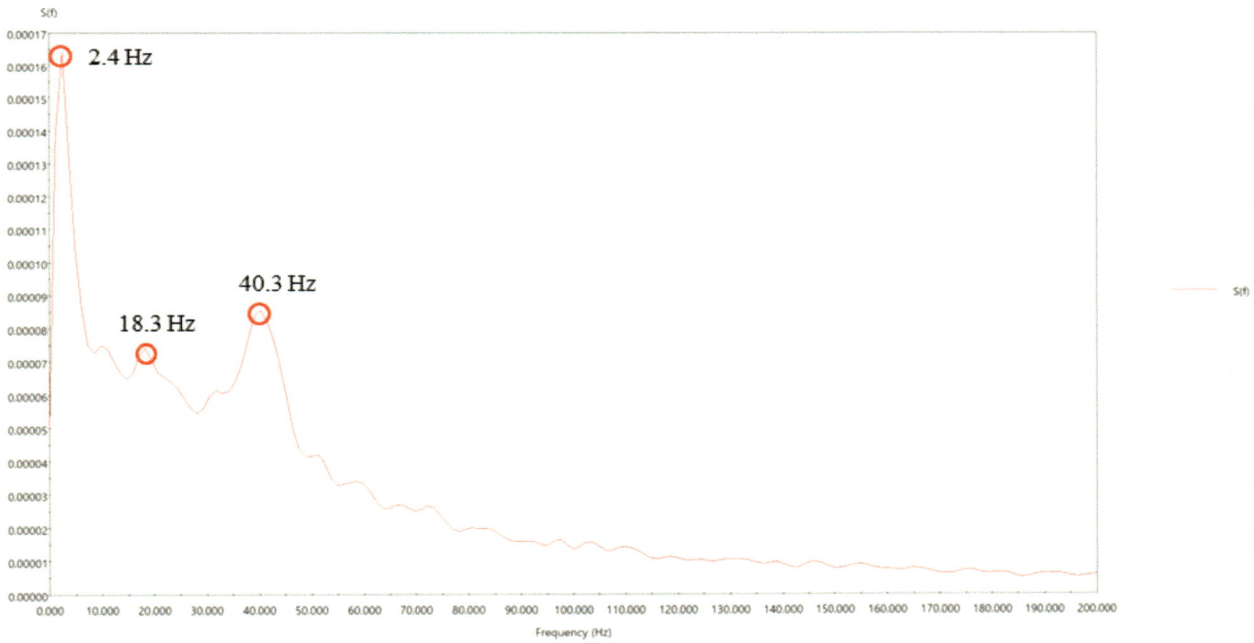

Fig. 18 CTA plot of the power spectrum of the voltage versus time signal shown in Fig. 17. The power spectrum was calculated after applying a Hamming window and using 4096 bins with 75% overlap. The frequencies at the circled peaks indicate the frequency content of the airflow.

Analysis

In this research, an experimental structure consisting of a cantilever plate fixed to a cylinder with an upper and lower mounting bracket was mounted in an AEROLAB EWT and characterized by performing a roving hammer EMA. The first three stable mode shapes were identified within a frequency band of 0-400 Hz, as shown in Fig. 7, which are consistent with

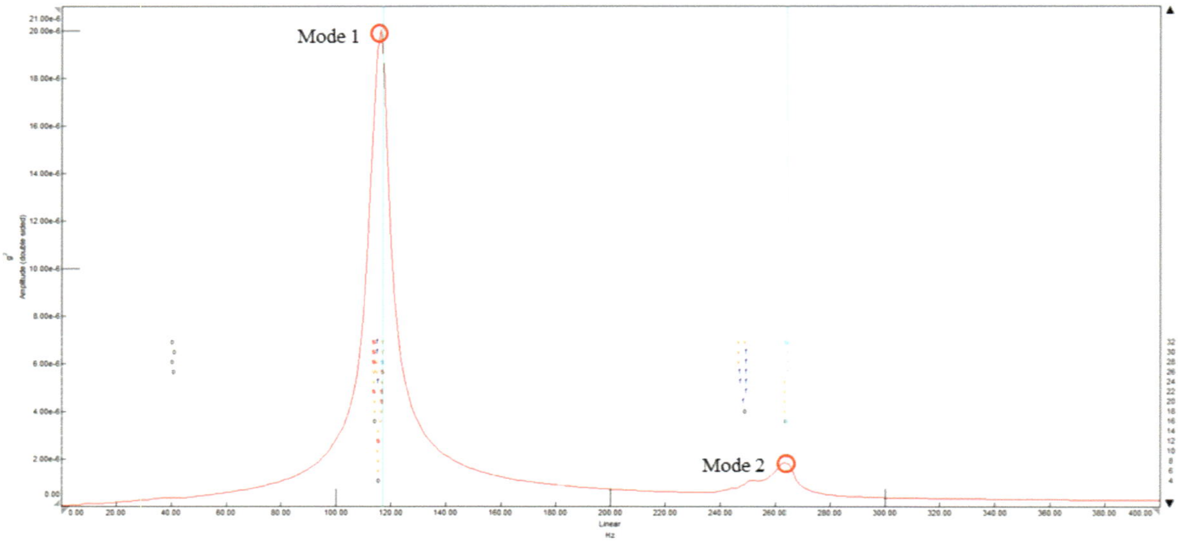

Fig. 19 Stabilization diagram using a curve fitting model size of 32 modes, where the first two stable operational modes between a frequency band of 0-400 Hz are indicated by red circles. The wind tunnel free-stream velocity was 10 m/s.

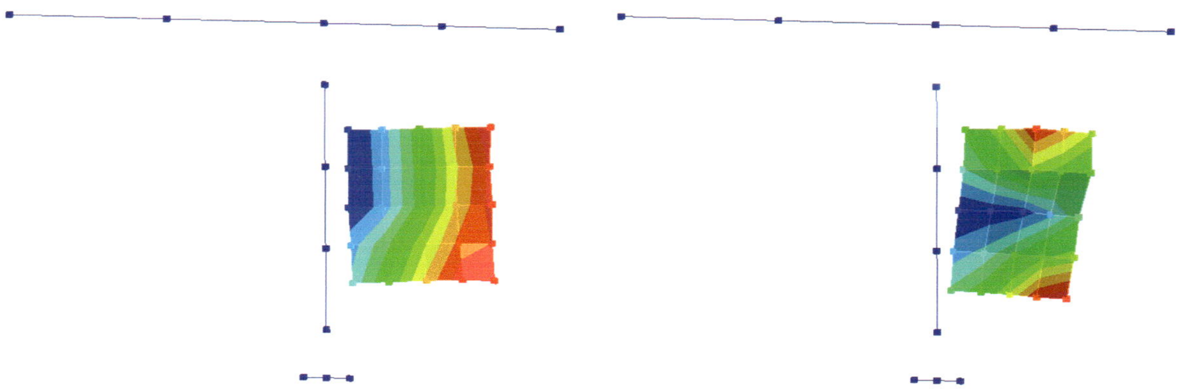

Fig. 20 First two stable operational mode shapes and their corresponding frequency and damping values within a frequency band of 0-400 Hz for a wind tunnel free-stream velocity of 10 m/s.

previous results [12]. Then, a CTA experiment was performed at a free-stream velocity of 10 m/s, allowing for visualization of the mean airflow velocity around the cylinder and cantilever plate. Fig. 12 shows that the mean airflow velocity is lower near the plate and increases to a maximum value exceeding that of the free-stream velocity at some distance away from the plate in the Z-direction, and then decreases back to the free-stream velocity. This phenomenon is due to a combination of boundary layer effects and vortex shedding, where in the former case the fluid velocity near a surface is lower than the velocity further away from the surface, and in the latter case the local airflow velocity is increased within a vortex. Similar results are observed in Figs. 13 and 14. An OMA was performed using a roving accelerometer and four reference accelerometers while the hot-wire probe collected data at a fixed position of X = 127.00 mm, Y = -31.75 mm, and Z = 25.39 mm. From the power spectrum plot in Fig. 18, the peak with the highest frequency of 40.3 Hz indicates the highest vortex shedding frequency observed at the probe location. Using Equation 1 or Fig. 2, the theoretical vortex shedding frequency expected for a 31.8 mm diameter cylinder in an airflow with a velocity of 10 m/s is 62.3 Hz. This case of reduced vortex shedding frequency observed in the experiment may be due to energy dispersion across several frequencies, as shown in Fig. 18 where there are peaks at 2.4 Hz, 18.3 Hz, and 40.3 Hz. From the results of the OMA shown in Fig. 20, the natural frequencies of the first two stable operational modes match very well with the first two stable modes captured from the EMA shown in Fig. 7. The percent difference between the mode 1 frequencies captured using EMA and OMA is 0.39% and the percent difference between the mode 2 frequencies captured using EMA and OMA is 0.29%. These results are expected because the structure will vibrate at the same natural frequencies regardless of the excitation source. Finally, the third mode that was observed in Fig. 6 using the EMA method was not observed using the OMA method, as shown in Fig. 19, because the free-stream velocity of 10 m/s was not high enough to excite this third mode. Additional observable modes should be expected in the OMA results with higher free-stream velocities.

Conclusion

The aim of this FSI work was to explore the vibration response of a stiff cantilever plate attached to a cylinder in an AEROLAB EWT under an airflow excitation. A roving hammer EMA was first used to characterize the structure by determining the first three out-of-plane natural frequencies and mode shapes within a frequency band of 0-400 Hz. Then, CTA was used to capture the mean airflow velocity around the cylinder and cantilever plate with a free-stream velocity in the wind tunnel of 10 m/s. Some interesting phenomena were observed in the mean airflow velocity plots that are attributed to boundary layer and vortex shedding effects. Lastly, the structure's response to a free-stream velocity of 10 m/s was captured by performing an OMA, where the first two natural frequencies had less than a 0.4% difference when compared to the first two natural frequencies captured using the EMA method.

Acknowledgments The authors would like to thank Dr. Zheng Li and Morgan State University for their support in allowing access to the AEROLAB EWT.

References

1. Modarres-Sadeghi Y (2022) Introduction to Fluid-Structure Interactions. Springer Nature, Cham.
2. Xie R, Yu L, Zhu W, Pan B (2020) Experimental study on flow-induced full-field vibration of a flexible splitter plate behind a cylinder using stereo-digital image correlation. J Vib Acoust. https://doi.org/10.1115/1.4048390
3. Wu J, Shu C, Zhao N (2014) Numerical study of flow control via the interaction between a circular cylinder and a flexible plate. J Fluids Struct. https://doi.org/10.1016/j.jfluidstructs.2014.06.002
4. Duan F, Wang J (2021) Fluid–structure–sound interaction in noise reduction of a circular cylinder with flexible splitter plate. J Fluid Mech. https://doi.org/10.1017/jfm.2021.403
5. Chutkey K, Suriyanarayanan P, Venkatakrishnan L (2018) Near wake field of circular cylinder with a forward splitter plate. J Wind Eng Ind Aerod. https://doi.org/10.1016/j.jweia.2017.11.019
6. Shukla S, Govardhan RN, Arakeri JH (2013) Dynamics of a flexible splitter plate in the wake of a circular cylinder. J Fluids Struct. https://doi.org/10.1016/j.jfluidstructs.2013.03.002
7. Ro KD (2014) Experimental characterization of the flow field of square prism with a detached splitter plate at high Reynolds number. J Mech Sci Technol. https://doi.org/10.1007/s12206-014-0621-5
8. Watine Y, Gabillet C, Lossouarn B, Deü JF, Astolfi JA (2023) Vortex-induced vibrations of a cantilevered blunt plate: POD of TR-PIV measurements and structural modal analysis. J Fluids Struct. https://doi.org/10.1016/j.jfluidstructs.2022.103832
9. Fernandez F, Cleaver D, Gursul I (2022) Unsteady aerodynamics of flexible wings in transverse gusts. J Fluids Struct. https://doi.org/10.1016/j.jfluidstructs.2021.103425
10. Ahn YJ, Eitner MA, Rafati S, Musta MN, Sirohi J, Clemens NT (2022) Experimental investigation of fluid-structure interaction in Mach 2 flow using simultaneous high-speed PIV and DIC. 20th Int Symp Appl Laser Imaging Tech Fluid Mech. https://par.nsf.gov/biblio/10357649
11. Abdi R, Rezazadeh N, Abdi M (2019) Investigation of passive oscillations of flexible splitter plates attached to a circular cylinder. J Fluids Struct. https://doi.org/10.1016/j.jfluidstructs.2018.11.001
12. Will DT, Zhu WD (2023) Experimental modal analysis and operational deflection shape analysis of a cantilever plate in a wind tunnel with finite element model verification. Exp Tech. https://doi.org/10.1007/s40799-023-00682-w
13. Massey BS, Ward-Smith J (1998) Mechanics of Fluids, 7th edn. Stanley Thornes (Publishers) Ltd, Cheltenham.
14. Munson BR, Young DF, Okiishi TH, Huebsch WW (2009) Fundamentals of Fluid Mechanics, 6th edn. John Wiley & Sons, Inc, Hoboken.

Chapter 17
Traveling Wave Generation Through Piezoelectric Shunt Damping

A. Omidi Soroor, S. Motaharibidgoli, and P. A. Tarazaga

Abstract Having many different applications in mind, traveling wave generation in finite structures has been studied extensively by researchers in various fields. Surveying the literature suggests that most of the published work applied to finite and continuous structures is based on the notion of exciting the structure at two different locations at the same frequency with a phase shift to produce such waves. Recently, another approach has been proposed where there is only one excitation source, and the second one is replaced by a discontinuity that generates the required counterforce for reflection absorption. Thus far, this method has been experimentally verified in solid media where a perfectly tuned mechanical discontinuity, such as a spring-damper set, was leveraged. The authors herein are interested in replacing the mechanical discontinuity with an adaptive element in the hopes of widening the excitation frequency bandwidth in which this type of response is achievable within a given structural configuration. As such, a shunted piezoelectric element is adopted, thereby enabling variable stiffness and damping coefficients that can be adjusted based on the excitation frequency of the incident waves. This methodology also provides the ease of tuning the system electronically as opposed to achieving this precise tunning mechanically, which has been shown to be very difficult.

Keywords Traveling Waves · Single-Point Excitation · Shunt Damping · Negative Capacitance

Introduction

Researchers have extensively studied methods for traveling wave generation due to their various applications since 1990 [1]. These applications include but are not limited to particle transfer [2], robotic locomotion [3], and propulsion [4]. The majority of the literature is concerned with the two-point (or two-mode) excitation method for generating such waves. In this approach, the structure is excited at two locations with a frequency between two vibration modes and a phase shift between them, such that traveling waves are obtained within the space between the two exciters [5]. However, the authors have recently attempted another approach to traveling wave generation in solid media, i.e., the single-point excitation method. This idea had been previously explored by Xiao et al. in acoustic ducts [6]. In this approach, one of the exciters is replaced with a highly tuned type of discontinuity, a spring-damper set in mechanical structures, as seen in [7]. One of the primary motivations for developing this method is to mimic the observations from the mammalian cochlea, wherein the basilar membrane undergoes a similar dynamic behavior, i.e., the sound entering the ear initiates a wave on the basilar membrane that travels towards its apex without any reflections [8].

A recent study [9] by the authors has suggested that adopting a mechanical discontinuity to generate the required counterforce for the incident wave reflection cancellation might not be a feasible solution as it may not address a wide excitation frequency bandwidth. The discontinuity has to be specially tuned to the excitation frequency, restricting the ability to address a large bandwidth solution. Therefore, in the present study, the authors introduce an adaptive solution to address an excitation frequency range similar to the basilar membrane responsiveness in the audible frequency range. As such, piezoelectric materials are chosen to replace the spring-damper set implemented in the prior works. In the following section, the details of this solution, as well as some of the preliminary results of a pilot study conducted by the authors, are presented and discussed.

A. Omidi Soroor · P. A. Tarazaga
J. Mike Walker '66 Department of Mechanical Engineering, Texas A&M University, College Station, TX 77843
e-mail: omidisoroor@tamu.edu; ptarazaga@tamu.edu

S. Motaharibidgoli
Department of Mechanical Engineering, Virginia Polytechnic Institute and State University, Blacksburg, VA 24061
e-mail: mostafa4@vt.edu

Brandon Dilworth et al. (eds.), *Topics in Modal Analysis & Parameter Identification I, Vol. 9*, Conference Proceedings of the Society for Experimental Mechanics Series, https://doi.org/10.13052/9788743801542-17

Methodology

The present method uses piezoelectric patches shunted with RC circuits instead of the mechanical discontinuity introduced in [7] and [9]. Figure 1 depicts the schematic of the proposed traveling wave solution.

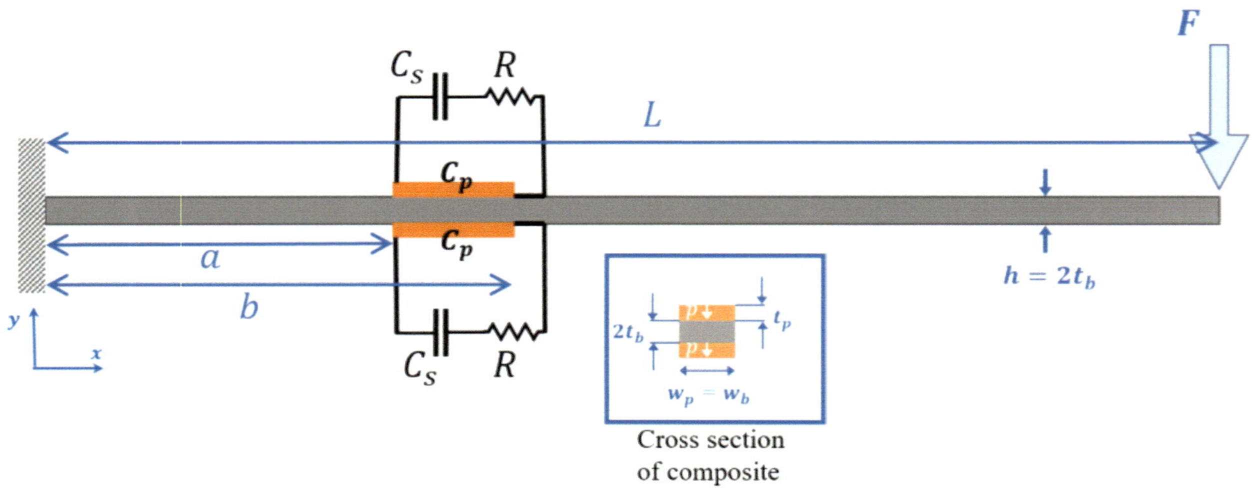

Fig. 1 Cantilevered beam with shunted piezoelectric patches [10].

In Figure 1, F denotes the harmonic excitation force. L, w_b, h, and t_b are the beam's length, width, full thickness, and half thickness. t_p and w_p represent the piezoelectric patches' thickness and width. Each piezo patch is shunted with a resistor and a capacitor with resistance R and capacitance C_s, respectively. C_p is the inherent capacitance of the piezoelectric element. The coupled electromechanical finite element formulation for the following system is developed as follows,

$$\begin{cases} M\ddot{u} + Ku = B_v V(t) + B_f F(t) \\ B_v^T \dot{u} + (C_p + 2C_s)\dot{V} + \frac{2}{R}V = 0 \end{cases} . \tag{1}$$

In Eq. (1) M and K are the mass and stiffness matrices, respectively. $\mathbf{u}$ and V are the nodal displacement vector and voltage, respectively. Finally, B_V and B_f are voltage and force influence matrices. The details regarding these matrices and vectors can be found in [10]. Interestingly, following some mathematical manipulation, it turns out that shunted piezoelectric patches induce external stiffness and damping in the system, which can be calculated as follows,

$$\bar{K} = \frac{R^2\omega^2 (C_p + 2C_s)}{4 + (R\omega (C_p + 2C_s))^2} B_v B_v^T \text{ and } \bar{C} = \frac{2R}{4 + (R\omega (C_p + 2C_s))^2} B_v B_v^T . \tag{2}$$

Using such passive electrical elements adds much more adaptability to the model compared to the cases considered in prior studies, as the equivalent stiffness ($\overline{K}$) and damping ($\overline{C}$) can be easily tuned now. Hence, with proper circuit tuning, high-quality traveling wave response can be obtained in the region between the excitation force and piezoelectric patches. In the following section, some of the preliminary results of this study are presented and discussed.

Preliminary Results

According to [7], a cost function is used to assess the wave quality in a given region. Pilot studies have suggested that optimal traveling wave response can be obtained in cases where resistive shunts are used, implying that $C_p + 2C_S = 0$. This suggests that

$$C_s = \frac{-C_p}{2}, \tag{3}$$

meaning a negative capacitance is required to meet this condition, as the piezoelectric material's inherent capacitance is positive. The cost function plot in Figure 2 asserts that a small optimal region exists where high-quality traveling waves exist for a given case. It is worth mentioning that a lower cost function value is associated with a higher quality of traveling waves.

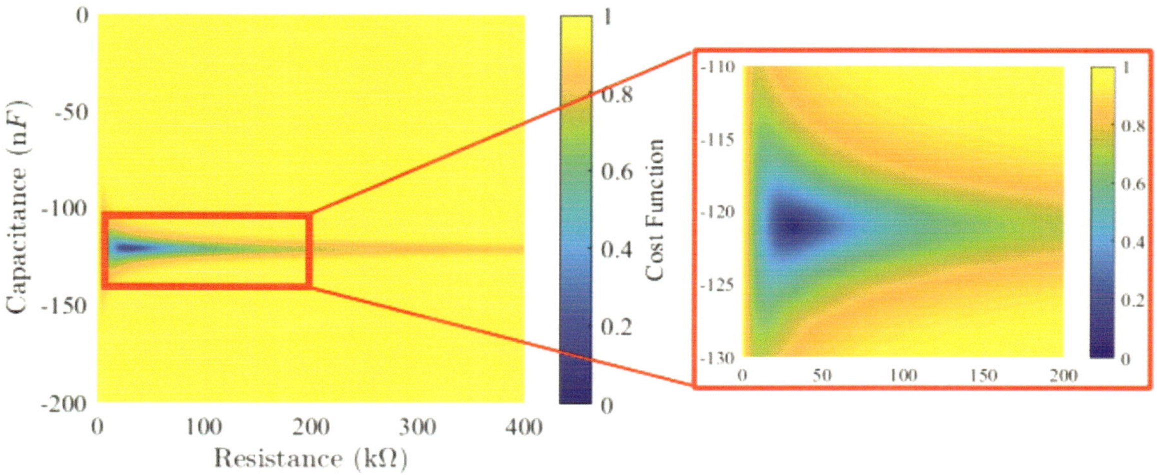

Fig. 2 Cost function contour for a case with an excitation frequency of 1700 Hz [10].

As highlighted in Figure 2, the cost function is minimized in the case where $C_s = -121\ nF$ and $R = 32\ k\Omega$. The system's response in this optimal condition is given in Figure 3.

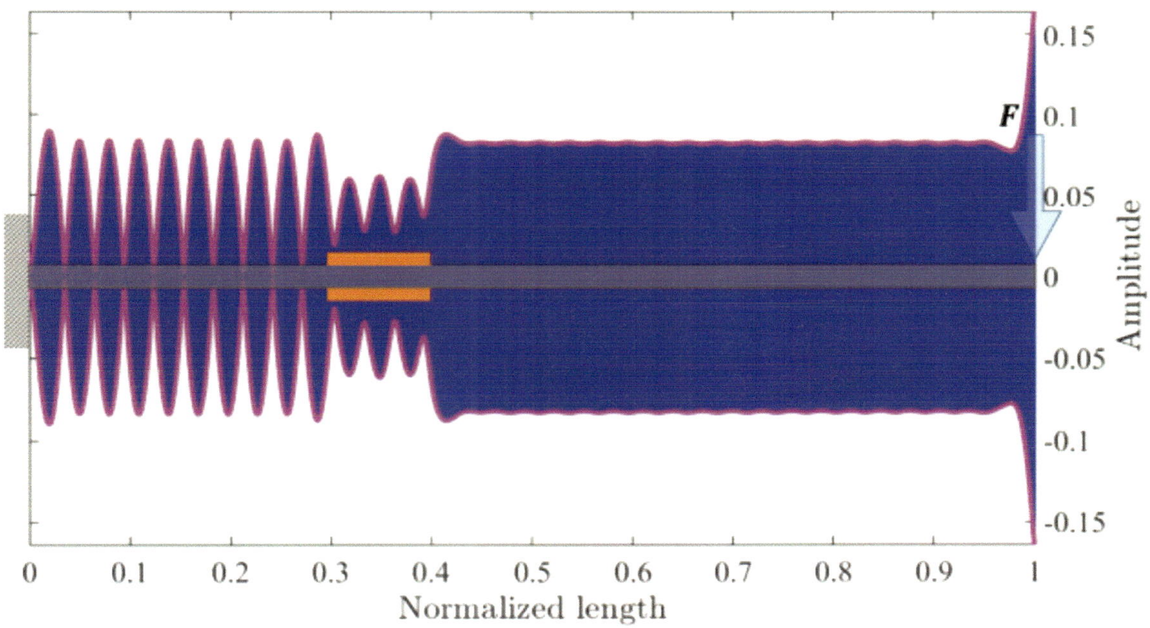

Fig. 3 Area swept by the wave and the wave envelope in the assumed optimal case [10].

Figure 3 suggests high-quality traveling waves can be obtained when the circuit parameters are optimized relative to the system configuration. Realizing the negative capacitance requires additional circuitry, which is extensively discussed in the literature [11]. Therefore, this approach is promising for improving the single-point excitation traveling waves model and relaxing the need for mechanical discontinuities such as springs and dampers in solid mechanical structures. In the last section of this extended abstract, we provide a brief overview of the ongoing research on this topic.

Ongoing Study

As the next step in the work discussed above, the authors are conducting parametric studies to understand the model's sensitivity to different parameters and configurations, e.g., unimorph or bimorph piezoelectric patch installment, series or parallel configurations of the circuitry components, etc. Efforts are being made to conduct an experimental study to verify the simulation results.

Acknowledgments The authors would like to recognize Texas A&M University's support through the Emil Buhler Aerodynamic Analog Fellowship and James J Cain '51 Faculty Fellowship.

References

1. Y. Tomikawa, K. Adachi, H. Hirata, T. Suzuki, and T. Takano, "Excitation of a Progressive Wave in a Flexurally Vibrating Transmission Medium," Japanese Journal of Applied Physics, vol. 29, no. S1, p. 179, 1990/01/01 1990, doi: 10.7567/JJAPS.29S1.179.
2. W. C. Rogers and M. I. Albakri, "Tailoring Structure-Borne Traveling Waves in Targeted Areas of a Two-Dimensional Plate for Particle Motion Applications," in ASME 2021 Conference on Smart Materials, Adaptive Structures and Intelligent Systems, 2021, vol. ASME 2021 Conference on Smart Materials, Adaptive Structures and Intelligent Systems, V001T07A004, doi: 10.1115/smasis2021-67804. [Online]. Available: https://doi.org/10.1115/SMASIS2021-67804
3. T. Nakamura and K. Sato, "Locomotion strategies for an omni-directional mobile robot using traveling waves propagation," in 2010 IEEE International Conference on Robotics and Automation, 2010: IEEE, pp. 3769-3774.
4. P. F. Musgrave, M. I. Albakri, and A. A. Phoenix, "Guidelines and procedure for tailoring high-performance, steady-state traveling waves for propulsion and solid-state motion," Smart Materials and Structures, vol. 30, no. 2, p. 025013, 2021.
5. V. V. N. S. Malladi, D. Avirovik, S. Priya, and P. Tarazaga, "Characterization and representation of mechanical waves generated in piezo-electric augmented beams," Smart Materials and Structures, vol. 24, no. 10, p. 105026, 2015/09/18 2015, doi: 10.1088/0964-1726/24/10/105026.
6. Y. Xiao, H. Lu, D. M. McFarland, A. F. Vakakis, and L. A. Bergman, "Inducing a nonreflective airborne discontinuity in a circular duct by using a nonresonant side branch to create mode complexity," The Journal of the Acoustical Society of America, vol. 143, no. 2, pp. 746-755, 2018, doi: 10.1121/1.5022777.
7. S. Motaharibidgoli, S. Davaria, V. V. N. Sriram Malladi, and P. A. Tarazaga, "Developing coexisting traveling and standing waves in Euler-Bernoulli beams using a single-point excitation and a spring-damper system," Journal of Sound and Vibration, vol. 556, p. 117728, 2023/07/21/ 2023, doi: https://doi.org/10.1016/j.jsv.2023.117728.
8. G. von Békésy, "Travelling Waves as Frequency Analysers in the Cochlea," Nature, vol. 225, no. 5239, pp. 1207-1209, 1970/03/01 1970, doi: 10.1038/2251207a0.
9. Omidi Soroor, A. and Tarazaga, P. A., 2025. Non-reflective traveling waves in finite thin beams: A parametric study. Thin-Walled Structures, 208, p. 112839.
10. S. Motaharibidgoli, "Generating Traveling Waves in Finite Media Using Single-Point Excitation via Passive Absorber," 2023.
11. M. Berardengo, O. Thomas, C. Giraud-Audine, and S. Manzoni, "Improved resistive shunt by means of negative capacitance: new circuit, performances and multi-mode control," Smart Materials and Structures, vol. 25, no. 7, p. 075033, 2016/06/14 2016, doi: 10.1088/0964-1726/25/7/075033.

Chapter 18
Experimental Modal Analysis of a 12 Inch Water Tunnel

Keith Rice, Megan Ewers, Sean Collier, and Nicholas Vlajic

Abstract Water tunnels are one of the most commonly used experimental research facilities for making hydrodynamic measurements of submerged structures. However, because the wave speed of water is close to that of steel, the structural dynamics of the tunnel itself can couple into the water in certain frequency ranges. This fluid-structure coupling may corrupt measurements and lead to errors in instrumentation data during measurements. A modal test was performed on The Pennsylvania State University Applied Research Laboratory's 12 inch (30.5 cm) water tunnel, and compared to acceleration measurements at a number of different flow speeds. These modal results give insights into the observed vibrations of the tunnel while under operation.

Keywords Modal analysis · Fluid-structure coupling · Flow · Measurements · Accelerometers

Introduction

Water tunnel test facilities are the keystone of controlled experimental measurements of structures in a flow field, and are used to characterize the hydrodynamic properties of submerged bodies as well as validate numerical models. The Fluid Dynamics and Acoustics Office at The Pennsylvania State University Applied Research Laboratory maintains and operates four different water tunnels to measure the hydrodynamic properties of submerged bodies in flow fields. The 12 in. (30.5 cm) cross section water tunnel[1] is one of the most widely used water tunnels due to its versatility to support a number of measurements and its cost-effectiveness. A description of the tunnel specifications can be found in Ref. [1], but a short summary is presented here. The water tunnel has two interchangeable test sections that include a circular test section that is 12 in. (30.5 cm) in diameter and 20.0 in. × 4.5 in. (50.8 cm × 11.43 cm) rectangular cross section. The closed-looped variable-speed tunnel can support velocities of 6 ft/s to 69 ft/s (2 m/s to 21 m/s) and pressures of 3 psia to 60 psia (20.7 kPa to 414 kPa), allowing for cavitation studies from cavitation numbers of 0.08 to greater than 350. Additionally, a wire-mesh grid can be inserted into the diffuser of the tunnel that generates turbulent flow within the working section to study the effects of turbulence on bodies. This tunnel has been used to support a number of measurements of two- and three-dimensional bodies such as those of Refs. [2–5].

The tunnel has a number of instrumentation capabilities that include pressure sensors, static and dynamic force gauges, accelerometers, hydrophones and acoustic arrays, and allows for various optical flow measurements. Power spectra data from the different instrumentation and experiments reveal features at common frequencies, leading to speculation that the these features originate from structural resonances of the water tunnel itself. These features are referred to as facility noise and can corrupt measurement signals in certain frequency regimes.

A schematic of the entire tunnel is shown in Figure 1 (left), while a photograph of the rectangular test section is shown in Figure 1 (right).

Keith Rice · Megan Ewers · Sean Collier · Nicholas Vlajic
Applied Research Laboratory, The Pennsylvania State University, University Park, PA, 16802
e-mail: kkr5496@psu.edu; mbe5377@psu.edu; smc604@psu.edu; nav5000@psu.edu

[1] The tunnel is referred to as the 12 in. (30.5 cm) tunnel since the circular cross section is 12 inches (30.5 cm) in diameter. The rectangular cross section, which has a similar area to that of the circular one, was the test section studied here.

Brandon Dilworth et al. (eds.), *Topics in Modal Analysis & Parameter Identification I, Vol. 9*, Conference Proceedings of the Society for Experimental Mechanics Series, https://doi.org/10.13052/9788743801542-18

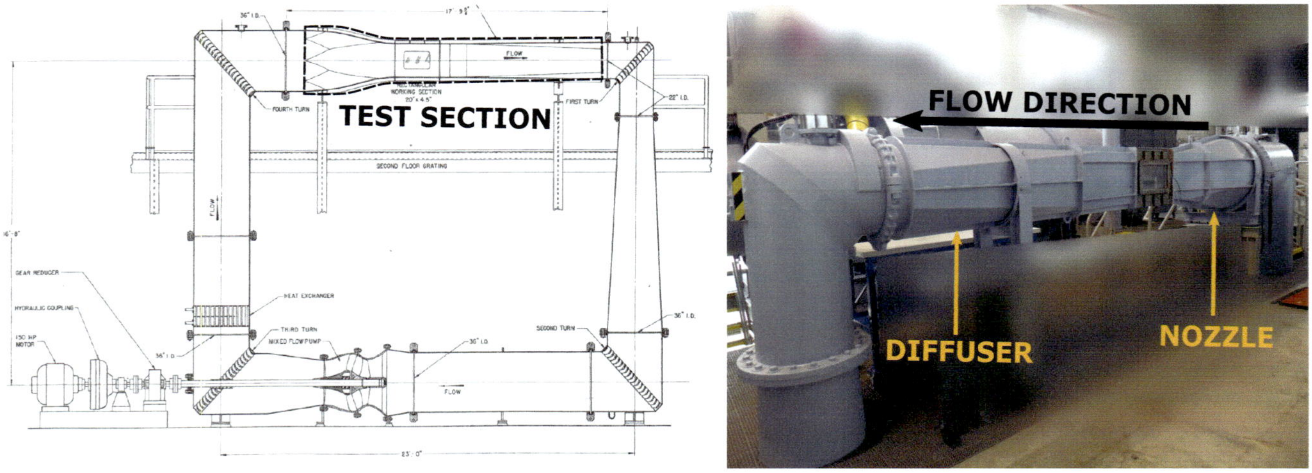

Fig. 1 (Left) Schematic of the entire 12 in. tunnel [1] and (right) photograph of the top portion of the test section that includes the nozzle, working section, and diffuser.

A modal analysis of this tunnel with and without water with the circular test section installed was presented in 2018 [6]. This study showed that the resonant frequencies were reduced by 10% to 15% and the amplitudes of the resonances were reduced up to 15 dB when the tunnel was filled with water. An interesting finding of this study was that the water did not introduce any significant radiation damping into the structure; the attenuated response was primarily due to mass loading. The study focused mostly on the spatial Fourier modes of the structure given its circular geometry. We note that a similar spatial Fourier analysis study is not appropriate for the rectangular cross section studied here given its geometry. For the current study, all data were collected with water in the tunnel.

The intent of this work is to characterize the structural dynamics of the 12 in. (30.5 cm) water tunnel with the rectangular section to gain insights into the origins of the facility noise. Once the nature of this facility noise is better understood, experiments can be designed to avoid certain frequency regimes wherein structural vibrations may be corrupting measurements. Moreover, vibration mitigation strategies can be designed to attenuate some of these undesired structural motions.

Analysis of Vibrations under Operation

Facility noise can originate from a number of different sources, but for the purposes of this study, can be considered as either electrical noise or mechanical noise. Electrical noise includes any electromagnetic interference from electrical utilities, lights, or motors. Mechanical noise can originate from the vibrations of the drive system, including the motor and impeller, as well as fluid-flow forcing on the tunnel itself exciting structural resonances. Initial characterization measurements were made with five accelerometers attached to the tunnel, while operating at six different drive speeds.

Power spectra from one of the accelerometers that highlights the effects of motor drive and structural effects at two different drive speeds are shown in Figure 2. Note that all of the acceleration data reported here were collected without a turbulence grid installed in the diffuser section. Harmonics of the motor at 94.5 RPM (1.58 Hz) (Figure 2 (left)) and 182 RPM (3.03 Hz) (Figure 2 (right)) are marked with numbered dashed lines. It is important to point out that the measured response in Figure 2 is a combination of both the drive amplitude and the structural response, so that the dominant harmonic frequencies may change with drive speed. Although drive speed can be expressed in Hz given some RPM, this is a separate quantity from the drive frequency of the supply phase voltage waveforms which control the drive speed.

In the 94.5 RPM data shown in Figure 2 (left), harmonics 5 and 7 are particularly notable, since they are likely excited by the three phases in the motor ($3\times2 \pm 1$) [7]. At 94.5 RPM, harmonics 5 and 7 are near 8 Hz and 11 Hz, respectively. At 182 RPM shown in Figure 2 (right), harmonics 5 and 7 are still present, but the 7th harmonic is not as strong. There is still a response in spectra near 8 Hz and 11 Hz at 182 RPM, which are likely resonant modes of the structure. At lower frequencies, when the harmonics of the drive system align with these resonances, there is an amplified response.

Power spectra from the same accelerometer as Figure 2 at six different flow speeds are shown in Figure 3. Low frequency spectra (under 50 Hz for this study) are shown in Figure 3 (left), while the broadband response (up to 1 kHz) is provided in Figure 3 (right). All data were collected with 100 second durations, sampling at 20.48 kHz. The low-frequency power spectra

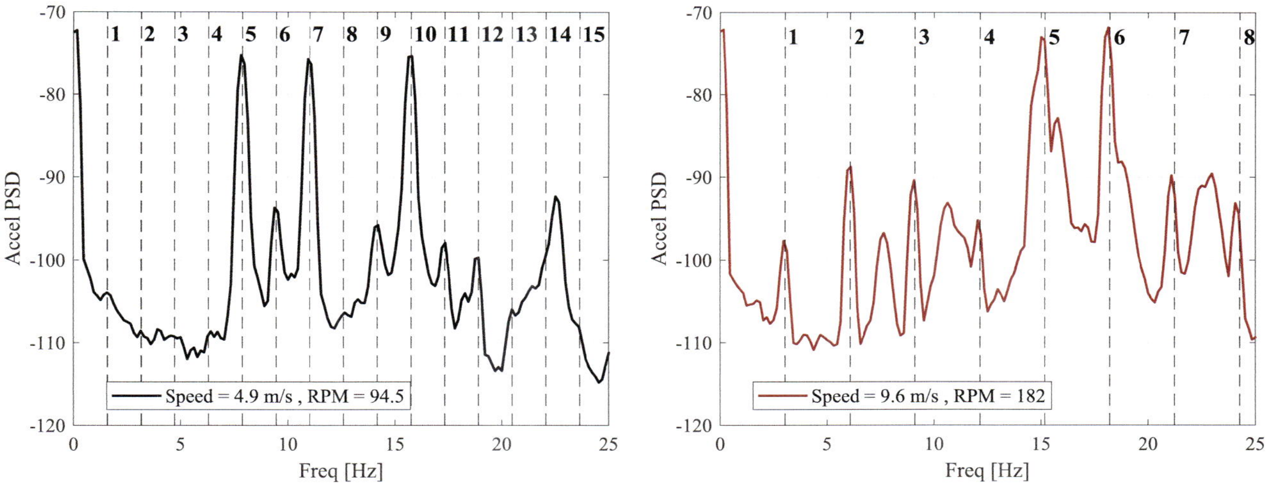

Fig. 2 Acceleration spectrum of an accelerometer mounted on the outside of the tunnel while the motor was operating at 94.5 RPM (1.58 Hz) (left) and 182 RPM (3.03 Hz) (right). Harmonics of the drive speed are shown as vertical dashed lines.

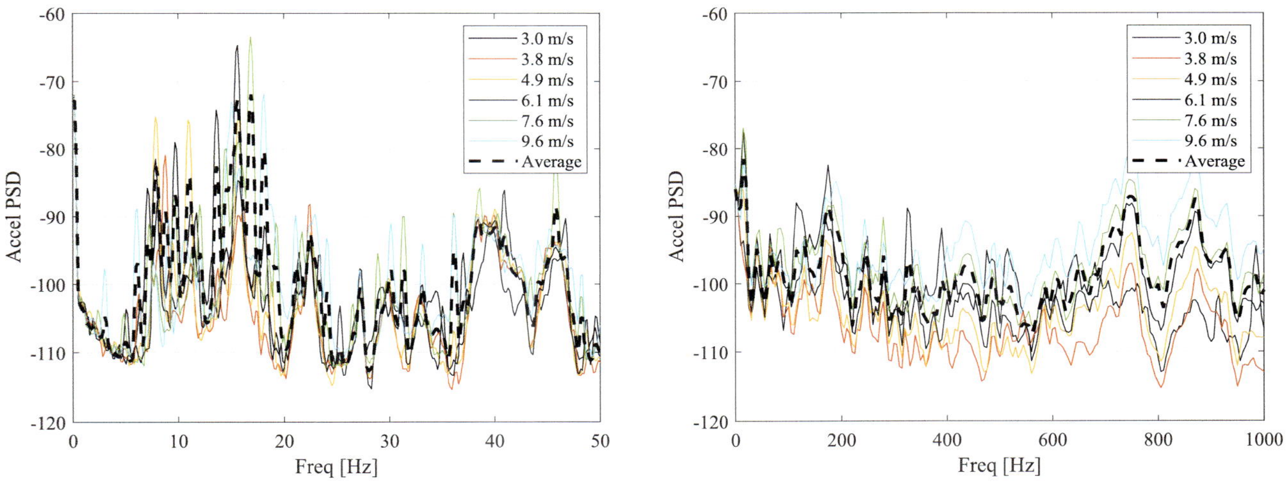

Fig. 3 Low (left) and high (right) frequency regimes of acceleration spectra at different operating speeds.

were calculated using 25 averages with 25% overlap, while the high-frequency data were calculated using 500 averages with 25% overlap.

When looking at the response spectra of the accelerometer, structural resonances excited by flow-induced forcing will not change with drive speed since the forcing is broadband. However, driving excitation from the motor and impeller are expected to generate tonal forcing that change with drive speed, even though the resonances will be unchanged.

As a first approximation to remove the tonal effects of the motor drive from the structural response, the amplitude spectra were averaged over all the drive speeds and the result is shown in a dashed black line.

When looking at the averaged response in the low frequency data (shown in Figure 3 (left)), prominent features in spectra occur at 7.8 Hz, 8.8 Hz, 10.9 Hz, 13.6 Hz, 15.6 Hz, 16.9 Hz, 18.1 Hz, with the two highest amplitude spectra being 15.6 Hz and 16.9 Hz. Note that although these results are averaged spectra, the individual spectra at each drive speed tend to vary around these frequencies. The spectral response between 25 Hz and 50 Hz tend to be more constant with respect to drive speed, indicating that excitation in this regime is likely from flow-induced forcing. The broadband data (shown in Figure 3 (right)) tend to have frequency components that do not change with flow speed, although the amplitude generally increase with flow speed above 600 Hz.

Experimental Modal Analysis

Due to the size of the structure and the nature of the anticipated modes, a roving hammer modal analysis was performed on the test section of the tunnel. Six single-axis accelerometers were affixed to the tunnel in three orientations which aligned with Cartesian axes as shown in Figure 4. This set of accelerometers contained the same accelerometers that were used in the drive speed testing and were thus at the same locations. The tunnel was filled with non-flowing water to account for fluid-structure coupling. Two tests were done separately, namely, a "low-frequency" test and a "high-frequency" test. The intent of the "low-frequency" test was to excite modes below 100 Hz. A 2.4 lb (1.1 kg) PCB Piezotronics 086D20 hammer was used to hit 114 points that were coarsely spaced since these modes of the tunnel will have low wave-numbers.

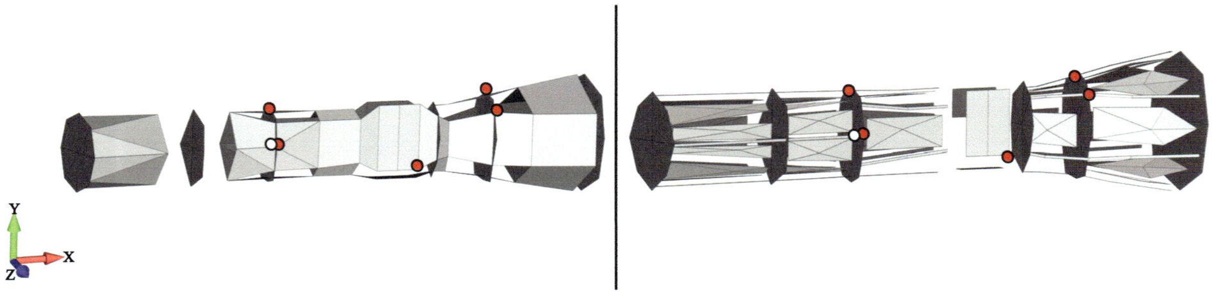

Fig. 4 Low-frequency (left) and high-frequency (right) experimental meshes with accelerometer locations marked. White dots were used to improve the visibility of two locations in close proximity.

For the "high-frequency" test a 0.7 lb (0.32 kg) PCB Piezotronics 086D05 hammer with a metal tip was used to excite the structure to identify modes up to at least 1 kHz. For this high-frequency test, the finer mesh consisting of 335 hit locations (including the 114 from the low-frequency test) was used to resolve the motion since the wave numbers are larger at the higher frequencies.

Each strike was performed three times to achieve an average spectrum. Note that accelerometers and hit points were only place along the test section and not the entire tunnel itself (see Figure 1 (left)). Care must be taken when analyzing results, especially any modal assurance criteria, since there may appear to be spatial aliasing as the entire tunnel was not instrumented.

The meshes were constructed using elements that had surface normal vectors that matched the direction of the surface being struck in order to move along the same vectors as the accelerometer data; faces of the tunnel that were not struck were omitted from the meshes because there was no data to reliably describe their movement.

The PolyMAX algorithm was used to identify modes from the data [8]. A mode order of 26 was used for the low-frequency test, searching from 0 Hz to 100 Hz. A mode order of 40 was used in the high-frequency test, searching between 100 Hz and 300 Hz. The identified modes were then cross-referenced with the experimental acceleration spectra from the drive speed testing in Figure 3 to identify modes that may be excited during normal tunnel operation.

Results

A comparison between the normalized surface average mobility from the modal test and the average acceleration of the operational drive-speed test at low frequencies is shown in Figure 5. The operational test trace has correlation with the modal test trace at several frequencies, most notably near 15 Hz.

Modes pertinent to both the surface averaged acceleration from the modal test and the drive speed accelerometer data are depicted on the following pages in Figures 6 and 7.

The low-frequency data contains modes at 7 Hz, 8 Hz, and 10 Hz, along the z-, x-, and z-axes respectively. Some of these low-frequency modes look like modes with free or fixed ends but in fact include motion of the rest of the tunnel. While the test section was sufficiently spatially resolved, there was modal participation from the lower sections of the tunnel which was not resolved. The tunnel has an unusual shape, namely, a cross-section that transitions from a circle to rectangle to circle with a decreasing and increasing effective area. Despite this atypical geometry, some of the lower order modes are representative of bending motions of a beam. The first bending mode on the z-axis (about the y-axis) occurs at 15 Hz. The first bending mode on the diagonal between the y- and z-axes occurs at 27 Hz, while 37 Hz represents the first bending mode on the y-axis but second on the z-axis.

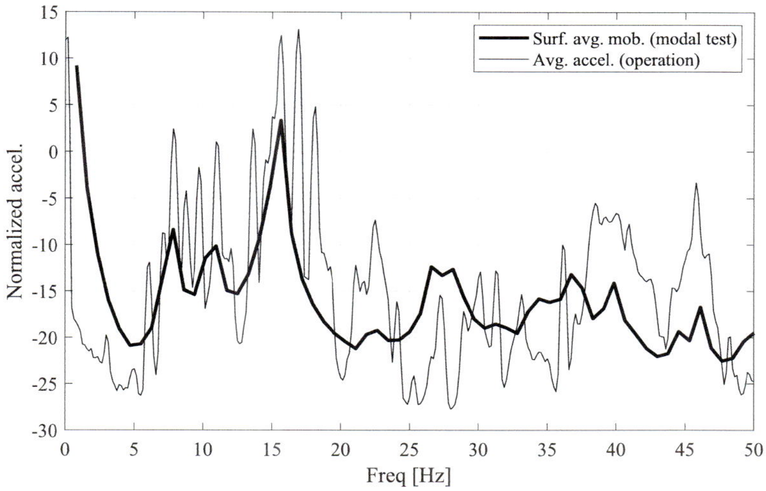

Fig. 5 Comparison of operational accelerometer data with low-frequency modal surface average accelerance data.

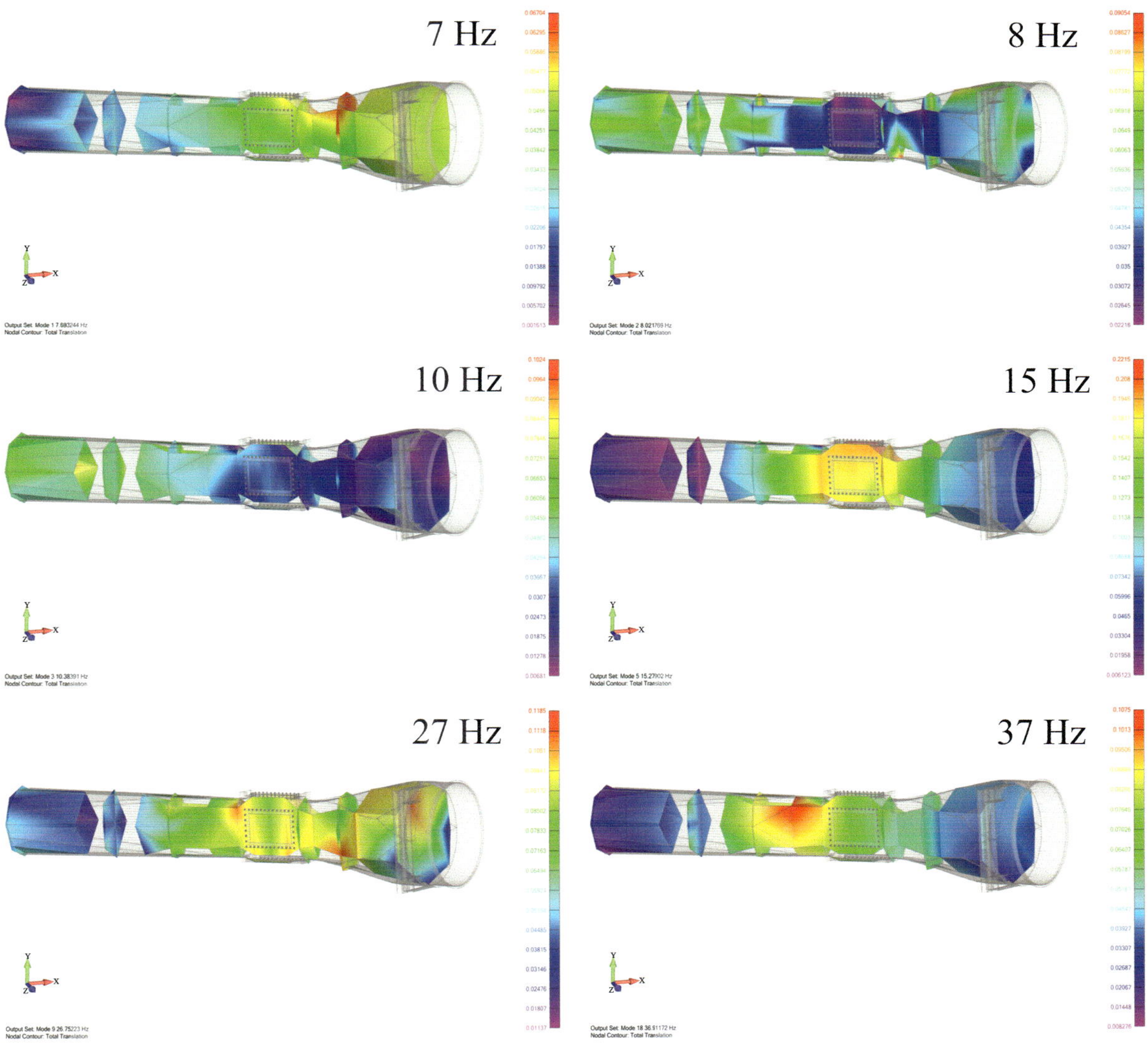

Fig. 6 Modes of interest below 50 Hz that correspond to higher amplitude regimes of operational acceleration data.

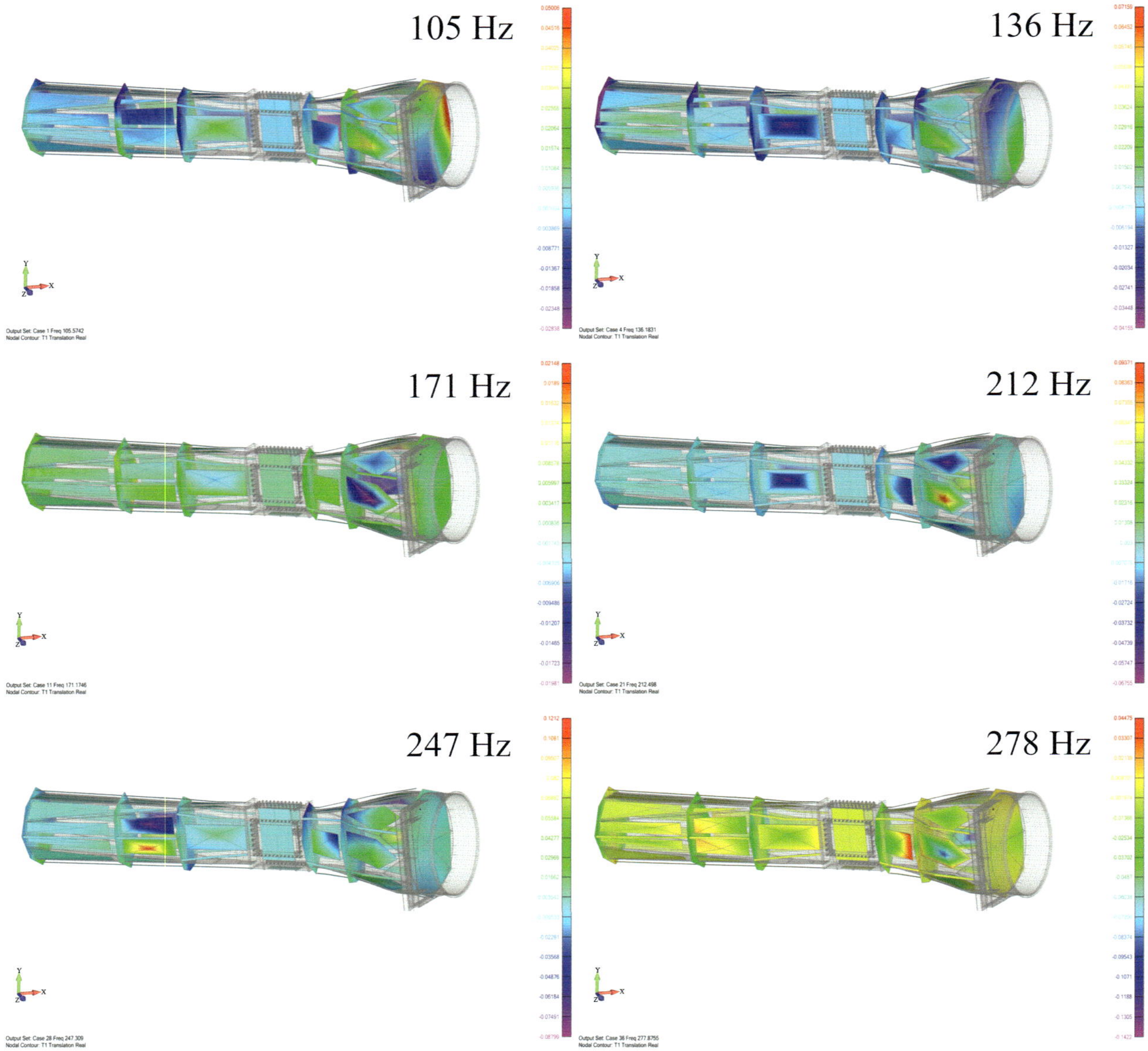

Fig. 7 Modes of interest above 100 Hz that correspond to higher amplitude regimes of operational acceleration data.

The identified high-frequency modes are documented in Figure 7. The modes in Figure 7 indicate tunnel vibrations nearest the following peak frequencies from the data in Figure 3: 100 Hz, 130 Hz, 175 Hz, 210 Hz, 245 Hz, and 280 Hz.

In this higher frequency regime, the modes don't necessarily behave as simple beam-bending modes and the motion becomes more complex. Not every peak in the operational acceleration data was reflected in the modal data, and vice versa. At higher frequencies, the system becomes modally dense and discerning real modes becomes difficult.

As noted earlier, the operational data in Figure 3 was taken without a turbulence grid installed. In conditions wherein the turbulence grid is installed, turbulent flow through the tunnel is expected to excite these high-frequency modes and create an amplified response in the accelerometer readings over a large bandwidth.

Discussion and Conclusion

The results presented here are useful for interpreting past data collected in this facility, as well as future tests. Acceleration spectra during tunnel operation contains both broadband characteristics, and tonal features from both the motor drive and structural resonances of the tunnel. The modal analysis performed on the tunnel showed that the the structural response of the tunnel is modally dense, due to the size of the tunnel and of the fluid-structure interaction. Errors in instrumentation located within the tunnel can be amplified when harmonics of the motor drive speed align with structural resonances of the tunnel at the lower frequencies, below 100 Hz. At higher frequencies, above 100 Hz, other resonances were observed and are assumed to be excited by fluid flow forcing through the tunnel. However, the acceleration spectra during operation is complex in nature and the presence of a strong response at a particular frequency in experimental acceleration data may not imply an excited vibration mode; similarly, an existing structural mode may not be excited during the course of an experiment. The data collected here did not have the wire-mesh turbulence grid inserted into the diffuser. The presence of this grid is expected to exacerbate the fluid flow forcing and introduce additional tonal features from resonances of the grid itself. Further analysis with and without the turbulence grid may yield additional insights. For example, asynchronous and synchronous averaging, as well as instrumenting the motor and performing coherent noise rejection may also reveal additional information to the nature of the spectral response of the tunnel.

Acknowledgments The authors would like to acknowledge Hruday Shah, Victor Baran, and Sierra Nelson for their assistance with the experiments.

References

1. Lehman, A.F. "The Garfield Thomas Water Tunnel". In *Bodarski Institut, Shipbuilding Research Institute Zagreb, Presented at: The Symposium on the Towing Tank Facilities, Instrumentation and Measuring Technique, 22-25 September 1959* (1959).
2. Stinebring, D.R., Straka, W.A., and Willits, S.M. "Hydrofoil test facility at ARL Penn State". In *Fluids Engineering Division Summer Meeting*, volume 41995, pages 603–607 (2005).
3. Reich, D.B. *Water tunnel experiments on a model scale helicopter rotor hub*. M.S. Thesis, The Pennsylvania State University (2013).
4. Brungart, T.A., Myer, E.C., Capone, D.E., and Campbell, R.L. "Hydrofoil vibration and noise reduction with leading edge isolation". In *INTER-NOISE and NOISE-CON Congress and Conference Proceedings*, volume 2005, pages 623–629. Institute of Noise Control Engineering (2005).
5. Lysak, P.D., Capone, D.E., and Jonson, M.L. "Measurement of the unsteady lift of thick airfoils in incompressible turbulent flow". *Journal of Fluids and Structures*, 66:315–330 (2016).
6. Myer, E., Bonness, W., and Fahnline, J. "Modal analysis results of ARL/PSU 12" water tunnel test section with and without water". In *Intenational Modal Analysis Conference XXXVI, Orlando, FL* (2018).
7. Gieras, J.F., Wang, C., and Lai, J.C. *Noise of polyphase electric motors*. CRC press (2018).
8. Guillaume, P., Verboven, P., Vanlanduit, S., Van Der Auweraer, H., and Peeters, B. "A poly-reference implementation of the least-squares complex frequency-domain estimator". In *Proceedings of IMAC*, volume 21. A Conference & Exposition on Structural Dynamics, Society for Experimental Mechanics (2003).

Chapter 19
Frequency Band Damping: Implementation and Innovations

Dagny Beale, Gregory Bunting, Nathan Crane, David Day, Clark Dohrmann, Payton Lindsay, Justin Pepe, and Julia Plews

Abstract This talk overviews a novel frequency-band-limited approach to tunable structural damping, building on previous work in this area [1]. In particular, this work will discuss numerical stability, practical code implementation considerations, and application to large-scale problems in structural dynamics.

The inclusion of damping in FEA is not merely a theoretical enhancement but a practical necessity. It bridges the gap between idealized representations and realistic structural response. By providing a more flexible approach to damping, we enable engineers and scientists to make fine-tuned, informed decisions in the design, analysis, and optimization of structures.

Keywords Frequency band damping · Frequency dependent damping · Damping models · Modal damping · Damping

Introduction

Finite Element Analysis (FEA) is a cornerstone in the engineering and scientific communities for predicting structural response. An understated yet crucial part of FEA is damping, which can heuristically capture real-world energy dissipation mechanisms in structures. Choice of damping model is critical, and directly influences the fidelity and robustness of the simulation.

Recently, Huang, Sturt, and Willford [1] proposed a novel approach to apply uniform damping across a spectrum of frequencies. The approach enjoys several benefits, including the ability to apply differential damping across subregions of a model.

This work builds upon the original publication's foundation, and details its incorporation into a massively parallel finite element code [2]. It delves more deeply into the derivation and implementation, examines some potential drawbacks of the approach, and proposes a potential path forward towards improving it. We also include an example on a multi-million element model, where we compare the new approach to direct modal damping approaches, explore the performance characteristics of the model, and make some recommendations for usage best practices.

Theory

In this section, we provide a brief overview of the theory of the damping approach, as well as some additional clarifying details and insights beyond what was given in the original paper.

We begin the discussion with the equation of motion, which is given by

$$M\ddot{u}(t) + f_{int}(t) = f_{ext}(t) \tag{1}$$

where the $f_{int}(t)$, the *internal resisting force*, consists of a constitutive and damping component,

$$f_0(t) + f_d(t).$$

Here we assume linear elastic behavior such that $f_0(t) = Ku(t)$, and adopt the notation $d = u(t), v = \dot{u}(t), a = \ddot{u}(t)$.

Dagny Beale · Gregory Bunting · Nathan Crane · David Day · Clark Dohrmann · Payton Lindsay · Justin Pepe · Julia Plews
Sandia National Laboratories, Albuquerque, NM 87185
e-mail: dmbeale@sandia.gov; gbuntin@sandia.gov; nkcrane@sandia.gov; dmday@sandia.gov; crdohrm@sandia.gov; plindsa@sandia.gov; jppepe@sandia.gov; japlews@sandia.gov;

Brandon Dilworth et al. (eds.), *Topics in Modal Analysis & Parameter Identification I, Vol. 9*, Conference Proceedings of the Society for Experimental Mechanics Series, https://doi.org/10.13052/9788743801542-19

In the frequency domain, the resisting force is defined as

$$F_{int}(\omega) = [K_1(\omega) + iK_2(\omega)]\, U(\omega) \tag{2}$$

We now introduce the concept of a *specific damping factor*, a dimensionless measure of damping given by [1, eqn 3.8.9], [3, eqn (5)]

$$\xi(\omega) = \frac{K_2(\omega)}{K_1(0)} \tag{3}$$

With these prerequisites, we may now restate the main goal of this approach more precisely: define a formulation for the damping force, $f_d(t)$, that approximates a *target specific damping factor* $\xi \approx \eta$ across a frequency range $[\omega_1, \omega_2]$.

Consider a damping force given by the following relation [1, eqn (7)]

$$f_d(t) = \eta \sum_{1}^{N} \frac{2\alpha_n}{\omega_{cn}} \dot{f}_{Ln}(t) \tag{4}$$

where ω_{cn} is the *n*th logarithmically-spaced cutoff frequency between $\omega 1$ and $\omega 2$.

The *n*th filtered force history, $f_{Ln}(t)$, is governed by the relation [1, eqn 9]

$$f_{Ln}(t) + \frac{\dot{f}_{Ln}(t)}{\omega_{cn}} = f_0(t) \tag{5}$$

Calculating the specific damping factor of the damping force given by eq. (4) yields the following result (see appendix A):

$$\xi = \eta \sum_{n=1}^{N} \alpha_n \phi_n(\omega) \tag{6}$$

where $\phi_n(\omega) = \frac{2\omega/\omega_{cn}}{1+(\omega/\omega_{cn})^2}$.

Recalling again the goal of approximating $\xi \approx \eta$ within $[\omega_1, \omega_2]$, we see that an optimal damping force is one which satisfies the following relation:

$$\sum_{n=1}^{N} \alpha_n \phi_n(\omega) \approx 1 \quad \forall \omega \in [\omega_1, \omega_2] \tag{7}$$

Thus, we may formulate the least squares approach to calculate the optimal values of α_n, ultimately leading to the following relations [1, eqns (19),(20)]:

$$\alpha = \mathbb{X}^{-1} \frown \tag{8}$$

where

$$\begin{aligned} y_i &= \int_{\omega_1}^{\omega_2} \phi_i(\omega) d\omega \\ X_{ij} &= \int_{\omega_1}^{\omega_2} \phi_i(\omega)\phi_j(\omega) d\omega \end{aligned} \tag{9}$$

Although not given in the original paper, the integrals given in eq. (20) can be solved directly, with the following solutions:

$$y_i = \int \phi_i(\omega) d\omega = \omega_{ci} \ln(\omega_{ci}^2 + \omega^2) \tag{10}$$

$$X_{ij} = \int \phi_i(\omega)\phi_j(\omega) d\omega = \begin{cases} 2\omega_c \left(\arctan\left(\frac{\omega}{\omega_c}\right) - \frac{\omega_c \omega}{\omega_c^2+\omega^2}\right) & \text{if } \omega_{ci} = \omega_{cj} = \omega_c \\ \frac{4\omega_{ci}\omega_{cj}}{\omega_{ci}^2-\omega_{cj}^2}\left(\omega_{ci} \arctan\left(\frac{\omega}{\omega_{ci}}\right) - \omega_{cj} \arctan\left(\frac{\omega}{\omega_{cj}}\right)\right) & \text{otherwise} \end{cases} \tag{11}$$

In fig. 1, we explore how well the chosen relation matches the goal ($\sum_{n=1}^{N} \alpha_n \phi_n(\omega) \approx 1$). Figure 1a shows the contributions of each component to the overall sum, and shows good agreement in the frequency range of interest. However, note that the plot is logarithmic in the x-axis, which can obfuscate the slowness of the drop-off outside of the desired range. This slow decay is because the formulation as outlined makes no attempt to minimize damping outside the frequency range of interest, and is one of the key drawbacks of this approach.

Figure 1b demonstrates this aspect more clearly, where there is nearly 20% of the maximum damping an order of magnitude above the high-frequency cutoff. This is an important clarification for potential users of this capability to keep in mind, and can lead to unintended behavior, for example when combining multiple frequency bands.

---

[1] $\omega_1 = 3.5$, $\omega_2 = 20$, $N = 4$

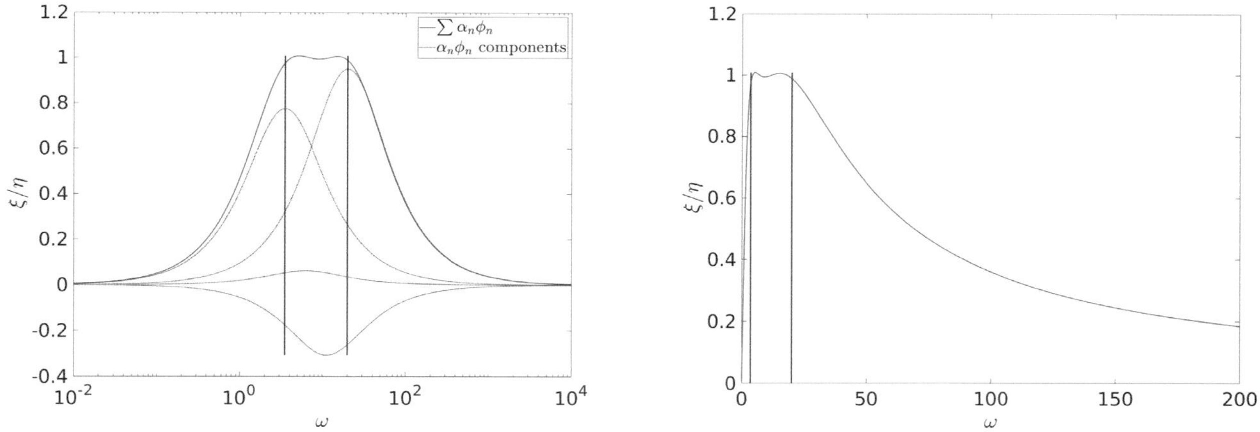

(a) Summation of components.

(b) Linear scale.

Fig. 1 Specific damping factor scale[1].

The results above motivate the need for an improved formulation that not only approximates the target damping within a frequency range, but also minimizes damping outside of it.

One natural modification to accomplish this goal is to optimize α_n to instead satisfy the following relation:

$$\sum_{n=1}^{N} \alpha_n \phi_n(\omega) \approx 1_{[\omega_1,\omega_2]}(\omega) \quad \forall \omega \in [0, \inf] \tag{12}$$

where the *indicator function* $1_{[\omega_1,\omega_2]}(\omega)$ is defined as,

$$1_{[\omega_1,\omega_2]}(\omega) := \begin{cases} 1 & \text{if } \omega \in [\omega_1, \omega_2] \\ 0 & \text{otherwise} \end{cases} \tag{13}$$

This leads to a similar formulation to eq. (8), but with the following definitions for $\mathbb{X}$ and $\curvearrowright$

$$\begin{aligned} y_i &= \int_{\omega_1}^{\omega_2} \phi_i(\omega) d\omega \\ X_{ij} &= \int_0^{\inf} \phi_i(\omega)\phi_j(\omega) d\omega \end{aligned} \tag{14}$$

(note the modified range of integration for X_{ij}).

We now regenerate fig. 1 using the above relations. In the resulting plots (fig. 2), while we do see a quick drop-off outside of the target frequency range, the match inside the range is significantly worse, and the scale actually drops below zero at several points, indicating that an intermediate range of integration may be optimal.

To explore this concept, fig. 3 compares the original range of $[\omega_1, \omega_2]$ along with several slightly larger ranges of integration, as well as the full range. These results indicate that separating the choice of integration range from the frequency range of interest is a viable option to address the inherent drawbacks of the existing methodology, and warrants more investigation. This simple modification provides a tunable parameter to choose between the best fit in the frequency range of interest, or the fastest decay outside of it, along with anything in-between.

Relation to viscous damping

In the outlined methodology, the level of damping is controlled by the target specific damping factor η. However, for the sake of usability, it is convenient to express damping in more familiar terms, namely, the viscous damping ratio ζ.

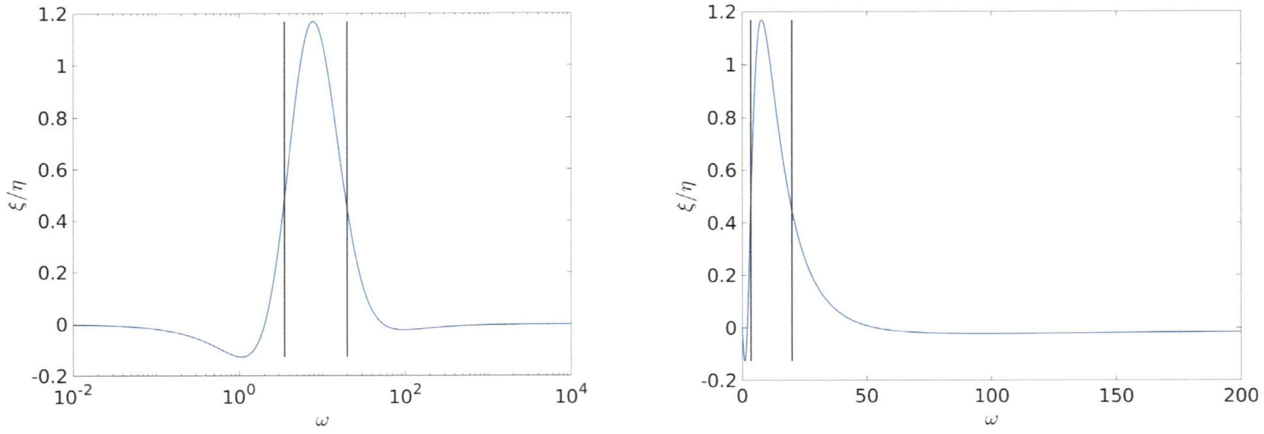

(a) Log scale. (b) Linear scale.

Fig. 2 Specific damping factor scale, modified formulation.

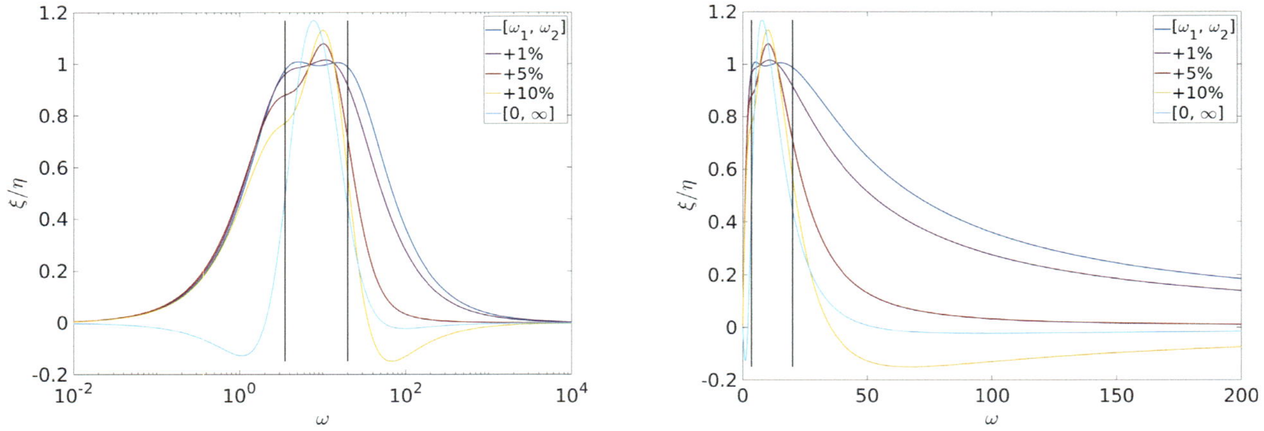

(a) Log scale. (b) Linear scale.

Fig. 3 Specific damping factor scale: range comparison.

The viscous damping ratio ζ may be defined as [1, eqns 5, 6]

$$\zeta = \omega_n \xi/(2\omega)$$
or
$$\xi = 2\zeta \frac{\omega}{\omega_n} \tag{15}$$

Plugging eq. (6) into eq. (15), we obtain the following relation:

$$\eta \sum_{n=1}^{N} \alpha_n \phi_n(\omega) = 2\zeta \frac{\omega}{\omega_n} \tag{16}$$

After substituting eq. (7), eq. (16) simplifies to the following, which relates the target specific damping factor η to the viscous damping ratio ζ

$$\eta \approx 2\zeta \frac{\omega}{\omega_n} \tag{17}$$

At the natural frequency ω_n, eq. (17) simplifies even further

$$\eta \approx 2\zeta \tag{18}$$

While eq. (18) is technically only valid at the natural frequency, it provides a comparable level of damping across a wide range of damping ratios, as seen in fig. 4.

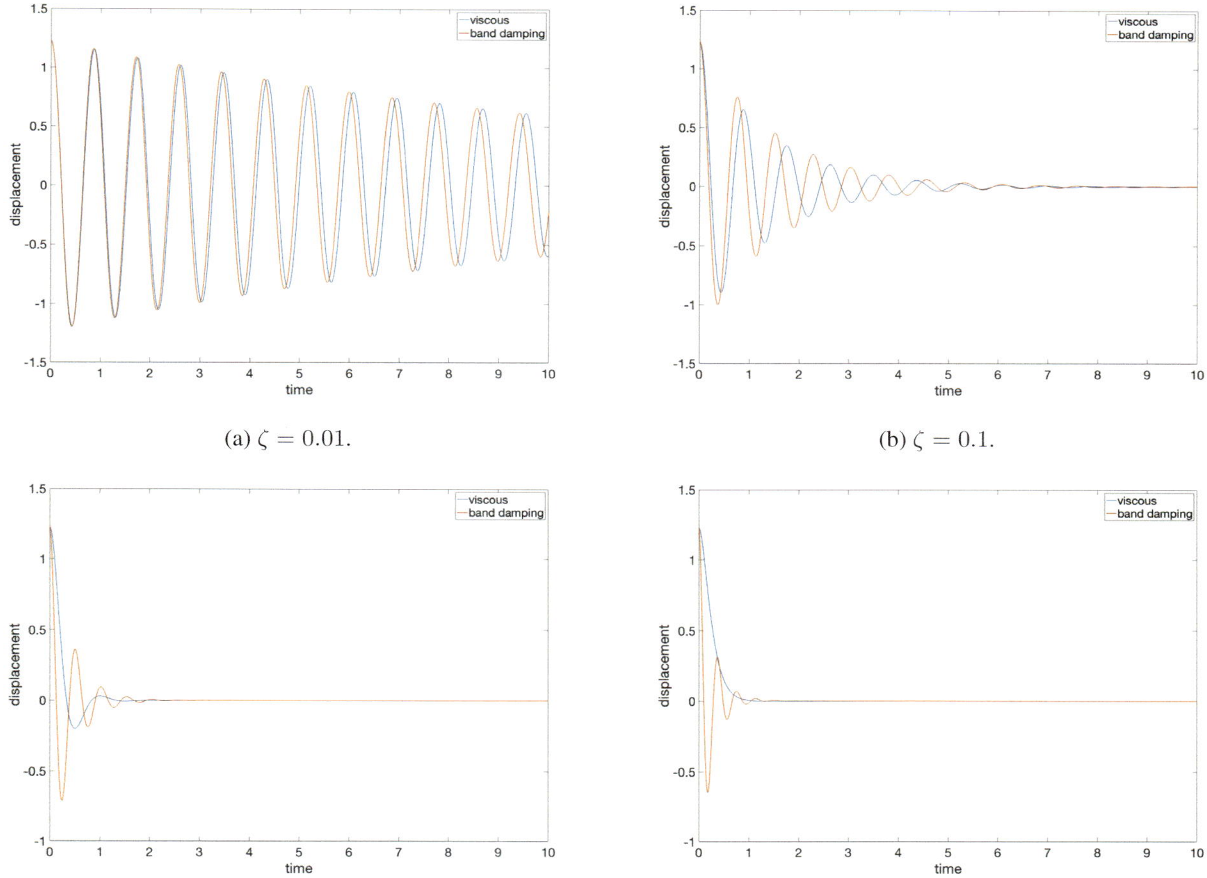

(a) $\zeta = 0.01$. (b) $\zeta = 0.1$.

(c) $\zeta = 0.5$. (d) $\zeta = 1$ (critically damped).

Fig. 4 Comparison of band-limited and viscously-damped response[2].

Taking the same system as fig. 4 and fixing $\zeta = 0.1$, we also see that eq. (18) remains a good approximation for a wide range of frequency bands in fig. 5.

Based on these considerations, eq. (18) was chosen to allow the convenient specification of band-limited damping given a desired damping ratio.

As an interesting aside, the band-limited methodology may also be modified to apply viscous damping across a limited frequency range.

To accomplish this, we modify eq. (7) in the following way:

$$\sum_{n=1}^{N} \alpha_n \phi_n(\omega) \approx \frac{\omega}{\omega_n} \quad \forall \omega \in [\omega_1, \omega_2] \tag{19}$$

which again leads to a similar formulation as eq. (8), now with the following definitions for $\mathbb{X}$ and $\curvearrowright$,

$$\begin{aligned} y_i &= \int_{\omega_1}^{\omega_2} \frac{\omega}{\omega_n} \phi_i(\omega) d\omega \\ X_{ij} &= \int_{\omega_1}^{\omega_2} \phi_i(\omega)\phi_j(\omega) d\omega \end{aligned} \tag{20}$$

[2]Spring-mass system in free vibration; $m = 2.34$, $k = 123$, $d_0 = 1.23$, $v_0 = 0$, $\omega_1 = 3.5$, $\omega_2 = 20$, $N = 4$

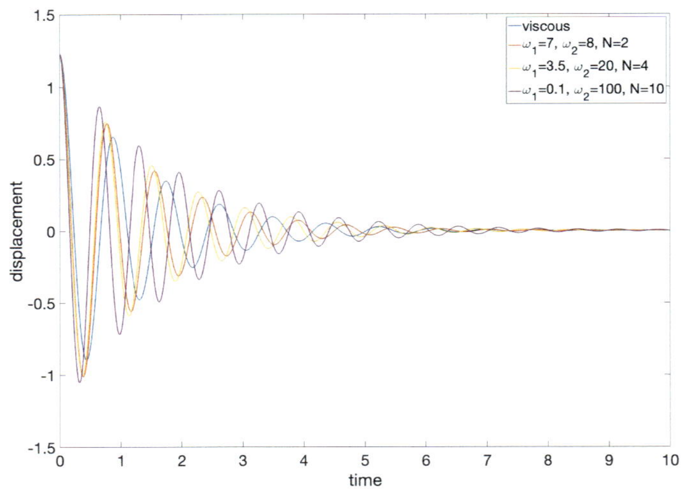

Fig. 5 Viscous Damping Ratio Comparison: effect of frequency bands.

Figure 6 compares the specific damping factor of this approach with the exact/viscous relation. Good agreement is seen with viscous damping in the frequency range of interest.

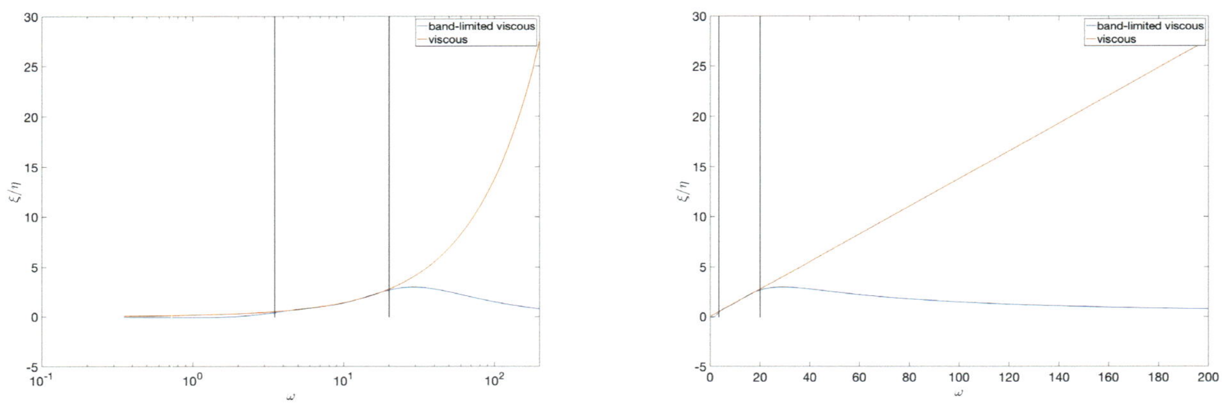

(a) Log scale.

(b) Linear scale.

Fig. 6 Specific damping factor scale: band-limited viscous damping[3].

Finally, fig. 7 compares viscous damping, the original band-limited damping approach, and the modified band-limited viscous approach as outlined above. The band-limited viscous results are a closer match for viscous damping, as expected.

Implementation

One important consideration when adopting this approach is the solution of eqs. (4) and (5). Here, we compare the ubiquitous forward and backward Euler approaches.

(Forward) Euler

We first divide the time domain into finite steps of length Δt. Subsequently, the solution to $\dot{y}(t) = g(t, y(t))$ at the ith

[3] $\omega_1 = 3.5$, $\omega_2 = 20$, $N = 4$

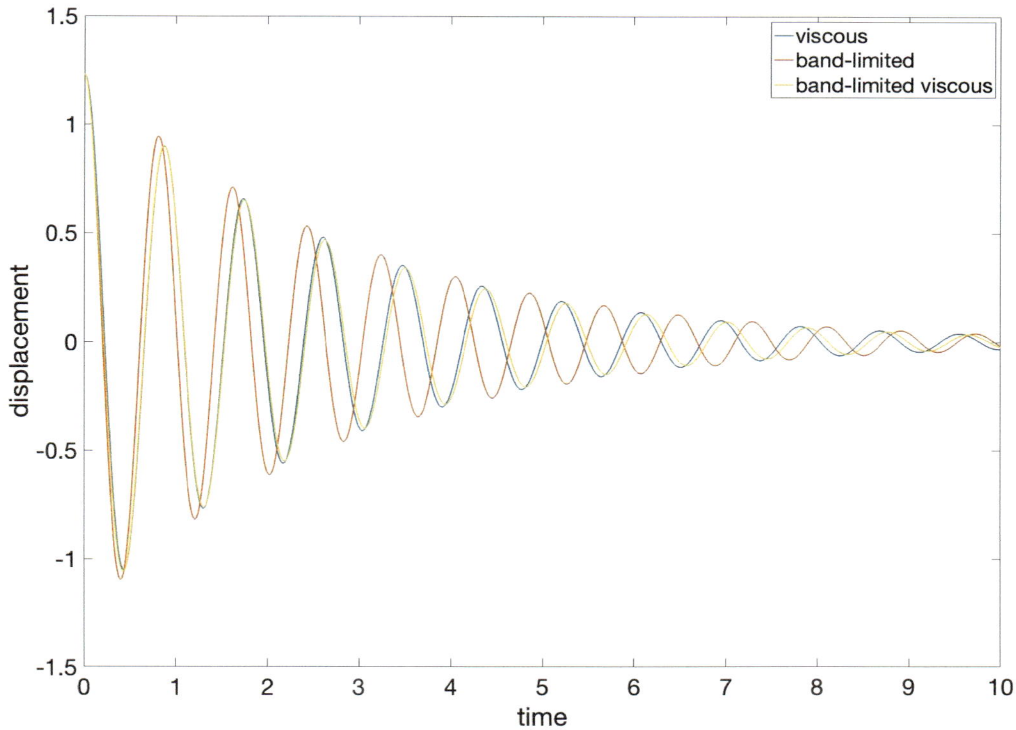

Fig. 7 Band-limited viscous comparison.

step may be approximated as:

$$y_i = y_{i-1} + \Delta t g(t_{i-1}, y_{i-1}) \tag{21}$$

Rearranging eq. (5), we obtain:

$$\dot{f}_{Ln}(t) = \omega_{cn}\left(f_0(t) - f_{Ln}(t)\right) \tag{22}$$

Applying Euler, we obtain:

$$\begin{aligned} f_{Ln(i)} &= f_{Ln(i-1)} + \Delta t \omega_{cn}\left(f_{0(i-1)} - f_{Ln(i-1)}\right) \\ &= f_{Ln(i-1)} + \Delta t \omega_{cn}\left(K d_{i-1} - f_{Ln(i-1)}\right) \end{aligned} \tag{23}$$

where we take $f_{Ln(0)} = 0$.

Finally, plugging the solution back into eq. (5) and then eq. (4), we can approximate the damping force as:

$$\begin{aligned} f_{d(i)} &= \eta \sum_1^N 2\alpha_n \frac{\dot{f}_{Ln(i)}}{\omega_{cn}} \\ &= \eta \sum_1^N 2\alpha_n \left[f_{0(i)} - f_{Ln(i)}\right] \\ &= \eta \sum_1^N 2\alpha_n \left[K d_i - f_{Ln(i-1)} - \Delta t \omega_{cn}\left(K d_{i-1} - f_{Ln(i-1)}\right)\right] \\ &= \eta \sum_1^N 2\alpha_n \left[K d_i - \Delta t \omega_{cn} K d_{i-1} - \left(1 - \Delta t \omega_{cn}\right) f_{Ln(i-1)}\right] \end{aligned} \tag{24}$$

Which leads to the following modified equations of motion at each step i:

$$M a_i + \hat{K} d_i = \hat{f}_{ext(i)} \tag{25}$$

where the modified stiffness $\hat{K}$ is defined as

$$\hat{K} = \left(1 + \eta \sum_{1}^{N} 2\alpha_n\right) K \tag{26}$$

and the external force is modified as:

$$\hat{f}_{ext(i)} = f_{ext(i)} + \eta \sum_{1}^{N} 2\alpha_n \left[\Delta t \omega_{cn} K d_{i-1} + (1 - \Delta t \omega_{cn}) f_{Ln(i-1)}\right] \tag{27}$$

Backward Euler

While in forward Euler the values at the previous step are used to update the new solution, the backward Euler method uses values from the new solution to calculate the slope:

$$y_i = y_{i-1} + \Delta t g(t_i, y_i) \tag{28}$$

Again rearranging eq. (5) and applying backward Euler, we obtain:

$$f_{Ln(i)} = f_{Ln(i-1)} + \Delta t \omega_{cn} \left(K d_i - f_{Ln(i)}\right) \tag{29}$$

or

$$f_{Ln(i)} = \frac{f_{Ln(i-1)} + \Delta t \omega_{cn} K d_i}{1 + \Delta t \omega_{cn}} \tag{30}$$

where $f_{Ln(0)} = 0$.

As before, we can plug the solution back into eq. (5) and then eq. (4), and approximate the damping force as:

$$\begin{aligned} f_{d(i)} &= \eta \sum_{1}^{N} 2\alpha_n \frac{\dot{f}_{Ln(i)}}{\omega_{cn}} \\ &= \eta \sum_{1}^{N} 2\alpha_n \left[f_{0(i)} - f_{Ln(i)}\right] \\ &= \eta \sum_{1}^{N} 2\alpha_n \left[K d_i - \frac{f_{Ln(i-1)} + \Delta t \omega_{cn} K d_i}{1 + \Delta t \omega_{cn}}\right] \\ &= \eta \sum_{1}^{N} 2\alpha_n \frac{K d_i - f_{Ln(i-1)}}{1 + \Delta t \omega_{cn}} \end{aligned} \tag{31}$$

Leading to the following modified equations of motion:

$$M a_i + \hat{K} d_i = \hat{f}_{ext(i)} \tag{32}$$

where the modified stiffness $\hat{K}$ is defined as

$$\hat{K} = \left(1 + \eta \sum_{1}^{N} \frac{2\alpha_n}{1 + \Delta t \omega_{cn}}\right) K \tag{33}$$

and the external force is modified as:

$$\hat{f}_{ext(i)} = f_{ext(i)} + \eta \sum_{1}^{N} 2\alpha_n \frac{f_{Ln(i-1)}}{1 + \Delta t \omega_{cn}} \tag{34}$$

Note that with both approaches, this damping approach is represented in the governing equations as a stiffness modification and external force contribution. However, for linear systems, the forward Euler approach involves only an initial stiffness matrix modification (eq. (26)), and the damping force contribution and filtered force update (eqs. (23) and (27)) may be accomplished in a single call prior to the solution step. In contrast, the stiffness modification for the backward Euler approach (eq. (33)) involves the timestep Δt, which might change throughout the simulation, and the filtered force (eq. (30)) must be updated after the solution step, as it depends on the new displacement u_i.

While the backward Euler approach offers stability benefits at large time steps (fig. 8a), the forward Euler approach was ultimately chosen due to the implementation benefits outlined above. Below the critical timestep, the results for both approaches converge with decreasing timestep (figs. 8b to 8d).

[4]Spring-mass system in free vibration; $m = 2.34$, $k = 123$, $d_0 = 1.23$, $v_0 = 0$, $\zeta = 0.05$, $\omega_1 = 3.5$, $\omega_2 = 20$, $N = 4$, $\eta = 2\zeta = 0.1$

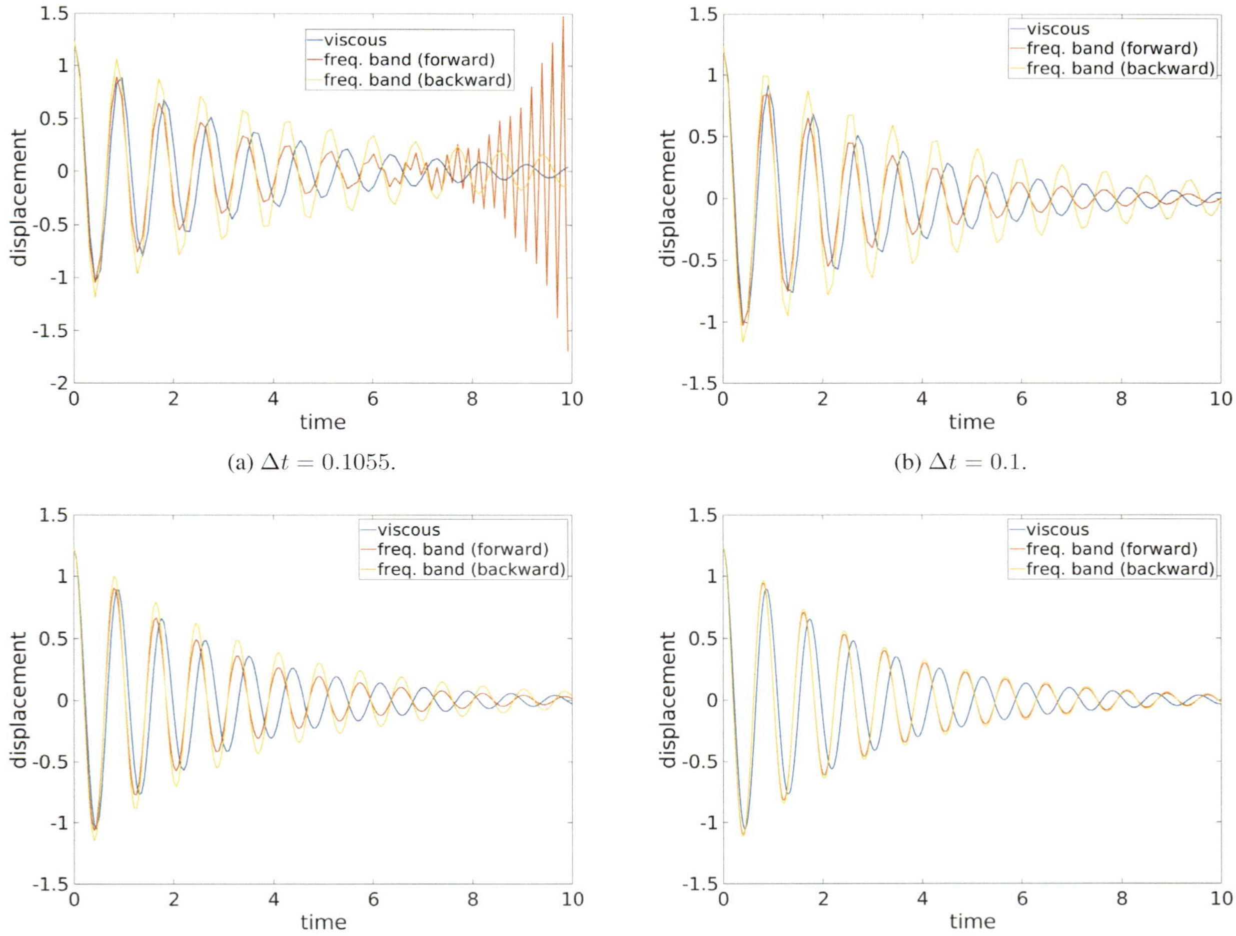

(a) $\Delta t = 0.1055$.

(b) $\Delta t = 0.1$.

(c) $\Delta t = 0.05$.

(d) $\Delta t = 0.01$.

Fig. 8 Comparison of forward and backward Euler for different time discretizations[4].

Results

We now examine some results for a large model, and offer some comparisons to modal damping approaches.

This model includes about 4 million elements, and was run on 800 parallel processors. While this example is fabricated, it has been tuned to be representative of the size and modal density of real models. Figure 9 shows several mode shapes of the model.

We will now use this model to compare the new band damping approach to direct modal damping. For modal damping, we further consider 2 approaches: direct transient simulation and modal transient (i.e., transient solution in the modal space). Note that even with a direct transient solution, an initial eigenvalue problem must still be conducted to compute modal information. For realistic system models with millions of degrees of freedom, the computation of modes can quickly become a performance bottleneck. Even worse, thousands of modes are often required to resolve the frequencies of interest, which frequently makes direct modal damping approaches prohibitively expensive. In this example, modal damping was limited to the first 5000 modes, which was enough to resolve frequencies up to around 7500 Hz (see fig. 10). In a direct transient simulation, this means that high-frequency content above 7500 Hz will be undamped. For modal transient simulations, high frequency content is zeroed.

In contrast, the new band-limited damping approach may be extended across an arbitrarily large frequency range with minimal overhead. In this example, we have damped frequencies up to 100,000 Hz, which would have been completely intractable using direct modal damping.

Figure 11 compares of the damping characteristics of each approach. Figure 11a plots the acceleration of a certain point

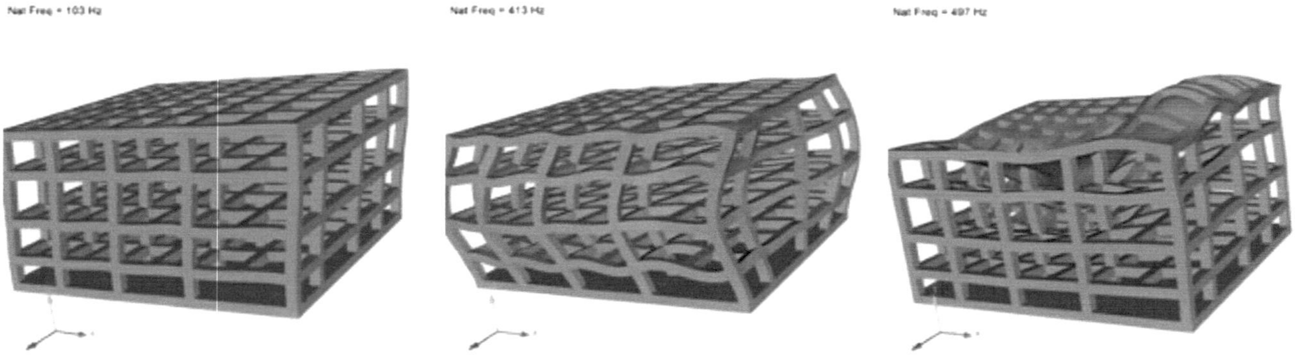

Fig. 9 Mode shapes of a large model.

over time, showing in broad strokes that all 3 approaches have similar damping characteristics. We also clearly see the lack of high-frequency content in the modal transient results. Figure 11b further reinforces this conclusion by examining frequency content. Below 7500 Hz, all 3 methods follow the same trends, with a slight shift between the modal and band damping approaches being attributable to the artificial stiffness contribution introduced by the band damping implementation (eq. (26)). Beyond the modal damping maximum of 7500 Hz they differ in the expected way, with modal damped transient trending more towards the undamped response, and modal transient results flattening out.

In table 1, we examine run times of a transient simulation, comparing both direct modal damping approaches with the new frequency band approach. The first 1 is a direct transient simulation with modal damping (10-7500 Hz). Column 2 is also a direct transient simulation, but with band-limited damping (10-100,000 Hz), and column 3 is a modal transient simulation with modal damping (10-7500 Hz). In all cases, the transient simulation included 20,000 steps, and a flat 2% damping was applied across the frequency range of interest.

Recall that the maximum frequency for modal damping is dictated by performance - uniform damping into the ultra-high-frequency range is completely untenable with this approach. However, even benefiting from a drastically reduced frequency

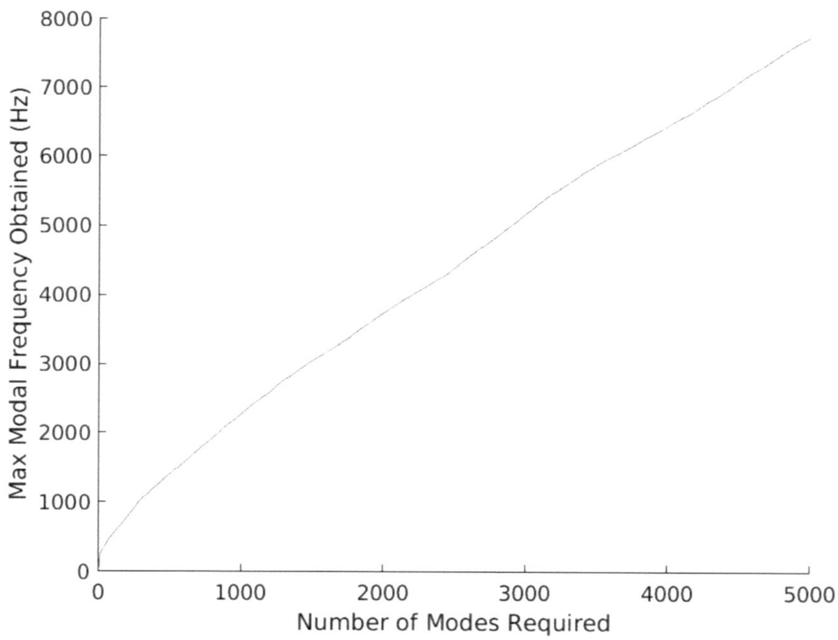

Fig. 10 Number of modes required to resolve a given frequency.

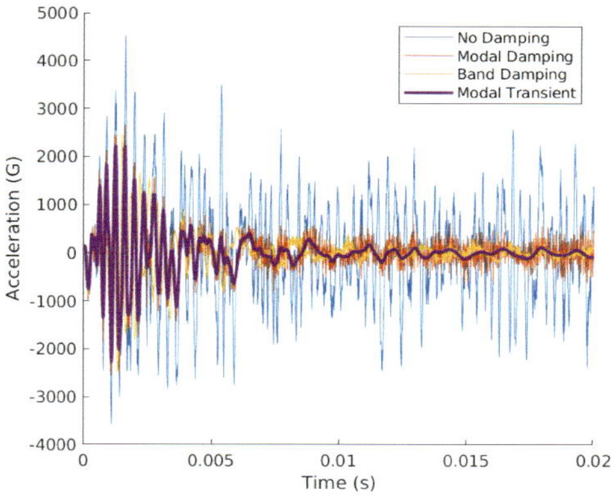

(a) Time domain.

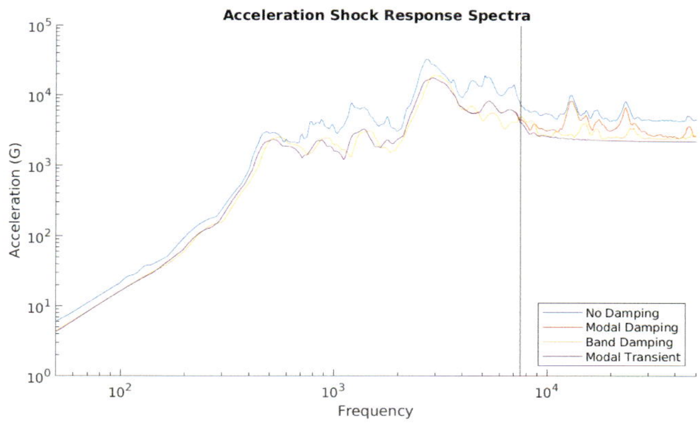

(b) Frequency domain.

Fig. 11 Comparison of damping approaches.

Table 1 Runtime Comparison of Damping Approaches.

	Modal Damping (10 – 7500 Hz)	Band Damping (10 – 100000 Hz)	Modal Transient + Modal Damping
Compute Modes	46 hours	-	46 hours
Transient Simulation	12.0 hours	12.5 hours	0.2 hours
Total	58 hours	12.5 hours	46.2 hours

range, both modal damping approaches are still significantly slower than the new band damping approach. This is due to the huge upfront cost of calculating modes. Even after modal computation is complete, comparison of just the transient simulation times (row 2) shows that the addition of band damping only incurs a minor overhead over a direct transient simulation (12.5 vs. 12 hrs, or around 4%).

Conclusion

In conclusion, this damping approach offers a convenient and efficient way to apply uniform damping over a frequency range. For large simulations, this approach enjoys a significant advantage over direct modal damping, where thousands of modes might be required to capture engineering-relevant frequencies, leading to prohibitively expensive simulations. However, it suffers from slow decay of damping outside of the range of interest, which hampers its effectiveness, especially when multiple frequency bands are used in the same analysis. This effect can be mitigated somewhat by an alternative formulation proposed here, which introduces a tunable parameter to choose between a better fit within the range or faster decay outside.

Acknowledgments Sandia National Laboratories is a multi-mission laboratory managed and operated by National Technology & Engineering Solutions of Sandia, LLC (NTESS), a wholly owned subsidiary of Honeywell International Inc., for the U.S. Department of Energy's National Nuclear Security Administration (DOE/NNSA) under contract DE-NA0003525. This written work is authored by an employee of NTESS. The employee, not NTESS, owns the right, title and interest in and to the written work and is responsible for its contents. Any subjective views or opinions that might be expressed in the written work do not necessarily represent the views of the U.S. Government. The publisher acknowledges that the U.S. Government retains a non-exclusive, paid-up, irrevocable, world-wide license to publish or reproduce the published form of this written work or allow others to do so, for U.S. Government purposes. The DOE will provide public access to results of federally sponsored research in accordance with the DOE Public Access Plan.

Appendix A: Derivation of the Specific Damping Factor

Beginning from eqs. (4) and (5), one may derive the specific damping factor, eq. (6).

In the frequency domain, eqs. (4) and (5) become:

$$F_d(\omega) = \eta \sum_1^N i\omega \frac{2\alpha_n}{\omega_{cn}} F_{Ln}(\omega) \tag{35}$$

and

$$\begin{aligned} F_{Ln}(\omega) + i\omega \frac{F_{Ln}(\omega)}{\omega_{cn}} &= F_0(\omega) \\ \text{or} \\ F_{Ln}(\omega) &= \frac{F_0(\omega)}{1 + i\left(\omega/\omega_{cn}\right)} \end{aligned} \tag{36}$$

Substituting eq. (36) into eq. (35), we obtain

$$F_d(\omega) = \eta \sum_1^N 2\alpha_n i\left(\omega/\omega_{cn}\right) \frac{F_0(\omega)}{1 + i\left(\omega/\omega_{cn}\right)} \tag{37}$$

which can be manipulated via multiplication of both numerator and denominator by $(1 - i(\omega/\omega_{cn}))$ to

$$F_d(\omega) = \eta \sum_1^N 2\alpha_n \left[\frac{\left(\omega/\omega_{cn}\right)^2 - i\left(\omega/\omega_{cn}\right)}{1 + \left(\omega/\omega_{cn}\right)^2}\right] F_0(\omega) \tag{38}$$

Recalling that $f_{int}(t) = f_0(t) + f_d(t)$, we may state the resisting force in the frequency domain as

$$F_{int}(\omega) = \left[1 + \eta \sum_1^N 2\alpha_n \frac{\left(\omega/\omega_{cn}\right)^2}{1 + \left(\omega/\omega_{cn}\right)^2}\right] F_0(\omega) + i\eta \left[\sum_1^N 2\alpha_n \frac{\left(\omega/\omega_{cn}\right)}{1 + \left(\omega/\omega_{cn}\right)^2}\right] F_0(\omega) \tag{39}$$

And finally, following eqs. (2) and (3), the specific damping factor is found as

$$\xi(\omega) = \eta \sum_1^N 2\alpha_n \frac{\left(\omega/\omega_{cn}\right)}{1 + \left(\omega/\omega_{cn}\right)^2} \tag{40}$$

or equivalently as stated in eq. (6).

References

1. Huang, Yuli, Sturt, Richard, and Willford, Michael. "A damping model for nonlinear dynamic analysis providing uniform damping over a frequency range". Computers & Structures, 212 101–109 2019.
2. Beale, Dagny Marie, Bunting, Gregory, Day, David M., Dohrmann, Clark R., Lindsay, Payton, Pepe, Justin, and Plews, Julia Anne. "Sierra/SD – User's Manual – 5.18" URL: https://www.osti.gov/biblio/24300362024.
3. Chopra, Anil K. Dynamics of structures. Pearson Education India, 2007.

For Product Safety Concerns and Information please contact our
EU representative GPSR@taylorandfrancis.com Taylor & Francis
Verlag GmbH, Kaufingerstraße 24, 80331 München, Germany